"James Hayes has achieved a rare and profound understanding of Hong Kong's New Territories by mastering the mountains of historical and ethnographical data with passion and intellectual energy while relating to the people who inhabit the land with humility and empathy. He is in a class of his own."

– Elizabeth Sinn
Honorary Professor at the Hong Kong Institute for the Humanities and Social Sciences, University of Hong Kong. Author of *Pacific Crossing: California Gold, Chinese Migration, and the Making of Hong Kong*

"This is treasure trove for anyone interested in the history of Hong Kong's New Territories. The essays focus on a wide range of topics, including land tenure, village organization, marriage, rural education, and government relations. Scholars who work on the British Empire and its colonial manifestations in South Asia and Africa will also find here a rich source of comparative ethnography."

– James L. Watson
Fairbank Professor of Chinese Society and Anthropology
Emeritus, Harvard University

A Pattern of Life

A Pattern of Life

Essays on Rural Hong Kong by James Hayes

Edited by Hugh D.R. Baker

ISBN: 978-962-937-553-9

Published by
    City University of Hong Kong Press
    Tat Chee Avenue
    Kowloon, Hong Kong
    Website: www.cityu.edu.hk/upress
    E-mail: upress@cityu.edu.hk

Printed in Hong Kong

*This volume is offered to Dr James Hayes
to honour his exceptional contribution over sixty years
to the work of The Royal Asiatic Society, Hong Kong,
and to mark the esteem and affection
in which he is held by its entire membership*

Royal Asiatic Society Hong Kong Studies Series

The Royal Asiatic Society Hong Kong Studies Series is designed to make widely available important contributions to the local history, culture, and society of Hong Kong and the surrounding region. Generous support from the Sir Lindsay and Lady May Ride Memorial Fund makes it possible to publish this series of high-quality works that are of lasting appeal and value to all, both scholars and informed general readers, who share an interest in and enthusiasm for the area.

Other titles in the RAS Hong Kong Studies Series:

Contents

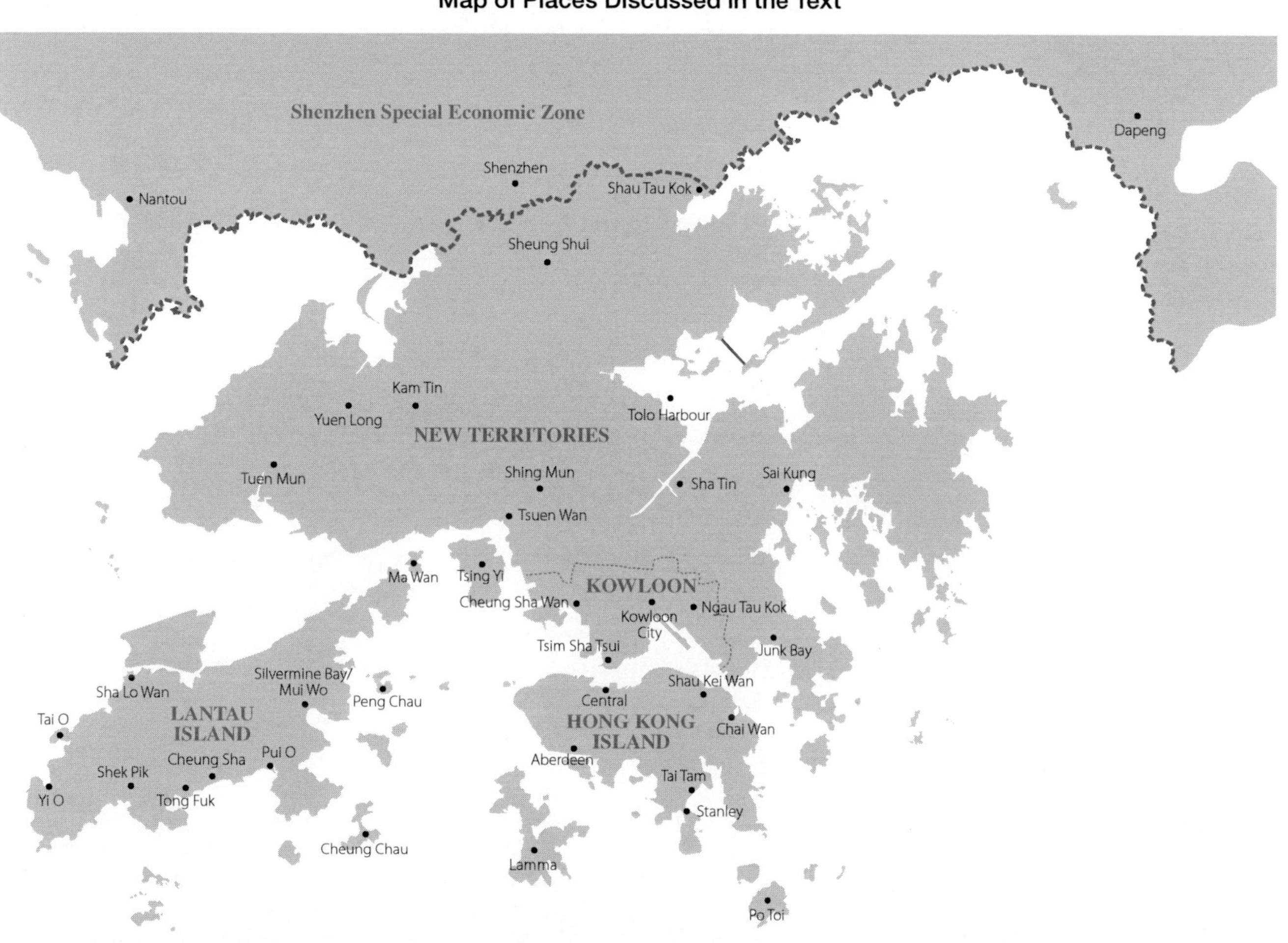

Map of Places Discussed in the Text
Shenzhen Special Economic Zone
Nantou
Shenzhen
Shau Tau Kok
Dapeng
Sheung Shui
Kam Tin
Yuen Long
Tolo Harbour
NEW TERRITORIES
Tuen Mun
Shing Mun
Sha Tin
Sai Kung
Tsuen Wan
Ma Wan
Tsing Yi
KOWLOON
Cheung Sha Wan
Kowloon City
Ngau Tau Kok
Junk Bay
Tsim Sha Tsui
Shau Kei Wan
Sha Lo Wan
Silvermine Bay/
Mui Wo
Peng Chau
Central
HONG KONG
ISLAND
Chai Wan
LANTAU
ISLAND
Pui O
Tai O
Shek Pik
Cheung Sha
Aberdeen
Tai Tam
Stanley
Yi O
Tong Fuk
Cheung Chau
Lamma
Po Toi

Acknowledgements

I am deeply indebted to Dr Colin Day who, in addition to compiling the Bibliography, has done a great deal of the support work that has made my job easier; and he in turn has enjoyed the able help of his wife Jenny. Robert Nield's contribution is very apparent and is an informative platform for James's own writings which follow. Heidi Dyer generously offered to help me with the proofreading and proved to have a natural flair and aptitude for the task, much to my benefit; and my family gallantly rescued me from the slough of computer ineptitude on many occasions. I am grateful to former colleagues of James who enriched my understanding with their insights, and I am also grateful to Professor David Faure for permission to use the photograph of James and a village informant which adorns the dust jacket of this book. Last but not least, I would like to thank Dr Abby Manthey, editor at City University of Hong Kong Press, and her team for their thoughtful and tireless help in seeing this volume into print at a time when working conditions have been particularly difficult.

Editor's Introduction

The life and career of James Hayes as a government official in Hong Kong were busy, fruitful and fulfilling. It could hardly have turned out otherwise: posting a natural historian with an anthropological bent, a strong sense of justice, and a pragmatic approach to problem solving into the quasi "living museum" of the 1950s New Territories was an inspired move. James relished his duty to the government he represented, but for the people for whose well-being he was responsible he developed a real and abiding affection. The love and the duty may not always have been easily reconcilable, but to read his many writings is to discover through his eyes that the two were more complementary than conflicting. Thanks to his active role in what he describes and analyses, the papers in this collection are themselves historical material, and carry value accordingly.

James's understanding of history allows him to transmit to his readers a reality that might otherwise be in danger of appearing quaint. He sees—and enables us to see—a coherent context that reveals the enduring values and motivations which shape and are shaped by societies and cultures everywhere. Of course, these vary in detail and in the nature of the challenges which face them, and the differences often tend to obscure the similarities so that we "cannot see the wood for the trees". Despite the accessibility of his writing style, he is an academic's historian, meticulous to a fault in showing his sources and always aware of the interplay of continuity and change. In addition, he has embraced insight from the sister discipline of social anthropology, and as a result, he has the breadth of vision to work backwards from what he can observe now to comprehend the past as well as to use his knowledge of the past to make better sense of what is happening in the world today.

It follows that this kind of history is not really an account of events. It does not turn on what happened or when and is more concerned with understanding the everyday norms upon which time and actions make their mark. Perhaps I can illustrate with a true anecdote: a history teacher at my school once asked the class "What happened in 1066?" and was gratified to hear a unison chorus of "Battle of Hastings, Sir". The next question was "And what happened in 1374?" A few wild guesses were met with a stern "Incorrect", and he finally had to give us the answer he was looking for—"Nothing". James could never have produced such a crass question, or conceived of its fatuous answer. Of course he acknowledges events and dates, but the extraordinary can only exist where there is an ordinary, and it is the latter which interests him more deeply.

Not that he is short of matters in which he is interested, as his published *oeuvre* attests.[1] And it is the number and wide range of his writings which made it necessary to think hard about the selection of pieces for this volume. How to organise it? Should it focus on his career as a Hong Kong government officer or on the topics he has dealt with as a historian? Is there any value in organising the material at all, or should the selection be randomly presented so as to demonstrate its richness and diversity? Having weighed various ideas, my choice fell on the one theme which predominates — Life in the New Territories of Hong Kong.

James has published six (English language) books on Hong Kong, mostly on the history of its rural people and communities. I was asked not to include excerpts from any of these, since printed books have longevity and can readily be found in general and specialist libraries, and because excerpts from full length works seldom do justice to a subject which has been carefully developed over many pages. The materials chosen therefore consist of articles from journals, conference papers, stand-alone chapters from edited volumes, and scripts for talks. The focus on Hong Kong means that interesting items such as "Book Publishing and the Popular Culture: Kwangtung and Shanghai", "Western Photography in China: the Historical Background", and "Calligraphy — a Very Fine Art" are also passed over. It may seem paradoxical that a number of pieces from *The Journal of the Hong Kong Branch of the Royal Asiatic Society (JHKBRAS)*[2] have been included: after all, many of the back numbers can still be purchased from the RAS[3] so that availability cannot be claimed to be an issue. However, James has been far and away the most prolific contributor to the *Journal* since the first volume appeared in 1961, and he was its Honorary Editor from 1967 to 1980. Thus, this publication would not do justice to his work if some of his most original writings were excluded. Other papers and articles found here are taken from publications which may not now be widely available.

In the end, the chapters have fallen into a pattern that is neither chronological nor, strictly speaking, topical. **Overviews** consists of treatments that, rather than being devoted to specific locations or issues, range over the whole of Hong Kong's New Territories or deal with broad topics. **Transitions** contains three papers which chart a traumatic process all too familiar to the people of Hong Kong: the planned obliteration of established communities and their resettlement elsewhere. In illustrating the kind of serious practical problems that James spent a major part of his career handling, these papers reveal a pragmatic caring official who is also a detached historian. **Communities** deals with individual settlements (especially Shek Pik, Cheung Chau, Tsuen Wan, and Shing Mun) which James has studied in greater depth and where he has addressed specific topics in finer detail. In part, this last section can be seen as a "tasting menu" of interesting shorter pieces, of which he has written many, principally for the *JHKBRAS*.

The date of original publication of each chapter is clearly shown in a footnote on the opening page, and readers are advised to take note of it so that they are not puzzled by apparent errors in the chronological order of presentation. Thus, the statement that "The main crop was and still is rice"[4] means that rice was still being grown when this part of the article was drafted in 1967: indeed, it was very unlikely to have been the case as late as when this version was published in 1984. The time-frame for each chapter is set by the date when it first appeared in print. Each chapter features an introduction to provide further context and rationale for the inclusion of the paper in this volume. Annexes have also been added to Chapters 1, 3, 13, and 15. These consist of other materials written by James that have additional light to throw on the topics of those chapters, and any notes have been numbered consecutively with those of the main chapter.

Further, the various pieces were written as free-standing items and for publications with different styles and demands. Little attempt has been made to homogenise their presentation, so there is inevitably a certain amount of repetition. To avoid this, I have, where possible, taken the liberty of editing out a few passages without indicating the excisions. The same applies to the copious accompanying notes, which owing to space constraints have been quite severely pruned. In compensation, the content of particularly informative notes has been transferred into the body of the main text, again without indication of the change. Even so, some of the notes are lengthy and placing them at the bottom of the page could prove distracting to the reader: they can all be found collected together by chapter at the end of the book.

For convenience and clarity, the Chinese characters for names, places, and other terms used in the text can be found in their full (i.e., "unsimplified") form in the Index under their English meaning or romanised spelling. Transcription of Chinese terms into romanisation has been handled using the Meyer-Wempe system for Cantonese (without tone-marks or aspirate markers). For Hong Kong locations, I have followed the spellings adopted by *A Gazetteer of Place Names in Hong Kong, Kowloon and the New Territories* (Hong Kong Government Printer, 1960), which essentially uses this same transcription system. The names of places elsewhere in China, as well as the names of dynasties and reign periods of Chinese emperors, are given in their official Hanyu Pinyin romanisation, while a few aberrant but widely accepted spellings (such as Macau, Kowloon, Confucius, Sun Yat-sen, and *kowtow*) are retained in their familiar standard form.

*****

Overviews

There was no doubt in my mind about what should open this volume. **The Pattern of Life in the New Territories in 1898** was the first piece that James published, and it focuses on the first year of the lease that transferred more than 366 square miles of land to the control of the United Kingdom. Initially negotiated almost as a casual exercise in "land grab", over the course of its allotted 99 years the New Territories (*San Kai*) acquired greater importance as the only space available for the expansion of Hong Kong's population, and ultimately the expiry of the lease in 1997 became the trigger-factor for the remarkably peaceful and orderly transfer of the entire Hong Kong territory back to China.

For much of his service in the Hong Kong government (1956–1988) James worked in the New Territories and, like the ideal "father and mother official" (*fu mou kwun*) of Chinese tradition, he extended his concern for those he administered far beyond the bounds of bureaucratic government. Many of the themes which are introduced in this chapter, notably clans (lineages), customary law, education, ethnic differences, land, and local leadership—the static picture of life that he has made his baseline—were again taken up by James in more detailed treatments (and can be found in the later chapters of this collection). In addition, changes which could not have been foreseen in 1898 are also important to him, and so urbanisation, enforced resettlement, and, rather less obviously, modernisation have not been neglected in the items selected for inclusion here either. **The Pattern of Life** remains a stimulating foundation study for anyone wishing to understand an important part of the total territory of today's Hong Kong. Appended to it is a short paper that James wrote early in his government career, the object being to try to clarify the confusing concept of the "customary land trust" which creeps into a number of the later chapters in one form or another.

In **Rural Leadership in the Hong Kong Region**, the lives and achievements of three leaders from different villages of Lantau Island (Tai Yue Shan) are examined and used as examples of the generality of local men of wealth and influence. The three men were all born between 1800 and 1850, two of them surviving until 1916 and 1922, respectively. One began as a humble shop assistant, one inherited a number of plots of land from his father, and one was an unsuccessful scholar; two were Hakka and one a Cantonese; all had energy and acumen; and each of them built and continuously nurtured a reputation and power base in his home community, investing in land and money-lending. Although they were able to a greater or lesser extent to be active and exert influence further afield, their main efforts were directed to running affairs in their own villages—big fish in small ponds, but very important to maintaining local order. This is described as "a form of genuine local self-government" necessitated by the inability of overworked officials to handle trifling rural matters in pre-lease times. It might be added that from the villagers' point of view it was also no doubt an advantageous way of avoiding unwelcome attention from officials.

In his working life, James was constantly confronted with problems of customary law, which fascinated and plagued him, but for which he had and has considerable respect. Imperial China had a long tradition of formal state law which laid down broad principles of right and wrong, sometimes in minute detail, but often with cavalier indifference to clarity. Thus, the *Tai Ching Leut Lai* [*The Laws and Statutes of the Great Ching*], in force throughout the time when all three parts of the territory of Hong Kong came under British control, was very precise as to who might be legally adopted to continue the family line, but it said nothing about what constituted a valid adoption procedure or ceremony, and no form of state registration of adoption existed. Similar lacunae characterised matters such as birth, marriage, concubinage, divorce, succession, and death, and for these and others it was customary law which determined practice, with variant (largely unwritten) rules observed in different regions and even in adjacent villages. In some parts of the New Territories, for instance, it was acceptable to adopt a son from a family of another surname, regardless of the fact that *The Laws and Statutes* prohibited cross-surname adoption and laid down severe corporal punishment for anyone who infringed. In other parts, the official prohibition is still observed to this day. James has visited the subject of customary law in a number of papers, of which the earliest is reproduced here. The original text of

Chinese Customary Law in the New Territories of Hong Kong was accompanied by an annex summarising a few actual case records found in District Office files, and, feeling that these will prove of interest and use to many, I have presumed to add more case descriptions cannibalised from three of his other articles. It will no doubt be noted that, over the thirty years that separate the first from the fourth set, the quality of case presentation becomes increasingly more elegant and confident, as might be expected. Customary law is an immense subject, even when its scope is limited to as small an area as Hong Kong, and any brave person who eventually attempts a full study will have reason to be grateful to James, along with a small handful of others, for recording their experiences in this field.

Education and Management in Rural South China in the Late Ching looks at questions of literacy rates, curriculum content, the uses to which literacy was put, and the written and printed materials which were available in rural areas of Hong Kong before and after the commencement of the New Territories lease. Again, this is a topic to which James has returned more than once, and it reflects his long-term interest in educational materials and in rescuing and collecting manuscript documents and printed works which by the mid-twentieth century were obsolete or meaningless to those who found them when turning out dusty cupboards. Libraries and academic colleagues have since greatly benefited from his "gene for preservation" and his generosity in making materials available to others. The paper shows that village life, no less than urban residence, was dependent on literacy. This did not mean that every villager was literate. Indeed, many women before the Pacific War were given no opportunity to be educated (as the frequent use of a cross in lieu of a woman's signature on old official documents demonstrates). However, comparatively few such "marks" were made by men, indicating some level of literacy. James comments that: "We can take a degree of male literacy in the villages of the Hong Kong region for granted."

Transitions

A Chinese Village on Hong Kong Island Fifty Years Ago — Tai Tam Tuk, Village Under the Water, as is clear from the title, is not about the New Territories, though the location was far enough from urban centres that it might as well have been. Tai Tam Tuk's fate in the early years of the twentieth century closely paralleled that of Shek Pik five decades later, and it makes sense that, being put in charge of the resettlement of the Shek Pik villagers, James should have investigated one of its antecedents. His technique of seeking out elderly survivors who can contribute their own life-stories to flesh out impersonal records succeeds in painting a convincing picture of a little known event.

Relentless urbanisation is the dominant theme of **Old Ways of Life in Kowloon: the Cheung Sha Wan Villages**. Again, James has relied quite heavily on "the recollections of old village people, all born before the [1898] lease." He has always valued and learned from such informants with no less enthusiasm than he has from old documents. This article is particularly rich in historical detail and records the destruction of vibrant communities "swept out of existence and redeveloped". Of course, this has happened to many areas of Hong Kong, but after his Shek Pik experience, James clearly felt for those affected, and this is poignantly reflected in his sympathetic account.

On a similar topic to the previous paper, **The Old Popular Culture of China and its Contribution to Stability in Tsuen Wan** examines another long-established area subjected to rapid development, but finds that cultural continuity helped to soften the deleterious effects of social change. James was district officer and town manager of Tsuen Wan from 1975 to 1982 and had ample opportunity to experience and appreciate the extent of the population's co-operation and what he dubs "right minded-ness" at a time when their entire environment was being redesigned as Hong Kong's first "New Town". The cynic may question whether the situation was quite as sweet and trouble-free as he depicts.

Were there no problems with secret societies, drugs, corruption, or other social evils? His concluding section shows that he himself has misgivings about the view that a legacy of Confucianism and acceptance of hardship is enough to explain social docility under stress. In this regard, James the Sinophile is an astute and knowledgeable historian and observer (and this is a thoughtful article backed by hands-on experience), but James the cynic (while not lacking justification for his opinion) must surely admit that, despite inequalities, colonialism, exploitation, and suffering, the people of Hong Kong have generally shown remarkable qualities of restraint and cohesion in creating a more civilised and prosperous society over the years.

Communities

The small island of Cheung Chau (sometimes known as Dumbbell Island) is unusual in that it evolved as a town without a rural hinterland of any significance, and for this and other reasons it tends to be *sui generis*, as distinctive in character as in physical shape. Its limited size and bounded nature would seem to make it attractive ground for sociological and historical research, but James is one of only very few to attempt it. In 1963, he produced **Cheung Chau 1850–1898: Information from Commemorative Tablets**, an exercise in building up a coherent picture from minimal pixel clues. It was followed in 1977 by a long chapter about the island in his book *The Hong Kong Region, 1850–1911*, but by way of contrast the second piece included here, **Notes and Impressions of the Cheung Chau Community**, did not appear until more than thirty years after the first. This paper draws attention to the differences that cross-cut the population, notably ethnic diversity, where Hoklo ("Fellows from Fujian Province"), Tanka ("Egg families": a disparaging name for Cantonese-speaking boat-dwellers), and other groups from various parts of

South China competed for space, livelihood, and political control. Including both articles here provides an opportunity to observe the increasing depth and sophistication of understanding resulting from the author's long exposure to New Territories society.

While Cheung Chau is inhabited and, to some extent, riven by different ethnic and homeland groups, in the Pui O Valley on Lantau Island there are nine villages, some Cantonese (often referred to as "Punti", a corruption of *pun tei* "indigenous"), some Hakka, and a few inhabited by households of both groups. **A Mixed Community of Cantonese and Hakka on Lantau Island** makes it clear that not only is there no record of animosity between the two, either now or at any time since the area was settled in the seventeenth century, but that there has all along been a considerable amount of intermarriage. In light of the long history of Hakka-Punti rivalry and warfare elsewhere in Southeastern China, this example of their peaceful co-existence is rare and not easily explicable.

Before its clearance to make way for a new reservoir, Shek Pik was a mono-ethnic settlement of Punti, but it was shared by different clans. **The Settlement and Development of a Multi-clan Village** looks at how these clans co-existed in a context where many other New Territories villages were each exclusively settled and controlled by a single clan. Much scholarly attention has been focused on "single-lineage villages", but James, perhaps as a result of having worked in areas where clans are less prominent, has been more interested in other kinds of settlement, and it is particularly useful to have this example of a different aspect of kinship in action. He reveals that there was some intermarriage of the clans within the village, a feature not reported as customary elsewhere.

Village Credit at Shek Pik, 1879–1895 is a short paper, and it is not likely to fully satisfy the curiosity of a reader who has never heard of a Chinese money loan association (*ngan wui*). However, it does add significant detail to the sum of what is already known on the subject. While it does not deal with the methodology of interest calculation, it does give the exchange rate between silver dollars and Chinese taels (*leung* "silver ounces") in the late nineteenth century. As with many of his other similarly short taster pieces, this paper contains knowledge that James has happened upon and preserved from extinction for the use of future scholars and, it has to be said, of anyone who finds cultural diversity or history fascinating.

By contrast, **San Po Tsai (Little Daughters-in-Law) and Child Betrothals in the New Territories of Hong Kong from the 1890s to the 1960s** is a much longer article. It deals with a custom that has been outlawed by enlightened modern society in Hong Kong, as also in China and, hopefully, elsewhere. A *san po tsai* (sometimes referred to as a "child bride") was a young girl already betrothed and, in most cases, living with her future husband's family until puberty and marriage. Needless to say, she had no choice in who her spouse would be (any more than he had), and it was normal practice for marriages to be arranged by the parents well before puberty (even if betrothal did not occur until after). This paper discusses the procedures and circumstances of such marriages and gives details from a number of areas in the New Territories, including Shek Pik and Tsuen Wan. It is particularly important because there has been little information published on *san po tsai* marriages in Hong Kong. That they existed is certain — indeed, James himself has reported that there were three in Shek Pik at the time of the resettlement[5] — and it is highly probable that, although it is seldom mentioned, there are still women alive today who were married in this way.

Shek Pik is again the setting for the next article, **Geomancy and the Village,** the first of two on the subject of *feng shui* ("wind and water", often called "geomancy" in English). Believers in *feng shui* hold that the natural landscape and the built environment influence both the fortunes of the people who live in them and the well-being of the descendants of the dead who are buried in them. That being so, it is a short step to thinking that inadvertent alterations to the physical surroundings can have a harmful or perhaps beneficial effect, and from there it is not illogical to conclude that features can be deliberately manipulated for good or evil by those who understand the complex system. Belief in the efficacy of *feng shui* can be found in urban Hong Kong and has even taken uncertain root in foreign cultures, but it is even more strongly felt among the villagers of the New Territories. James encountered it frequently during his work, and in this paper, he describes some of the instances with which he had to deal. The second piece on geomancy, **Feng Shui and Road Works at Tong Fuk Village, South Lantau, in 1958,** recounts similar experiences in the nearby village of Tong Fuk. It includes extracts from a minute that James wrote to the district commissioner at the time expressing his irritation and frustration at the continual use of *feng shui* as an obstacle to change. It is the voice of James the government official which speaks loudly through both these articles, but even here James the compassionate Sinophile sits at his shoulder quietly writing: "My experiences convinced me that the local response to what was taking place was based on genuine feeling, whatever subsidiary motives there may have been in addition." He has also written: "It is always easy to assert that Feng Shui is merely an excuse for squeezing money out of Government, but … it is rarely the case that there is no underlying fear of disturbing the local Feng Shui."

We began with a review of the New Territories at the time it was leased to Britain in 1898, and it seems appropriate to close with James looking back on his own first year in the New Territories Administration. It is forty years since **The New Territories Twenty Years Ago: From the Notebooks of a District Officer** was first published, and it now serves as a historical waymark in much the same way as "The Pattern of Life in the New Territories in 1898", albeit less broad in coverage.

* * * * *

This collection is necessarily not representative of all James's interests, nor is it by any means a complete record of his published work on Hong Kong. It aims to be an illuminating sample of his expertise, understanding, and long experience, as well as a useful reference book for those who would like to continue the study of a unique area of considerable political, cultural, and historical interest. There have been other scholar-officials of Hong Kong, such as Sir James Stewart Lockhart, Dr E.J. Eitel, and K.M.A. Barnett, who have left a legacy of thoughtful, insight-rich works, but the Hong Kong writings of Dr James Hayes are unequalled in scope and academic value.

Hugh D.R. Baker
Emeritus Professor of Chinese at London University's
School of Oriental and African Studies (SOAS)
October 2020

Learning All the Time, Sharing All the Time: Biography of Dr James William Hayes, ISO, JP

The first contribution by James Hayes to the Royal Asiatic Society's Journal was in Volume 2, published in 1962. The most recent is in Volume 57, fifty-five years later. There have been countless others in the intervening half-century. His work is everywhere. No Journal contributor has been more prolific. It is a privilege, therefore, to present this brief biographical essay about the man who has been of such help, support, and encouragement to so many Hong Kong and regional scholars.

Early Life

James was born on 8 November 1930 in a small house adjoining a stable block on the Cairnie estate, in Fifeshire, Scotland, where his maternal grandfather was employed as a gentleman's gentleman. James's mother was responsible for, among other tasks, the laundry of the big house and its many servants. For

James, childhood in these austere-sounding conditions was not all work, nor was it joyless. His grandfather was an active, cheerful man and had been in the army. Indeed, a strong military thread runs through James's family. His father, a keen horseman, enlisted in a cavalry regiment in 1926 and was posted to Cairo. There he met James's mother, who was working as a nursemaid for a British military family. They married in 1928, and James was born during a period of home leave.

By 1937, James had already attended two primary schools in Scotland and was to attend three more in England. One of these, in 1938, was the Albert Road Junior School in Romford. A report by his class mistress records that James was: "A gentleman — can always be relied upon to carry on quietly and efficiently." She added: "It has been a joy to teach such an interested scholar." But the family's stay at Romford was brief; with the onset of war in 1939, pressure mounted on mothers with young children to seek shelter away from the big cities that had become targets of German air attacks. In September 1940, James and his mother returned to Scotland. From 1942 to 1944, he attended Waid Academy, a private secondary school not far from where he was born.

In early 1944, with the war still in progress, the young family returned south, to Kingston. There James attended Tiffin Boys' School until 1949. He remembers a schoolmaster taking him under his wing and recommending history books for him to read, many of them military, sowing the seeds for his life as an historian. James would note down the names of all the army officers who featured in his reading and ask his mentor to look them up in Hart's Army List; he still treasures the letters the master wrote in reply.

Gaining entry to the University of London, James graduated in 1952 with a BA (Hons) in history. For his studies, he selected British colonial and empire history, and the development of dominion status. These would stand him in good stead in his future career—but first came compulsory National Service. After a period of training, James was posted to Korea, where war had been raging since June 1950. As a newly commissioned second lieutenant, he arrived on the front line in early June 1953, narrowly missing one of the last major battles of the conflict.

On his way to Korea, James's unit was stationed in Hong Kong for six weeks of preparation. This, and his war service in Korea, became the catalyst for a life-long interest in East Asia, particularly what he saw of its old-style rural life. His National Service completed, in 1954, James returned to London to resume his studies. Initially embarking on a doctorate programme, he soon decided to cut this short and settle for a master's degree; his travels had made him long for adventure. An application in 1955 to the Colonial Office was successful, and he was permitted to complete the remaining year of his study.

Hong Kong Government Service

Having expressed a strong preference for Hong Kong, James boarded the P&O ship *Canton*, reaching Victoria Harbour in August 1956, ready to take up his duties as a "Cadet Officer Class II". Cadets, a small group that formed the core of the colonial government, were expected to move regularly between different departments, gaining experience as they went. In general, cadets had a sense of honesty and integrity, and played an important role in ensuring that the people were well governed. China had had a similar system since about the sixth century, and it was inevitable that Hong Kong cadets, particularly in the rural areas, came to be seen as the traditional Chinese *fu mou kwun*, or benevolent father-and-mother officials. This expectation was to suit James well as he began to develop his role.

The Hong Kong that James came to help govern was very different from today's modern and bustling city. Victoria Park was newly opened, having been reclaimed from the harbour. Construction of the new runway at Kai Tak had started; it was expected to cost HK$100 million. The number of maternity beds in Tsuen Wan had just doubled—from thirteen to twenty-six. More poignantly, the population of the colony had increased four-fold since the end of the Second World War.[1] This fact, and its repercussions, was to present James with significant challenges in his work as a district officer.

Initially, James was attached to the Social Welfare Department, accompanying social workers on their daily rounds. He was soon posted as assistant secretary in the Colonial Secretariat, the nucleus of the colony's government. There, covering for someone who was on leave, he had temporary policy responsibility for the Royal Observatory, the Fire Brigade, and the Agriculture, Fisheries, and Forestry Department. This challenging introduction to the work of a government officer was but filling in time before the commencement of a Cantonese language course at the University of Hong Kong. Cantonese is a notoriously difficult language for foreigners to master, and conversancy in it was a requirement of the job. A year's induction was considered sufficient to arm James, by October 1957, for his first posting in the field—district officer (south). The role of the district officer was multi-faceted and extremely demanding. He was the visible face of the government, responsible for the welfare of the people in his district. He had to balance the need to improve the people's living conditions with respect for their traditions.

The "south" in James's title was something of a misnomer. His district comprised Tseung Kwan O, Clear Water Bay, southern Sai Kung, and most of Hong Kong's Islands, excluding Victoria. Indeed, the district officer (south) was known as "Lord of the Islands". James believed that he had to know how the people in his district lived in order for him to help improve the quality of rural life and engender a sense of belonging to Hong Kong. Accordingly, within his first six months, he visited nearly all the district's 180 villages, making detailed notes about each one. He did not realise it at the time, but those visits provided the last opportunity to witness and record Hong Kong's centuries-old rural economy and its people. In one village he even met an old gentleman who had been a scholar-official in the Qing government. James's exploratory walks became legendary among his colleagues, both for the energy required to keep up with him and for James's expectation that he should be accompanied. Stephen Selby recalls: "He walked far and fast. It was never an invitation."

The standard garb for district officers at that time was white shorts, white shirt, long white socks, and perhaps a solar topi, giving the wearer a "faintly eccentric" appearance, according to Sir David Akers-Jones. Seemingly anachronistic today, these symbols of colonial Hong Kong toured their villages, their authority accepted by the rural leaders as they adjudicated on local disputes, such as the boundary between one padi field and the next. James recalls that his first case as district officer involved a disagreement regarding the colour of a pregnant cow. An understanding of the people and their traditions was essential in such an alien environment. Indeed, the government's policy in the New Territories was minimal interference with the indigenous legal system. This was to develop in James a keen desire to study and document that system.

Returning from home leave in August 1961, James found that he was now district officer (islands), as the Sai Kung area had become a separate district. District officers were generally left to get on with their jobs, with little interference from above, meeting together once a month to exchange ideas. Rachel Cartland, a newly arrived administrative officer, some years later was secretary to those meetings. She recalls that James did more listening than speaking. However, Gordon Jones, a contemporary of Rachel's, remembers that if James felt something was wrong, he would say so.

In addition to compulsory part-time duties with the Royal Hong Kong Regiment, where James served as captain until 1966, there was much to occupy his time. However, two particular interrelated projects dominated most of James's time as district officer and stimulated his interest as an historian: the Shek Pik Reservoir and the "New Town" of Tsuen Wan.

In the early 1950s, it had been decided to build a reservoir at Shek Pik on Lantau Island, and this required the removal of four villages. The island being within James's district, he was closely involved. Preparation work, which commenced before James's arrival, gathered pace during the late 1950s. One village dated from the fifteenth century immediately sparking James's interest. Finding that virtually nothing had been written about it, he started interviewing the villagers and recording the inscriptions on their ancestral tablets and memorial plaques. He also collected land title deeds and genealogies. He encouraged his colleagues to do likewise, soon building up a considerable archive of oral and documentary materials.

This project introduced James to the challenge of balancing the demands of a difficult job with his interests as an historian. Meanwhile, the Shek Pik villagers had to be convinced that removal from their ancestral homes was for the greater good. Tact, diplomacy, and empathy with Chinese traditions were all required in large quantity, and James proved equal to the task. It had been decided to rehouse the villagers in newly constructed concrete buildings in Tsuen Wan, and James led a group of elders there to inspect them.

However, given the requirement to rotate between different departments, before he could see the Shek Pik project finished, James was posted to the Resettlement Department. From 1963 to 1965 he was in charge of the many resettlement estates, including that of the Shek Pik villagers in Tsuen Wan. A major aspect of this job was clearing Hong Kong's squatter areas and preventing others from appearing. Returning once more from home leave in January 1966, James found he had been posted to the Central Government Secretariat. Initially, he was placed as acting chief assistant secretary in the Secretariat for Chinese Affairs (SCA). This body was responsible for advising the government on matters relating to Chinese law and custom, a very broad brief but one ideally suited to James's interests and abilities. In 1967, after spending a few months at the hub of government as assistant colonial secretary, he was posted back to the SCA. He remained there until 1971, witnessing the 1967 "disturbances" and becoming one of the architects of the City District Officer Scheme. He then served in the Commerce and Industry and Urban Services departments from 1972 to 1974, a period that saw great changes in Hong Kong's public housing policy and the beginning of the New Towns programme.

James returned to Tsuen Wan in 1975 as district officer. He held this position until 1982, also acting as its town manager for the latter five years. Governor MacLehose (1971–1982) was strongly promoting the development of New Towns, of which Tsuen Wan, with its community of Shanghai manufacturers, was the most complex. James had already seen the removal of the Shek Pik villagers to the new seven-storey blocks in Tsuen Wan. He was now responsible not only for them but also the many knitters, silk-weavers, tin-beaters, and plastic-flower factories that occupied similar buildings.

The complexity of the job increased in 1977 when it was announced that the Mass Transit Railway (MTR) would run through Tsuen Wan. Although the Shek Pik villagers were safe in their new accommodation, many other old villages had to be removed. There were also the squatter areas, containing various commercial undertakings as well as tens of thousands of post-war settlers. One of the more significant sites that had to be cleared was the Hakka walled village of Sam Tung Uk. James persuaded a group of local elders to finance its relocation and preservation. It now stands, as a testament to James's influence and concern, near the Tsuen Wan MTR station.

James was responsible for Tsuen Wan for seven years. In an environment where capable people tended to drift automatically upwards, this was an unusually long period. Indeed, he recalls that Chief Secretary Philip Haddon-Cave was surprised that James had been in Tsuen Wan for so long. Inevitably, the powers that be decided that James's talents should be shared more equally. Besides, despite preferring to work in the field rather than at the Secretariat, he says he was "not entirely devoid of ambition". Moreover, he felt an obligation to serve more fully the system that had given him so satisfying a life among a population for whom he came to have such affection and respect. It was therefore with mixed feelings that he was promoted to be deputy commissioner of labour in 1982. Although he was desk-bound for much of the time, he was still able to interact directly with ordinary people in his supervision of evolving employment, safety, and factory regulations.

James's last position in government, from 1985 to his retirement in November 1987, was regional secretary for the New Territories. The urban area was the city south of Lion Rock; the New Territories encompassed everywhere else. Although perhaps having less freedom in this more senior position, James nevertheless encouraged innovation in others. For example, district officers were trying to settle issues concerning family succession in accordance with customary Qing law and practice, but with little knowledge of what that law and practice was. Therefore, in 1986, James commissioned a working group to produce some definitions. The result was a ground-breaking publication that served to assist various government officers in the conduct of their duties in the rural area.[2] As regional secretary, James also contributed to the development of the New Territories "Small House Policy", by which indigenous residents had a right to build themselves a house. James saw that building restrictions and pressure on the availability of land meant that villages could not grow, and that they were consequently dying out as people moved away. This thorny issue has by no means been resolved, even today.

In 1987, James was told that he would have to retire on his fifty-seventh birthday; the government was committed to reducing the number of senior expatriates. "This left me decidedly vexed", he recorded, his hopes and obligations regarding the New Territories only partly fulfilled.[3] However, he felt he had contributed to Hong Kong's development. "It sounds very egotistical, but it wasn't really." He rose to the occasion simply because Hong Kong had that effect on him.[4] Former Governor Wilson (1987–1992) told me that James was

> the archetypical example of those remarkable Colonial Service officers who became fascinated by, and deeply engaged with, the territories and people which it was their task to administer. They have been one of the glories, and sometimes oddities, of the old British colonial system.

James the Scholar

James's historical instincts were aroused when he attended the inaugural lecture of the newly re-established Hong Kong Branch of the Royal Asiatic Society (RAS). In April 1960, Frederick Drake, professor of Chinese at the University of Hong Kong, spoke on "The Study of Asia: A Heritage and a Task". This experience engendered in James a commitment to "learn all the time, and share all the time", something he describes as his guiding beacon. Given James's academic grounding in history, Drake's lecture was a clarion call for him to take a serious interest in the history and culture of Hong Kong.

To his advantage was that whatever research there was into Hong Kong studies was being performed by civil-service enthusiasts, such as Ken Barnett. No one would challenge the right of a district officer, even an expatriate one, to ask questions, whereas university academics did not have the same access. According to Elizabeth Sinn, James's first RAS Journal article, "The Pattern of Life in the New Territories in 1898", marked the beginning of a deep commitment to local studies on the part of the Society.[5] What James described to me as his "absorbing interest in the people of the towns and villages of [his] district, and their history" was reflected in his research and writing. He credits Professor Maurice Freedman of the London School of Economics with giving his work international recognition in the early 1960s. Freedman also encouraged James to take his academic pursuits further, and in 1975, his thesis on the history and institutions of the Hong Kong region earned him the PhD from London that he missed out on twenty years earlier.

James's "absorbing interest" was more akin to a passion, seen in both his work and his studies. He found the people in Hong Kong's rural areas of particular interest. Most families had lived in the area for hundreds of years, leading the same life generation after generation.

> It didn't matter where you went in the New Territories in the late 1950s, and it didn't matter that you were a European and an official; if you spoke even a little Cantonese, you were treated with great courtesy. People always seemed completely at their ease.[6]

James maintains that his job had to come first, and that the opportunities for study arose from it. His work in the New Territories and the Resettlement Department provided a rich environment for developing his academic enquiries. Kowloon's old villages were also part of his responsibilities in the SCA. In all three postings, his interests enabled him "to get closer to the ordinary folk", helping him to do a better, more informed, job. The result was research that helped his work, and work that inspired his writing. And he is still writing. Before he submits anything for publication, James drafts it and re-drafts it many times. He admits that editors then have to grapple with his notorious scribbled notes, written in his own inimitable and incomprehensible shorthand.

This account of James the Scholar must also touch on the sharing part of his "guiding beacon". Patrick Hase, himself a leading historian of Hong Kong's New Territories, told me: "James has taught me most of what I know of the New Territories, and has been generous with his time and views whenever I have needed them. He is [my] Master and Mentor." James has for many years maintained an active correspondence with a range of scholars in shared fields of interest, giving assistance and advice wherever it is sought.

He has also long been generous with his various collections. Elizabeth Sinn remembers him scouring old book stores and second-hand shops. He would also collect old account books, shareholder registers, and other company records from Chinese businesses that either did not want to keep them or whose premises were being redeveloped. People would put things aside for him because they knew he would visit and want to keep them. He would then collect the items and place them in the back of his car, which Elizabeth described as a mobile clearing house. According to Stephen Selby, James's office was also full of odds and ends that he had collected over time. Elizabeth went on to add:

He would identify what he had collected as: "This would be useful for Elizabeth, or David Faure, or Patrick Hase." He would collect things even if he did not know what he would do with them. If he had had to pay for them, he would never charge when he passed them on.

James was one of the first people to see the historical value of such items. Collecting them required the coming together of two attributes: a real interest in Hong Kong's history and culture, and an ability to gain the trust and friendship of the Chinese donors.

The Royal Asiatic Society

James's commitment to sharing is also apparent through his membership in the RAS. He had been in Hong Kong only a short while when the Society was resuscitated in 1960. Attending the inaugural address that year, he became one of the earliest members. From 1967 to 1980 he was the honorary editor of the RAS Journal, piloting through the production of fourteen volumes. He became vice president in 1970 and served as president from 1983 to 1990.

James's contributions to the Society are legion. Apart from countless journal articles, he was an active leader of local visits for the benefit and education of members. Patrick Hase, arriving in Hong Kong as a district officer in 1972, joined the RAS on James's encouragement. Patrick told me with great clarity of his first RAS visit, led by James; it was through the then marshes and duckponds of Tin Shui Wai. Another outing, to the Kowloon Walled City in 1989, was so popular that it had to be run three times. James describes these activities as being "a labour of love", as was his commitment to the expansion of the Society's substantial library, adding to it significantly himself. He wrote: "My work with and for the Society has been among the most meaningful and satisfying of all my various activities."[7] He only stepped down as president because of his decision to relocate to Australia.

Family ties in Sydney prompted James to leave Hong Kong in 1990, something he describes as "a very traumatic uprooting".[8] Notwithstanding, he has flourished in his new home, continuing his scholarly pursuits. In 1991, he became secretary of The Asian Arts Society of Australia, giving talks on Chinese topics and writing numerous articles for the society's journal. In recent years he has been finding new homes for his collections. For example, many of his Qing scholar-official manuscripts are now with the Hoover Institution in California. He has also donated items to Sydney's Museum of Applied Arts and Sciences, the Art Gallery of New South Wales, and the National Library of Australia. To quote long-time friend and fellow book-lover Sally Burdon, James is "as engaged as ever".

James the Man

In preparing this essay, I have asked many people to describe James to me. Responses showed a remarkable consistency: "a chivalrous man of the old-world type", "charming and self-effacing", "has a smile of self-deprecation", "a scholar-official from the old school", "a friend rather than a senior officer". James has touched the lives of countless people. He described to me, with some emotion, the "good men" who were among his early superiors in Hong Kong, men such as Ken Barnett and Ronnie Holmes. "They were all-round absolutely first-class persons and gifted administrators. Throughout my life, I have been helped by amazing people." There are many who would say the same about James.

Even though "the odd fright" he says he encountered in Korea might have prompted a typical response such as "My word!", former colleagues remember him as being "not always the gentle pussy cat". Stephen Selby recalls that James could "F and Blind with the best of them—a real squaddie"; but he added that he only did this for effect. James admits that he does get angry, but he gets over it quickly. Patrick Hase recalls an occasion when James had sent out bailiffs to remove some illegal graves from a hillside above Tsuen Wan. In their enthusiasm, they also removed an ancient grave of the leading Tsuen Wan clan, taking the remains to be cremated. "The whole clan invaded the office, yelling and screaming. James was so angry that his staff could have been so stupid. His colour went from pale to red to deep purple, he was unable to speak for some moments."

At all other times, James was approachable to his junior colleagues. If any showed an interest in local history and culture, he gave them "huge encouragement", remembers Stephen Selby. Hugh Baker attests to James's generosity with his materials.

> His energy has been extraordinary over the years, holding down onerous jobs in government and contriving at the same time to be prolific in writings and activities outside his day job. I am far from being the only person to benefit from his help.

As an aside to me, James countered this with: "I am privileged to have the time, energy, and opportunity to expand my knowledge. It makes one realise how little one knows."

James's affection for the Chinese people with whom he interacted is evident through his writing. The notes on his village visits as district officer include such informal comments as: "a good, intelligent chap" and "a nice old boy". He was "genuinely accepted by the indigenous people against the background of arrogance and superiority exhibited by some expatriates".[9] Patrick Hase recalls James taking him to the New Year Dinner of the Apleichau Kaifong in 1975. To some, this might have seemed a chore, but to James, it was not only an important part of his job but also a pleasurable way to get to know Chinese people and their ways better. To the end of their lives, James retained a close friendship with many of the village elders he had worked with during the construction of the Shek Pik Dam.

One lady has played a pivotal part in James's life for almost half a century. James saw a picture of Mabel Wong on the desk of a female colleague; Mabel was also in the Administrative Service. "Who is that?" he asked. "You can't meet her", he was told, "because she has just gone to Oxford on a course." James waited until Mabel got back, and fell for her straight away. They married in 1974. Even though, according to James, Mabel repeatedly says to him "you are conspicuous for promising much but delivering little", he feels the same way about her as when they first met. In these enlightened times, it is hard to understand the difficulties that James and Mabel faced when their engagement was announced. The stigmas and taboos of early colonial Hong Kong lived on into the 1970s. James recalls being "strongly advised by a European lady against [marrying] a Chinese female colleague". The lady in question, a long-term Hong Kong resident, spoke of Chinese girls in very disparaging terms, "in a way that blended fear, dislike, and scorn in almost equal proportions".[10]

From an earlier marriage, James has three daughters, all leading international lives. No doubt they, like so many people, have been strongly influenced by their father.

Other Qualifications and Honours

In recognition of his long service to Hong Kong, James was made a Companion of the Imperial Service Order (ISO) in 1986. He served as an official Justice of the Peace (JP) from 1961 to 1987, and of course retains that title for life. Too numerous to describe here in detail, other qualifications and honours that he has accumulated over the years include honorary research fellow, Centre of Asian Studies, University of Hong Kong (1968–2010); and honorary fellow of the Hong Kong University of Science and Technology (since 2008).

Perhaps the award of which James is most proud is the honorary doctorate (DLitt) presented in 1992 by the University of Hong Kong for services to Hong Kong culture. Typically, he sees this as recognition of the efforts of a number of people to study Hong Kong. "I like to think the award, although a personal recognition, signified that Hong Kong studies and those who pioneered them in my generation were at last being recognised."[11]

Conclusion

A 2018 article in the *South China Morning Post* described the problems that some New Territories residents have in establishing their legal ownership rights, saying that they have merely been tolerated by the government.[12] "It's easier said than done", said a commentator, an excuse that has been repeated often since 1898. Another said: "Our city really needs to think long term about how to build communities, not just how to house people. ... It's time for the government to be more courageous and adventurous, and try something new." James was tackling similar problems sixty years ago; many of his efforts leave their mark still.

The first part of James's guiding beacon, "learn all the time, and share all the time", is something that he has clearly achieved; his many publications and other scholarly works are evidence of his continuing thirst for expanding his already prodigious knowledge. So many times during our conversations, he would say: "I have written about this somewhere." It is uncommon, however, for one who has achieved so much to live up to the second part of his beacon, the sharing. From the beginning of our relationship, spanning over thirty years, James has shown himself to be always encouraging to neophytes such as myself. He has a way of giving young researchers the impression that they are talking to an equal, when they certainly know that is not the case.

Perhaps the most fitting way to round off this essay is to echo part of the citation for James's honorary doctorate from the University of Hong Kong in 1992, which quoted Laozi's *Dao De Jing*:

> As he does not like to show off, he is enlightened. As he is not prone to be self-righteous, he is distinguished. As he does not blow his own horn, he acquires merit. As he does not extol himself, he is fit to be a leader.[13]

I am grateful to James, and to the many other people who have generously shared with me their recollections and experiences.

Robert Nield

Past-President of the Royal Asiatic Society Hong Kong,

author of *China's Foreign Places: The Foreign Presence in China in the Treaty Port Era, 1840–1943*

and of *The China Coast: Trade and the First Treaty Ports*[14]

October 2020

A Pattern of Life

Essays on Rural Hong Kong by James Hayes

Overviews

1

The Pattern of Life in the New Territories in 1898

This article launched James's writing career, and it remains an excellent introduction to the history of the Hong Kong area, broad in coverage and interesting in content. The New Territories became part of the British Crown Colony of Hong Kong in 1898 on a temporary and finite lease, but this is not an introduction to the area's colonial history — it barely mentions Britain — James sets out to describe and explain the workings of Chinese society and culture upon which British rule was imposed. As the bibliography of James's many writings (at the end of this book) shows, the majority of his oeuvre has this Sino-centric focus, and this piece was as much a sample of his own future interests as it was a crafted exercise to enlighten the innocent foreigner.

In 1898, Great Britain signed the Peking Convention which established the lease of the New Territories for 99 years. The world has made such material progress since that time, and urban Hong Kong has itself seen so many changes that it is difficult for us today to imagine the rural part of the colony

* Originally published in *JHKBRAS* 1962, Vol. 2, pp. 75–102.

as it then was, without roads or wheeled transport other than the wheel-barrow, with inhabitants who knew nothing of cars, aeroplanes, or weapons of mass destruction. Having made this effort, we must think back further still if we wish to obtain a proper appreciation of the situation, as James Stewart Lockhart[1] told the Hong Kong government in 1898. At the end of his report on the "New Territory", as he styled it, he said: "Under Chinese rule enterprise has been at a discount, and progress has been at a standstill for centuries. The Xin'an District of today must be much the same as it was four or five hundred years ago."[2]

The report is a valuable first-hand account of the area as it was in the year of its acquisition and covers the points in which the government would be most interested such as topography, communications, trade and natural products, population, industries, and the existing civil government. It also gave its author's recommendations as to how the New Territories should be governed and looked after in the future. This article, whilst making use of Lockhart's report, tries to give the background which he, of course, would take for granted. It does not pretend to deal with every part of the backcloth but only touches on those parts which seem worth mentioning for their share in fixing life in its accustomed mould: the village, the people themselves and their history, the clan system, ancestral worship, education, the district government, the background of affairs elsewhere in the province, the prevalence of disturbance and epidemic, popular religion. All of these were factors which made for integration or disruption in a life that could never have been easy.

The New Territories comprised an estimated 376 square miles of hill and plain situated on the mainland of China and a number of offshore islands, large and small, some of which were inhabited and some were not. For the purpose of this article it is sufficient to say here that in 1898 it was primarily an agricultural district consisting of a few broad valleys and many pockets of farm land among the hills or at their foot, both on the mainland and on some of the larger islands. There were a few market towns here and there—namely, Tai Po, Yuen Long, Tai O, Cheung Chau, Sai Kung, and Tsuen Wan. In 1905, Governor Sir Mathew Nathan reported that Yuen Long had "seventy-four shops of which twenty-five are large and deal in rice, oil, samshu, etc. The remainder belong to barbers, doctors, jewellers, vegetable sellers, piece goods dealers etc." Tai Po Market consisted of twenty-three large shops and fifteen smaller ones. Tsuen Wan had "a few shops supplying the local needs".[3] The present New Territories towns were not the largest in the Xin'an District. Pride of place went to Shenzhen, now on the Chinese side of the border, with sixty-one large shops and three hundred and twenty-three medium sized shops.

The emphasis was on farming, though there were a few small industries in operation. Village life was bounded by the two rice crops in summer and autumn and the winter season, when most land lay fallow; and by the occasional visit to the market town, often two or three hours away and over the hills, always on foot, and frequently laden with produce and livestock to sell or exchange.

It goes almost without saying that this small slice of territory, only half the size of the district of Xin'an, which was one of the smaller administrative districts of Guangdong Province, and 1,500 miles from Beijing, was an insignificant part of the Chinese Empire. However, despite its minute size and remoteness from the central provinces and the seat of government, it was fundamentally Chinese and essentially Confucian in its component parts, two features which are worth noting. One of its former district magistrates made an observation covering both these points in a Confucian discourse which he contributed to mark the restoration of a school at Kam Tin in 1744 when he wrote: "In this era of prosperity, culture has spread to even this remote place near the sea. Here the Book of Poetry is read as early as sunrise."[4]

The integrated life in which everything under Heaven has its place and plan is a recognisable feature of the Confucian code which was evolved and formulated in an agricultural society over 2,500 years ago. A study of the daily life and background of New Territories people in 1898, which was also placed in an agricultural setting, though one based on the cultivation of rice and not of wheat, leaves me with the impression that the high degree of mental and environmental integration attainable within a Confucian framework had certainly been attained here. Life was lived generation after generation according to a set pattern. The disciplined life imposed upon an agricultural community by the seasons was reinforced and coloured by the Confucian system of ethical behaviour which included filial piety and ancestor worship, two fundamentals that were re-expressed every New Year and at the two annual grave festivals. Both operated through the closely knit organisation of the clan, a group of families of the same name linked by descent from a common ancestor. This internal bond was further tightened by the restrictions of thought and movement imposed by poverty and poor communications.

I have always felt that this essential unity of life and thought is reflected in the traditional village scene, whose component parts are laid out in accordance with a general pattern whose essential beauty and simplicity leave an impression on the mind. Most of the present villages in the New Territory existed in 1898 and it is only mainly in the last ten or fifteen years that their original outline has been cluttered up with additional buildings in a semi-European style and their surrounding fields covered with wooden shacks put up by immigrant vegetable farmers. Clear all this away and in a good many cases you can still see what Stewart Lockhart and the gentlemen of his party saw as they travelled through the Territory in the month of August some sixty years ago. You will see a village whose houses are laid out in close rows on the higher ground. Behind them will be a thick grove of *feng shui* trees and to their front will extend terrace after terrace of rice fields, the one sliding almost imperceptibly into the other, the whole layout shaped for the purpose of seeing that a water supply can be led to each field for the planting periods of the year. On the slopes of the hills there may be pine trees and, occasionally, crops like pineapples and peanuts. You will also notice a few prominent horseshoe-shaped graves, some green or brown burial urns glistening in the sun, and areas on the higher slopes which look as though they have been shaved recently; as they virtually have by the women of the village who cut grass to sell for boat breaming and brushwood to burn in their own stoves. Entering one of these larger villages you will still see what Lockhart had to report:

> The houses in these villages are, as a rule, well and solidly built. The foundations and lower courses of their walls are, in many cases, of granite masonry, the upper courses being made of blue or sun-dried bricks. The door posts and lintels are of dressed granite slabs with tiled roofs on rafters made of China fir. The floors are generally concreted, and frequently paved with red brick or with granite. Well-built and handsomely decorated temples exist in all the important villages, and in many places large and expensively constructed buildings, in which the ancestral tablets are kept, were seen. As usual in China the streets are narrow and paved with large slabs of stone. Such drainage as exists is on the surface, underground drains never being used in Chinese villages.

In their surroundings and the generally peaceful life they led, everything conspired to make the people of the New Territories a conservative minded and generally amenable body, and Lockhart said of them: "Taken as a whole the inhabitants may be regarded as an industrious, frugal and well-behaved people." It may be appropriate at this stage to mention who they were. He found 161 Punti (Cantonese) villages with a population of some 64,000 persons and 255 Hakka villages, most of them smaller and more remote than the Cantonese ones, with a population of 36,000 people. He also mentions the boat people of whose numbers he was unable to obtain an estimate. He does say, however, that they formed a class by themselves and were looked down upon by the land population. Neither Punti nor Hakka are native to the district or to the province. The former, says Lockhart, are supposed to have come from the provinces bordering on the south of the Yangtse River and made their way to South China during the early periods of Chinese history. They were firmly established in the south during the time of the Southern Song dynasty (1127–1278) and, as he observes, it is a fact that most of the Punti inhabitants easily trace their descent from ancestors who were settled in the Xin'an District in that period, or elsewhere in Guangdong Province. The Hakka, or "strangers" as the term signifies, are, he says, supposed to be descended from the Mongols and to have reached the southern provinces when the Mongol dynasty was overthrown about the middle of the fourteenth century. They are regarded by the Punti as aliens, and speak a dialect quite distinct from the Cantonese. They are a hardy and frugal race and are generally found in the hill districts. As a rule, Cantonese and Hakka kept themselves to themselves in different villages and there has been a general antipathy between them until recent times.

Whether Punti or Hakka, the villages were inhabited by clans: either in groupings in which there were only persons of one clan descended from a common ancestor; or in villages in which lived several groups of families of different name, that is, several clans, having come there together or at different times. Examples of both kinds of villages, large and small, can be found all over the New Territories. Both Punti and Hakka clans have a history of wandering from the north throughout the last ten centuries at least, and it is clear that for all the families who came to what is now the leased territory it was the end of the line, the end of a chapter of wandering that was often interrupted for centuries in some location elsewhere in the province.

At Fan Pui, for instance, a small village on Lantau Island, lived the Fung clan who arrived there in the eleventh generation after the first ancestor had entered Guangdong Province. The twenty-second generation are living there still in an adjoining bay, having had to make way for the Shek Pik reservoir scheme. The family came from Ma Tau Wai in Kowloon and had made their way there from the Nam Hung District in the extreme north of the province after spending some time in the district of Hok Shan on the way south. Their neighbours, the Tsui clan of Shek Pik, claim twenty-seven generations in Guangdong and fifteen in Lantau: that is, nearly four hundred years. The first ancestor came from a village in the Nam Cheung District of Jiangxi Province and settled in the Dongguan District. Eventually, following the example of other members of the main branch who gradually moved southwards, a Tsui of the thirteenth generation came to Shek Pik and was buried there. Their clan history mentions that members of successive generations before the move to Lantau were officials and military officers who won the imperial favour in the Ming dynasty, whereas the Fung genealogy makes no such claims to fame for its progenitors. Both these clans are Cantonese. The condition of the peasantry impressed Lockhart favourably on the whole,

> The inhabitants, though by no means wealthy, seem to be, as a rule, comfortably well off and able to earn an honest livelihood without difficulty. Few signs of anything approaching destitution were seen, and only a few beggars were met.

The reason for this general standard of well-being was undoubtedly the universal ownership of land which was clearly shown by the land survey made in the first years after 1898. It was carried out by surveyors and staff on loan from the government of India. The survey sheets and the Crown Rent Rolls which form the schedules to them can be found in the District Offices of the New Territories Administration and they are a valuable record of land ownership and land classification at the time of the lease.

For example, at Shek Pik and Fan Pui in 1958, out of sixty-six families, four owned between 3–4 acres, nine between 2–3 acres, nineteen between 1–2 acres, fourteen between 0.5–1 acres, twelve between 0.25–0.5 acres, and eight between 0.10–0.25 acres. Except a few late arrivals, therefore, every family owned land. The position was much the same as it was in 1898.

Punti and Hakka alike, most families in every village owned some fields, and because of the joint succession to ancestral property by all male descendants in the direct line, nearly everyone had a joint and undivided share, a stake, in the land. There was also clan land which could be farmed out to poorer members. In land matters the clan had priority over the individual. This was reflected in Chinese deeds of sale or mortgage which, if the New Territories is anything to go by, appear to follow the same form in Guangdong as in far Shandong.[5] Where a sale was contemplated, a reason always had to be specified, and the land always had to be offered first to all relatives (which meant practically anyone inside the clan) before being offered to an outsider. Mortgages were more common than sales and were redeemable at any period after the original mortgage so that land need not pass outside the clan forever. There is no doubt that this tight rein on sales assisted the general preservation of the clan and the village and was a powerful factor in the continuance of a static and integrated life. These matters were regulated by the clan elders in conformity with immemorial custom.

To meet clan needs, amongst which was the proper worship of ancestors as well as the needs of the living, such as education of the young and the care of the old, certain fields and houses were set aside in trust, and the trust so created was known as a *tong* or *tso* (see the annex to this chapter). These are commonly found in the New Territories and many were registered at the land settlement which followed the grant of the lease to Great Britain. The *tso* is the more closely connected with the clan. Anyone can form a *tong*, but a *tso* is definitely a clan affair and of the nature of a serious ancestral trust.[6] It is set up to ensure that property is not divided or disposed of without due thought and is designed to circumvent the acts of foolish or spendthrift descendants, in the interests of all that the Confucian system holds most dear: the rearing of sons, giving them a proper education, seeing that forebears are duly respected in a fitting manner, assisting with weddings and funerals, repairs to the ancestral temple, and so on. Another and less formal method of securing these aims is the setting aside of "joss and oil fields", sometimes known by the obscure title of *ching sheung*, whose proceeds, again, are used for the proper observance of ancestral rites and other family needs. One need hardly emphasise the integrating effect of these land measures.

To understand the people and their outlook and background it is necessary to see to what sort of government they were accustomed. The government of the Xin'an District was essentially Confucian, like that of every other administrative division; by which I mean that Confucian principles were ostensibly followed. This was sealed by the state worship of the sage. In every district city there was a temple to Confucius styled a *man miu* in which the district magistrate, his senior staff, and the local gentry paid the customary respects to the sage and his seventy-two disciples on his birthday (the twenty-seventh day of the eighth moon) and at the spring worship, or *chun chai*, in the second moon. The same thing happened at the prefectural and provincial capitals. At the head of the Xin'an District was the district magistrate whose superior was the prefect of the Guangzhou Prefecture, which embraced at least five large districts. The latter was subordinate to the provincial governor and he in turn to the viceroy of the Two Guang provinces of Guangdong and Guangxi. The nature and duties of the provincial officers had been established since the Tang dynasty and for well over a millennium the pattern of government had been cast in an identical mould. The district magistrate was usually a scholar who had taken one of the metropolitan examinations at Beijing and he was always a native of another province than the one he served in, this being a long-standing rule. He spent three or six years in one post and was then moved elsewhere, and was promoted in due course to be prefect or to higher office through merit, connections, or good fortune. Some persons began and ended their official careers as district magistrates.

The district magistrate's duties were many and his competence was most extensive. He was, in truth, the "father-mother official" or *fu mou kwun*, so called by them and also so styled in official documents because of his authority over all their affairs, criminal or civil. He certainly regarded himself as standing *in loco parentis* to the people of his district. An instance of this outlook is a proclamation issued by the Canton viceroy in April 1899 in which he told the people of the New Territories that the English government had agreed that "the people are to be treated with exceptional kindness". On the reverse side of the medal, the magistrate could use his authority to evil purposes. Such an official might be referred to as being *yu fu* "as (fierce as) a tiger"[7] or a *kau kwun* "dog-official" whose extortions and venality were a byword in the district. When I asked an old scholar about extortion and venality among magistrates, he replied in distinctly extenuating tones: "Some did; but then they had so many people to look after." He observed that there were some rich districts in Guangdong in which a magistrate had to do nothing to obtain money as it came rolling into the office in the way of presents, inducements, additions to land and other taxes, etc., whilst there were others so poor that the magistrate could squeeze little from them even if he tried very hard.

In his government, the magistrate was usually assisted by an indoor and outdoor staff. The former might consist of personal adherents from his own home district who followed him from post to post, and partly of local personnel of the tribunal or *yamen*, such as a legal adviser, secretaries, and land clerks whose local knowledge it would be difficult to dispense with. All these were entirely dependent upon the magistrate for their livelihood, and upon what they could pick up in the course of their duties. To maintain his position and put food into the mouths of the members of his personal staff and their families, the magistrate was given an inadequate salary by government. In addition, there were the outdoor staff which comprised a considerable number of police, watchmen, runners, and the like, who may have been paid by government despite what Lockhart says to the contrary, but used their opportunities as they came.

In the Xin'an District, the magistrate's *yamen* was at Nantou, which lies beyond the northern or further shores of Deep Bay on the far side of the Nantou peninsula. This was the district city where the treasury, jail, and examination halls were also situated. It also contained a Confucian temple. The seat of government therefore lay outside the borders of the New Territories, which was served by several subordinate officers. The assistant magistrate's office was at Dapeng northeast of Mirs Bay and outside the New Territories; and there were two deputy magistrates one of whom was stationed within the walled city of Kowloon. They had power to make arrests and conduct preliminary enquiries but were bound to refer most cases to Nantou for final decision. The Kowloon deputy, like his colleagues, had a lock-up for detaining persons pending trial and there was also one each for the local divisions of the district, or *tung*, several of which were within the present boundaries of the New Territories. These lesser officials were appointed from Beijing but had limited powers and, as with the magistrate himself, were transferable every three years.

There were also military officers in the district, a battalion commander at Dapeng, who also had quarters at Kowloon in which he was more often to be found. He had subordinates with him at Kowloon City and also in the islands, at Tung Chung and at Tai O on Lantau, whilst there appear to have been other subordinate officers on at least Lamma and Cheung Chau.[8]

In addition to the military posts (Lockhart does not mention any naval forces) there were the police of which there were two kinds. First, there were the *chai* or "runners", of whom there were about sixty, stationed in Nantou under the direct control of the magistrate. Lockhart states:

> They are sent, as occasion requires, throughout the district for a variety of purposes, including the making of arrests, the collecting of the land tax, and acting generally as the eyes and ears of the Magistrate. They receive no pay from Government, but manage to earn a fair livelihood by illicit squeezes.

There were also village constables, from two to six, according to the size of a village, appointed by the village and paid by village contributions levied according to the size of a villager's landholdings. "Their duty is to keep watch, especially at night. They have the power of arrest, which is deputed to them by the gentry and elders of the village."

The elders played a great part in maintaining the *status quo*. Together with the headman of the village and the local gentry they formed a local tribunal which dealt summarily with all minor matters in the *tung* and *heung* into which the district was divided.[9] Inside the villages the headmen and elders acted likewise. A form of genuine local self-government existed in 1898. Its *raison d'etre* was probably nothing more high-flown because the district magistrate, traditionally an overworked official, would have been completely swamped with work of a trifling nature had they not existed. J. Dyer Ball in his *The Chinese at Home* says:

> The life of an official in China, if he occupies a high position and rules over a populous district of country, is arduous in the extreme. He knows no hours. His work is never done. He is up before dawn, and official receptions take place in the small or

early hours of the morning. The health of many a man is injured by the incessant toil and unremitting anxiety.[10]

He calls him "often hard worked, harassed with many cares, and loaded with responsibilities". His is experienced and impartial testimony. To quote Lockhart:

The gentry and elders in the village council determined summarily cases of theft, disputes about land, domestic squabbles, and cases of debt. As a rule the decision of that council is accepted as final. But if either of the parties to a case is dissatisfied, he can appeal to a council of the Tung, or to a general council, made up of representatives of the different Tung. ... Each council of the Tung contains representatives of the villages which make up the Tung. In addition to a council of a Tung there is a general council for the whole of the Tung Lo or Eastern Section, which is practically that portion of the district of Xin'an contained in the map attached to the Convention. This general council is styled the Tung Ping Kuk or Council of Peace for the Eastern Section. It has its council chamber at the market town of Shenzhen which is regarded as the centre of the Eastern Section. If the decision of the council of the Tung, or of the General Council is not regarded as satisfactory, an appeal lies to the Magistrate of the district.

Villages must occasionally have made their own rules. There is an interesting survival of these written on a wooden board which hangs in one of the side rooms of the Yeung Hau Wong Temple at Tung Chung on Lantau Island. It is dated in the third moon of the nineteenth year of the Guangxu reign (1893). The text refers to the passing of the good old days and lays down measures to deal with offenders. For stealing crops, for cutting down pine trees and bamboo, and for letting pigs or buffaloes graze on other people's fields there were fines in cash, a proportion of which went to the person who caught the culprit. He was to be escorted to the *heung* council office, and should he refuse to pay after a hearing there, he was to be taken before the magistrate. It was drawn up by the Tung Chung Hap Heung, or all the villages of the Tung Chung Valley.

A few words on the elders and gentry may be appropriate here. An elder was an older villager whose character, influence, and senior generation in the clan entitled him to a say in its affairs. He was more to the fore in the remoter villages of the district, which were generally the poorer ones and could not afford to support *literati*, as they are sometimes styled, which is what the gentry really were in the Chinese context. These were persons of considerable influence who came generally from the larger, richer villages of the plains which had one or more village schools where the elements of a classical education could be obtained. In course of time by dint of hard study at home or in Guangzhou the cleverer among the local scholars, after successful examination by the district magistrate at Nantou and then by the Guangzhou prefect, proceeded to the viceroy's *yamen* in the same city where eventually a favoured few would manage to pass the first degree of *sau choi*. This in theory entitled the scholar to qualify for an official post. In practise there were many more *sau choi* than there were posts and a scholar had to pursue further study and pass other examinations before he stood a real chance of becoming an official. In every district, there were *sau choi* who would never obtain posts. Many became local schoolmasters. Others by virtue of wealth and position became the local gentry who, by report, were sometimes a help to the magistrate and frequently a nuisance, both to him and to the litigant or criminal public.

In his 1901 book *Society in China*, Sir Robert Douglas has hard things to say of these men:

[Their] mental activity, ... not having ... any power to operate in a beneficent way, exerts itself with unprecedented vigour and hardihood in local affairs. No dispute arises but one or more of these social pests thrusts himself forward between the contending parties, and no fraud on the revenue or wholesale extortion is free from their similar influence.[11]

They sat on the local tribunals (*kuk*) and advised the magistrate on local affairs. Being *literati* like himself they had ready access to his *yamen* and to his ear. Sometimes they even outranked him. Elders, on the other hand, rarely sat on the *kuk*. Lockhart estimated that there were one hundred and fifty *sau choi* in the whole district. In 1898 the elders of important villages like Ha Tsuen and Ping Shan were *literati*. Several of them played a leading part in the planning of operations against the British take-over.

Sometimes the wealthier village elders enhanced their position by purchasing degrees. In the late Qing period, the sale of examination titles appears to have been considerable, and I have come across several such persons in villages in the Southern District of the New Territories. They were usually comparatively wealthy villagers. Such a one was Chan Tak-hang of Cheung Kwan O in Junk Bay who died in the seventeenth year of Guangxu (1892) at the age of sixty-four. According to his descendant, the present village representative, he was a man of substance who built a guest house in the village which is still standing today, gave money for the upkeep of the stone tracks which linked the villages of the area with Kowloon, and was well known locally. His portrait, painted at the age of fifty-seven, shows him in his borrowed finery as a *kwok hok sang*, or "Student of the National College", for which he paid an unknown consideration to the Qing government. A man such as this would obviously play a considerable part in the affairs of his immediate neighbourhood.

Despite the presence of troops, military posts, and police of two types in the territory, besides the assistance of the local *kuk*, the magistrate's power to prevent crime appears to have been limited. Piracy, in particular, was rampant at different times, and ranged from the anti-dynastic activities of Koxinga in the mid-seventeenth century on behalf of his former masters the Great Ming dynasty (which occasioned the forced evacuation of the coastal population from 1662 to 1669), through the widespread depredations of large pirate bands at the beginning of the nineteenth century,[12] to the milder but still disconcerting activities of the period under review.

It is necessary to emphasise the prevailing unrest, since until quite recently the only striking difference between the New Territories in 1898 and the territory we know today was the imposition of the *pax britannica*. Until the British government got into the saddle and established its police stations and patrolling launches, the people were subject to piracy, robbery, and other forms of violence as from time immemorial. The governor specifically mentioned in a dispatch to the secretary of state in April 1899 that

> the (Tai Po) district is well known in Canton (i.e., to the Viceroy) to be turbulent, that to the N.E. of Mirs Bay being noted for piracy, and so ill-disposed that I am informed no Customs Official dares to land there except with the support of a revenue cruiser.

Of course, the local population were sometimes not averse to such efforts themselves, and as a British Consul wrote at the time: "The old free-booting spirit still survives among many who are now apparently peaceful traders and fishermen [of which] we occasionally get startling proofs in some unexpected daring act of piracy on the high seas or along the coast." Smuggling was also common, whether of salt or opium.[13]

Looking outside the district to the province and its capital city Guangzhou, the political scene, as revealed by the Trade Reports to the Foreign Office of consuls in the several British treaty ports of Guangzhou, Amoy, Samshui, and Pakhoi was the reverse of satisfactory. Though written by a succession of men of obviously varying temperament and outlook they reveal a sad state of affairs. Everywhere there were disturbances which the civil authorities were slow or incapable to correct, and clear signs that the dynasty was held to have exhausted its mandate from Heaven. In Guangzhou itself there was a serious plot to seize the city in October 1894, which led Consul Fraser to write in his next report that there was "little doubt that dissatisfaction with the administration of their native country is growing among the Southern Chinese, and if no attempt at reform is made, may result in a serious insurrection".[14] He mentioned the plot but remarked that its failure was due more to the ineptitude of its organisers than to the vigour of the local authorities. His colleague at Pakhoi, in the southeast of the province, was more critical:

> Such as is Chinese civilisation, Pakhoi is of its outskirt only and shows a lower level than I have seen anywhere else in this country. Piracy is in the blood of the race. A glance through the year's diary shows a monotonous record of petty coast raids, hoverings of pirate junks (which still terrorise the neighbouring coastline) and robberies of every degree of dignity from the sacking of the larger pawnshops to the plunder of a returned emigrant from the Straits or Sumatra. ... Of Chinese local authorities at Pakhoi itself there are practically none, the highest native Civilian within 20 miles being an officer of the rank of Sub-district Deputy Magistrate armed with an amount of authority that barely enables him to call in question the theft of a matchbox. It would be invidious to say this much of the Pakhoi neighbourhood without adding that most of the adjacent areas are worse.[15]

Whilst these reports were confined to individual districts there can be little doubt that the general unrest was known and felt in the New Territories. It will be recalled that Sun Yat-sen was a Cantonese, and some of his followers are credited with swelling the ranks of the village bands which offered resistance to the British troops who entered the New Territories in 1899. This tale of unrest and lawlessness, and weakness on the part of the civil authorities, provides a background to the unsuccessful reform movement of 1898, sponsored by the southern party at Beijing, whose sequel was the incarceration of the emperor by his formidable aunt, the Empress Dowager, the stringent capital measures against the reform party, and their dispersal overseas or in foreign concessions in China. The leader of the movement and adviser to the emperor was Kang You Wei, a prominent scholar and mandarin, and himself a Cantonese.

Disturbances apart, the common people preferred to be left to themselves. They rarely had anything to do with the magistrate and his followers and preferred it that way. The magistrate, in his turn, was glad to leave routine affairs to the local tribunals. The price paid for these attitudes was the prevalence of crime. Poor communications were no help. The magistrate was often rendered powerless by unrest and disturbances of all kinds. Robberies and descents on shore by pirate gangs could take place with impunity since, even if help came, it invariably arrived far too late. Crime might eventually be punished but it was seldom prevented. No one would inform on disturbers of the peace for fear of reprisals or being entangled in the meshes of the law. Commenting on coastal piracy in 1897 Consul Brenan wrote:

> The boat people never attempt to effect an arrest; there would probably be bloodshed and they would then be involved in judicial proceedings almost as unpleasant for themselves as for the pirates. They are thankful enough if they can get rid of their dangerous passengers, and persuade them to go off and try their fortune elsewhere.[16]

However, it is only fair to state that the people of the district were also apt to create trouble among themselves, especially when circumstances conspired to make life difficult, as in the dry season. This was especially true of the more closely populated agricultural areas, with villages in close proximity to each other, often sharing the same water supply for their fields and personal needs. The volatile Cantonese temperament is not suited to a cautious settlement of complicated personal problems: it is easier by far to fly off the handle and strike an attitude than to sit down and think. Hence difficult situations often were made intolerable by proximity and a quick temper, and clan fights were not uncommon, especially in the Yuen Long area.[17] A tablet in the Tin Hau Temple at Miu Kong, Tsuen Wan, refers to the death of seventeen male villagers during an armed conflict between this village and Shing Mun Pat Heung in three years of intermittent strife which began in 1861. To these disturbances between the Punti villagers can be added a general antipathy between Hakka and Punti which sometimes erupted into violence and was still smouldering after the Hakka rebellion thirty years before.[18]

The education of the people was not calculated to improve matters, either over their own disputes or in taking a sensible attitude towards trouble from outside. I have already mentioned the educational process by which the *literati* obtained their degrees. The great majority of the people, by contrast, were illiterate and superstitious and for the most part were bereft of any formal education. Cattle tending and crop watching came first, schooling a bad second. Education was the result of parental initiative and favourable circumstance. As I have already said, there appear to have been schools in the larger villages, but they were private and were usually attended by a small proportion of village children, those whose fathers were willing and could afford to educate them. At Ho Chung near Sai Kung, for instance, a large village of nearly a hundred families in 1898, the number of children in the school, which was held in the schoolmaster's private house, was around twenty. The children came and went, some spending three years there, others less, and none but the brightest spent longer. Many children received no education at all, since in addition to the cost of tuition, parents had to pay for books, desk, pen, ink, and stationery. Study consisted of portions of the Four Books and Five Classics and reading, recitation, and dictation based upon them. The number of characters learned at school was limited and the classical terms and characters learned by rote were not always of much use in daily life in the country, whilst practical subjects such as arithmetic and geography were unknown. Only clever children with well-off and determined parents continued their education and, by going mostly to Guangzhou, learned something of the outside world.

Life was therefore constricted and uncertain, dependent as it was to a great degree on a lack of natural disasters, and the epidemics which invariably followed in their wake, and sometimes did not require such prompting. There is a catalogue of such things in the District History.[19] Life was also essentially local and personal. It was not therefore surprising that disputes over land, whether rents or taxes, were considered of great moment in the minds of the people. There is evidence for this throughout the New Territories where court cases relating to land were sometimes held to be of sufficient importance to warrant their being inscribed on stone tablets inside the more important temples in the area, where presumably they would be seen by the worshippers who congregated there in large numbers at festival times.

There is a spirited account of a dispute between tenants and a new and rapacious landlord at Kat O in 1802 which was complicated by the clerks of the *yamen* who, obviously for a consideration, deluded their magistrate and were in collusion with the landlord. The tenants petitioned no less a person than the viceroy of the Two Guang provinces in his *yamen* at Guangzhou and his instructions, relayed through the governor and prefect, are set out in stone so that justice could be done, and seen to be done, ever after. Everything worthwhile, every precedent or decision of importance, seems to have been set forth on stone: "to ensure compliance"; "for observance by both parties"; "to follow the judgment"; "for fear that this would be forgotten as time goes by, thus leaving endless troubles in the future"; "for the general information of the people"; and so on. The tablets were either set up by the people or, as in most of these cases, by order of the magistrate with the written approval of the viceroy; by the community of Tung Chung, Sai Chung, Keung Shan, etc.; by the fishermen of Peng Chau "since approval had not been given for the erection of a tablet by the Viceroy" (later given by the magistrate); by the provincial governor and so forth.[20]

Perhaps to compensate for the severities and uncertainties of this life, the inhabitants of the district fortified themselves by a devotion to religion that was marked by its generous diversity. To the usual galaxy of gods such as Tin Hau, Kwun Yam, Hung Shing, Kwan Tai, Pak Tai, Tam Kung, and Yeung Hau Wong they added local officials who had acted as their benefactors and anyone else who took their fancy. Whilst there may be some who are not so well known and whose memory has faded in the minds of the people, the two who have left an indelible mark in the New Territories are Wong Loi Yam and Chow Yau Tak, successive viceroys of the Two Guang provinces, who were responsible for obtaining the cancellation of the edict of 1662 which ordered all inhabitants of coastal areas to remove fifty *li* inland in order to deny their assistance, forced or otherwise, to the pirate bands attacking the new dynasty in the name of the Ming which it had supplanted eighteen years before. Great hardship was encountered which is hardly surprising, and the people were eternally grateful to their benevolent officials and commemorated them in several temples dedicated in their honour. One of these was burned down in 1955 during the fire which destroyed Shek Wu Hui near

Fanling, and others are to be found at Sha Tau Kok and Kam Tin, and Sai Heung in Chinese territory. In addition, a school was named in their honour at Kam Tin, and when it was repaired in 1744 the Xin'an magistrate of the time composed a Confucian discourse which was inscribed on the wall of the restored building to instruct the pupils and their parents. An interesting survival which still existed in 1898 was the appearance of an old beggar in the Yuen Long villages every Chinese New Year who brought statues of Wong and Chow for the people to worship, and incidentally to supply him with food and money. To these men-become-gods for whom the construction of a temple was necessary to ensure their better worship and resulting favours, there must be added an equal and possibly much older faith in sacred tree spirits and the multitude of earth spirits known as *pak kung*, *tai wong*, and ordinary *she tan*, who look after villages and localities, such as passes, bridges, and fords over streams. Tree spirits are quite common in the New Territories where many old trees have joss sticks and red paper inscriptions placed under them on a rough altar. There is, in particular, a very large old banyan tree a few miles from Sai Kung Market which must surely be the oldest tree in the Southern District. This is visited regularly by devotees, and I can say with confidence that belief in tree and earth spirits still exists today, and might indeed be said to flourish.

The reliance on the spirits who ruled this world and would assuredly be encountered in the next was expressed in the continual reconstruction of temples. A great many of the temples in the New Territories today owe their present fabric, or a great part of it, to repairs made during the last fifty years of the Qing dynasty. It was evidently a highly necessary part of the proceedings that the god should be informed of the names of the contributors so that his benefits should not pass anyone by, since their names, and often the amounts they gave, were scrupulously inscribed on the commemorative tablet which was always let into the wall to mark the occasion. Sometimes over a thousand names had to be recorded in this way, most of them in respect of trifling amounts, even for a small and out of the way temple, as in the reconstruction of the Tin Hau Temple at Cheung Chau in the second year of the last Qing emperor (1909).

The magistrate, too, was expected to play his part in warding off disaster. The District History mentions that the incumbent in 1630 wrote a prayer for divine help to the City God of Nantou after a dark mist resembling the shadow of a black dog haunted womenfolk in the third moon; and the magistrate in 1673 wrote the "Lamentations" or odes and addresses burnt in sacrifice when a severe typhoon hit the district city: this was preserved among the literary works recorded in another chapter of the History. There is no mention of later imitations.

Besides this preoccupation with spirits of all kinds and a general disposition to ensure against all possible acts of ill will on their part which was, one almost thinks, a by-product of the bad times and the uncertainties which usually surrounded the Chinese peasant and his city counterpart, there was a regular and intense devotion to the ancestors of the clans which was carried on through the centuries. This, of course, was Confucianist, as opposed to the Taoist and animist forms of religion to be seen inside temples and on the fields and hillsides. There is no doubt that the clans were kept together by the regular attention that was paid to the ancestral duties and the particular reverence accorded to the first ancestor who had settled in the village. I have already explained how, on the material side, management of land by the clan for the clan assisted in keeping both land and people together. On the spiritual plane the ancestral duties had the same effect.

At the heart of the clan was the ancestral hall.[21] Here the soul tablets of past generations were arranged in rows on an altar: these can still be seen in a few ancestral halls today, notably at Ping Shan and Ha Tsuen, two villages of the Tang clan, whose green and gold tablets date back to the Song dynasty. Most villages in the New Territories, large and small, appear to have had ancestral halls at the time of the lease. Many of them are standing today and I have traced the presence of others which have mouldered away since 1898.[22] Each clan had its own hall and here its members gathered to perpetuate its corporate identity on occasions like births, weddings, and funerals, and regularly each year at the New Year festival.

As an adjunct to the tablets in the ancestral hall, the graves of ancestors were also the subject of regular attention by the villagers, particularly the grave of the first ancestor and his wife.[23] The graves were visited without fail at the two major grave festivals of Ching Ming and Chung Yeung in spring and autumn respectively, and to them came all male descendants who could walk unaided, or on a friendly arm, or be carried, in order to sweep the graves, offer food and drink, and make the obligatory *kowtow*. These ceremonies were carried out near the village on the slopes of the surrounding hills where the clan graves were usually to be found; but sometimes filial piety was tested further since the dictate of a geomancer would place the first ancestor's grave, and others, at some distance from the village. This could mean considerable inconvenience at the grave festivals. This is the case at Pa Mei, a small village in the Tung Chung Valley on North Lantau, where the first grave is at Cheung Sha on South Lantau.

At New Year the burden could be much heavier. Not every village had its own ancestral hall. Sometimes the parent village from which the first ancestor had come was near at hand, and in these cases it was often felt unnecessary to build an ancestral hall in the new village. Instead, the able bodied members of the clan, male and female of every age, sallied forth at New Year and at the time of the grave festivals on a journey to their relatives in their native village.[24] Frequent examples of this can be found in the New Territories, and at the time of the major festivals in 1898 the hill tracks and little ports and market towns of the colony must have been full of persons travelling to and from their homes on ancestral duties.[25]

The whole ethos and action of the clan was practically one hundred percent Confucian in its workings. In 1898 the clan system appears to have operated in the New Territories in the traditional ways and with all the latent powers and vigour at its command. It regulated what happened within and helped to determine what went on outside itself. Its heads who were educated to the Confucian tenets were part of the mechanism of local government. The government of the province, prefecture, and district were also Confucian to the core, in precept if not always in practice, and both government and people knew how they stood in their traditional relationship to one another. Disturbances, lawlessness, and unrest were mere *trivia*, annoying but of no real import to the discipline of the land and the clan. The popular religion too, was but an ephemeral thing, something to meet the needs of the moment; something that was not so respectable as the austere worship which fell within the Confucian canon. In short, the impression left by the brief excursion into the past which forms the basis of this article has left me with the firm impression that Confucianism was the dominant influence over people and government in the New Territories in 1898. I hasten to point out that in itself this is not in any way surprising: but in view of the remoteness of the area and its late settlement by Chinese of different race with their undoubted absorption of earlier inhabitants, this impression of its pervasiveness and brooding presence everywhere in the Territory at this time is probably worth restating.

Chapter 1 Annex
Tong and *Tso* in the New Territories

Originally a cyclostyled memorandum, signed "J.W. Hayes", this analysis was produced for use in government offices in approximately 1961. It served as guidance for handling New Territories land dealings and was cited in a 1995 Supreme Court Judgment and its subsequent appeal. Tso and tong crop up in writings on the New Territories so often that it seems right to explain them as early as possible in this collection. Although this piece was never formally published, its survival is testimony to its usefulness.

These two traditional Chinese organisations are confusing to foreigners especially as their immediate object is the same: namely that property should be perpetuated and should not be disposed of without due consideration and the consent of those persons currently involved in its communal ownership or management. Little has been written on the subject.

Of the two, the *tso* is especially concerned with the clan. A *tso* can only take the name of a deceased person. It can originate with a man who, for various reasons, does not want all his property divided among his descendants, perhaps to avoid disputes or to prevent it from being broken up into minute parcels, but always to perpetuate his own memory and those of his direct ancestors. Alternatively, it can be initiated on behalf of a certain ancestor by a descendant who buys land which is registered as a *tso* in the ancestor's name. The title of the *tso* is simply a man's name with the word "*tso*" tacked on at the end. *Tso* land is more likely to be bought than inherited land and the benefactor must be more prosperous than his forebears if he can afford to set aside bought or ancestral land in his own or ancestor's memory. He was generally the founder or an early member of the clan in a particular village; which, in the New Territories, can mean that he lived anything from one to eight hundred years ago, depending upon the age of the settlement.

The profit deriving from *tso* property — in the past usually in the form of *kuk* ("unhusked rice") being rent from the fields — is used to further family worship and for the repair and maintenance of the ancestral graves. A surplus is usually eaten up in feasts given at the main Chinese festivals of the year, though traditionally it was supposed to assist with the education and welfare of descendants, and in some cases may still be.

Tso property can be large or small, and will obviously vary from clan to clan but in every case, managers are elected to manage the property. This was the case both before and after 1898. Ideally the property should not be sold or mortgaged, and should descend to future generations intact, but the New Territories Ordinance Cap. 97 (19), provides for this contingency provided a request is made to the district officer (as assistant land officer) to deal in the property and his consent is forthcoming if the usual notice of intention, which is posted locally to ensure that all concerned know about the forthcoming dealings, has expired without objection.

The *tso* is something personal to the direct male descendants of one ancestor; so much so that even the descendants of the originator's brothers by the same mother have no share in the property or its management. It is this highly personal element and this narrow intent to benefit the ancestor and his direct descendants in the male line which differentiate *tso* and *tong*.

The *tong* is the more flexible organisation and is not linked to ancestor worship and little else besides, as is the case with the *tso*. It is a business association as often as not, and can, in fact, be a registered company. Indeed, a new *tong* with over twenty members is not, by implication, exempt from the legislation of 1910 Cap. 9 (20), which gives exemption to "any clan family or *tong* owning land on the twenty eighth day of October 1910 in respect of which a manager has been duly registered under the Ordinance". The same exemptions and restrictions presumably apply to *tso*, since these are family organisations. However, old New Territories organisations, both *tso* and *tong*, which have prospered and grown since 1910, to the extent that they have over twenty members since that date and so put themselves outside the scope of the exemption, rarely registered themselves under the Companies Ordinance, Cap. 32 and the government seems never to have enquired too closely into the matter. New organisations of the traditional type, large or small, do not seem to register under the Companies Ordinance either, unless it suits their convenience.

However, it must not be imagined that *tong* are only business organisations. At the time of the lease there were four recognisable types. The first was a purely business organisation between friends or business associates with no common relationship (e.g., Shui Shang Tong of Tai O, which was formed by several otherwise unrelated Tai O businessmen, shopkeepers, and farmers to buy land in the locality and share in the profits). The second was also a business organisation but one formed between family members and clansmen (e.g., Chi Wing Shing Tong of Shek Pik, which originated in the Chi clan of that place and was, among other things, a money loan association). There was also the religious *tong*, usually Buddhist, in which the members of a *chai tong* ("vegetarian hall"), *chi* ("monastery") or *am* ("nunnery") formed a *tong* to further and simplify their internal relationship in respect to land ownership and routine management; especially since membership was always changing due to deaths, disputes, and the recruitment of new inmates (e.g., the Kwong Sin Tong, a *chai tong* at Luk Wu Tung, which owned a considerable amount of property locally on which it supported its existence). However, very few Buddhist halls form themselves into *tong*, more's the pity. In all these cases the name chosen for the *tong* was purely decorative and, it was hoped, an auspicious one, as Chinese shop signs and company names contrive to be to this day.

There was in addition the family *tong* which in many ways is akin to the ancestral *tso* though usually with a wider scope of activity. It is not always easy to differentiate the two since their objects largely coincide. The name, too, seems at first sight identical in form though, in fact, the difference lies in the *tso* using the personal name and the family *tong* using the ancestor's business or lucky names in the title (e.g., Li Tun Yan Tong of Shek Pik).

The ancestral *tong* is a convenience and can be formed not necessarily by one man but by several brothers or clan cousins who do not wish to divide all their ancestral or newly purchased property (ordinarily the latter) but desire to set all or a part of it aside for the benefit of their descendants, with an obligation, as in a *tso*, to carry out the required sacrifices etc. as a matter of course. The descendants would share the profits on a pre-arranged scale that is subject to change over the years as shares are inherited, bought, or sold from other members of the *tong*.

Welfare matters (e.g., education and the relief of old age) are more usually handled by a family *tong* rather than by *tso* which relate mainly to the requirements of ancestral sacrifice for which they generally require less land than the family *tong* with its wider responsibilities and greater need of funds.

Whatever its welfare or family functions, whatever its ends and policies, the *tong* is mainly a business venture concerned with profit and losses on which the continuance of its activities depends. Some of these *tong* are very large and are extensive landowners (e.g., Li Kau Yuen Tong of Sha Wan, Guangzhou, before the lease, which was the tax lord for the whole of Lantau).

In all these cases, a list of members of the *tong* is required by the assistant land officer, and managers reported to him by the members can be registered in the Land Office provided no objections are raised when the assistant land officer posts the usual notices of intention to register. Proposed dealings are handled in the same way as for *tso*.

2

Rural Leadership in the Hong Kong Region: Village Autonomy in a Traditional Setting

Much has been written about the mandarins of China, unsurprisingly since they were selected from among the best educated and were most interested in writing about their own kind. Such leaders had little or no contact with the rural areas where the vast majority of people lived, and it is doubtful if any one of them as high as a district magistrate had set foot in what is now the New Territories for centuries. The leaders that James examines here were not grandees imposed as governors, prefects, and magistrates by the imperial court, they were home-grown men of energy, acumen, and strong will who rose to power and influence through success and achievement in their own local area. The state and its apparatus of government may have had ultimate power, but the everyday running of the country was carried out by unelected, unappointed men of action and initiative — not necessarily well educated or amiable or scrupulous, but capable, persuasive, and identifying first and foremost with their family and their native village.

* Originally published in Göran Aijmer (ed.), *Leadership on the China Coast* (London 1984) pp. 32–52.

This is an amplification of an article I published in 1967 and which was written round three area leaders from the village communities of Lantau Island. The present expansion of the paper is more concerned with the wider and general context, though still with local application. In it I seek to emphasise the immense support afforded to local leaders by the family and lineage organisation and by the customary law, as well as by the frequent occasions inside the lineage and the village for the exercise of leadership functions.

In this fringe area of the Chinese Empire we are no doubt dealing with what one of the mid-Qing provincial mandarins of Guangdong Province described as residents of "the huts thinly scattered along the shores of the ocean, ignorant and disobedient", but even after discounting the hyperbole, the ordered situation in these settlements revealed by detailed investigation is surely remarkable.

Lantau, the largest offshore island of the New Territories,[1] is roughly fifteen miles long by five-and-a-half miles broad. It takes the form of a mountain range which runs, with breaks, along its whole length on a northeast-southwest axis. The main peaks of this range are around three thousand feet high. Most of the cultivated land is situated around the coast, and at the time of the British lease amounted to a little less than 2,660 acres; that is, only a few square miles.[2] The main crop was and still is rice, harvested twice, in July and November. In 1898, the island possessed one market town (population two thousand) situated at its western extremity. This place was a salt-producing centre and a considerable fishing-port. There were also about fifty small villages on the island. At a carefully conducted census taken some years after the lease, four of these villages had populations in excess of two hundred persons (the largest 363) another seven had more than one hundred inhabitants, whilst the remainder were under that figure. The total land population was then over 6,700 persons, mainly Cantonese. Most of the villages were inhabited entirely by Cantonese or Hakka lineages, though some of them were of mixed settlement. There was also a boat population of around 5,500 persons whose craft were based on the market town and other anchorages along the coastline.

Before 1898, Lantau was part of the Xin'an District of Guangdong. Though it was not far by sea from the district city, it was not under the district magistrate's direct rule but was under the charge of one of his deputies. This officer's *yamen* was in the walled city of Kowloon and he was responsible for many other villages besides those on Lantau. There was no civil officer resident on the island before 1898, though one imagines that runners would visit it from time to time to chase in taxes and, perhaps less frequently, to make an arrest. The military authorities were most in evidence. A Captain commanded a detachment in the fort at Tung Chung (a large valley in the north-central part of the island), and a junior officer was in charge of another body of troops in the market town of Tai O. There were supposed to be others in certain small posts in other scattered locations. Their presence was perhaps more due to European activities in the local seaways, and to pirates, than to any disturbances likely to take place on the island, especially in the latter half of the nineteenth century when there is no memory of internal trouble.[3]

The people of Lantau were left mainly to their own devices by the government, military, and civil alike. From evidence collected locally it appears that as elsewhere in China the lineage and village elders kept the peace in the villages, and the kaifong (street association) did the same in the market town and paid for watchmen to bar and walk round the principal streets at night. Anything more serious than minor disturbance and petty crime, such as piracy or armed robbery, was reported to the military, though by that time it was usually too late for anything effective to be done. Disputes were settled locally as far as possible. Besides these, the elders handled a variety of duties which, irrespective of the size of the community, were sometimes arduous and complex since much depended on handling individuals so as to produce a fruitful result. They organised small public works of benefit to their communities, such as the digging of a well or the construction of an irrigation dam or a small pier; they managed the local temples and arranged the details and financing of all festivals and much else connected with the popular religion in its community aspects; they were responsible for finding suitable premises for village schools and engaging teachers, and so on. These persons came forward by a combination of such factors as age, experience, ability, ambition, leisure, wealth, lack of anyone else willing to do the job, and so forth. However, it is also true to say that they had to be acceptable in their communities, since without local support and goodwill they could hardly operate.

It is fortunate that the Hong Kong government was interested in the question of local leadership and how it could assist the new administration by continuing to deal with local cases. In 1899, it drew up a Local Communities Ordinance, divided the New Territory (as it was first called) into districts and sub-districts, and issued circulars "to all villages and hamlets in the islands, requesting the villagers to send in the names of such persons as they wished to recommend for appointment as Committeemen of the Sub-districts under Section 4 of the Local Communities Ordinance". The names of villages and their leaders were published in the *Hong Kong Gazette* in July 1899. Whilst the other provisions of the Ordinance, especially the establishment of local tribunals, were not brought into effect or were later repealed, these lists provide an invaluable guide to local leadership at the time. The Hong Kong governor of the day wrote: "The Committeemen as a rule are those who possess influence in their own immediate neighbourhood, whose advice is listened to, and whose lead is generally followed." My research confirms that they are lists of men who mattered, and not just of dummies put forward to placate an insistent and largely unknown colonial administration. Evidence collected from Lantau, Cheung

Chau, Tsuen Wan, and the like shows that market towns and villages nominated their important men; in effect, the latter must have listed themselves, the natural leaders of the day. It indicates, too, that a detailed investigation of the listings by reference to genealogies, land registers, grave tablets, temple and lineage trust account books, and the like, supplemented by oral history where still possible, would produce a voluminous and accurate profile of the rural leadership of the time.[4]

A scattered community of peasant farmers and petty shopkeepers might seem, educationally speaking, incapable of taking a lead in public business, and too engrossed in their own affairs to wish to do so, thus creating a power vacuum which might be filled from outside. However, inquiries into local history in the period under review show that outsiders seem to have taken no part in organising local affairs. This was not because there was a lack of interested outsiders. Two very different parties had an interest in the island and might conceivably have taken the initiative. There were the shopkeepers and fishmongers from the neighbouring market centres on the islands of Cheung Chau and Peng Chau who had an economic interest in the people of the island's southern coast and its affairs. There were also more likely candidates for local leadership in the family of scholar-gentry from near Guangzhou that collected rents in silver from the island's population every year. The Li Kau Yuen Tong appears to have received rent for centuries by virtue of a grant of land which went back to the Song dynasty (960–1278), but in the nineteenth century its interest in the island seems to have been confined to securing its income and — on the evidence of commemorative tablets — making occasional contributions to the repair of local temples at the request of the organising committees. No one living can recall or has heard tell of its taking part in the arbitration of local disputes in the last quarter of the century — which is the only period for which there is reliable first-hand information. As for the shopkeepers and other commercial people in the market centres, the surviving evidence, oral and documentary, points to a degree of financial exploitation through foreclosure on debts by taking fields and property in pawn, and by usury, but little in the way of directing local affairs.

Instead, local leadership, other than the internal or village leadership exercised within the various lineages which in some cases constituted an entire village, and in others shared the settlement, was provided by such village persons as rose above their local environment by reason of business acumen and personal ability and can be said to have created their own wider area of influence on the island.

With regard to the principal sub-soil owner, the Li Kau Yuen Tong, I have not found any evidence in my later research to contradict the view that the *tong* played little or no part in the management of local affairs. Whilst this may not mean that it did not do so at an earlier time, it would appear that, by the late eighteenth century at least, its authority over its Lantau tenants was eroded and its area coverage reduced. We may deduce this from a few surviving land papers and tax receipts which indicate that some land was held direct from the provincial authorities, the sharper tone of the later of two (1765 and 1807) wood-block printed leases issued by the *tong* to its tenants indicating growing difficulties in controlling them, and by the assertions made and attitudes taken by another in 1899 when they persuaded the Hong Kong government to register property in their names instead of the *tong*'s. Thus, in the overall context of local leadership at that time, prominent villagers were fortunate in not having to contend with the rivalry or opposition of greater forces. Of course, this material is entirely one-sided, coming as it does from the peasant side, and from Hong Kong government sources which were sympathetic to the cultivators. It remains to be seen from the further evidence that must still, one day, turn up from the Li family's side what the position was as viewed by them. The lineage itself, though seemingly long, landed, and powerful, with scholar and official members, is still something of a mystery. I have not yet been able to trace a genealogical record. Even the late Professor Jen Yu-wen, normally a mine of information on Guangdong subjects, did not know of one, though he was able to refer me to several sources of information about the family's early members, and told me that towards the end of the Southern Song dynasty, in about 1265–1275, an ancestral hall had been built on an island south of the city of Guangzhou, but it had been demolished for development before the Pacific War.

Then, who were these leaders whose names assumed prominence on an "island" or supra-village basis? Three such persons have come to my notice. One of them flourished in the middle years of the nineteenth century, and the other two in its second half. It is fairly certain that there were other persons exercising a similar authority in the course of the century, but I have not yet learned who they were.

Chan Fu Shing (circa 1800–1860) was a Cantonese from the village of Sha Lo Wan in North Lantau. He was the eldest of three sons who were brought there by their mother at the beginning of the nineteenth century from Sai Heung not far from the district city of Nantou (about eighteen miles away by sea). The mother was presumably a widow. Why she came to Sha Lo Wan is not known—perhaps a married aunt or sister lived there—but when they did arrive it is more than likely that the family had no land of their own because of the circumstances of their coming and the fact that the oldest village lineages of peasant farmers claim a depth of settlement that indicates arrival in the seventeenth century.

Family tradition has it that the boy was put to work in a grocery store in the market town of Tai O six miles away. Being able and diligent he made himself indispensable to his employer and eventually became a partner in the business. By this means he obtained the small capital that was essential for speculation. He appears to have used this money to make loans to village people either at the customary high rates of interest—documents show that fifty percent per annum was common—or in return for mortgages on land.[5] He was also able to buy land when the opportunity presented itself and gradually built up an estate for himself and his descendants. It was not a large one. By the time of the British lease, the Chan family, all descended from himself or his brothers, owned nineteen acres in and around Sha Lo Wan. Most, if not all of this property, must have come from Chan Fu Shing. It is interesting that almost half of these fields were placed in common ownership in two ancestral trusts with one or more managers. This ensured that the land would not be divided into small segments every succeeding generation and would not be at the mercy of a spendthrift or gambler. By way of an aside, it is, in my experience, unusual—at least on Lantau—for so high a proportion of land to be preserved in this way and this prescience must have been exercised by Chan Fu Shing. The Chans' ancestral hall, used as a village school for almost a century, was also supported by Fu Shing and his money.

He also had land interests on Lantau outside his own village and entered into a business speculation with two other persons, who were probably his fellow merchants in Tai O. Land was purchased wherever it could be obtained by sale, or mortgage leading to possession, from needy farmers—some of whom were likely their customers—and registered in the name of a *tong*. In 1899, this Shui Shang Tong owned over twelve acres of farmland in various parts of the island and still exists today. An account book for the years just before the Japanese war is extant and shows that the Chans' share of the rents was forty percent of the whole. A more detailed investigation of the *tong* reveals that in 1962 it was registered as owning 12.19 acres of fields on the island, in scattered locations as follows: Tai O and surrounding villages 7 acres; Shek Pik 1.96 acres; Tung Chung 2.79 acres; and Shui Hau O 0.44 acres. This land was reported to number about 150 separate lots. According to the rent book of 1939, mentioned above, the rent from these fields was one hundred piculs of unhusked grain (*kuk*), to be divided among ten beneficiaries in accordance with their several and joint interests. These totalled 10,000 parts divided as follows: 2,000; 2,000; 1,500; 667; 222; 222; 222; 1,581; and 919. There had been transfers by sale between 1939 and 1948, whereby the descendants of Chan Fu Shing sold away their rights to 4,000 parts. In the Block Crown Lease registers for these areas drawn up after the land settlement that followed the lease of the New Territories to Great Britain, no managers are listed for the *tong*'s properties. The earliest list available in the District Land Registry is dated 1939.

In due course, Chan Fu Shing's growing wealth enabled him to devote himself to public duties such as the management of village affairs, the arbitration of local disputes, and the organisation of small public works. One of these was the repair of the village temple in 1852. A tablet commemorating the work shows that he donated a considerable sum to its repair, in addition to being the leading spirit in the work. This self-made man set the seal on his position by purchasing the title of *kam sang* or "Student of the Imperial Academy" for which he would have paid the Provincial Treasury upwards of one hundred ounces of silver. This title would have given him standing among the gentry of the Xin'an District, and enabled him, if so inclined, to mix on favourable terms with the civil and military officers of the local administration. This bears out Professor Ping-ti Ho's estimate that

> in late Ming and the entire Qing period it may be said that men above average economic means almost invariably purchased at least an Imperial Academy studentship ... by which they could acquire the right of wearing students' gowns and caps and exemption from corvée, thus differentiating themselves from ordinary commoners.[6]

If, however, *kam sang* were two a penny elsewhere it was not so on Lantau. The island was a poor place and there were few other *kam sang* to steal Fu shing's thunder there.

The second of these local notables, Cheung Kwong Chuen (circa 1850–1916), was a Hakka from one of the smaller villages of the Pui O group in South Lantau. Unlike Chan, who had been a newcomer, Cheung's family had been settled in the area for upwards of two centuries before his birth and his father possessed a small number of fields which had descended from his ancestors. The Cheung lineage, too, was the most powerful in the sub-district. Its members were settled in five of the nine small villages of the group — all their villages were multi-lineage — and included one or two degree holders by purchase among its immediate forebears.

Like Chan, Cheung went into business, though not in the market town and not as an errand-boy, but locally and on his own account. He opened a shop in a small house situated outside the main village of the group and stocked it with goods which he brought over by sampan from the nearby island of Cheung Chau, the local market centre and a fishing port. He also sold supplies to the many Tanka boat people who frequented the creek and anchorage outside the villages and worshipped at a large temple dedicated to one of their favourite deities there. Again like Chan, Cheung had a good head for business and used whatever money he obtained from his shop to lend sums to other villagers. As usual the loans were made for interest at high rates or in return for mortgages of land. The deeds relating to about a dozen of his mortgages have survived in an old account book. One of them, dated 1898, shows that he was capable of lending to a farmer what was then the considerable sum of $120 — the equivalent of ninety ounces of silver — in one single transaction. As happened more often than not in deals of this sort, the land, consisting of an acre and a quarter of good padi fields, was sold to him seven years later.

Cheung's career developed along much the same lines as that of Fu Shing. He settled disputes over a considerable area, including villages outside his own group, and helped to arrange various public services, including a regular ferry to Cheung Chau. Again, he also took the lead in managing the affairs of the local temples and in repairing them when this became necessary. For instance, his name heads the list of twenty-six persons who presented a commemorative red and gilt board on the occasion of the last major repair to the Tin Hau Temple at Ham Tin, Pui O, dated the equivalent of 15 January–13 February 1915. It is not certain whether he purchased a degree, but he may well have done so because, as has been said, this was the normal thing for a prospering villager to do at this period.

Cheung Kwong Chuen exemplifies the type of rich peasant whose socio-economic impact on his own community needs careful study wherever it can be attempted. Unfortunately, I cannot take this too far, as his activities are not fully known and are tangled in with his duties as manager of one or more of the lineage trusts.[7]

The third member of the trio, Kung Fong Chai (circa 1850–1922), was a Hakka from a village a few miles from Tai O. An interesting account of his life is given in the Lantau gazetteer compiled in 1955 by Rev. Fat Ho, abbot of the locally well-known Po Lin Monastery. Here his name is listed as a *kui sai* or prominent lay Buddhist, a reminder of the religious beliefs and activities of some local leaders. It may be translated as follows:

Mr. Kung Fong Chai was a *kam sang* in the Qing dynasty. His ancestors came from Put Hoi to settle in Yi O on Lantau Island, and for seven generations had been engaged in farming. Mr. Kung spent his spare time in study and established a school. In his middle years, he spent his time travelling around. Later he was chosen to take part in the provincial examinations and passed. In calling over the names of the candidates it was reported that

Lantau was his native place. The chief examiner regarded Lantau as a remote place inhabited by uneducated persons and struck his name off the list, replacing it with that of another candidate. Consequently Mr. Kung could only attain the *kam sang* degree. After the establishment of the Chinese Republic he stayed at home and led a quiet life, devoting his time to calligraphy … He died peacefully at home.

It is interesting that village opinion took the view that the chances of a local man attaining rank and position through scholarship were slight. The information obtained by Abbot Fat Ho, presumably from members of the Kung lineage, was that the examining officials were themselves prejudiced against persons from Lantau, as coming from such an uncivilised, remote area and other villagers echo what one Sha Lo Wan elder told me in 1962: namely that Lantau's *feng shui* (geomantic influences) were not favourable in this regard.

Like the Cheungs, the Kung family had been settled on Lantau for a long time.[8] Fong Chai had a better start in life than either Chan Fu Shing or Cheung Kwong Chuen. His father was a schoolmaster with a business turn of mind who, besides owning land in his own village, had built up a small estate in the neighbouring settlement of Shek Pik where he had taught for many years. After being educated by his father he was sent to the district city to continue his studies in the academy there. As we have seen, fate was against him. Despite this favourable beginning he does not seem to have obtained the first degree by examination after all, and had to purchase the title of *kam sang* later on.

Being literate and neither a shopkeeper nor a farmer he probably possessed more of the external attributes of a gentry member than the other two. As the 1955 biography states, he was well known in the area as a scholar and calligrapher, and his services were in demand for writing presentation scrolls and for composing suitable inscriptions for temples, monasteries, and private houses. He was also a geomancer or expert on *feng shui* and was often called in by local people when they wished to site a new grave. All these were gentlemanly occupations. Kung was also a teacher and taught for some years at Shek Pik like his father before him. Later on, he also taught in the school run by one of the district associations in Tai O Market. However, he did not forget the business side of his life, on which his superior position depended, and continued to act as a money-lender and land-broker. At the time of the lease of the New Territories he owned or managed eight acres of land in the Shek Pik Valley and was recorded as holding mortgages on thirty plots of farm land there. It was left to his nephew, who succeeded him in the property, to dissipate the estate which had been built up by Kung and his father. This man was known locally as a gambler but when I saw him in 1962, aged seventy-two, three weeks before his sudden death, I was impressed with his appearance and manner, and could well imagine that his uncle and great-uncle had been public figures in the area.[9]

What point of interest can be made from what is known of the origins and careers of these three men? In the first place it is interesting that two of them were Hakka at a time when Cantonese must have formed the great majority of the population of Lantau and when the Hakkas in this part of Guangdong were generally considered to have been under the domination of the Cantonese.[10] In passing, I am inclined to think that this point has been over-stressed.

Second, it is interesting that all three came from villages and not from the market town. One would have expected that its shopkeepers and tradesmen would, in the aggregate, have been better off than most villagers and that a place which had a population anything from ten to twenty times larger than those of the neighbouring villages ought to have provided more pupils and hence a superior type of teacher, resulting in better-educated boys who were more qualified to become rural leaders.[11]

However, and third, their importance must be assessed against the realities of the social and geographical background of Lantau at this time. There were no wealthy, numerous powerful lineages on the island to compare with those living in the mainland area of the present New Territories. The Cheungs were very small fry compared with the Tangs of Yuen Long. Apart from the shop-keepers in the market town, some of whom were themselves villagers or were of village descent, the rest of the land population of Lantau were peasant small-holders few of whom seem to have owned more than one or two acres of land and were intent upon making a living from the soil.[12] Communications were restricted to village tracks over difficult country or to boat travel round the coast, usually by village rowing-boat. The terrain hindered social, economic, and political intercourse among the penny-packet group of villages and could only be spanned by energetic leadership, motivated by private interest and backed by personal visitation. Another factor which increases the impact these men made on their communities is what I am convinced, from my later experience, must have been the ignorance of the outside world and the massive involvement in traditional beliefs and rituals on the part of most village people at this time. Easily paralysed by fear and indecision in times of danger, and harassed by doubt and incapacity when there were important issues to decide, the quality of leadership possessed by the few is highlighted by the condition of the many.

It is not surprising, then, that men of the calibre of the three I have mentioned appear to have handled everything in their sphere of influence. Old men living today still remember the Hakka Cheung Kwong Chuen very clearly and state, with great conviction, that he managed all the important affairs of the group of villages over which he exercised a personal influence; and I have already mentioned the impressive bearing of Kung Fong Chai's nephew. Yet there is a paradox. Despite the drive and ability which removed them from ordinary villagers by many degrees, these three persons were otherwise very close to them. They came from the same farming stock, had many kinsfolk among them, and had been brought up and educated together with them in the same place. They all had village wives who had been chosen for them by their parents in their early manhood in accordance with custom, and though like most rich men in old China, they may have taken concubines later on, they do not seem to have gone outside the island for them. Moreover, they lived in ordinary village houses which were scarcely different in size or outward appearance from those of other villagers. Perhaps because of these ties they appear to have made good landlords, whether through fear of family and local opinion or because they were so close to a farming life and stemmed directly from farming stock.

My fourth point concerns land as a decisive factor in local leadership. Land played a major part in the emergence of these three men. One factor common to all three is that it appears to have been essential to build up an estate in order, through receipt of rents, to obtain the funds and leisure needed to become a substantial money-lender. Rents were usually paid in kind locally but could thereafter be converted into cash. Once the capital sufficient to embark on this course was acquired it seems to have been comparatively easy to profit by the desires, needs, or misfortunes of others. Many mortgages led to eventual ownership by the money lender, who could also purchase land with the proceeds received from his interest loans. Yet these men were not large landowners and their holdings were very small by comparison with the total areas of cultivated land in the various localities. At Shek Pik, for instance, the Kung family owned only eight acres out of a total of 180. They held, in addition, a considerable number of mortgages from Shek Pik people. The 144 outstanding mortgages recorded in the 1904 Block Crown Leases for the Shek Pik Valley (out of some four thousand individually recorded plots of land) may well be fewer in number than in 1899 because, in the intervening years, it was reported that mortgagers were making great efforts to recover unencumbered ownership.[13]

What was important was not so much the size of the estate as the fact that the average villager's holding was much less. Once possessed of land and capital one was in the position to act as a man of affairs when setting out, or being called upon, to become one.

Fifth, land was indirectly of the greatest importance for a man's emergence as an area leader. Through acquiring land other than in his native village a man became known outside it. If he was a landowner renting out the land and clearly a person of ability and presence, then the way was paved to an extension of his sphere of influence because the local people would, in time, call on him to assist in solving disputes in which no decision could be reached. In a mountainous island where bad communications resulted in the growth of isolated communities the purchase of land or operation as a money-lender was almost the only way in which personal influence could be extended without a charge of unwarranted "interference" being made. This much is obvious on a moment's reflection, but it is not always apparent without personal knowledge of an area and its geographical characteristics.

Sixth and last, it is probable that the rural gentry of Lantau Island in the earlier part of the Qing dynasty were similar in origins and career to these men.

At this juncture we must mention the external and more formal side of their activities: that is, their relations with other gentry of the whole administrative district and with its civil and military officers. There is a lack of definite information with a local content. One imagines, however, that they would have been on good terms with the officers of the military garrison and the naval patrol vessels that called at the island from time to time, combining with the village leaders and the shopkeepers of the market town to entertain them on certain festivals and on public occasions. By way of a return, the officers contributed to local repair projects such as the reconstruction of village temples and gave something towards the cost of local opera shows and festivals. This much is certain because many repair tablets and commemoration boards show this pattern. Besides, the basic nature of government in rural areas has changed very little to this day, being founded on the creation and retention of goodwill wherever possible—as true for the Hong Kong government today as for the Chinese district government seventy years ago.

The position is much less clear on the civil side. There were usually four councils of local gentry in any administrative district, for the east, south, west, and north sections or *tung*, as Lockhart calls them in his 1898 report on the "New Territory".[14] He states that the council for the eastern *tung* embraced most of the territory and sat in the market town of Shenzhen just north of the 1898 boundary. One imagines that men such as the three who form the subject of this paper might have been members. Here I have the benefit of conversations with a former mandarin, now deceased, who served as a *Zhou* and then as a *Fu* magistrate in Hubei for some years before the Revolution of 1911. He told me that the councils of the poorer districts were augmented by prominent non-literati of the type to be found on Lantau, the normal restrictions on scholar membership being waived in order to secure the presence of persons who carried weight in their localities. If practised in Xin'an, then this realistic approach, in part occasioned by the need to obtain their help in chasing in and securing the payment of the land tax, would probably have brought in local leaders like Chan, Cheung, and Kung.

I must record that this is conjecture since no information on their participation in the council, their work there, or their relations with the district magistrate and the true gentry of the district has yet turned up—though I am by no means sure, given local conditions, that it ever will. However, an account of these men would be lacking unless one hinted at the possibility of their participation in local councils, especially as it is probable that the rural gentry of Lantau and similar fringe areas in South China and elsewhere in the Qing period were similar in origins to these three men.

Clearly, one important aspect in considering local leadership, since it defines the conditions in which leadership had to operate, is the nature of settlement in these men's home villages and others on Lantau. As was usual on the island, their villages were all multi-lineage settlements; and thus the local communities to which the three leaders belonged were essentially village rather than lineage.[15] It follows that in such settlements, leaders had to operate in the village at large and not only in their own lineages; and in view of the need to carry leaders of other lineages with them their approach to leadership must have been strongly influenced by the need to take consensus into account. This sometimes elusive quality can only be established by face-to-face contacts and much sifting of views and opinions to identify and gain acceptance of solutions to problems. Above all, it needs time, grafted on experience. Thus, leadership was essentially a matter for personal involvement and participation, not something practised from the side-lines — probably more so in multi-lineage villages than in single-lineage settlements. We may reasonably assume, then, that the location of the three leaders in such settlements was a feature that, given their basic talent, contributed to their emergence and aided development of a capability to act on a wider stage.

Turning to the background of leadership, we must be prepared to grasp the idea that even on Lantau Island, and notwithstanding the disdain of our mandarin already quoted, we are considering a highly organised local society. There was a strong institutional structure beneath our leader's feet, within lineages and in the village at large. In the first place, and fundamentally, there is the undoubted strength of family and lineage. On Lantau, the family was an organisational reality, based on such manifestations as written records; individual, branch, and lineage land ownership; ancestral halls;[16] ancestral graves; and lineage trusts to provide funds for the regular worshipping ceremonies and occasional repairs. Lineage and family generated a range of tasks to be carried out at various levels, and indeed, our leaders would have been performing the major responsibilities of the day within their own lineages as a matter of course.

Some readers will urge that I am here dealing with small lineages and that these are in no way to be compared with the larger ones so plentiful in Guangdong. Certainly, there was a striking contrast between the villages inhabited by small lineages, individually or with others, and the home villages and village complexes of the large lineages. However, in my view an important caveat must be entered. My research among small lineages in this part of the province and knowledge of larger ones through study of their family genealogies,[17] leads me to the tentative conclusion that the extremes of Freedman's model of a continuum of structural complexity from simple groupings of a few families sharing common ancestry ("Model A") to massive virtually self-governing organisations grown to wealth, size, and influence as a group, despite great variation in the social and economic status of their members ("Model Z"),[18] may indicate a greater polarity in institutional and social organisation than existed in practice. Put another way, the basic motivation and organisation in both great and small lineages was more similar than the extremes of size and wealth would seem to allow. Among the small lineages of Lantau and similar parts of the present New Territories, the emphasis on family, lineage, ancestors, and continuity of the line, and reliance on the traditional ethics that energised them through generations, was just as strong.[19]

The Lantau lineages can be shown to have had this character in 1899. In the three villages from which our area leaders came, most lineages had established ancestral halls and landed trusts, were providing education and had a village temple. Preliminary research into the Tsuen Wan Sub-district reveals that practically all lineages there had small ancestral halls and landed trusts for associated ritual purposes, and that matters of common concern were centred on a number of community temples. Family records were common in both areas, though all in manuscript. Forty years later, on the eve of the Japanese Occupation of Hong Kong, institutional initiations in education, repairs, and other acts relating to ancestral graves, and the updating of written family records, show that concern for the lineage, past, present, and future, was still tenacious, whilst my experience in the last four years in the Tsuen Wan Sub-district shows that it continues to be a force that moves village communities even today. Thus, local leaders were, at all times, well grounded in family and village responsibilities, and had a lifetime's experience in handling them. Finally, it may be concluded that the order that would characterise a well-regulated and well-behaved lineage—not always found in practice but apparently the ideal[20]—would greatly assist men in carrying out the duties of leaders in the village at large.

The customary law was another major force that was a powerful aid to local leadership. It is largely to be seen in the papers drawn up in connection with land transactions and family affairs. Here we must turn to the documents that survive from the late Qing countryside. In land and property matters alone, on the evidence available, there must literally have been millions of these in existence in Guangdong before the Communist land reform, and they constitute a vital source of primary information on the functioning of local society. The provisions built into the different types of documents indicate a means to order and settle multitudinous situations in family, lineage, and village that must have been of the greatest help to village leaders. The many examples that I have seen from Hong Kong and Guangdong incorporate much detail designed, one must suppose, to help leaders buttressing transactions with set formulae and reducing the area for possible dispute by mentioning the obvious things that could cause disagreement. Deeds for the sale or mortgage of fields specify the terms of the transactions, while deeds selling hill land for grave sites allow for repair using nearby earth, and prohibit "mounting" by their own or others' graves (a serious cause for dispute) and so on. These documents embody the customary law of that part of China to which they belong, and though they were not officially recognised transactions until they were registered and "chopped" (officially sealed), they were given universal recognition by villagers and townspeople and formed an essential part of the local machinery for regulating routine affairs. All carry plenty of signatures, with independent writers and middlemen in case of query, irregularity, or failure to carry out the agreed terms. In this region, the middlemen were paid a percentage of the purchase price by both buyer and seller, which presumably helped to inculcate a sense of responsibility and obligation to assist if disputes occurred. Naturally these various provisions did not prevent disputes, but it must have given the leaders a solid basis for their efforts. Local leaders could (and were perhaps expected to) modify and add to local custom, as circumstances changed and situations required.[21]

For the most part, local leadership comprised action in everyday routine or occasional events. On the mundane level, disputes could occur between families or between whole villages, on account of irrigation, forest rights, land, and moveable goods, as well as the treatment of or quarrels between women. The construction of a grave or of a new building could alter geomantic harmony, and when discovered (not always immediately) could give rise to strong feelings and over-hasty actions. Disputes were enriched, and in part caused, by the legacy of past animosities that in many places continued latent into the present. Prudent folk would walk warily, and thoughtlessness or temper could precipitate trouble. Hence the need for sensible leaders who were prepared to go to the scene of a contest or matter in dispute. Drama was an essential part of the proceedings. Solutions initially demanded were usually extravagant in nature or downright impossible to meet: I remember a call for an alleged offender to provide ten thousand strings of fire-crackers as evidence of his "guilt" in a case between parties from different villages involving disturbance to a grave in 1957. Where the issue was not deadly it was often, one supposes, enjoyed by participants and onlookers alike, furnishing suitably embroidered material for teahouse and shade tree gossip thereafter.

Fear of supernatural forces was another very strong element in rural life. Religious rituals were commonplace at every level, for routine protection or in emergencies, or for granting favours or desires for families, lineages, or the whole village community. Leaders at different levels were involved both by determining the need and in arranging the event. One of my village friends has emphasised the great reliance placed pre-war on placatory ceremonies known locally as *tun fu* and *nuen fu* ("protecting" charms and renewing — literally "heating" — charms) to put right any fear. I have made the point above that ignorance and massive involvement in traditional religion handed down through generations of local settlement, had increased the gap between leaders and the led in the mid- and late-nineteenth century. This reflects how I saw this in 1967. I now think that I underestimated the extent to which Lantau leaders, too, shared the views of their fellows, especially as the attitudes and beliefs of their womenfolk — often the principal repositories of local religious lore — would have been a determining factor in most households and a continuing strong influence upon succeeding generations. Fear came to the fore in emergencies, especially those brought about by sickness and death, and there was then much talk and plentiful opportunity for leadership activities.

Such a time of trouble was brought about locally by the over-population that seemingly occurred in the mid-nineteenth century. The times became out of joint for many communities, a situation that lasted for sixty years and more. The disasters of this time were not attributed to their probable rightful causes — among them malnutrition, poor living conditions, an impure water supply, and the fiercely malarial qualities of the local earth — whilst the nature of the expedients adopted to counter disease was not calculated to restore health. Nor was it uncommon for villagers to move bodily to new locations. Removals to poorer quality houses on other "less dangerous" sites, or to huts in the fields built to serve as shelter and storage places during planting and harvesting seasons are recorded in a number of Lantau villages, but whatever they might have done to restore good fortune they did not necessarily assist a return to good health.

To conclude, it is evident that village leadership in late nineteenth century Lantau and adjoining areas operated across a spectrum of various situations, usually recognisable in advance and experienced previously. It was greatly influenced in its actions and decision-taking by the transmitted ideas and precedents of previous generations. There was probably not much room for manoeuvre, but the capacity of the individual leader made a great deal of difference in the handling and outcome of different problems.

3

Chinese Customary Law in the New Territories of Hong Kong

This was the first of James's series of essays on Chinese customary law. Contrary to what its name seems to imply, "custom" in this context is not static but evolving, and a flavour of change can be tasted in some of the case histories that James has published. They are collected together and annexed to this paper as illustration of the types of problem with which district officers and their staff have been dealing since the New Territories were first leased and right up to the present day.

In Hong Kong, a place was made for customary law when, after 1898, the Hong Kong government found itself having to administer its then "New Territory". This was the area leased to Great Britain by the Qing dynasty under the Convention of Peking on 9 June 1898.[1] Essentially a rural area with some seven hundred villages and a few market towns, its inhabitants,

* Originally published in *Proceedings of the Tenth International Symposium on Asian Studies* (Hong Kong: Asian Research Service 1988) Vol. 1, pp. 455–462.

hitherto governed with a loose rein under the system of district administration practiced in the Chinese empire, had been obliged in the main to manage their own affairs.

Not having high expectations of revenue, the Hong Kong authorities did not wish to spend heavily on their "New Territory". After providing for policing and better communications, they left its administration to a district officer with wide powers over land and people. Life in the villages continued much as before, and the management of local affairs with it. Customary rights and practices were, of course, at the heart of the old system, which was managed by the elders of lineages, village leaders, and sub-district notables, and monitored by the bulk of law-abiding people with their strongly implanted sense of right and wrong.

Customary Law in the Hong Kong Region

The customary law included established practices which had won acceptance among people of a locality and over many years had been enforced as needed by local leaders with the approval of the inhabitants. Customs could vary, but in any one locality there was a range of accepted forms which transactions and the relationships resting on them had to take if they were to be accepted as valid and the obligations arising out of them secured. Where land and family were concerned, this was usually expressed through written documents which followed long-established formulae.[2]

By the nineteenth century, many of the customary practices of the Hong Kong region had long been reduced to writing. Even in peasant lineages, there were sometimes written as well as verbally transmitted rules concerning land and the ancestral cult. Other local regulations directed at protecting the village community were also written down. They could take the form of actual instructions, but more often they appeared in documents that followed a long accepted format.

A considerable body of specimen documentation was available for my research. It was mostly embodied in manuscript handbooks kept by leading villagers, copied and recopied over time. An important element of the documents, especially those relating to land, was the provision for consultation and attestation. All concerned in a transaction were to be consulted and had to put their names to the paper recording its details.[3] As Dr David Faure has shown, the Chinese district magistrate expected to see such documents when disputes were brought to him for settlement. Despite the loss of much of this documentary material, enough remains to show very clearly that the provision of written support for customary law and practice was commonplace in the New Territories before the Lease of 1898.

Having decided that it would use the customary law, it became the Hong Kong government's task to make provision for the continuance of local practice. This it proceeded to do: not by setting down in detail what the local practices were, but by providing a new ordinance for the land officer and the district officers to apply them in their administrative work and in their courts, and to register their decisions on ownership and related matters in the land registries. However, the colonial administration did introduce a set of documents for use in its District Land Registry in regard to all land transactions, giving them legal status by including them in a schedule to the ordinance. Perhaps they perceived that unless they did so, the people would continue to use the customary forms of documentation long in use in the region.

The regulating ordinance first passed by the Hong Kong Legislative Council in 1905 authorised the application of the customary law in matters relating to the ownership of land and the management of the many lineage and village trusts to be found in the territory. It was to be cited as the New Territories Land Ordinance, 1905. The new law, revised and augmented as the New Territories Regulation Ordinance, 1910, and many times amended since, remains to this day the main instrument governing the succession to and management of village land there.

The Changing New Territories

However, time does not stand still. Hong Kong has seen dramatic changes in recent decades. This has been especially the case in the New Territories, where "New Town" and other development has brought a population of nearly two million into the area. Furthermore, the planned population by the mid-1990s will be some three and a half million. This large-scale development will continue to require the removal and resiting of many villages and the resumption of much village land.

Not all villages have been, or will be, moved. In fact, the majority of old settlements will remain *in situ*. However, the rural economy and the occupations of the villagers have already changed by degrees over the past twenty years, and with them the life styles and expectations of most village people. Because of the modernisation accompanying development, the overall context of life for most villagers, and especially the young, is now very different from what it was in the past, with ongoing implications for the family and the lineage. Yet paradoxically, the village communities remain conservative, paying close attention to such traditional concerns as the ancestral rites and the protective rituals of the popular religion, especially the periodic celebrations of those which protect the village and its inhabitants.[4]

The New Territories Ordinance Today

Despite the revisions noted above, the clauses through which district officers working in the New Territories region administer the customary law have not been changed in essentials from the early years.

Attention should be drawn to section 12 which gives the High Court and the District Court jurisdiction in land matters in the New Territories, and to section 13 which gives them power to enforce Chinese customs. Section 15 provides for the registration of managers for land in the name of a "clan, family, or *tong*", and section 17 for registration of successors to deceased landholders where no probate has been granted. Section 18 gives power to appoint trustees for minors.

The Land-related Customary Law in the New Territories before the Onset of Large-scale Development

Succession to Landed Property

With the passing of the New Territories Land Ordinance in 1905, succession to landed property held in private hands continued to be subject to the rules of the customary law. After approval by the district officers acting as assistant land officers, the legitimate successors were registered as the new owners.

The general practice in succession matters was for all sons to share, including those of secondary wives (concubines). Also, adopted sons were to be treated as natural sons for purposes of succession and division of property. Thus, registrations of ownership were usually in multiple names and undivided shares.

Succession to a deceased father often brought division of property, so that these were linked subjects, but sometimes division had already taken place during the father's lifetime, by mutual agreement between those concerned and with his consent. Complications were sometimes experienced by the District Office when processing applications for succession. The reasons could be various, such as (a) the lack of a male heir, requiring the adoption of a successor where this had not already been provided for, sometimes done by the widow after her husband's death; (b) non-recognition of an adopted son by other sons; (c) non-recognition of the male offspring of concubines; (d) the need to provide for widows and concubines from the estate; and (e) the potential successor's absence abroad for many years without reliable information as to whether he were alive or dead, had male children, etc. There were also (f) cases of intent to deny rights, and (g) cases where the true facts were no longer ascertainable due to the passage of time. Harmony through compromise was prudently sought in such cases but was not always attained within the family, lineage, or village. All such situations continue to occur at the present time, together with others resulting from today's changed circumstances.

Customary Land Trusts

These trusts comprised a variety of types and served varied purposes in a lineage or village. The ancestral trusts, known as *tso*, were intended to provide for the worship of a particular ancestor and the upkeep of his grave, as well as for educational and welfare purposes if funds allowed. The objects of the bodies styled *tong*, were more varied and could cover business ventures and religious bodies, but they could also be ancestral in intention. The village trusts usually related to worship at a temple or shrine, or for other common purposes in the village, and could bear a variety of names. This description continues to apply at the present time.

After 1905, as before, the properties of the customary land trusts were to be controlled by managers appointed by the members and registered by the district officers. The managers were provided by customary practice, being selected from among the male members of the trust by those males already serving as managers, and usually by co-option and consensus rather than by election. The main difference from the past was that the managers were now given full power under section 15 of the 1984 Ordinance to deal in the property as if they were sole owners. (This was, on the face of it, very different from their limited powers under the customary law, which emphasised consultation and agreement before any sale or mortgage of trust properties.) However, the section also required the giving of notice and the consent of the land officer, so that, in practice, they continued to be as restricted in their actions as before, for the members usually insisted on consultation, and the district officers scrutinised every application for alienation.

In the past, before the onset of development, management of these trusts did not present many problems, save where neglect or criminal intent were evinced by their managers. Indeed, in 1905–1960, the situation was generally so quiet and unchanging that many trusts did not bother to appoint more than one manager or report deaths and nominate successors, although this is required under the Ordinance. The situation changed dramatically with development and the widespread resumption of private land for the New Town programme and other major public works beginning in the late 1950s. The compensation money or land exchange entitlements received by the managers aroused intense interest among their members and sparked off many disputes as to distribution of the proceeds. Because of the uneven distribution of males among branches in many lineages, the debate often focused on whether the proceeds should be distributed *per stirpes*, that is equally among the branches, or *per capita*, that is by head. It appears that the former was the customary practice, but intense pressure often led to the adoption of the latter method, or of a mixture of both.

At the same time, and especially in areas as yet unaffected by development, there are many customary land trusts that have not experienced these problems. Others have solved them through the perspicacity of the managers and elders.

How Do Villagers View the Customary Law Today?

Today's New Territories villages vary extremely in their situation. Some have been rebuilt on new sites by the government to make way for development, and have no other land left to speak of. Others in remote locations in the hills have been abandoned by their inhabitants. Many find themselves hemmed in by old, miscellaneous squatter development or new construction projects, especially those on the fringes of the New Towns. Much land in the environs of all villages with road access is now occupied by modern village houses built under a concessionary policy introduced by government in 1972 to soothe villagers' resentment at restrictions on the use of their land for private development.[5] Agricultural land near towns is often left uncultivated and untenanted pending hoped-for applications by commercial companies to lease and fill it for open storage. Indeed, more and more land in the mainland New Territories is being used for temporary and short-term purposes connected with development of all kinds, and much of the central area has become a glorified "builder's yard". Along the main roads, many villages live in the midst of these unsightly sprawls, often built on their own land.

It might be surmised that this hotchpotch of situations could give rise to an equally diverse spectrum of opinion among villagers as to the appropriateness of the customary law. Yet it would seem that this is not so. Even the re-sited and other villages within New Town boundaries, which have lost most of their former landholdings, place strong emphasis on the place of the ancestral hall within the lineage, and as mentioned above, conservatism is the prevailing characteristic of the indigenous population. There is a keen sense of tradition and identity, and a general desire to hold to the traditional succession by males only, so as to protect and maintain the solidarity of lineage and village.

My enquiries on the subject in the past few years, whilst still an official in the administration, are reflected in the following summarisation of the general position.

Succession and Trusteeship

In matters of succession there is, as stated, no pressure for change from male members of the indigenous population; and the great majority of women and girls seem to accept that, once married, they are outsiders with no claim upon their own families or the property of their fathers. Widows and unmarried girls expect some provision, but by cash payment or regular income from property. Well-educated single adult women sometimes make claims to a share of land, but are bought off by payments in the end. Such girls are aware of the different legal status of their sisters in Hong Kong and Kowloon, and resent their own less favourable position. However, as one of my male informants has said, the great majority of village women have long been "brainwashed" to expect little or nothing from their fathers' estates, and this is not likely to change until the increasing number of non-indigenous wives — mothers of the next generation of daughters — exert more pressure than their present-day counterparts.

Even then, there may still be reluctance to transfer to or share land with females because of its disruptive effects upon the family and lineage. It may simply be that more fathers will execute wills that make financial provision for their daughters; like an old friend of mine now deceased who, rather surprisingly for someone of his generation, thought that the customary practice was unfair. For the present, whether unmarried females or married daughters get anything from an estate is entirely up to their brothers' attitudes and the nature of their personal relationships, or sometimes to their own persistence and initiatives.

Trusteeship does not normally arouse as much debate or dissension as succession. It is temporary, conveys no rights of disposal, and its purposes are well understood and generally accepted. On occasion, however, a woman may try to cling on to rights to property or income derived from it, obtained under trusteeship whilst a minor or unmarried, or as the trustee.

Customary Land Trusts

As already stated, many of these land trusts are small, but others are of major importance since they control a significant part of the larger lineages' local landholdings. The thinking on them is fairly clear. In all lineages, large or small, adult males continue to exclude women from membership and voting rights, retaining management firmly in their hands. However, there has been a general shift in regard to the distribution of income.

Money, or anything that brings in money, is a hot topic: whether it be cash compensation from government resumptions of trust land, the disposal of "Letters of Exchange" given for earlier resumptions,[6] rental income from land, or from proposed sales of trust land. There are also debates over whether cash received from whatever source should be banked or invested to bring in a higher return.

As stated above, the distribution of money is perhaps the hottest topic of all. Most managers are unable to follow the old practice of distributing it equally among the branches, and have to resort to part allocation to branches and part to individual males of the *tso* or *tong* concerned. I have been told that the number of persons in each branch — and not just the adult males as before — together with the amounts to be received from each source in individual families, are factors that will influence agreement on the allocation ratios, or impede it. It can also happen that a father may agree with the managers' suggestions but his sons do not. Failing all-round agreement, the cash compensation may remain uncollected and be left with the government treasury for years, yielding little or no interest.

Disputes over *per stirpes* and *per capita* distribution apart, there have been many debates about whether females should be included in the distribution of compensation and other moneys. Some managers are prepared or obliged to include widows and unmarried girls in cash distributions. In Tsuen Wan and Tsing Yi, even babies of either sex have been included in disbursements! Sometimes the pressure may have come from women, but it is more likely that the idea has come from men seeking every avenue of gain for their families. At times, even married women have been included in cash distributions, though custom gives them no rights in the matter. It would seem that expediency has played a large part in bringing about the changes that have affected distributions in the past twenty years.

Managership of customary land trusts has thus been highlighted, together with the character of the managers. Some are autocratic and unyielding, others weak or merely realistic. Some hold out, some compromise, others do exactly what the younger members want, now and over the past thirty years. In the smaller lineages whose land has been affected by development, managership itself has become highly prized, instead of being something that was often ignored and left to a single person. Having more than one manager became highly advisable, to protect interests and to prevent fraud. In the large lineages of the region, by way of contrast, managership had always been important because of the large amount of land held by their trusts.

Before and after the establishment of a separate Lands Department in 1982, district officers have been drawn into these disputes, not always successfully, because of the intransigent stand taken by the opposing parties and because they are no longer magistrates with judicial powers over land. The Rural Committees have also helped over the years — some even established mediation committees — but have had the same experience. It is reported that in some cases there has been a total deadlock, with large sums payable by government left unclaimed pending agreements that never materialise.

The District Officer's Duties in regard to Succession, Trusteeship, and Managership

Some of the material assembled in the annex following this chapter is taken from case files from the Tsuen Wan District Office that came to my attention whilst serving there between 1975 and 1982. They indicate some of the responsibilities then being discharged by the district officer in respect of customary succession to land and of managerships of land in the ownership of lineage and village trusts, as provided for by the New Territories Ordinance. They illustrate the administrative case work of the office and the sort of problems encountered in this field.

The work was usually straightforward. Applications for succession were processed in accordance with set procedures. Besides other standard checks, these allowed for the posting of notices of intention in appropriate places, to enable persons with an interest or knowledge of the case to object or inform if all was not as represented by the applicants. The same procedure was used for applications for trusteeship or for the registration of new managers for customary land trusts.

Applications could be initiated by the interested parties, but they were often set in motion by official prompting when payment had to be made for land being resumed by legal process for a government project. Without securing a new owner for land owned by a deceased person, no extinguishment of title could be obtained and entered in the District Land Registry, nor compensation effected. The same problem arose if a registered trust had no living manager, or if there were vacant manager posts where the members had not bothered to appoint and register a successor.

Occasionally, these administrative duties within the scope of the New Territories Ordinance involved the district officer and his staff in disputes over, and arising from, land ownership and management. Where there was no urgency, it did not matter if cases could not be resolved by the local leaders or by the District Office. The courts were available at need, as provided by section 12 of the 1984 edition of the Ordinance, and were required to settle cases of dispute over village land in accordance with Chinese custom, as in section 13. Where land was required for a public purpose, as explained above, the district officer was obliged to do his best to secure an early agreement through mediation, if those concerned were amenable. Such intervention was needed to make progress with the administrative chores arising from resumptions and to fulfil the government's legal obligations to owners.

At other times—and in no way connected with resumptions for development—individuals, families, and members of trusts or their managers brought forward problems for solution to the District Office, as the time-honoured place to obtain redress or assistance, but since, from 1961, the district officers had no judicial powers, mediation was all that could be offered. Where mediation duties were undertaken by the district officer in customary law matters, it is important to note that acceptance of the decision by both sides to a dispute was a vital element.

The Part Played by Village Leaders in Customary Law Case Work

Here, long established practice was a help to both sides. For those involved in voluntary mediation, or in any disputed succession or associated matter taken up by the District Office in connection with government business, acceptance of the official's decision was encouraged by their own awareness of local opinion, and by their knowledge that the district officer was likely to know both the custom and how their communities felt. On his side, he could expect to obtain this crucial information from the village representatives and the Rural Committees, either of their own volition or upon his request. No district officer could operate successfully for long in this complex arena without the co-operation and support of competent and public-spirited local leaders.

Of course, the district officer had always to be on the lookout for bias or worse in their reporting and advice, and on occasion he would also have to discount untrue accusations of such behaviour on their part. He could allow neither to obscure the major role played by trustworthy men in this field, and the reliance of himself and his staff on their continued contribution.

Notably, these leaders were seldom autocrats. They relied heavily on their fellow clansmen and villagers for support and co-operation. When, in their view, local opinion was misinformed or wrong-headed, they had to work to alter it, or else accept it. Where the District Office was involved, they had to advise on the position frankly, if their status with either side allowed, or remain silent and let the official draw his own conclusions. Many were very good. Some were masters of the art of knowing when to keep quiet — their influence temporarily eclipsed or their advice discounted — and when to renew the fight and conclude a settlement. This was so in a family or village dispute, or in a difference of opinion with the government over matters affecting the village.

Their parishioners were not the easiest of people to manage, in my experience and observation. They were often opinionated and voluble, striking attitudes and playing to the gallery as if on a stage. The "operatic" element of Chinese village life has been remarked on by many observers. Picturesque language characterised both verbal exchanges and their letters to the District Office. It enlivens the accounts of many dispute cases. Sometimes, too, the parties to a dispute were obstinate to a degree. Time and effort, not always successfully applied, was required on many occasions, inside and outside the village.

Something of the flavour of these local cases, and of the role of the elders in the customary law work of the District Office, is conveyed by the material given in the annex following this chapter. Its contents are not comprehensive, only indicative, and are taken from cases that I was either involved with or had got to know of from conversations with local leaders or from reading the office files.

Conclusion

The customary law of the New Territories is not a well-researched subject. Indeed, it has been largely neglected by local and overseas scholars to date. It is hoped that this preliminary account, which is no more than an introduction to the subject, will quicken interest in it, and lead to much needed research while it is still possible to collect materials and to interview persons who have played a part in administering it from government offices and others from the rural population who have first-hand experience of dealing with its complex human problems on the ground. There is still much to learn that will add to our understanding of traditional Chinese rural life and the part played by the customary law in its management, as well as its interface with the imperial codes and the bureaucracy.

Chapter 3 Annex
Customary Law Cases

Varying from brief summaries to detailed accounts of more complex problems, the examples with which James chose to enrich his papers cover "Family" (Cases 1–8) and "Customary Land Trusts" (Cases 9–16). They reflect his long-term interest in and understanding of these issues, and by and large the length of his treatments grew as his experience deepened. The cases can be found in the following four publications:

"Chinese Customary Law in the New Territories of Hong Kong", *Proceedings of the Tenth International Symposium on Asian Studies*, Vol. 1, *China* (Asian Research Service, Hong Kong 1988) pp. 474–476.

"Chinese Customary Law in the New Territories of Hong Kong: the Background to the Operation of the New Territories Ordinance, 1899–1987", *Asian Profile*, Vol. 19, No. 2, April 1991, pp. 132–136.

"Chinese Customary Law: Family Cases from Shek Pik, Lantau, New Territories of Hong Kong", *JRASHK*, Vol. 57, 2017, pp. 208–217.

"Chinese Customary Law: Family and Customary Trust Cases from Tsuen Wan District and New Kowloon 1961–1982", *JRASHK*, Vol. 59, 2019, pp. 190–199.

Family Cases

Case 1 (Shek Pik)[8]

The first of these cases originated with a tragedy, the death in custody of a young husband during the Japanese Occupation of Hong Kong between 1941 and 1945. It concerns a normal adoption, but introduces a *chiu long yap she* ("beckoning a groom into the household" — uxorilocal marriage) case as well, arising out of unusual circumstances. It is, for this reason, of special interest.

As the couple had a daughter but no son to carry out the customary sacrifices to the deceased, a suitable boy from within the lineage was adopted for this purpose post-war, with the approval of the lineage head and elders. Some years later, the adopted son and the widow began a sexual relationship. Warned by the elders but to no avail, she became pregnant. The document drawn up to describe the ensuing situation states that as it was impossible for their fellow clansmen to condone such unseemly behaviour, the lineage elders decided that their connection with the deceased should cease and that they must immediately leave the village—in other words the pair should be expelled from the lineage. The property pertaining to the deceased husband and father was to be re-allocated to the daughter, now of marriageable age, in accordance with customary *mores*. Signed by a senior kinsman from the same branch of the lineage and the daughter, as well as by three lineage elders, it was witnessed by the village headman. Copies of the agreement were to be kept by the senior kinsman and the daughter, and all parties thereto were to observe its contents. This paper, dated September 1959 and described in

Cantonese as a *hip yi shue* (agreement), was sent to the chairman of the Tai O Rural Committee and to the district officer (myself).

The arrangements made for the estate by the elders of the lineage are illuminating, since they embody one of the local customary practices that provided flexibility in dealing with family situations beyond the norm, and also highlight the enormous importance attached to the ancestral cult and the performance of its rituals. Should the unmarried girl accept a husband chosen for her by them and he is willing to come into the family under the *chiu long yap she* arrangement, then he could succeed to the family property in lieu of the expelled adopted son. Should she marry outside the lineage in accordance with usual practice, the estate was to revert to the lineage "to set up an ancestral tablet [for her deceased father], keep incense burning for the departed soul, and sweep his grave at the Ching Ming Festival", whilst any cash compensation for crops, fruit trees, cattle, etc. due to be paid by the government upon removal would become her dowry.[9]

Case 2 (Shek Pik)

This case occurred in Fan Pui, the smaller of the two Shek Pik villages, a single-lineage settlement. In 1959, its inhabitants were resettled, still as a farming community and of their own choice, in the adjoining bay to the west, Tai Long Wan. Like Case 1, it too involved a man killed during the Japanese Occupation and, as the widow had been left with no son, a boy from the same lineage had been adopted. However, he proved himself to be of bad character, and in 1955 was forced from the village by the deceased's clan brothers because he was misbehaving with the wife of a clan cousin who had gone to work in Borneo. Within a few years he had married a woman from urban Hong Kong and did not return to the village thereafter.

This all happened before work on the reservoir began. The errant son's misbehaviour notwithstanding, he was still the properly adopted and recognised heir, and he received the housing entitlements and compensation due to his adopted father, plus others due to him as the recognised successor to a long-deceased great-uncle in whose name some property was still registered.

Case 3 (Shek Pik)

In the absence of the adoption papers in Cases 1 and 2, it is fortunate that one in the traditional format was available in a third family case, coming from the same lineage and village as the second. This was for the adoption of a boy from outside the valley, approved by the elders of the adopter's lineage, and dated in 1959. As with Cases 1 and 4, this one brought up other information and documentation, which make this case particularly interesting.

The circumstances were as follows. Just before the village removal, one of its former headmen, now elderly, had married an outsider who already had an adopted son. Having no surviving male issue from his first marriage, he had in turn adopted this boy as his own heir. He reported his remarriage to the district officer, enclosing two customary documents. One was the boy's previous adoption paper dated in 1948, the other, drawn up in mid-1959, was his own adoption of the boy after first, and unsuccessfully, asking his kinsmen (as required by custom and as so recorded in the document) whether they were willing to provide a suitable lad to be his heir. The paper was signed by the adopter and by the lineage and branch heads and other elders, and was witnessed by the village heads of his own and the Shek Pik village. Like the paper in Case 1 above, it had been written by the schoolmaster of Shek Pik.[10]

The interest of the boy's earlier adoption paper lies in showing that he and his mother were boat people, locally known (in Cantonese) as *shui sheung yan* ["people who live on the water"], from Cheung Chau, a nearby major anchorage and coastal market centre. Even in the late 1950s, intermarriage with adoptions between land and sea people would not have been common. Personalities apart, wishing to bring a woman and boy from the boat population into a traditional and very small, single-lineage village like Fan Pui was unlikely to find favour — to say the least — because such persons came from a very different background and in any case would not have possessed the skills required for a farming life. Therefore, it was in no way surprising to find that the former headman with his new wife and adopted son had elected to be rehoused with the Shek Pik people in Tsuen Wan instead of accompanying his own clansmen to the new village.

Case 4 (Shek Pik)

This case involved bringing an outsider into the Fung family, but for a different reason and a different purpose than in Case 1. Whereas (to recapitulate) the earlier arrangement had been the *chiu long yap she* one used when a man from another lineage was to be brought into a family to marry an unmarried girl, here the customary arrangement known as *yap mun kung* was being used when a man came into a lineage with the consent of the elders to marry a widow.

In this particular instance the purpose of bringing in the man was to be two-fold. The widow for whom the man was intended had two young children. Because her son had a diseased spine, the grandfather had feared he might be unable to have children of his own, and thus the incomer was also intended to become the old man's heir to ensure continuance of the family line. No doubt for this reason, the document recording the arrangement was described in Cantonese as a *chuk shue* (a will).[11] Whilst there is no mention of the *yap mun kung* by its name, the facts are certain as I learned of them through the village head (he happened to be the widow's brother) and lineage elders, who provided me with a hand-written copy of the document and discussed the case with me.

Dated February 1946, this paper was signed by both the grandfather and his wife as the principal parties concerned and, it would seem, by the man in question. It had been witnessed by four other kinsmen, two elders from another local lineage, and by the village headman. The man (from one of the South Lantau villages) entered the lineage and the occasion was marked by the customary feast. As usual in *yap mun kung* arrangements the man had kept his own family name, Tsang.

Unfortunately, the widow's new husband-cum-father-in-law's intended heir was an addicted gambler, and the old man had seen fit to disown him along the way, though (it was said) this was not made known to the elders at the time. Meanwhile, the widow stuck by him and continued their relationship. They had two more children, and after the old grandfather died, the adopted son became the registered owner of his properties and received the replacement housing units in the specially built Shek Pik New Village in Tsuen Wan. There he continued to gamble away the proceeds of the rents and had even talked of selling or mortgaging the properties. In desperation, the village headman asked me to assist, and with help I was able to persuade the man to include his wife as a registered co-owner and hopefully save the day.

Regarding *chiu long yap she* and *yap mun kung*, the Shek Pik elders told me in 1962 that, whilst cases were not common, they were not unusual in the villages of their part of Lantau Island. Among the cases they recalled for me were the following. During the wartime Japanese Occupation a Chi of Shek Pik had gone to a Tsang family of Upper Cheung Sha in a *chiu long yap she* relationship, and in similar fashion a man from Tai Ah Chau, a small offshore island south of Shek Pik, had entered the Ho lineage of Fan Lau. Pre-war, around 1930, a Shek Pik Chan had married a widow of the Law lineage of Shek Mun Kap Village, Tung Chung, as a *yap mun kung*. In the early post-war years, another man from the Chan lineage had entered the Kung lineage of Yee O to become the second husband of a widow with children, whose husband had been shot by bandits during the Occupation. This man had been expelled from the Kung lineage later on for failing to support his new family.

I recall another *yap mun kung* case from the Japanese Occupation period coming to light in 1961. It arose from a disputed succession case at Upper Cheung Sha Village, some four miles east of Shek Pik. Under this kind of family arrangement, a man from Chinese territory (not stated but likely to have been from one of the islands south of Lantau) had married a young widow of the Tsang lineage of that place after her husband had died during the Occupation, and he had been taken into her clan. However, this was only *after* she had adopted a boy from Lap Shap Mei, another of the islands in the same area.

The succession claim was not made until 1961, when the widow discovered that the husband (who had taken a concubine after five or so years but had all along stayed in the village to farm and bring up his children by both women together with the widow's adopted son) had claimed the property descending from her late husband. She had come up to the District Office to object, with a fellow objector who was none other than the *yap mun kung* surnamed Tsang from Shek Pik.

Upon enquiry, the District Office found that the widow had left the husband ten or more years before the claim was made, and had gone to live and work elsewhere on Lantau. However, her claim on behalf of her adopted son, now 22 and working in a textile factory in Tsuen Wan, was supported by a senior elder of the Tsang family and the village headman, who each confirmed that the boy had been properly adopted with the payment of adoption money in rice and the holding of the customary celebratory meal, and that the claimant had entered the lineage as a *yap mun kung* shortly after. When all the facts had become known, the case was decided in favour of the adopted son, in line with established local custom.

The Shek Pik elders clearly distinguished these two kinds of locally known male marriage into a woman's lineage; the one to an unmarried girl, the other to a widow. In both, the man had to *kowtow* to the bride's parents, if living, or in front of her forbears' ancestral tablets, if deceased, as she would have done to her husband's ancestors in the usual marriage ceremony.[12] In the former, the man had to take his wife's lineage name, whereas he had no need to do so in the latter. However, in the *yap mun kung* arrangement, the second son would take the husband's original family name and succeed to his property, if any. This would be the case even if the father's property was much greater than his wife's, whilst the latter's family would have no claim on it. Were there to be younger sons as well, disposal of their father's personal property would be a matter to be settled between both parties to the agreement. I was unable to discuss with other persons involved in either of these interesting relationships at the time, so as to obtain corroborative material, a fact I now regret.[13]

Case 5 (Shek Pik)

This concerns a division of family property in 1782 (two identical documents) and an appeal of considerably later but unknown date. Whereas the previous four case studies and the uxorilocal marriages were all more or less contemporary with my early years in Hong Kong, Family Case 5 takes us back over one-and-a-half centuries to earlier generations of the same (Chi) lineage in Shek Pik. Notwithstanding this time difference, I decided to include it here, since in dimensions other than time, ways of doing and thinking appear to have changed little within the community, which in any case had been in existence since the fifteenth century. The three surviving documents are the undated appeal, and the two later (as deduced for the reasons given below) are copies of the property division of 1782.[14]

The main feature of this case is the marked difference between the actual content of the division and the alleged facts as stated in the appeal, such that it is hard to see how the two can be related. Without their context (how they came to hand and from whom), genealogical aids, and expert advice in regard to calligraphy and the paper on which all three documents were written, it might not have been possible to relate them and then to tease out the strands of a complex tale, which thereby becomes all the more interesting.

The gist of the matter is the assertion of the plaintiff (as we must call him) that the 1782 division had involved the property of *two* brothers, not one as stated in the surviving copies, and *twice* the area of land shown in them; and his claim that as the successor to his adoptive father (the only son of the elder of the two brothers who had arranged the alleged "double" division), he was still being denied part of his rightful share of the properties. The only problem was that he could neither produce a copy of the claimed "double area" division document to support his appeal, nor (while he seemed to have a garbled notion of its contents) was he in possession of a copy of the actual "single area" deed of division document against which he was now appealing. This, it appears, was produced by the lineage heads and the village elders during their hearing of the appeal. In effect, the plaintiff was arguing that the division was made in his grandfather's time a generation earlier than shown in the 1782 division, but without any proof. Besides making these claims, the plaintiff's story introduced him and other persons not named in the actual "single area" deed of division document, leaving myself and Dr Patrick Hase with the difficult task of identifying them and confirming their place in the still existing lineage in question.

Whilst the outcome of the appeal is not known for sure, nor whether the case might not ultimately have gone to the magistrate, I think it was a decidedly shaky one, and I concur with Dr Hase's view that it was likely that the elders had not agreed with the plaintiff but had managed to achieve some kind of compromise solution, which had kept the peace inside the lineage. They had also, we think, allowed the plaintiff to make copies of the original document.[15] Otherwise how could these papers have been passed down the generations and survived until 1960 in the hands of one of his direct descendants?

The interest of this much older customary law family case is three-fold. First, there is the manner in which the actual (as opposed to the claimed) division was drawn up. Whilst the decision to divide the property was taken by the father and mother, and in their lifetime, it had been arranged by two branch elders of the Chi lineage and by two village elders from two of the other major lineages in this old multi-lineage settlement. Second, the appeal was made to the same parties, although the intervening passage of time made it likely that at least some of the four leaders in question, although holding the same positions, may not have been the same men. Third, the plaintiff had laid emphasis on the fact that he had not taken the case to the district magistrate but had elected to keep the matter within the lineage and the village. This seems to bear out Philip Huang's assertion that ordinary villagers of the time were aware of the local magistrate's jurisdiction in civil law matters and would resort to the courts at need.[16]

Case 6 (Tsuen Wan)

This case is based on a letter dated 18 November 1977 from the manager of the Chan Yam-chun Tso of Ham Tin Village, requesting incorporation of the property of two brothers, one of them deceased and the other long departed for Malaysia without trace or news, into the main *tso* estate.[17]

A widow, a daughter, and a step-daughter from the widow's first marriage survived. The letter stated that it was traditional New Territories practice for a widow to have the estate until death in the absence of a male heir, but that married daughters had no such entitlement as they were expected to be cared for by their husbands' families. This was mentioned in the letter "in case the female members of our clan are ignorant of the accepted practice and cause conflict".

Case 7 (Tsuen Wan)

Another case based in Tsuen Wan involves a statement dated 13 February 1978 by the chairman of the Tsing Yi Rural Committee in regard to a dispute case from San Uk Tsuen, Tsing Yi, in which a natural son had refused to share his father's property with an adopted brother and persisted in this stance for over ten years after his father's death. Even though the adopted son was a *mai tsai* "bought son", taken into the family when he was still small many years before, he was entitled to his share, said the chairman. He added that ninety percent of Tsing Yi villagers disagreed with the natural son's behavior.

The chairman instanced his own elder brother, another "bought son", who had been brought into the family by his grandfather but had an equal share of inheritance in accordance with custom.

Case 8 (Tsuen Wan)

The focus of this case is an issue in which a daughter's temporary interest in her deceased elder brother's share in land in joint ownership was contested when she applied for removal of trusteeship exercised on her behalf whilst unmarried and a minor, and requested its registration in her own name.

This is a complex case, but it shows that the unmarried women in a family, as well as widows, were allowed rights under customary law. In this particular case, the Tsuen Wan Rural Committee supported the objection from the male trustee and the other males with an interest in the jointly held property, but it would seem from their letter to the district officer that, even after marriage, women in this situation could expect to receive income from such property:

According to village custom, a married woman is not entitled to succeed to the property left by her ancestors, and she is only entitled to enjoy the income derived from such property until she dies. In the light of this, [the named person's] party is justified in opposing the proposed removal of trusteeship in order to prevent unauthorized disposal of the property in question.

Source Material and Further Observations on Family Cases

Four of the above case studies are based on documents that came to my notice during work at the reservoir site, augmented by information obtained from my discussions with lineage and village elders. The documents dated from the fifteen-year period from 1946 to the village removals in 1959–1960. The discussions, being recollections of events within living memory, took in the five decades going back to the early years of the century.

The subject matter has partly to do with adoptions of male minors for the purposes of ensuring continuance of the family through the male line and, in two of these cases, to provide for the performance of the ancestral rites for young married men who had died in custody during the Japanese Occupation of Hong Kong without leaving male children behind them. Adoptions were usually from within the lineage, or by default or sometimes by preference outside it, and not infrequently by purchase. In general terms, adoptions were central to Confucian philosophy and Chinese custom, feature in both the imperial code and customary law, and were a common feature of Chinese social life.[18]

The other cases have to do with local practices involving adult males of other surnames who were brought into households under arrangements made by family and lineage elders to become a husband for an unmarried girl or a new husband for a young widow with or without children. However, being outside the (virilocal marriage) norm, they were resorted to only when unusual or special circumstances required. Known respectively in the local Cantonese as *chiu long yap she* and *yap mun kung*, they are described and their use and purpose explained in their particular contexts in Cases 1 and 4.[19]

Although infrequent, they were also found elsewhere on Lantau. My discussions with the Shek Pik headmen and elders revealed specific instances of each kind known to them from villages in nearby places during the previous 50 years. The actual number is likely to have been more, and it is highly probable that these forms of marriage had also taken place in the remoter past.

Besides the documents and information available for family cases of those sorts, there were also three historical documents pertaining to a disputed inheritance case at Shek Pik that was the subject of a belated appeal to the village and lineage elders in the early nineteenth century, perhaps several decades after a division of family property in 1782.[20]

During our discussion, the elders and headmen had assured me that documents were still being drawn up and kept for all adoptions and cases of taking-in. As with individual transactions in land, particularly with regard to sales and mortgages—all of them invariably in deed (contract) form—it is quite likely that many of the divisions of family property at the village level were similarly recorded in writing, like the one drawn up in 1782, which is the subject of Case 5.[21]

The written record was meant to ensure clarity, and to promote performance and continuance in an uncertain world in which the desired outcomes were often subject to adverse events and human shortcomings. In the documents I have studied, it is common for the circumstances and the means devised to meet them to be described, and the consent of all those concerned, either as principals or witnesses, is recorded. It was also intended that they would provide proof that a transaction had been entered into willingly and before witnesses, in case of later denial and dispute.

The number of case studies has been limited here to those coming to my notice at the time. However, to my mind, this seems more than compensated for by the complexity — one might say the "duality" — and interest of their contents, as described with the help of the lineage and village heads. Without their explanations I could not have fully understood either their details or their significance.

Taken together, what else can we say about this group of case studies? To me, they embody two major themes that characterised this part of Guangdong under imperial rule during middle and late Qing, and which, in regard to the first of them, had continued well into the mid-twentieth century, long after it became the British-ruled New Territories of Hong Kong in 1898–1899.

First, there is the self-management that was for long the norm in its villages and townships, and which has impressed itself so deeply on those of us who have studied parts of Southeast China in depth.[22] Second, there is the fact that whilst the arrangements for adoption, marriage, and inheritance were, as herein stated, made within local communities and supervised there by lineage, village elders, and village headmen, they were also national in their nature and coverage and, being included in Qing imperial statute law and its case law, were within the purview of the imperial bureaucracy.

Generally speaking, buttressed by local custom and public opinion, civil matters like these would remain the everyday business of village and lineage leadership unless and until dissatisfied plaintiffs or parties in dispute would decide to take them to the district authorities, or until actions deemed criminal in these areas of civil law would bring them within the scope of the magistrates' courts. Whilst the force of custom and prevailing opinion might well have been a powerful deterrent to going outside the community, in the past two decades the published researches of Philip Huang and his associates[23] into surviving court records have shown that there were indeed many plaintiffs who had sought redress at the district magistracies notwithstanding.

Customary Land Trust Cases

Case 9 (New Kowloon)

The New Kowloon area is part of the territory leased from China in 1898, but in 1900 it was separated from the remainder of the New Territories for administrative purposes. One of its old villages, Nga Tsin Wai, has a *tso* with four branches. When, in 1964, the *tso* was to receive a grant of land for a new ancestral hall (replacing one demolished for development), there was a problem over the manager for the First Branch. He had been living in Guangzhou for over ten years with his mother, wife, and children and was unlikely to return to the village. He had given a power of attorney to another member of his branch, but this was contested by a third person who wished to be the manager in the place of the absent one.

The correspondence on the matter contains some interesting statements. When consulted by the government, the managers of the three other *tso* of this Ng lineage said that in their clan managership was for life and that authorising another to act in his place was quite in order. They also said that the concurrence of managers of other branches was necessary when any branch changed its manager. Their letter contains the following statement:

> Our clan is divided into four *fongs* (branches), and from each *fong* a manager is elected to handle jointly the properties of the clan. In order to protect the interests of the [i.e., all] clan members, a person who is elected manager by other members of the same *fong* must also obtain the unanimous approval of managers from the other three *fongs* before he can assume the post of manager. According to the normal practice of our clan, once a manager is elected, he will remain so till his death even though he may not live in Hong Kong. If for any reason he is unable to carry out his duties, he has the right to authorize someone worthy of his trust to act on his behalf and other members of the same *fong* will have nothing to say against him ... [the objection] in violation of the traditional rules of our clan is without ground and we do not agree to this contention.

It is worth noting that the person authorised to act in the manager's place said in a statement taken from him at the time that "it is not customary in my village to change a manager unless the manager has done something wrong". These passages are taken from Appendices E and F to Secretary for Chinese Affairs' memorandum (66) in SCA 2/586/57 Part III, dated 16 March 1964. The papers are not without bias, but I think there is a ring of truth to the passages quoted above.

In the Nga Tsin Wai case, the government found itself in a dilemma. Despite the Ng clan's very long settlement, there were only five adult male members in the first branch, of whom two were abroad. Also, it appeared that whatever the traditions of managership, three of the five wanted to have a new manager, albeit one of this group was—naturally—the contestant. Another difficulty was added to this indeterminate situation, in that even if the government was prepared to accept the old manager and his empowered representative, the power of attorney given by the registered manager in Guangzhou was not considered by government lawyers to be adequate for the representative to sign the new grant.

Case 10 (Tsuen Wan)

In regard to not changing managers of ancestral trusts, even if abroad, I also recall the case of the main *tso* of Muk Min Ha Village, Tsuen Wan, in the 1970s. This was a single-lineage settlement of 250 years' standing, with a large ancestral hall. The whole village was being removed for development and was to be rebuilt in another place. Its remaining fields were being resumed and compensated, and the managers of the various lineage landed trusts had much business to transact with the District Office.

Unfortunately for the village leadership, one of its *fongs* had left the village for Malaya pre-war. In the absence of its manager from Hong Kong and his alleged neglect of their common business — not for the first time, said the elders darkly — the managers of the other branches of the lineage found it next to impossible to act in matters that concerned them all.

Up to the time I left the District Office, they had not been able to persuade him and the members of his *fong* to provide a successor or even an authorised representative. I think there was a "history", or at any rate a "story", behind the impasse. However, all was well by the time the lineage's new ancestral hall was opened in 1986. The overseas branch had been co-operating — it was, of course, in its own interests to do so — and the registered manager had authorised his elder brother to represent him in all official transactions connected with the trust properties of the lineage, old and new. The elder brother was also present at the opening ceremony.

Case 11 (New Kowloon)

In another case in New Kowloon, the primary document is a letter of 23 January 1977 from four villagers of Kau Wah Keng who objected to the sale of ancestral land registered in the name of a *tso* and mentioned that the eight plots in question had all along been cultivated in rotation by the descendants of this *tso*.

Case 12 (New Kowloon)

A letter dated 19 August 1965 from a villager of Kau Wah Keng is the focus of this case. It explains that two plots of land bought from fellow villagers and members of the same *tso* as himself were in fact registered as *tso* property. However, the *tso* property had been divided among its members at some stage [said to be a long time before 1898 in fact] and as he wrote in his letter: "The division has not been registered in your office because the members can keep their shares without interference." He was writing to state the position because the *tso* could not act to register the change owing to an internal dispute among its members.[24] Confirmation of division of land among branch members without official registration is provided in Case 3. The objection letter states

> As a matter of fact, a portion of the properties left by our ancestors has long been divided among the various *fongs* (branches) of the family. However, the division has not been registered with the Land Registry of the District Office, which is not uncommon in the New Territories.

Case 13 (Tsuen Wan)

This case is based on a letter of 8 November 1961 from a villager of Yau Kam Tau. It was sent upon seeing a notice posted by the District

Office about the intended sale of *tso* property. "We were shocked to learn that an unworthy descendant of the *tso* [the manager] intended to sell, without calling a meeting of the families and obtaining their consent ... Upon learning of this the descendants were extremely angry." The letter continued:

> The *tso*'s estate was founded by our ancestor through the hardest toil during his lifetime, in order to provide his descendants with the expenses of the spring and autumn sacrifices annually, and for their education and welfare. No change has ever been made to this practice over the years, and it can be verified at any time as the account books and the minutes of meetings of the families can be produced upon request.

The letter in Case 10 of 23 January 1977 from Kau Wah Keng also touches on this important point: that there should be no sale of ancestral land without consultation and consent from interested parties. The letter states: "The managers ... have sold this land without our consent, which is against procedures. We will not recognize or ratify such sale ... please protect our rights and interest in the ancestral property."

Case 14 (Tsuen Wan)

In a letter dated 20 January 1962, the village representative of Yau Kam Tau requested the district officer to pay compensation for *tso* property resumed by the government for development to the branches and not to individual males, as he was under pressure to do (he was also manager of the *tso*). He stated that

> it has been a village tradition for the inhabitants of the New Territories to distribute the public funds of the village (meaning in this case the surviving lineage among several previously settled there) equally among the branches. The various rural committees

in the New Territories have been mediating disputes of this nature on this basis. If funds were to be distributed to villagers on the basis of all male adults, the number of disputes would increase in future.

He was going against the request of some members of his *tso* who, at a meeting held two days before, had asked for distribution to all adult males. He added that he dared not approach the Tsuen Wan Rural Committee because they would have mediated on the old basis, which would have further exacerbated matters within the village.

This man, then aged 60, was a well-educated and experienced village representative who later became chairman of the Tsuen Wan Rural Committee. He would have been well aware of customary practices in the New Territories.

Case 15 (Tsing Yi/Tsuen Wan)

In 1982, I made further enquiries into how managers of customary land trusts in the districts of Tsing Yi and Tsuen Wan were dividing cash among their members, and recorded the following notes:

i. Tsing Yi: The managers divided the cash compensation from resumptions of *tso* property among all members of the lineage (i.e., *per capita*), leaving a balance to be distributed among the branches (i.e. *per stirpes*). In one case, eighty-eight percent of the compensation money was divided among individuals, including babies and unmarried females. The remaining twelve percent went to the branches in equal shares.

ii. Tsuen Wan: Here, too, where money was received, it was now usual practice for the managers of trusts to make a division between individuals and branches. The allocation was variable and dependent upon the number of persons in the lineage. If large, the allocation to the branches was less. Again, at the time of enquiry, unmarried females and babies were included in the *per capita* distribution.

In both Tsing Yi and Tsuen Wan, it was usual for the branches to divide up their shares among members.

Case 16 (Tsing Yi/Ma Wan)

I have found other material about lineage trusts from Tsing Yi. This is the more interesting because there were several very old trusts involved, with membership spread across two places. There were also interested parties on the adjoining island of Ma Wan which, unlike Tsing Yi, had not been affected by development. Members of the same Chan lineage had settled there 300 years earlier, about the same time, as the other part had established themselves on Tsing Yi. Both groups had equal rights to the trust properties on Tsing Yi, under the Chan Wing Li Tso, Chan U Hing Tong, and Chan Yue Hing Tong. These three trusts appear to be the oldest of their kind in the Chan lineage, stemming from the founding ancestor and his sons.

The properties on Tsing Yi were all affected, one by one, as the government's New Town development programme progressed. The Tsuen Wan District Office file dealing with the trusts (TW 23/541/63) contains interesting material on the way in which the members of the lineage, in both places, reacted to the resumption of the properties and how they arranged the distribution of the cash compensation paid by the government and the income from sale of "letters of exchange entitlements" taken by the managers in lieu of cash.

The Ma Wan Chans were suspicious of their Tsing Yi cousins long before any resumption of land for the development programme began on the island in the 1970s. In 1963, they wrote to the District Office explaining their descent from the

Wing Li Tso and stating their legitimate interest in its land and assets, and their right to information and consultation should any transactions in the trust properties be proposed. They stated that they had only one representative among the five registered managers of the *tso* and that "in order to be fair and to avoid disputes" they should have the same number as their Tsing Yi clansmen in the future. The district officer responded by instructing his staff to make sure that the Ma Wan Chans were kept informed of whatever transactions or government requirements affecting the common property were received by his office, and this continued as standard practice. The matter of appointing extra managers was not so easily dealt with, since this was something for agreement within the Chan lineage.

However, it is clear from the file that the Ma Wan Chans did share in the benefits obtained from land resumption. A short minute from the District Land Registry describes one such case:

> The 3 managers of Chan Wing Lee Tso of Tsing Yi Island requested [the district officer's] consent to sell 1975 Letter B agricultural land of 40,509 square feet. Notices were posted. Verbal objections have been received from members of the *tso* in Ma Wan. Letters have [since] been received withdrawing their objections. I understand from Chan Sai-lung, one of the managers, that the Letters B will be sold at $17 per sq. ft., of which $2 will be distributed among the members of Tsing Yi and $2 among the members of Ma Wan. The remaining proceeds will be invested in tenement flat property in the name of [the] Chan Wing Lee Tso.

Obviously, the Ma Wan people were watching the Tsing Yi folk like hawks and used their objections to force an acceptable distribution whenever money or money's worth was at stake.

One interesting distribution took place in 1979. One of the properties of the U Hing Tong, comprising a building lot with five houses on it, was needed for development. The District Office agreed to provide them with five new houses. This lot was but one of nine owned by the *tong*, albeit the rest, together with the remaining part of the building lot, were in agricultural status and therefore less valuable. Originally, at meetings of the lineage, it was agreed to divide the five new houses among representatives of the four branches of the lineage, and in at least two cases the persons allocated these holdings were to be registered as managers of the stated *tongs*. However, two months later, it was decided to register the houses in the names of the selected persons; numbering two, one, four, and four, respectively. What went on inside the lineage is not known. There had been a written objection from two Chans, but it was overcome by consensus and a further posting of notices. A two-month interval did not lead to further demurrals. The wishes of the *tong*'s members were respected and the allocations approved and registered.

The case is interesting because the managers described it as "an issue" and the assistant district officer (lands) concerned stated that "this section have already done the best we can [*sic*] to settle this very complicated *Tong* case". The managers had dealt with the objection firmly, because the allocation had been discussed and agreed at a formal meeting held in the ancestral hall, and they told the District Office that one of the objectors, the son of a manager of the *tong*, was "not a welcomed person in the village". Reporting to the district officer, the officer added that "the writer [there were in fact two] has no firm ground to object as the decision is agreed by the *Tong*'s meeting and agreed by this *Fong*'s [other] members". Nonetheless, the writers had tradition on their side when they wrote: "It is deemed that the property of the *Tong* or any part and parcel of the said property, should never be privately owned by a single descendant." In fact, the houses were mostly to be registered in multiple names by persons who were clearly leading members of the several entitled branches and must be deemed to have had certain obligations to their branch members.

The Ma Wan Chans must have had entitlements from this property as with other lots in the U Hing Tong's ownership, but it is not clear what they received on this occasion.

In passing, it would appear from the file that one of the two related *tongs* may have owned land on Ma Wan until it was sold to a development company about 1974. It would seem that the Tsing Yi members got wind of this, and in their turn asked the District Office to keep them informed. It would be interesting to know whether they got anything.

The file contains other information relating to the appointment of managers for this *tso* and two *tongs*, either to replace deceased ones or to add extra ones to complete representation by all entitled branches. Members in both Tsing Yi and Ma Wan were involved, both at their own request and because it was District Office practice to keep both sides in the picture, although leaving them to sort out what should be done. The last of these concerns the U Hing Tong's managers, and relates to an objection to a new manager, which was settled by appointing two, the second of whom was to represent a branch that did not yet have a manager on the *tong*. There was apparently a similar situation in the Chan Yue Hing Tong.

Despite their early promptings on the subject, the Ma Wan people do not appear to have gained parallel representation on the Wing Li Tso and the two *tongs* (i.e., their own set of managers). Just four and five registered managers are listed for the U Hing Tong and the Chan Yue Hing Tong, respectively. So the best they could do was to keep on their toes, objecting in writing when proposals for replacement managers were made, or when compensation was likely to be paid, in order to gain leverage in negotiation. Finally, in 1986, they returned to the charge by writing again about having their own set of managers in both the U Hing Tong and Chan Yue Hing Tong.

Conclusion

The inference I draw from the above case records is that, with changing times, managers of customary trusts and village representatives were faced with new problems in what had always been a difficult area of lineage and village business. They had to be scrupulously fair and neutral in their handling of their fellows, their own loyalties notwithstanding—that is, if they wished to have any chance of successful mediation in disputes, and not even then when financial gain was at stake in the face of steadily increasing cash compensation from the government and profits from the growing value of letters of exchange entitlements when trust properties were required to be surrendered for development projects.

Individual greed and increasing pressure and dissent from female members of the lineages (ever excluded from membership of customary trusts) were other factors in the new mix.

4

Education and Management in Rural South China in the Late Qing

That China was possessed of a literate culture is undeniable, and the high respect in which the literati *were universally held, plus the reverence for the written word which prompted charities to pay collectors to salvage and ritually dispose of paper with writing on, vouch for the strength of that sentiment at all levels of society. This essay examines the historical role of the written word in New Territories villages and offers evidence of considerable reliance on documentation in various rural activities, notably in nuptial contracts, deeds of property sale, in rituals, taxation matters, family records, public notices, keeping accounts, and so on. It was far from the case that everyone could read and write, but almost everyone it seems had access to and an understanding of the benefits of, indeed the necessity of, literacy. How this was achieved at the village level may have been somewhat haphazard in organisation, but it permitted a reasonable degree of self-sufficiency.*

* Originally published in *Proceedings of the Sixth International Symposium of Asian Studies 1984* (Hong Kong: Asian Research Services 1985) Vol. 1, pp. 575–592.

There has long been a debate and an interest in the extent of literacy among peasants in China. The latest work on the subject is by Evelyn Rawski, who in her book *Education and Popular Literacy in Ch'ing China*[1] concludes that in eighteenth and nineteenth century China, a broad range of the male populace, including peasants as well as urban dwellers, learned to read and write. The spread of a basic literacy was encouraged by its usefulness in everyday life and by the low cost of tuition, teachers' salaries, and text books. I am more interested here in South China and in particular the Hong Kong region than in the whole country, and therefore it was with some interest that I noted her quotations from various estimates of male literacy in South China in the nineteenth century.

Ms Rawski quotes an 1830s estimate that "not more than four- or five-tenths of the men" could read and the result of a census taken in Hawaii in 1896 which showed that slightly under fifty percent of all Chinese in Hawaii over six years of age were literate. Ms Rawski goes on to give a few examples of the various purposes for which literate persons were needed in the Qing dynasty. She mentions the police, security, and tax collection systems which were an important part of the system of local control by the State, reminding us that the government relied on written notices in town and country to put over its requirements and make them known to the populace. She also notes that written materials were common in Chinese society and that it was important to have persons who were able to read, and sometimes to write, documents required for many occasions in village life; as at marriages, funerals, the division of family property, paying and allocating taxes, and sales transactions. There were, too, some management schemes in the countryside, particularly those involving water control systems, which required a certain level of basic literacy. Even money loan societies needed someone to keep the books. There was also the fact that not everyone living in the countryside was a farmer. A number of persons were engaged in other occupations, some of them requiring a basic knowledge of reading and writing.

In my own published work, I have demonstrated a management structure in all the local villages and market towns, regardless of size.[2] I have also commented on the persons who performed the duty of "middleman" in land transactions, but have not gone into the subject of who wrote the documents required to make it work. I have left the reader to assume that, with the existence of schools in most villages of any size, the managers and their assistants had the capacity to write in connection with their duties, perhaps with assistance from the local schoolmasters. Ms Rawski has not gone into this point either, having established that the extent of literacy was fairly general and its level sufficient for the ordinary purposes of government and people alike.

Our enquiries should be carried further, and our assumptions tested. Who were the writers of documents and papers in everyday use? Were they professional specialists as Ramon Myers has suggested on the basis of enquiries elsewhere?[3] Did these specialists come mainly from the market towns and larger villages, in accordance with Professor Skinner's theory that services and the cultural influences were provided from within the standard marketing community?[4] Were they the schoolmasters and elders acting as semi-professionals? Alternatively, were there no professionals as such, but only villagers providing their own documentation at will, owing to the spread of basic literacy in the villages?

In this article, I shall turn from the larger scene to look more closely at some of the communities which are known to me in the Hong Kong region, and especially some which I have written about in previous work. I shall examine whatever written material is available from these places, try to establish who the writers were, and attempt to show more clearly how education and management were linked. I am less interested in education itself than in showing that it was seemingly effective in providing writers in many ordinary families who, virtually unaided, were capable of drawing up the papers required for most social and economic activities.

Village Education in the Hong Kong Region

We can take a degree of male literacy in the villages of the Hong Kong region for granted. My enquiries over the years have shown that practically all my informants born from 1880 to 1910 had been to school for at least a few years.[5] A few examples from the areas in which deeds and papers are available for study will indicate the sort of education that village leaders received in the late Qing.[6] Take, for instance, the present village representative of Shek Pik, a village on Lantau Island which over twenty years ago was removed to Tsuen Wan to make way for a reservoir project. Born in 1899, this man attended the village school for two years when he was eleven to thirteen years old and then went to the outlying islands to work for a fish dealer there for the next three or four years at $3 a month. At Shek Pik, the school consisted of a village house with a small courtyard, providing two classrooms. Up to fifty pupils, all from Shek Pik, attended school. The school day began one hour before dawn, with a break from 9 to 10 a.m. for breakfast. It continued to 12 noon, and then from 2 to 5 p.m. This happened every day, except at festival times and during the planting and reaping periods for the rice crops twice a year. The annual cost to his father was $4. When he began his education, he was taken to the Hau Wong Temple next to the school to worship at the altar, and then into the building to bow before a picture of Confucius. Every day the pupils took turns to light the joss sticks. The boys studied the Chinese classical books, starting with the Three Character Classic. The school had a teacher's quarter and kitchen attached to it. The building was already old when he studied there and was in a poor state like most of the village houses at that time. The village headman looked after it, because it was common property belonging to the village temple, and like the temple itself, it was periodically repaired by subscription whenever necessary.

Another village leader, born in 1885 in the village of Sha Kok Mei (population 346 in 1911) near Sai Kung Market began his education at the age of ten and studied for five or six years in the village school. Sha Kok Mei was a big village, and like Shek Pik had a proper school building.

This man finished school at fourteen because his father died. The family experienced financial difficulties, and he was sent to Kowloon to work as an apprentice in a piece-goods shop. The family was not well off, and in addition to his mother consisted of himself, his brother, and three elder sisters. There were about thirty students in this school, all from the same village. Classes began at 6 a.m. and breakfast was taken between 9 and 10 a.m. They continued until 12 noon, with a break until 1 p.m. for lunch, and did not finish until 6 p.m. There were lessons in reading, recitation, and penmanship, and the books studied were the usual classical texts. Normally, school began in the second or third lunar month and closed in the ninth month, and where they could the students taught themselves in the intervening period. These breaks were intended to enable students to assist their families with their farming livelihood. In this respect, the Sha Kok Mei School was unlike the Shek Pik one, where no such lengthy intermission occurred.

In another large village of the Sai Kung Market area, Ho Chung (1911 population 418) in Hebe Haven, the school operated all year round, except for the main festivals and busy farming periods. The times for daily study, with intervening breaks, were more or less as in the other places, and the texts studied were again the classical books. The school was operated in a private house belonging to the village schoolmaster. There were around twenty-five children in the school at the time my informants were there in the last years of the nineteenth century.

The cost was $3 a year per student, and most of my informants only studied for a few years. As at Shek Pik, they bowed to the picture of Confucius and then to the teacher upon entering the school room each morning. When lazy or dull, they were beaten on the head with a heavy ruler.

In the Tsuen Wan Sub-district, a village leader born in 1902 who went on to become chairman of the Rural Committee, probably received a better education than most boys of his time, though he came from one of the smaller villages of the area (Yau Kom Tau, 1911 population 52). Studying between the ages of ten to eighteen *sui* he was sent to three different schools in three neighbouring villages. At the last, he studied under a *sau choi* scholar from Guangdong — "a very good teacher" as he described him — who was also a Chinese herbalist. Less gifted boys from his clan studied for a few years in a small school room attached to its ancestral hall. In an adjoining settlement (Tsing Fai Tong, 1911 population 90), the former village representative, born in 1898, studied in his family's ancestral hall for four years from the age of eight *sui* with ten other boys, which was the more usual educational experience. All teaching in these schools was in Hakka, their native tongue, and the books were the usual classical texts, together with the popular *Yau Hok*.[7]

It is clear from these accounts and from many others taken from old people who attended school in local villages at the end of the last century and the opening years of this, that although many were educated, the average villager would not have had an extensive schooling.

The Papers Available for Study and Their Relevance

My enquiries into literacy for rural management, as I have stated above, relate to a number of small villages in the Hong Kong region. Other than being located in the areas I have been able to study intensively, the choice for present purposes has been further limited by the availability of documents. These comprise papers recording transactions in land. Other material of a miscellaneous nature, such as family documents and the village handbooks, also survives but is less suitable for present purposes as the writers are mostly not identified. Not that the number of papers available for study is very large. There are some forty land documents from the village of Shek Pik, and twenty other deeds from the Tsuen Wan Sub-district of the mainland New Territories. Of the latter, only a small group from Tsing Yi is suitable for this study. There are, besides, over forty land papers from villages near Sai Kung Market in the eastern New Territories, which date from the years of the Japanese Occupation (1941–1945) and serve as a late commentary on the earlier material. I have brought in this later group of papers because of the sparse body of documentation, and wish to emphasise that together, for the large area covered by my enquiries over twenty years, they represent the only groups of deeds that I have been able to find. Apart from individual papers from scattered locations, amounting to no more than a few tens of documents in all, nothing more has come to light.

This dearth of materials is the more striking in light of the large mass of papers that must have been produced. The region contained hundreds of thousands of individual fields and pieces of land all in private ownership and subject to sale and mortgage. The writer of "A General Report on the Survey of the New Territory from November 1899 to April 1904" in *Sessional Papers for 1904* stated:

As the cultivation in the hilly Districts remaining to be surveyed consisted of small terraced fields running up hillsides and narrow valleys, the average size of field was so small that it was found impossible to represent such minute detail on the 16-inch scale with any degree of utility; the government therefore decided to increase the scale to 32 inches to the mile.

The Shek Pik papers came from one family in one lineage in a multi-lineage village, from a valley that contained over four thousand individual fields.

The Tsing Yi papers likewise came from one family and relate only to their holdings of hill land, not their fields and houses. Practically all village families owned some land, and it represented one of their few disposable assets. Sales, and especially mortgages, were prompted by economic hardship, family requirements (including paying for marriages and funerals), and personal foolishness that included gambling. All the evidence indicates a lively market in land. In these remnants that have survived by chance into the present, we clearly have but a minute percentage of the total production of papers of all kinds, especially those pertaining to land and property.

The shortage of material is due to the events of the last eighty years. The land settlement of the New Territories, following its lease to Britain in 1898, led to the handing in of many land documents to establish claims to land, and it would seem that most of the owners did not get them back.[8] Again, the Japanese Occupation was a time of destruction for many records, not necessarily by the action of the incoming Japanese forces and civil administration, but also because local villagers were fearful of retaining them under a change of regime; this much is certain from the weight of evidence that is available across the New Territories.

Consequently, our enquiry has to make do with a smaller number of documents than one would really expect, and certainly wish, to have for present purposes. On the other hand, because field research has been possible in Hong Kong, we can obtain a good, rounded knowledge of the society to which these documents belong. The Block Crown Leases drawn up in 1904, following the land survey and settlement of titles to property, provide detailed information on landholdings and ownership, whilst genealogies and grave tablets give details of the families settled in the villages.

It has also been possible to supplement these basic sources with material from government reports, newspapers, and miscellaneous written work; and not least, by interviews with old persons. In this way, it is possible to put the documents into something like their full context, something that is difficult to do from library research. Best of all, through being able to identify them with certainty, it becomes possible to relate the persons involved in land transactions to their clan and village. We can then know whether they are villagers or outsiders, belong to a major or minor clan, are newcomers, or have been long settled, and whether the fields are located in the village area or in an adjoining one. In short, the matching of documents with field research and other documentary sources breathes life and meaning into these relics from a bygone era.

The Traditional Format for Land Papers

The land papers in question all relate to sales or mortgages, usually of fields and houses but sometimes of hill land or farming structures and cow-sheds. There was a customary form and phraseology for these transactions whose recording followed a general format. After stating the name of the seller or mortgagor, and the occasion for the sale or mortgage, the document would recite the property in question and its location and whether it had come down from ancestors or been bought by the seller. The deed would continue with a recital that the property had been offered to relatives who had declined or were unable to purchase, after which, directly or through a middleman, an interested buyer had been secured. A price had then been agreed and was stated in the document, together with the affirmation that it had been handed over in full to the seller and witnessed. The property and its boundaries had been identified and pointed out. The usual deed concluded with a statement that this was final and irrevocable, that neither side, their relatives nor descendants, could go back on the transaction, and that the transaction had been put in writing lest words proved insufficient.

It was usual to involve a number of persons in the transaction besides the buyer and seller. The middleman has been mentioned, and there were also witnesses, especially to the handing over of the purchase money. Sometimes one of the witnesses was a clan or village head. A writer was also essential. Where one was not engaged or was not readily available, the seller might draw up the document. At other times, the middleman would act as writer. All parties to the transaction, including the witnesses, were listed on the document and sometimes, if illiterate (like the mothers who were party to some), they added their mark or finger print. The reason for involving a number of persons in the transaction was to enable any subsequent dispute to be quickly settled by reference for information or corroboration to those parties who had taken part in it.

The Shek Pik Papers

The Shek Pik land documents date from the 1830s to the 1890s. With one exception, they are all white or unregistered deeds.[9] Information collected from varied sources over many years has enabled me to provide a comprehensive account of the settlement pattern, livelihood, and managerial arrangements of this village, from which it is clear that the persons involved in these transactions were mostly Shek Pik villagers. There were also villagers from other settlements, including some from adjoining villages on the east and west, and from over the hills in the north-central and northwestern part of the island.[10]

Sometimes these persons were selling or buying into property at Shek Pik. In other cases, the land was located elsewhere. Its sellers or mortgagors were villagers of those places whilst the interested parties were Shek Pik natives who were increasing their holdings.

The format and attestation of the Shek Pik documents are in line with the general practice reported in the previous section. Besides the sellers and purchasers, mortgagors and mortgagees, there are middlemen, writers, and witnesses. On some deeds, the writer and middlemen serve or double-up as witnesses, but on others there are proper witnesses, mostly close relatives of the seller. Out of thirty-two transactions—the rest of the collection comprise family division and loan papers without the same helpful detail—twenty-five had stated writers who in nineteen cases came from the seller's clan. Of the remaining seven deeds, five were likely to have been written by the sellers, and in only two cases is the writer's identity uncertain.

These papers came to me from an elder of the Chi clan and only relate to his branch of the lineage, and especially to his direct line of succession in the branch. A partial genealogy was also available, and comparison of the two makes it possible to identify and provide details for some of the individuals whose names appear in the deeds. The oldest of these was born in 1779 and was the purchaser in a transaction in 1843. Some others are named in the partial genealogy and others are not, but it is possible to identify the generation to which they belonged and hence their approximate life span. The same can be done for a few persons in other clans for which genealogical information is available. Ultimately, given time and the availability of these types of information together with (for the later generations in the deeds) registers of ownership for the 1900–1904 British land survey and settlement of titles, it would be possible to make complete identification for all persons involved in these transactions, in whatever capacity.

However, such complete devotion to detail is hardly necessary. There are more than sufficient indicators to show that, whether from Shek Pik or adjoining villages, the persons listed in the deeds are all village people, many of them linked by marriage in their own and earlier generations as can be ascertained from the genealogies and my interviews with their descendants up to twenty-five years ago. As I have indicated, the writers came mostly from the families to which the sellers belonged. Thus, the general impression must be that these are village documents drawn up by village people. Partly through their concern for education and also because there was a clear need for persons who could write, these rural communities on an outlying island had, through their village schools, produced a fair, perhaps even considerable, number of men who were able to record day to day transactions in writing.

The standard of writing on the documents varies considerably. Some parties are obviously not very well skilled in penmanship, but others have passable and even good calligraphy, indicating not only that the village training had been successful in bringing forward calligraphic skills, but that there was a genuine capability in this line among village people at that time.

The Tsing Yi Papers

The small collection of deeds from nineteenth century Tsing Yi Island, Tsuen Wan, deal with the sale and mortgage of hill land in possession of the village families under customary law arrangements.

The island was offshore and small in size, and was always considered a poor place. There were only some six or seven small villages on the island at this time and their total population could not have been more than four hundred (374 in 2011). The community was thus small and isolated and not free from internal strife. Again, there is conclusive proof from genealogies and other information about the settlements that the parties who wrote and witnessed the written agreements recording these transactions were all village persons.[11] Moreover, though few in number, these deeds are well written and provide confirmation of the educational standard reached by village schools on the island at that time.

Clearly, it was more than sufficient to provide the documentation required to carry forward, in an independent way, the social and economic life of this small community.

The Sai Kung Papers

As already stated, the papers from the Sai Kung area are from a later time. They relate to transactions entered into by villagers during the Japanese Occupation of Hong Kong between 1941 and 1945. The plots of land which were the subject of sales and mortgages during that period had previously been registered in the District Land Office of the New Territories Administration at the time of the 1904 land settlement, and later transactions were recorded on the official forms provided for the purpose.[12]

In contrast, the transactions entered into during the Occupation were drawn up in the traditional form and do not appear to have been taken to the Japanese Military Authorities for either endorsement or registration.[13] However, they were brought into the Land Office of the British District Administration after the war, not necessarily immediately but when the need to register succession arose. The official practice of posting notices about an intended registration sometimes brought forward the purchaser in an as yet unregistered transaction, and on these occasions the seller, or more often his widow or sons, might dispute the sale. This was encouraged by the villagers' knowledge that there was a general feeling in the British Administration that transactions entered into during the Occupation had been in some way forced, and that collaborators and speculators might have taken advantage of the situation to buy land from impoverished and starving villagers. Therefore, it was the practice for the district officers to scrutinise such deeds carefully before confirming the transaction and entering it in the registry in the normal way.[14] In retrospect, and certainly insofar as these and other documents I have seen are concerned, these transactions had nothing special to them. They were drawn up in the traditional format and were perfectly genuine in most cases. Apart from the difficult circumstances of the war, there was nothing to differentiate them from those which had been customary in the area before the British lease of the New Territories in 1898. They had still been in use in outlying districts far from the District Land Registry well after that time, when villagers either did not know that they should take them into the British Land Registry and record the transactions on the forms provided by the administration, or could not be bothered to do so, knowing that local custom would recognise their validity anyway.[15]

For our present purposes, this group of documents is another useful indication of villagers' capacity to perform the written work and ancillary duties that were customary in traditional land transactions. The twenty-seven papers come from villages near or at some distance from Sai Kung Market. They relate to the sales of padi fields and, in some cases, of waste and hill land to other villagers. The parties mentioned by name on the deeds have been readily identified from my own notes and other reference works as being residents of local settlements, and some of the documents actually state the villages of the buyers and sellers. Writers are mentioned in twenty-one of the twenty-seven deeds. A total of thirteen of them came from the same clan as the sellers, seven from the same village, and three more from another village. Thus, there can be no doubt that we are again dealing here with villagers who are managing their own affairs. They were engaging middlemen and or writers from among their relatives, friends, and fellow villagers who would draw up the necessary papers. Some were perhaps writing the documents themselves. There is little to show any difference between these deeds and the Shek Pik group, save that the standard of calligraphy is generally not as high.

How Knowledge of Documentation Was Transmitted

Generally speaking, village children were not taught how to write these papers in school, despite their importance in rural life. Knowledge of the format of land deeds and papers used in important social events, such as weddings, celebrations, and funerals, were spread by two means. The first was by reason of the local practice of passing on old land documents to the new owner or the new mortgagee, whereby all owners had models to hand. The second was the practice adopted by village school teachers of making certain their brighter pupils obtained knowledge of all matters relating to the forms of local ritual and practice in social and managerial matters. This was done by giving the material in dictation or by allowing certain pupils to copy books which they themselves had obtained in the same ways from their own teachers when young. A third means, though one as yet less certainly established, was through the printed guides to form and ritual which I have purchased in Hong Kong from second-hand shops and stalls.[16]

Hardly any of these have been found by enquiry in villages, and therefore I have no mean of knowing whether these guides were really used to supplement village education and the copying or handing over of village handbooks from teacher to pupil. Nonetheless, these books were produced in considerable numbers and in many editions, particularly in the late Qing and early Republican periods.

Perhaps the most interesting aspect of the situation is that there seems to have been such a great reliance on manuscript village handbooks.[17] They were certainly treated with respect, and even today, when the need for them has long since passed, they are still kept by old men, usually former teachers or elders who have played a part in village management in their time. They are not discarded, like so much else in old village houses subject to modernisation or rebuilding in these modernising times.

The Village Schoolmaster

I have mentioned the village schoolmaster and his importance in the transmission of the documents that were essential in village management and social ritual. My enquiries about the teachers in the schools in the areas best known to me indicate that they were often local villagers, coming either from the same village or an adjoining one. There was, seemingly, a sufficient body of educated persons able to take up the burden of village scholar in the many things that had to do with writing and documentation. The village teacher was in truth an indispensable person, and in remote parts of the New Territories has remained such to this day.[18]

Elders and Village Helpers

The schoolmaster, despite his important role, was not the only person who transmitted the village handbooks or assisted in the writing of documents and the reading of related papers. This part was also played by the village elders, many of whom appear to have been sufficiently literate to carry out their duties.

Some of the persons owning village handbooks in the Tsuen Wan and Lantau Sub-districts fall into this class. Though they might often have had brothers and uncles who were schoolmasters, they themselves were not. There were also other younger men who appear to have been competent in writing documents and acquired managerial skills which were often in demand by fellow villagers. These I call "village helpers".[19] They were sometimes called forward by rotation for various duties, especially in assisting with protective rituals and celebrating festivals at the community level, but there were, in addition, others who, by inclination and ability, performed miscellaneous duties all the time. Such persons might well be able to read and write. Together, the schoolmaster, the elders, and the "village helpers" carried on the written work necessary for the smooth operation of village life. They were seemingly available in every small village: at least that is the impression obtained from my widespread enquiries in the region.

Conclusion

From the facts available about rural education in the century before 1940 it is clear that local villagers, in most cases, would not have had an extensive education. Yet, in the context of education for management, the documents used in this study seem to show that, even in the smaller villages of the Hong Kong region, there were sufficient persons able to undertake the considerable volume of written work required in connection with the social and economic activities of everyday life. In the late Qing, at least, this capability was quite widely distributed among families and lineages, thus seeming to endorse and perhaps better the estimates cited by Ms Rawski for Southeast China at the beginning of this paper.

Transitions

5

A Chinese Village on Hong Kong Island
Fifty Years Ago:
Tai Tam Tuk, Village under the Water

This article shows James in his element, the subject being closely associated with his own working life and experience, while his ability to combine documentary research with face-to-face interviews with elderly people who had lived through life-changing events brings into focus an episode of history which would otherwise have faded from public consciousness.

Tai Tam Tuk — the name means "the edge of the big water-way" — is a reservoir and boat anchorage on the southern side of Hong Kong Island. It is a favourite beauty spot and its bay is still in permanent use as a boat people's anchorage and is well known to weekend yachtsmen. It was a village long before it became a reservoir. The Hong Kong government's printed reports related to the construction of the

* Originally published in I.C. Jarvie and Joseph Agassi (eds.), *Hong Kong: a Society in Transition: Contributions to the Study of Hong Kong Society* (London: Routledge 1969) pp. 29–51. Reproduced with permission from Taylor & Francis Books UK.

reservoir in the second decade of this century show that a village community of some eighty persons was removed to make way for the scheme, whilst other records reveal that the Tai Tam Tuk families were supposed to be removed to the adjoining rural area of Chai Wan a mile or two away.

In their turn, most of the former inhabitants of Chai Wan were removed into the new resettlement estate which was built there when redevelopment of this hitherto outlying area of Hong Kong Island began a few years ago, and the estate office records facilitated contact with the sole surviving member of Tai Tam Tuk Village who still happened to be living at Chai Wan at the time of this second removal. She had been born in the neighbouring village of Stanley in 1890 and had come to Tai Tam Tuk to be married in 1905. Together with the rest of the villagers, she had moved from the reservoir site in 1914. In good health and with a retentive memory, she was able to give a full description of life in the old village. She was also able to refer me to another old lady (born in 1885), now living in Shau Kei Wan, who had lived in the village from 1900 until her first husband died in 1909 and she remarried one of the labourers working on the reservoir. These two old persons have been of great assistance in creating a picture of Tai Tam Tuk in the last years of its history.

Enquiries among the boat population confirmed that the older fishermen and their fathers had been born at Tai Tam Tuk, which shows that it has been used as a permanent anchorage by a group of Tanka boat people for at least the last eighty years. The mother of one of them is still alive. She was born there in 1884[1] and has been able to supply additional information concerning the relations between the boat people and the villagers. She referred me to a brother several years younger than herself, who has also given much help.

As might be expected, the government's printed records supply a considerable amount of information about the village. This is mainly contained in the "Blue Books" forwarded to the British government every year since 1844, three years after the foundation of the colony, and in the annual reports of various government departments. These records, together with miscellaneous information collected from elsewhere and the recollections of the four old persons mentioned above, make it possible to give a fuller account of this small village during the latter part of its history than might be expected in light of its extinction fifty years ago. Thereby, the curtain is partly raised on the village side of Hong Kong's history, a subject which has been generally neglected by western writers.[2] To this extent, a study of Tai Tam Tuk, otherwise a village of no significance, is of greater interest than might be the case.

There is an epic quality about the locality of Tai Tam Tuk. Its scenery and the fate of its village are equally compelling. The village was situated at the head of a large inlet of the sea and was bordered on three sides by steep hill slopes which rise in places to a height of well over a thousand feet. Behind the village the lower reaches of the hills were thickly wooded in the mid-nineteenth century, probably more so than any other part of Hong Kong Island at that time. The grandeur of its scenery is still impressive today and can best be appreciated if one stands half-way along the Shek O Road and looks down towards the reservoir. Equally, it is not difficult to conjure up the growing and inchoate sense of uneasiness experienced by the villagers in the years after 1883 when construction work for the first of the Tai Tam series of reservoirs began in an upland valley at some distance from the village (though it was not until thirty-one years later that the village had to move for the last and biggest of the three reservoirs that were constructed in this place).

Tai Tam Tuk has to be seen in its proper perspective. When it first came under British rule in 1841 it was a small and remote village situated on an outlying and sparsely populated island off the long coastline of Guangdong. At that time, it had a population of about fifty persons.[3] This number suggests that the village was established sometime in the eighteenth century. Its inhabitants were Hakkas, and by the time of its removal in 1914, there were two clans living in the village. The Chung clan with its ten families was then in the majority. There were also two families of the Yau clan, amounting to a dozen persons. A few years before, a third clan had been living in the village. Two Chan brothers, who like their father had been born in Tai Tam Tuk, had recently left to live in Stanley. Whether the ancestors of these Yau and Chan families were living in the village in 1841 is not known for sure: the Chung clan must certainly have been.[4] The first Chung to settle there is said to have come direct from the Mui Yuen area of the Ng Wah District, over one hundred miles away, but it is no longer remembered what brought him to Tai Tam Tuk, and, as happened in so many cases, the family record[5] was lost during the Japanese war. The origins of the other families are no longer remembered.

What did the village look like? A government paper of 1887 shows that there were still only twenty houses in the village by that time. Of these, thirteen had been included in the first land survey presumably made some forty years before. These dwellings were one-storey and small, averaging four hundred square feet in size. My informants tell me that the houses were constructed of mud brick made, as elsewhere, by the villagers themselves with earth from their own fields. The foundations and the actual work of construction were probably left to masons and carpenters from Shau Kei Wan and Stanley, the two nearest market centres. As is common in the villages of Hong Kong and the New Territories, the door jambs, entrance posts and lintels of the houses were cut from local granite, and the roofs were made of red tiles. The floors were of beaten earth. The Chung family had an ancestral temple among their houses, but the Yau and Chan families, being fewer in numbers, had not. There was a small temple just outside the village dedicated to the goddess Tin Hau. To the rear of the village there was the usual grove of large trees, mainly banyans. The houses stood beside the main stream which provided the villagers with water for drinking and daily use. It was tidal below the village and was crossed by a wooden bridge erected by the village people.

The houses stood in two rows, rather in the manner described by Chadwick in his report on the sanitary condition of Hong Kong in 1882, where he wrote: "The usual type of village consists of a double row of houses facing a street. The back of one row of houses is at or above high water mark."[6] Tai Tam Tuk had no surrounding wall. Some of the houses were in a ruinous condition in 1914, which is usually the case in the smaller and poorer villages in South China where frequent typhoons and heavy rains combine to shorten the life of these simply constructed dwellings. Perhaps in consequence, most families in the village had several houses. For instance, one of my informants, her husband, his parents, and his younger unmarried brother shared three houses and one shed, but ate together as one household.

The villagers were farmers and their principal crop was rice which was cultivated on the terraces that stretched up the sides of the valley behind the village. These fields were fertile and are said to have produced a good yield, because the land was well-watered by the perennial flow of water that came rushing down the ravines and joined the mountain stream which flowed into the sea near the village. Indeed, it was the quantity of water available locally which ultimately spelt disaster for the village. An account of harvest time in one of the Hong Kong villages appeared in the *Illustrated London News* for 16 January 1858 and is worth repeating here, not only because it is possible that Tai Tam Tuk was the village in question,[7] but also since it describes village routine at one of the important seasons of the year:

On the 1st of November [1857] I took a walk with a friend into the interior of Hong Kong and saw the process of rice-harvesting, beneath a bright, hot sun, the entire village population hard at work getting in the second crop of padi. The principal part of the labourers are women, owing probably to the fact of the men being generally engaged in fishing. The padi rice grows to a height of about two feet six inches. The fields are little patches of about fifty paces, on account of the unevenness of the ground. The rice is thrashed out of doors: first, in a tub with a screen, by a man, who takes a bunch in his two hands to strike the ears against the edge of the tub and then gives the rice again to be thrashed on a floor made hard with chunam, the Chinese asphalt. Ploughing is here done with a very primitive plough and a wonderfully small bullock, as the ground is soft and does not contain a single pebble ... After being harrowed, it may receive a crop of sweet potatoes, or ground nuts. The women work with children on their backs. No one appears too young to take a part in the work. In the next fields are sugar-canes.

This extract mentions the cultivation of sugar-cane and groundnuts. These crops were not grown at Tai Tam Tuk during the time my informants lived in the village, though they recalled that they had been cultivated until fairly recently, together with vegetables such as greens, sweet potatoes, garlic, onions, and various kinds of yam. The quantities for this produce and of the rice yields for the second half of the nineteenth century are recorded in the annual "Blue Books" produced by the Hong Kong government. They supply yearly figures for Tai Tam Tuk and the other Hong Kong villages year by year over a period of some fifty years. One must presume that these figures are reasonably accurate. Since some of the early land records of the colonial administration are also available,[8] the two together provide some valuable material for the study of the agriculture of a group of Southern Chinese rural villages that could be unique for this period.

In 1914, the Chung households owned about forty fruit trees of various kinds, mostly tangerine and pumelo, but, curiously, no lichee or mango, two trees commonly found in the village orchards of this area. These trees were private property and not, as in some villages, a communal venture where the fruit was collected under common arrangements and either shared, or else sold and the proceeds credited to clan or village funds. The Chan and Yau families had no fruit trees.[9]

The Tai Tam Tuk villagers were accustomed to stripping the lower branches of the hill pines as a source of fuel for their stoves, but towards the end of the nineteenth century the government forest guards and sentences of fines or imprisonment imposed on villagers who were caught deterred them from following this ancient but unsatisfactory practice. However, Tai Tam Tuk was remote, and these pines were planted by the villagers, so these deterrents may have had less impact. Indeed, it is obvious from reports in *Sessional Papers for 1888* and *1894* that the small number of forest guards and difficulties in getting them to do their duty meant that for many years the villagers must have done as they pleased on the hillsides. Timber and brushwood were a marketable product and it is likely that the village people sold it in Shau Kei Wan in addition to using it at home. It has been estimated that the annual output of one acre of forest was approximately eleven piculs (twelve cwt.).[10]

In the extract from the *Illustrated London News* quoted above, it is mentioned that the village men were generally engaged in fishing. This is a useful reminder that the sea provided a supplementary source of food for the inhabitants of coastal villages which could be exploited as needed. At the end of the nineteenth century, the villagers of Tai Tam Tuk did not fish from boats — though they may well have done so previously — but mainly used throwing nets. These were made by the villagers from a kind of hemp, which they were able to buy in the shops of Shau Kei Wan. Such nets were common in this region at the time, though they are rarely seen today, having gone out of general use during the Pacific War (1941–1945). I have been told that, fishing in this way, a man standing up to his chest in the shallows could catch fish up to a catty in weight. Such fishing was normally carried out in the first half of the lunar year, but could obviously be resorted to whenever food was scarce or when the villagers fancied a change of diet. The Yau families had a stakenet which was operated from one of the headlands during the season. The sea also provided the villagers with seaweed which was washed in fresh water, mixed with tree leaves and rice or its husks, and fed to the pigs. It was commonly used in this way and was sometimes dried to keep for later use.

Though to a great extent self-sufficient, as was still the case in the first decade of this century, the villagers visited the nearest market town fairly regularly to purchase additional necessities. In the case of the Tai Tam Tuk people, the nearest market centre was Shau Kei Wan,[11] a fishing port three miles east of the village, which had probably served the villagers as such before 1841, as well as since. Shau Kei Wan also served Tai Tam Tuk's neighbours, including the villagers of Chai Wan and the inhabitants of the more distant villages and hamlets of the Shek O and Stanley peninsulas.[12] Communications were rudimentary up to 1914 when the road from Tai Tam Tuk to Shau Kei Wan was still a mud track.

Around 1910, my informants say that the villagers paid weekly visits to Shau Kei Wan where they bought clothes and other manufactured goods, peanut oil for their lamps, salt fish, preserved vegetables, and meat. The villagers could also obtain the services of specialists like blacksmiths, herbal doctors, fortune tellers, coffin-makers, and so on, and would generally sell any surplus produce and livestock to shops there which sold such articles. It should be noted that the pigs which were kept by most families were not generally reared for their own use, but were regarded as a source of additional income.

Shau Kei Wan also represented a place where the village men — those of them who remained at home and did not seek employment in Hong Kong or further afield — could seek company and relaxation in the tea houses and other places of entertainment. The Tam Kung Temple[13] here was always an attraction to nearby villagers at the celebrations on the god's birthday in the fourth moon when Chinese opera performances were held for the customary four days and five nights. There, too, the Tai Tam Tuk people could meet villagers from neighbouring places, with many of whom they would be linked by marriage, either in the present or past generations.

As was customary with any Chinese rural community, the male villagers married the women of surrounding settlements to which, in turn, their sisters and daughters went as wives. For instance, Mrs Chung and her mother-in-law both came from the Stanley villages two miles away and her sister-in-law was a Chai Wan woman. Wives came not only from the Hong Kong villages. Some of those whose names were given to me came from over the water, two from Kowloon villages and another from Hang Hau in the present New Territories. These marriages were all arranged, and like Mrs Chung, who did not know or see her husband until she had arrived in his village by bridal chair, these women had no say in the matter. However, widows did remarry, and in the two cases quoted to me had pleased themselves about a husband.

Though evidence is not complete on this point, it appears that the small size of the village led the families to look outside for wives and not to seek for them among the other clans since this might lead to quarrels and bad feeling between persons whose lack of numbers, as well as the remoteness of the place, made it advisable for them all to be on friendly terms. In one case known to me from a Hong Kong village, this was taken as far as the erection of a special wall between the two sections of the village inhabited by different clans in order to lessen disputes caused by children.

A second point should be made. Tai Tam Tuk was a Hakka settlement and seems to have remained so during its history. The marriage links of the old persons to whom I have spoken, and those of their relatives both in their own and immediately senior generations, show intermarriage with Hakka settlers from adjoining villages and not with displaced families from the town, whether Hakka or Punti. This is what one might expect, because of the network of contacts resulting from marriages in previous generations — the local villages had a seventeenth- or eighteenth-century origin, perhaps earlier in some instances — as well as the obviously greater suitability of village wives for village work. In this direction, then, the proximity of the city had made little or no difference to custom up to 1914.

From marriage I now turn to religion which, in one of its forms, the Confucian, is very much related to family life. First of all, there were the religious ceremonies connected with ancestral worship. In Tai Tam Tuk, where the Chung clan accounted for three-quarters of the villagers, their ancestral duties were centred on their ancestral temple. The members of the Chung family burnt paper and lit joss sticks at the family altar on the first and fifteenth days of every month and also on the main Chinese festivals throughout the lunar year. The New Year and the dates of birth and death of the first male ancestor to settle at Tai Tam Tuk were the occasions for particular celebrations within the clan, and at Ching Ming, or the first grave festival, the families went to the tombs of their forebears. Most of these were situated in a lucky site about two miles from the village. The will to fulfil the ancestral duties was strong and could involve considerable inconvenience. A man whose mother had remarried when he was a boy had taken him to Tam Kon Shan, one of the Lema group of islands. These lie over ten miles off Hong Kong, separated by seas which can sometimes be very rough. Notwithstanding the difficulties, this man returned regularly to worship at the tombs until increasing age and the Communist Occupation of the Lemas put a stop to his visits.

Another form of worship was carried out at the Tin Hau Temple not far from the village. This had been established by the early settlers and was the special property of the village. It was used by the villagers and occasionally by passers-by on their way through the valley. Here again, paper and joss sticks were burnt on the first and fifteenth days of each month, but the biggest celebration of the year took place on the ninth day of the third lunar month, which was celebrated locally as Tin Hau's birthday. On this day, every family in the village took it in turns to worship in the temple and the occasion was marked with special feasting.

A natural feature that was also an object of worship was a stone weathered into the shape of a lion. This was visited as a kind of local place god[14] all the year round, and at the important festivals during the lunar calendar it came in for its share of offerings of food, whole chickens, pieces of pork, etc.

However, these types of worship were not rigidly separated. From what I have gathered, it seems that, despite differences of emphasis, practically every festival day was taken as an occasion to pay some respects to all three objects of veneration, the ancestors, the temple, and the shrine.

At this point it is convenient to bring in the boat people, for, as mentioned in the opening paragraphs, the villagers were not the only inhabitants of the area. There were about twenty families of boat people permanently based on the bay at the time the village was removed.[15] This was an entirely separate community from the land people. They lived on boats and not on the shore and spoke a form of Cantonese, whereas the villagers spoke Hakka. About half these boat families were named Cheng, whilst the remainder belonged to four or five other clans. The boat people in the Tai Tam Tuk anchorage had their own family and other celebrations and did not join the village people in the worship at the Tin Hau Temple. This belonged to the village and had no significance for the fishermen who regarded it only as a nameless small temple or *miu tsai*. Neither did they worship the stone lion that was venerated by the village people. Instead they worshipped at two local shrines to gods styled *tai wong ye*, which were located at different points on the coastline of Tai Tam Bay. Their worship was rather peripatetic depending on where their fishing took them in local waters, though they always went to Aberdeen at New Year and for the celebrations on the birthday of the Hung Shing god at his temple there in the second lunar month.[16]

I have had an opportunity of discussing relationships at Tai Tam Tuk with each side and it is clear from what has been said that in daily routine, as in religion, the two communities went their different ways. The boat people had very little to do with the village people, and vice versa. This is reflected in how little each of my informants knew of the other's daily life in places like Tai Tam Tuk despite long settlement side by side.[17]

There is evidence that in some places the fishermen were exploited by the land people.[18] This was apparently not the case at Tai Tam Tuk in that they were not charged when they attempted to bream their boats on the beaches, which was usually required twice every month, nor were they asked to pay for grass and firewood when they collected them from the hillsides. The only restriction which seems to have been placed upon them was that they were not allowed near the village in their search for fuel; presumably because, on grounds of personal convenience, the villagers wanted the areas around the village for their own use instead of having to go further afield for their supplies. This is understandable and cannot be considered as an oppressive measure.

Besides breaming, the shore was also used for dyeing and drying nets. A visitor to Hong Kong in the 1870s writes of a nearby locality:

In "Deep Bay" [Deep Water Bay] we found a colony of fishers boiling their nets in an exceedingly tall vat, containing a decoction of mangrove-bark, which produces much the same rich brown colour as our own fishers extract from alder bark. Here, however, it is considered necessary subsequently to steep the nets in pig's blood to fix the colour. Those in common use are made of hemp, but others are made of a very coarse silk, which is spun by wild silk-worms, which feed on mountain-oaks. In order to give these additional strength, they are soaked in wood-oil.

We saw nets of very varied shape and divers-sized mesh hanging up to dry all along the shore, beneath the weird screw-pines. I am told that at the beginning of every fishing season they are formally consecrated to the Queen of Heaven, the protectress of fisher-folk, to whom sacrifices and incense are duly offered, while the nets are outspread before her to receive her blessing.[19]

Relations between the two communities were apparently limited to an exchange of basic commodities. The boat people occasionally sold fish to the land people who, in turn, sometimes sold produce to the fishermen, though such economic interdependence as existed was lessened by the villagers' own fishing activities. The land people also sold grass and firewood to the boatmen when the latter preferred to buy them instead of collecting them for themselves. The boat people's main markets for selling fresh fish were the more popular centres of Shau Kei Wan or Stanley, and it is interesting to note that they did not always sail to those places but often walked there over the hills, carrying their fish in two baskets hung at each end of a pole. At this time, however, the bulk of their catch was salted and sold to salt fish dealers in Hong Kong.[20]

The way of life described in the preceding paragraphs was not, of course, unique to Tai Tam Tuk but, with variations, could be found in the other Hong Kong villages and in all the coastal areas and islands of the Xin'an and adjacent districts of Guangdong Province. It was characterised by self-reliance in most things that concerned their daily life, the extent largely depending upon the remoteness of the district. This was largely the case at Tai Tam Tuk after 1841, despite the proximity of Victoria and its trading marts, though there was a general decline of self-sufficiency as the century drew to its close.

My informants state that the villagers of Tai Tam Tuk were accustomed to doctoring themselves with herbal remedies when they were indisposed or fell ill. This reliance upon herbal treatment is mentioned in an authoritative report on the adjacent area of the New Territories dated 1912 in which there is a list of efficacious herbs which could be gathered from the local hillsides.[21] These were prepared for medicinal purposes by knowledgeable persons, of whom there were always a few in each village, either persons who showed a special skill in this direction or had inherited it from preceding generations.

Turning from caring for the body to nurturing the mind, self-reliance usually extended to the field of education. In nineteenth-century China, the burden of providing education for village children lay with the elders of the villages acting, no doubt, in conjunction with the parents of children of school age. My enquiries into the villages of the Southern District of the present New Territories lead me to conclude that they took these responsibilities seriously. However, a village as small as Tai Tam Tuk would not usually attract a teacher because of the small number of potential scholars and the ensuing small stipend. Rev Wilhelm Lobscheid seems to indicate that there was no school at Tai Tam Tuk before the Hong Kong government established one there in 1857. Writing in 1859, he says: "This romantically situated village is inhabited by Hakkas, all uneducated, and in a state of great poverty."[22]

The new school got off to a good start with twenty-one scholars but soon dropped to about a dozen due, says Lobscheid, to the fact that "parents have not yet learned the value of education and are consequently unwilling to make great sacrifices for their children". He would have recommended closing the school had not the village headman solemnly promised a regular attendance of at least ten or twelve pupils. He goes on: "I have therefore engaged an humble, willing teacher, who is satisfied with a small salary, and who will, I trust, by degrees raise the people from the low ebb of their deplorable ignorance."

This unpromising start appears to have characterised the school at Tai Tam Tuk, for it seems to have a chequered history and was not regarded highly by the authorities. When the inspector paid his annual visit in 1879, he found the school closed when it ought to have been in session, whilst an earlier Education Report (1868) mentioned that the school was closed because the teacher had been indicted for highway robbery. The government school there seems to have been closed in the first decade of this century, though my informants tell me that a private school was still being conducted at the time the villagers moved from the valley.

The early records of Hong Kong and the surrounding area show that the local inhabitants had an unenviable reputation as pirates and robbers. There are many unflattering references of the kind which make this point. However, these early reports tend to overlook the fact that, unlike the mass of immigrants to the new city of Victoria and its suburbs, who were largely single men with nothing to lose from occasional riot and unlawful activity, the majority of the inhabitants of the farming villages of Hong Kong Island must have been generally indisposed to violence on account of their families, fields, and houses and an established way of life.

In fact, the village people had a good reputation. A guide to navigation on the South China coast published in 1806 quotes a report on Hong Kong and its approaches dated September 1793 which says of the island:

You will be supplied here with almost every kind of refreshment; especially fish, hogs, beef and poultry. We found the Inhabitants very civil and were daily on shoar at the Villages, and fowling in the interior parts of the Islands [*sic*].[23]

A few years after 1841, the botanist Robert Fortune wrote:

> In all my wanderings on the island, and also on the mainland hereabouts, I found the inhabitants harmless and civil. I have visited their glens and their mountains, their villages and small towns, and from all the intercourse I have had with them I am bound to give them this character.[24]

Another observer, K.S. McKenzie, speaking particularly of the Hong Kong villages, stated:

> The inhabitants, from our knowledge of their character, appear to be industrious and obliging ... From all accounts they seem in general to have been very peaceably disposed; nor did they exhibit any marked approbation or disapprobation, on their transfer to the British sway.[25]

In this connection, it is also interesting to note that when the Kowloon Peninsula was taken over by the British government in 1860, the proclamation addressed to the inhabitants of the area was at pains to distinguish between "the old inhabitants of this site who are indeed orderly people" and newcomers who were suspected of being "thieves and outlaws".[26]

From various accounts these people were under the control of their own elders when the island and, in due course, the adjoining area passed under British rule. In his *Closing Events of the Campaign in China*, Captain Loch writes (again, possibly of Tai Tam Tuk):

> The path now wound round a tongue of land to the left into a small dell, where there were a few houses built in a line. The patriarch and ruler of this community was standing foremost, ready to receive us. This universal custom of acknowledging the superiority of age has been recognized by us throughout the island.[27]

McKenzie also mentions being entertained by a village elder "during an excursion into the interior" of the island.

The Hong Kong authorities were at first happy to adopt this method of government in the villages and elsewhere and gave these men official recognition as *tepos* or village constables. In 1858, they instituted a salary for these men in order to brace them to their duties. These sums appear in the yearly *Colonial Estimates* of the time. Because of the small size of the village, the *tepo* for Tai Tam Tuk received a salary of £12 10s. per annum which was one of the lowest salaries for these officers. However, this system was discontinued only a few years later when the governor of the time introduced a cadet scheme for European officers whereby, it was considered, direct control could be exercised over local people.

Notwithstanding the abandonment of the *tepo* system, there is evidence to show that the elders of the villages continued to exercise their authority as they had done long before 1841.[28] In a report on the land system of the colony presented in 1887, the commissioners remarked that this was the case though they noted, with regret, that the people were more prone to take their problems for settlement to the triad elements in the local community rather than to the government. At Tai Tam Tuk just before the village was removed for the reservoir, the oldest man in the Chung clan was regarded as the head of the community. He looked after the ancestral hall and took charge of the village weighing scales, though the negotiations with the government seem to have been handled by Mrs Chung's father-in-law who was younger and more active. Generally, however, there were few problems of organisation in the village because of its small size, and except in a crisis the villagers went about their own business individually, even in matters of ancestor worship.

By way of comment on the foregoing, the value of historical reconstructions of village life in Hong Kong fifty years ago and more is perhaps open to question on the grounds, some might say, that they cannot be considered typical of the pattern of life in Chinese villages outside British territory. On the other hand, the detail of life in the Hong Kong villages is given in the local government's printed records, where information as to their population, land tenure, agriculture, health, education, etc. is available in considerable detail for a continuous period of sixty years that begins soon after the establishment of the city of Hong Kong in 1841. This is not the case with villages in nineteenth-century mainland China — nor even with those in the New Territories after the lease of the territory to Great Britain in 1898.[29]

But whilst this information is undeniably valuable for students of history and sociology, it is necessary to decide the extent to which it loses its intrinsic value because the island was under British rule. To answer this question, one must establish the extent to which, if any, British rule and its effects removed any similarity in daily life and background between the Hong Kong villages and similar villages on the mainland. Whilst the final answer requires a detailed study of the Hong Kong villages of a kind that, so far as I know, has not yet been attempted, certain differences are obvious.

It is certain that greater security resulted from British rule because it was direct and close at hand: this is attested by many reports for the early years of the colony which show the gradual diminution in crimes of violence and of the unwelcome attentions of gangs of hill robbers or pirate bands. Though remote, Tai Tam Tuk must have benefited from the police station which was situated at Stanley from 1845 onwards, and from the considerable number of troops that were stationed there in the nineteenth century.[30] Equally, piracy in local waters, planned and executed from British territory, seems to have become less common after 1866 due to the measures then taken by Governor McDonnell.[31] Of course, the Hong Kong villagers themselves were probably not entirely blameless beings. Though basically settled, with much to lose from unrest and actual disturbance, they were probably not above taking opportunities for gain and resorting to violence if the need arose or was thrust gratuitously upon them. However, as was the case with violence imposed from outside, villagers' own opportunities for unlawful gain and riotous conduct diminished considerably with the imposition of settled British rule.

Certain other important characteristics of Chinese rule were also removed. In the matter of land administration, the British government seems to have put a stop to the general "overlordship" of absentee landlords and their practice, apparently without proper justification, of levying charges on a greater area of land than was actually registered in their name—though this seems to have been tolerated by the Chinese authorities. Such levies were apparently a feature of land tenure on Hong Kong Island before 1841 and something which villagers had perforce to accept whatever the rights or wrongs of the situation. They continued to be made in many of the present New Territories villages until this considerable area was added to the colony in 1898, after which the British government put a stop to it there also.[32]

The significance of these charges and the fact that they were stopped in Hong Kong after 1841, and in the New Territories after 1898, is that, in this and other ways, the villagers were rid of the (for them) close and frequently harmful connection between the land-owning scholar-gentry and the local authorities that was an established feature of Chinese rule in the districts. To this extent, therefore, it must be accepted that the background of "interest" and influence which so frequently dictated events in Chinese villages was different in Hong Kong after 1841.

However, it also appears that the daily life and internal affairs of the villagers were otherwise little affected by the change-over. This enhances the value of the returns relating to the Hong Kong villages, and since the main differences are obvious enough, accounts of these communities may still be presumed to have some value for historians and sociologists.

6

Old Ways of Life in Kowloon:
The Cheung Sha Wan Villages

This is a detailed reconstruction of a settled rural community totally destroyed, first by overwhelming squatter influx, and then by the planned urban development which was carried out by the government in order to remedy the many problems that ensued. As elsewhere in his writings, James constantly comes back to the human element, unable to ignore what extensive experience taught him, that the comforting baby of tradition gets thrown out with the dirty water of slum clearance. Cheung Sha Wan is extinct. There are plenty of people there now in their place, but they are people who live in Cheung Sha Wan, not a Cheung Sha Wan community.

Writing in 1889 of sporting opportunities in the Far East, Lieutenant Christopher Cradock, RN, advised any of his messmates who happened to be in Hong Kong that "if at any time you are in want of a good 'constitutional' and will be content (at the outside) with a couple

---

* Originally published in *Journal of Oriental Studies* 1970, Vol. VIII, No. 1, pp. 154–188.

of brace, you cannot do better than land ... at the foot of the hills on the mainland immediately behind Stonecutter's Island".[1] Partridges were not the only wild life in the area as, some twenty years later, two tigers were reportedly killed by some Chinese in a cave in the hills near Sham Shui Po.[2]

Such were the environs of rural Cheung Sha Wan about the turn of this century. The area was Chinese territory up to 1898 when, with the rest of the present New Territories, it was leased to Great Britain to form a second extension to the small British Crown Colony of Hong Kong first established in 1841. Situated in the northwestern part of the Kowloon peninsula south of the Kowloon hills the old villages of Cheung Sha Wan have now all vanished and the farming area is heavily urbanised and largely occupied by two large public housing estates with a combined population of nearly 100,000 persons.

These villages, some half dozen in number, were of comparatively late settlement and had only some five hundred inhabitants in 1898. Their known history seems remarkably uneventful, and this article therefore focuses on the ordinary events of village life. It is concerned with, among other things, the diversity of settlement, the period in which settlement took place, the management of village affairs, and the ownership of land. Any lack of drama may be attributed to the facts of their situation towards the end of the Qing dynasty. It is necessary to stress their comparative isolation during most of their history. Though within sight of Hong Kong and not far from British Kowloon, they were situated in an isolated pocket of agricultural land at the base of the Kowloon peninsula, hemmed in between the sea and the steep Kowloon hills to the north. Communications with adjoining areas were confined to mud tracks over the hills and along the coast; and, beyond journeys made by brides on their marriage, visits between villages were usually confined to the immediate neighbourhood. Despite a sparse population, the villages of East and West Kowloon seemingly knew little of each other.

For these reasons, the area was relatively remote until fifty years ago when the sudden expansion and modernisation of the market centre of Sham Shui Po swept away the small town of that name and brought urban development almost to the doors of the villages. Even then the area continued to be mainly rural in character until the influx of refugees from mainland China after 1949 when, because of its proximity to urban Kowloon, it quickly became a large squatter colony. Successive fires, the health hazards, and the urgent need to provide land for redevelopment led to the clearance of the squatter area in 1954–1956 and the construction of a large resettlement estate by the Hong Kong government. The old villages, already buried under the squatter expansion, disappeared in the process.

This upheaval has rendered the area largely devoid of the written records related to the time when they were under Chinese rule which are sometimes found in rural villages to this day, records such as clan genealogies, the evidence of grave stones, memorial tablets of one kind or another (usually commemorating the periodic repairs of local temples but occasionally on more interesting topics), old land deeds, and so on.

The Hong Kong government's printed papers carry only a few references to it. Scraps of information may be gathered from other printed sources, but to my present knowledge the sum total is not very large. There is, in addition, the manuscript schedule of land ownership attached to the survey which followed the lease of the New Territories in 1898, but, for reasons unknown, the schedules for New Kowloon are less informative than those for the New Territories proper.[3] In consequence, this article is based largely on the recollections of old village people, all born before the lease, with whom I have spoken about the area as it was when they were young, whilst the printed sources have provided material for checking their statements and prompting questions.[4]

Before the British

Despite its limited extent, the area has an interesting diversity of settlement. There were long-established groups of Punti and Hakka farmers on land, Hoklo dwellers on the beaches, and Tanka boat people in the anchorages, all of whom had been settled for a considerable period. In this respect, however, it is typical of the coastal parts of the New Territories.[5]

If a Hong Kong resident had decided to visit the area in 1898, he or she might have crossed over from Hong Kong to the little market town of Sham Shui Po, which possessed several streets with various shops and manufactories, a pier, a street market, and several temples, one of which is still standing today. Situated on the 1860 boundary, it is said to have been in its origins a Hakka village, but it had grown considerably in the years following the development of British Kowloon when, though on the Chinese side of the line, its business opportunities had attracted a growing number of Cantonese shopkeepers.

Clear of the town, our visitor would have travelled along the long beach described in 1844 by the Rev. George Smith, later Bishop of Victoria 1849–1865, as "fine, spacious and sandy". Passing through a squalid settlement of twenty to thirty families of Hoklo duck and pig breeders whose long, fast shrimp boats were drawn up on the sand, the visitor would have seen, close by, some Tanka boat people busily employed in burning the marine growth from their boats using grass sold to them by the villagers, with more of their boats anchored off-shore.[6]

Turning inland to the rising ground leading up to the Kowloon foothills, he or she would then have entered the area of the farming villages. The largest of these was the single-clan settlement of So Uk, which was a village of Punti farmers. At no great distance, were other settlements, separated from each other by two to three hundred feet of rice and vegetable fields and the two streams which crossed the area. These were all settlements of Hakka farmers, principally of the Li family, who gave their name to the locality and lived in two of the villages there, Sheung Li Uk and Pak Shue Leung. The population of the two larger villages, So Uk and Pak Shue Leung, was around 150, but the remainder were each around fifty persons. Several other small settlements made up the rest of the land population of Cheung Sha Wan.[7]

Although the area has been settled for a long period, the village settlements which still existed until a few years ago were of late origin. Whereas the main Punti villages of central Kowloon date from the Ming period and before, these date from the eighteenth and nineteenth centuries. The most likely reason for this is the marginal nature of the area.

The Cantonese village of So Uk was the largest of the group and was probably the first to be established. The only genealogical record of the area which seems to have survived belongs to a branch of the So lineage of this village. By good fortune this states the year in which the first So arrived in the area. This was in 1739, in the fourth year of the Qianlong emperor, when he arrived from a village near Nantou twenty-five miles away, to which an earlier ancestor had removed from a village in the Dongguan District in the sixteenth century. He was then forty-nine years old. No reason is stated for his removal to Kowloon, though a farmer, as this man probably was, does not move to new ground when he is nearly fifty save for some compelling reason. His forty-four-year-old wife, and presumably their children, came with him and she died at the age of eighty-seven in 1782. By 1911, the descendants of their five sons then living in the village numbered 157 persons. Present day members of the lineage say that for most of its history So Uk was not known by this name but was called Mau Tin (rough grass field), perhaps a commentary on the undeveloped state of Cheung Sha Wan when the first So arrived on the scene in the early eighteenth century.[8]

It is not known for certain when the Hakka settlers arrived in the area; but on various grounds, such as the pattern of land ownership in 1898, the reported age of its two ancestral halls, and information known to the Li family (the main Hakka clan), their founding ancestor probably arrived within a generation of the first So. Other Hakka families arrived later. For instance, a surviving grave of the Ling clan of Cheng Uk indicates that their first ancestor would have arrived in the early nineteenth century. The immediate origin of these various Hakka clans is not known in every case. Several of them, including the Li family, had come thirty miles to Kowloon from the Sha Yue Chung area of northeast Xin'an near the market town of Tan Shui. As with the first So to arrive in Kowloon, it is not now known what prompted most of the Hakka arrivals to uproot themselves and begin a new and undoubtedly hard life in this area. In the case of the Li clan, their family tradition has it that the move was due to unspecified disturbances in the region of their old home and subsequent hardship. In others, a desire for more land and greater independence would appear to have dictated a move; and in one case, at a later period, personal foolishness like gambling led the father of one of my informants to leave his home and work as a casual labourer in Kowloon.

Turning now to the Hoklos, it is more difficult to state with any certainty how long they had been dwellers on the beach at Cheung Sha Wan. Their mat-sheds and other makeshift accommodations were less permanent than village houses of stone and mud brick; but since they have always lived on or near beaches in this way (and still do in various parts of the New Territories), their temporary appearance would be no true guide to the length of Hoklo settlement. In his *Europe in China*,[9] Eitel appears to place their first permanent appearance in Hong Kong and Kowloon in the late Ming dynasty, but on what authority he does not say. Undoubtedly, they have been a feature of this area for several hundreds of years, maintaining, as is their way, a dual existence on land and sea.

By 1898, the various clans had had time to get well established. According to my informants and the visual evidence of the few remaining houses at So Uk, their homes were substantial structures of mud-brick on stone foundations, with tiled roofs. As usual, each village consisted of a close group of houses built, often with party walls, in one or more rows. So Uk had five rows of houses. The following description of the use and ownership of village houses, though it comes from an adjacent area a few decades later, typifies the Cheung Sha Wan situation:

> Most of the houses of the inhabitants of the New Territories are for owners' occupation. Besides those used for habitation some of these houses are used for keeping cattle or storage of grass, etc. Some are ancestral and joss temples which are for worshipping purposes, and most of these were left by their ancestors.[10]

It was usual for a family to own more than one small house in a row and for its members to spread into several whilst still feeding as one household. When one of my informants (born in 1892) went to the Ling clan of Cheng Uk as a child-fiancée (*san po tsai*), at the age of eight, her future husband's parents occupied five houses in a row. In the years that followed, she slept in one with her mother-in-law, two adult but unmarried sisters-in-law slept in another, her father-in-law and two adult unmarried sons in the third, an old uncle and aunt in a fourth, and the family's hired labourers in the last. In Sheung Li Uk, when the oldest Li was a boy (born in 1890) his family occupied five houses next to the clan's main ancestral hall. One of these houses was an additional ancestral hall, built to honour his own grandfather, whilst the first of the other four was used at night by his mother and father and himself; the second and third were used by his unmarried brothers in their twenties; and the last by a married brother, his wife, and their small daughter. All these persons fed together. Their domestic animals were housed in a wooden barn, though, as stated in the passage quoted above, it was common for dwelling houses to be used as cow-sheds and pig-sties and also for storage of grass and firewood, agricultural implements, and farm produce. These two families appear to have been quite prosperous, but the families of other informants occupied only a pair of houses.

At Yeung Uk, which old Mr Li often visited as a boy to see his father's sister and her family, there were five persons occupying two houses and an ancestral hall. His relatives consisted of a widowed aunt in her late sixties, her son aged forty, his two boys, and a small daughter. There was also another clan, the Yeungs, after whom this small settlement was named, with six families and their own ancestral hall. Both clans were rice farmers and also fished by stakenet and sampan.

Ancestral halls have been mentioned. Most of the clans in these villages had an ancestral hall. The Li family of Sheung Li Uk and Pak Shue Leung had two, one in each village. These buildings were each situated in a row of village houses which they closely resembled, though they were better decorated than the ordinary dwelling houses with granite posts and lintels at the doorways and carved and painted wooden eave boards. The ancestral halls of the main clans who lived in these villages appear to have dated from the eighteenth and early nineteenth centuries, and those of the lesser clans from later in the century. In the normal run of events it is unusual to establish an ancestral hall until the second or third generation, by which time the family has prospered sufficiently, both financially and in numbers, to be able to devote a building to ancestral worship. Sometimes it has to come later since, though used quite frequently as school premises, they are rarely lived in, and to that extend are a luxury which cannot always be afforded.

There were no public buildings in the Cheung Sha Wan villages other than a separate school building erected by the elders of So Uk behind their village in the second half of the nineteenth century or possibly before. The land records show it to have been larger than the village houses and it is supposed to have accommodated up to fifty children. None of these villages possessed a Buddhist or Taoist temple, though each of them had the usual altar to the earth spirits at the edge of the houses. There was the usual grove of *feng shui* trees, some of them large and aged banyans, behind each village. None of these villages had protective walls, which is significant for the discussion of security and inter-village relations in later paragraphs.

The villagers relied on the streams which flowed past their homes for drinking water (which they invariably boiled), washing clothes, preparing food, and other domestic purposes. Sanitation inside the villages was elementary and largely neglected. The missionary Charles Gutzlaff's complaints (1832) of a village further up the coast of Guangdong could probably be also applied to the So Uk group:

> In the afternoon we visited some villages at the entrance of the bay. Viewed from a distance, their appearance is most romantic; the houses, built of brick, rise up among the high trees, of which there are a multitude overshadowing them. But on a nearer approach the charm vanishes. Large quantities of manure, near the houses, affect the air; the houses themselves have scarcely any furniture, and are exceedingly filthy; the lanes are narrow, and the whole built without plan or convenience.[11]

In this however, they would have been little different from many villages in South China, including those at Cheung Sha Wan.

The economic life of the people of these villages about the time of the British lease was apparently still very similar to that of more remote rural areas. Rice was grown for private consumption. If a family had no rice fields, or if its rice production was insufficient, it bought imported rice from rice shops in the nearest market town, in this case Kowloon City or Sham Shui Po. At that time, there was no way they could exchange a smaller quantity for a greater quantity of poorer quality rice and thus overcome an insufficiency, as is generally the practice in the New Territories today. Even at the turn of the century, however, there was probably a greater production of vegetables than was usual for a rural area where, normally, vegetables were only grown on some of the rice fields during the winter months for home consumption. This deviation from the norm is explained by the proximity of Hong Kong with its large urban population. Already, some families (mainly the later arrivals) grew only vegetables and sold them in Sham Shui Po as well as in the Central and Western Districts of urban Hong Kong Island. It was usual for the villagers, men and women alike, to pick their vegetables before dawn and, using the public ferry or their own sampans, to take them across to a wholesale vegetable dealer (*lan*) on the Hong Kong side. They would return in the afternoon with pig swill.

Pigs were reared for profit, and not, in the main, for home consumption, and like the vegetables they were also taken to Hong Kong for sale to a *lan* rather than to Sham Shui Po where the demand was less. The pig food seems to have been brought mostly from Hong Kong, and even on days when there were no vegetables to sell the women had to go to Hong Kong to fetch it. This was usually obtained from the restaurants and eating houses, where for $1 a month, the cook would give the women the waste food when they came around. On their return home, they had to pass through the Chinese Imperial Maritime Customs post at Sham Shui Po where, according to one of my informants (born in 1888), their pails and baskets were usually prodded with iron rods or otherwise inspected to make sure that they were not smuggling opium or other goods.[12]

A third source of income came from grass and firewood which were largely used for cooking purposes at that time. They were cut from the hillsides by the village women who took them to sell in the streets of Sham Shui Po and British Kowloon, from which some of it would find its way to Hong Kong.[13] The finer grass was sold to the boat people for breaming their pine-wood boats, which they did regularly on or about the first and sixteenth day of each lunar month.

Although the outlet for their produce was largely in urban Hong Kong, the market town for these and adjoining villages was Sham Shui Po, and it was from its shops that the villagers bought their clothes and necessities like cooking oil, kerosene, salt fish, pork, and vegetables. A few of these shops were owned by village people. Sometimes pedlars came into the village from Sham Shui Po selling kerosene, cooking oil, cakes, candies, and so on. Villagers also bought their agricultural implements in Blacksmiths Street (*Ta Tit Kai*) in Sham Shui Po and took them back there if they needed repair. If they wished to build a new house or repair an old one, the stone masons, builders, and carpenters came from the same place or from Kowloon City. The growth of Sham Shui Po had been gradual, and in 1898 it was only just displacing Kowloon City as the main market centre for local villagers.

Besides their rice and vegetable fields, pig rearing, and cutting grass and firewood for sale, the villagers grew various fruit trees. A mango orchard was started about 1870 by the villagers of Sheung Li Uk, headed by my informant's father. Lai-chi trees were common, and papaya and pumelo trees were also tended. There were, however, no fish ponds, no cultivation of wild tea bushes, and no sugar cane production in these villages as could be found elsewhere in the New Territories at that time. Nor, despite the proximity of the sea, did the people from the main villages fish by stakenet or sampan, as is common in other places to this day, though as mentioned above, the Hakka villagers of Yeung Uk, only a mile from the So Uk group, combined fishing with padi farming.

As in most country districts, and, in this case, despite the proximity of Hong Kong, with its opportunities for employment of various kinds, the women did not seek employment outside the village. In addition to their household duties, they worked in the fields, reared the pigs, and fetched their foodstuffs. On the other hand, they had more than their fair share of outdoor work because, as was usual at this time, many of the men had gone abroad or were working as seamen.

The existence of a Hakka-Punti complex of villages is interesting, since it poses the question of their relationship. Any clans living together in a confined area of this small size where the villages were only a few hundred yards apart would be subject to potential trouble, over such matters as family feuds or ill-feelings arising out of marriages, trespasses on land, interference with orchards or graves, field crops, distribution of water, and so on. When added to the additional difference of dialect, trouble was even more likely to occur. This was particularly the case between Hakka and Punti settlers in view of the severe fighting which had taken place between them in various places in Guangdong Province between 1840 and 1860. These acute differences were known and had their echoes in Hong Kong at the time. The authors of *The Treaty Ports of China and Japan*, published in 1867, wrote that fights between Hakka and Punti were common in British Hong Kong and that many Hakka labourers had come to Hong Kong with vivid memories of ill-treatment in their native place.[14] It seems that these fights were not confined to immigrant labourers with scores to settle. Eitel records that for several days in August 1862 "the peninsula of Kowloon presented ... the novel aspect of an animated battle field, as the Punti inhabitants of the neighbouring villages were engaged in a bloody warfare with the Hakka settlers at Tsimshatsui".[15]

However, there seems to have been little or no trouble in northern Kowloon between the two groups in the recollection of those persons who were born in the last quarter of the nineteenth century. Their views must reflect the position in their fathers' day since they would surely have heard from them of any disturbances which might have occurred. Quite independently of each other, my informants expressed surprise when I hinted at possible troubles. They affirmed the settled conditions in which they passed their early years, and before, and attributed them to the fact that the villagers, Hakka and Punti alike, were interrelated and, as they put it, "*tai ka tou haî chi kei yan*" (all our own people).

This last point is a significant one. In this area, Hakka and Punti have apparently been accustomed to intermarriages for a long time, frequently enough to make it an acceptable and not uncommon thing by the mid-nineteenth century. To take a few examples from among the families of my informants: in about 1840, a Hakka from Mong Kok in British Kowloon married a Punti woman from Chuk Yuen Village near Kowloon City. His grand-daughter, a Hakka woman, married a Punti from So Uk in 1903, whilst her father-in-law married a Hakka woman from the nearby village of Kowloon Tong in about 1870. Old Mr Li's father, a Hakka born in 1817, married a Punti woman from Kau Kong in about 1870 when they were both living in America. I have been assured by old Hakka and Punti people from this group of villages and elsewhere that intermarriage was quite common in their parents' day, and this seems to be so judging from the specific instances of intermarriage in the nineteenth century which have been quoted to me both from this area and elsewhere in the New Territories. Moreover, it seems not to have been unusual elsewhere in areas of mixed settlement. Writing in 1897, and clearly recalling his own experience at Swatow in the 1850s, Rev. James Johnston of the Presbyterian Church of England Mission wrote of the Punti, Hoklo, and Hakka of Northeast Guangdong: "While these three divisions of the population are distinctly marked, and kept up from generation to generation, there are frequent intermarriages between them and intermixture of the people in their different localities."[16]

Dialect-group differences, then, were apparently not necessarily an important factor in any quarrels which might have occurred, and what evidence there is suggests that Punti and Hakka in this area were more likely to quarrel with the Hoklo villagers than with each other. So far as the more ordinary causes of dissension are concerned, there were, for instance, no difficulties whatsoever about water. There was plenty for all, even after the area was used by the Hong Kong government as an immediate source of water for Kowloon soon after the lease of the New Territories. There were bound to have been minor differences of opinion between families arising out of intermarriage, and occasional difficulties over trespasses and damage to crops, but these matters were traditionally handed to the elders for settlement, and generally ended by them since, though disputes could be taken to the deputy magistrate at Kowloon City, few persons would wish to do so because of the known severity of legal proceedings under imperial rule.

A sensible attitude seems to have prevailed between villagers who were well aware of the causes and evils of disputes. In Pak Shue Leung, for instance, though the Li and Ling clans were on amicable terms, inviting each other to weddings, birthday feasts, and similar celebrations, they did not intermarry as this was held to be unwise in such a small community. Also, when one of my informants was a girl, there was a stone wall between the two sections of the village designed to keep apart the children of each clan, otherwise a likely source of trouble. I was told, too, that the elders of the upper villages used to urge consideration for others in keeping the stream clean for the lower villagers.

However, it was probably the relatively low density of settlement and the fact that most families were in possession of private land which had descended to them from their fathers and grandfathers (so that most of them did not have to rent land from others) which accounted for the lack of trouble in the area; and why the unrest and, on occasion, serious fighting which occurred elsewhere in the province were not repeated in this mixed settlement. There was no economic reason for disturbance as was apparently the case in more densely populated areas where there was a pressure of people on the land and its resources.

These, then, were the main factors explaining why it was that in this small group of villages daily life continued in a calm and orderly routine which was not disturbed by many fights or squabbles among the villagers themselves or with other groups of villagers or lawless bands from the outside. This was despite the lawlessness which appears to have prevailed around the coastal waters at this time, of which a hint is given in the autobiographies of L.C. Arlington, an officer of the Chinese Imperial Maritime Customs who was stationed on Cheung Chau between 1893–1899, and W.F. Tyler, another Customs officer who was serving on revenue cruisers in local waters about this time.[17]

There are hints of past troubles, however. One of the deeds brought forward for confirmation at the time of the land settlement soon after the lease concerned some fields which had changed hands as the price stipulated by a victorious clan for agreeing to desist from its attacks on a weaker one.[18] None of my informants had heard of this, which probably places it fifty or more years earlier than 1898, or in a different part of Kowloon.

How were these villages governed in the nineteenth century before coming under British rule? The area lay within the boundaries of the Xin'an District whose district magistrate had his headquarters in the walled city of Nantou on the further shores of Deep Bay, some twenty-five miles away from Kowloon in a direct line. In Kowloon itself, however, there was the small walled city of that name, with its sub-district deputy magistrate and its military garrison. The district magistrate was principally responsible for public order in his district, the administration of civil and criminal justice and the collection of the land tax, beyond which he was little involved with local people. The extent of his deputy's authority was severely limited,[19] and the extent to which the officers at Kowloon City affected the villagers of the surrounding area, and whether for good or ill, cannot be determined by the sources of information at my disposal.

It is certain that in the later years of the nineteenth century each of the villages described in this article had its elders (*fu lou*) who managed clan and village affairs as well as being responsible for a wide range of business, including education, minor public works, the settlement of disputes, and the organisation of popular religion. The influence of some of these men went beyond village boundaries. For instance, in Sheung Li Uk old Mr Li's father is said to have been consulted by his own clan and villagers of the surrounding area in their petty quarrels and other difficulties. Such men were usually consulted if the elders of complainants' own villages had failed in their efforts to "speak peace", or were considered biased. Though resorting to this arbitration was at variance with the accepted method of settling disputes within the clan or the village, it would be unrealistic not to suppose that wealth, judgement, manner, and experience helped men to determine where to take their troubles for settlement.

Within these villages my informants have told me that there were no set rules to determine fines for petty offences, such as survived until recently on a board dated 1893, which hung in a temple at Tung Chung on Lantau Island. This may only have been necessary in hard or troubled times, falling into disuse when daily life was easier, as it appears to have been in this area at the time of the lease.

Looking further afield, the market towns of Kowloon City and Sham Shui Po also had their own local government in the shape of the usual kaifong or association of neighbours which regulated the internal affairs of these small communities, a mixture of Hakka and Punti.[20] There is conflicting evidence on this point, but it appears that the elders of the surrounding villages, though not members of the kaifong, were consulted on any matter of common concern. This is not, in itself, surprising and is paralleled at the present day in some of the remoter market towns of the New Territories.

In addition to the elders and the kaifong, there was another body of elders and notables in the Kowloon District. This was the Lok Sin Tong established by officials and village gentry in about 1879 to perform charitable works in the surrounding district, such as the provision of free coffins for the destitute, the services of herbal doctors for the sick, and the encouragement of local public works, such as paths and bridges. It seems also to have been used for consultative purposes by the Kowloon officials.[21] It is not certain whether the villages of Northwest Kowloon were represented, though they were in the area from which its leaders came, albeit generally from the larger settlements.

The extent of inter-village co-operation is difficult to determine at this distance of time. Villages appear to have kept to themselves, beyond exchanging their womenfolk with other villages, sometimes quite far afield, in the traditional form. It appears that they would rarely combine in public works unless under the influence of a prominent person or under the pressure of a common and vital need. It is said that there was combination between the related villages of Sheung Li Uk and Pak Shue Leung in the repair of stream banks, wooden bridges, and village paths, but that, generally, the villages looked after their own sections. Personal friendship accounted for private co-operation between persons of different villages, such as borrowing cattle for ploughing. The money associations, which were common at the time of the lease, also brought men together from different villages.

Co-operation was apparently most common in matters of religion and education. So Uk, Kowloon Tong, and Kowloon Tsai—the first Punti, the other two Hakka settlements—though tending to be mixed in practice, are known to have held joint *ta chiu* ceremonies to allay restless spirits in 1900, 1910, and 1920, because one of my So Uk informants took part on these three occasions and a Kowloon Tsai woman on one of them before she left the village to be married. The villages were jointly responsible for financing and organising the proceedings and their co-operation in the project appears not to have been a new development but to go back to their earlier history. Similar examples of joint participation in these ten-year religious ceremonies are reported from six Punti villages of central Kowloon.[22]

Ruination by typhoon or long neglect of a popular temple was another occasion for villagers to combine resources, though the organisers were usually out for the big subscribers and not so much the small villager who could only afford to contribute very little, despite the usual sententious phraseology of the memorial tablets which often record that "a fur mantle is made out of many pieces of fur". The Mo Tai Temple at Sham Shui Po was repaired in this way a few years before the lease.

Education was another means of bringing people together since the smaller villages did not possess regular schools, though teachers, often from outside the local community, were sometimes invited to set up a small school in the ancestral halls and stayed as long as they could make a living. In consequence, parents who wished to educate their sons had to send them elsewhere. As previously mentioned, So Uk had a large school which, in the memory of the present elders, was attended by children from outside as well as from the village, some of them even from the Hakka villages. Hakka parents did not always wish their children to attend Punti schools and would send them to schools in other Hakka villages, where the teacher was invariably one of their own. This much is clear from what I have been told by different persons. However, to whichever school they went there seems to have been a good deal of movement by children of the smaller villages at the time of the lease, and this would surely help to establish friendships and ease inter-village relations.

Whilst on the subject of education, lest one might think that the pupils of such schools, in this remote corner of Guangdong, never attained academic distinction, it is worth quoting an extract from Rev. George Smith's account of his visit to Sham Shui Po in 1844:

> Near this little temple was a house, with a long inscription over a gate, leading into the principal court, which resembled a small farm-yard. This was to inform the passer-by that some relative of the inmate was a successful candidate for literary distinction, and had obtained a keu-jin [*kui yan*] degree.[23]

In the period under discussion, one of the Li family had a reputation of academic distinction and died whilst serving in an official capacity at Swatow in about 1890, presumably as a clerk or private secretary to a mandarin.

Our discussion would be incomplete without a glance at land tenure. When the Hong Kong government conducted its land settlement shortly after the lease of the New Territories, land was registered in the names of those persons who could give satisfactory proof of possession. The registers attached to the survey of fields and houses which was completed at this time provide interesting information about the Cheung Sha Wan area.

In the first place there is an interesting diversity between villages in the registration of ownership of land. The single-lineage Punti village of So Uk saw fit to register all houses and all agricultural land, padi and dry cultivation alike, in the name of their first ancestor, So Ting-hing (1690–1759), and not in the names of his living descendants. However, enquiry has shown that this is somewhat misleading, since my informants state that even at that date the land was not, as one might expect from the manner of its registration, regarded as one holding administered by a council of elders composed of representatives from each *fong* (branch). The great majority of the lineage land was shared between its five branches and only a relatively small proportion of the total holding, approximately one-twelfth, was reserved in common possession. Described in local terms of land measurement, this amounted to ten to twelve *tau chung* or nearly two acres. Again, the land in possession of each branch was not managed as a whole, but was permanently distributed among the various families and descended from father to son.

In the Hakka villages, land was registered in the names of the individual possessors belonging to the various clans and no land at all was registered in the name of the first ancestors or of any ancestral trusts, *tong*, or *tso*, of which there appeared to be none, at any rate on paper. Thus, no land was retained in common possession to defray the cost of ancestral worship. This is the more surprising because practically all the Hakka clans had ancestral halls and, as already mentioned, the Li family had two. It seems that individual families made their own arrangements for ancestral worship, and that, if there were any communal ceremonies at the time of the lease, they were not paid for with funds derived from land set aside for this purpose.

Turning now to individual tenure of land, it is possible, in the case of So Uk, to work out the average landholdings. This can be done by dividing the totals derived from the schedules by the number of persons listed at the 1911 Census. Despite the gap between the census and the land settlement, which was in some cases completed nearly a decade before, it is fairly certain that by 1911 there were very few outsiders in the village and that the village population had not increased much in the interim. Further, little or no land had changed hands in that time. It is therefore possible to give figures for the landholding per capita and per average household of six persons with tolerable accuracy. The general average for So Uk is 0.135 acres per capita and 0.810 acres per average household of six persons.[24]

It is more difficult to give figures for the Li clan of Sheung Li Uk and Pak Shue Leung, and for the other Hakka clans, because they occupied multi-clan settlements and the numbers of persons belonging to individual clans are not stated in the printed census papers. However, in the case of the Li clan, thirty-five individual possessors were listed for a total of 14.51 acres of agricultural land; which gives an average holding of 0.41 acres per land occupier. The So and Li clans are said to have possessed sufficient land for their needs, and more besides. This was apparently not the case with later arrivals, some of whom had to rent land from them. The Ling clan of Pak Shue Leung is stated to have rented fields from the Li families in the same village, whilst land set aside for the So ancestral hall was rented out to Cheng Uk people.

One interesting aspect of land tenure in these villages at the time of the lease which was not permitted to continue under British rule remains to be mentioned. This was the payment of regular charges on land to an outside family, the rich and powerful Tang clan of Kam Tin, a walled and moated village about eight miles to the northwest, which sent its men once a year to collect a levy reckoned in silver. One of my informants clearly recalls their visits since they stayed until they were paid and had to be housed and fed in the meantime, so it was cheaper to get rid of them quickly. In paying these levies these villages were by no means unique, as it appears that many villages on Hong Kong Island, in Kowloon, and in the New Territories paid rent to the Tangs in the nineteenth century and before.

These rent charges are mentioned in various reports of the New Territories Land Court which determined the possession and registration of land after 1898. It is not certain on what basis the Tang clan made its charges for the So Uk area, but reliable information in respect of other places makes it clear that the Tangs were almost certainly the recognised owners of at least part of the land for which they took payment. For instance, in 1860, when the southern part of the Kowloon peninsula passed into British hands, 169 "red deeds"—that is, registered land documents bearing the official red chop—were produced on demand to the

Anglo-Chinese Land Commission. Of these, seventy-eight were held by the Tang clan. Possession had previously been disputed between two of its branches, and had, at an un-specified date, been decided in favour of one of them. It is interesting to note that the ninety-one deeds not belonging to the Tang family involved 176 acres, whilst the Tang deeds, though fewer in number, involved 276 acres, including the sea-board.[25]

However — and this is the point — it seems that the Tangs were sometimes exacting charges for more land than was actually registered in their name, and that, without justification, they included hill and forest land in their calculations. The Tangs do not seem to have held any land on good title at Cheung Sha Wan, so it is likely that the So and Li villagers were paying them on demand, being in no position to do otherwise. Evidence of this is unfortunately lacking for Cheung Sha Wan, but a good example comes from a nearby area. The whole island of Tsing Yi, which amounts to 3.020 square miles or approximately 1,933 acres, was claimed by the Tangs after 1898. They could only produce "red deeds" in respect of 36.2 *mau* or a mere 7.5 acres, though in evidence given before a member of the New Territories Land Court they said that the whole island had been their property for the last two hundred years. The officer in question, H.H.J. Gompertz, reported:

> It appears from evidence I have taken that no members of this family reside on the Island — that they have no cultivation there or houses, nor have they any other interest than the collection of a fixed annual rent charge from the cultivators. This rent consisting nominally of 40 piculs of grain is regularly commuted into a money payment based on the current price of padi in Hongkong at the Winter Solstice. It is not pretended that this payment has ever been increased within the memory of any of the inhabitants, although it is quite certain and freely admitted by the cultivators

that additions have from time to time been made to the area of land under cultivation. Its incidence is shared among the various family [*sic*] cultivating padi on the Island according to the area and value of their holdings.[26]

There are two aspects of this interesting situation. In the first place the rental had never been increased, though more land had been taken into cultivation by the local people. In the second, from the calculations, it seems that the old-established rental for even the 36.2 *mau* owned by the Tangs was below average for the late nineteenth century.[27] At a time when agricultural rents were about fifty percent of the produce, the payment due to the Tangs apparently represented no more than about twenty-five percent of the crop. Hence, there is a paradoxical element in the situation, in that Tang pretensions to a larger area of land than they owned were not followed up by heavy charges. This is seemingly confirmed by the Cheung Sha Wan elders who, though they can recall little but the memory of the Tang levies, do make the point that, cumulatively, the Tang charges were not heavy. From this I think we may reasonably conclude that their practices at Tsing Yi and Cheung Sha Wan were typical of their transactions elsewhere.[28]

One further thought crosses the mind. Light charges may have been the result of local opposition, for it seems that the Tangs were not always successful in making these wider claims even in the Kowloon area, where, as we have seen, they owned a lot of land. In Nga Tsin Wai, a walled and moated village going back to late Song or Yuan times, two elders born in 1884 and 1885 have told me that the Tangs' claims to levy charges there were rejected long before their time by determined men who, so the story goes, undid the ancestral money bags in the presence of the Tang emissaries and, clinking the silver, announced their intention of spending it all in defence of their independence.

Under the Lease

When the Hong Kong government built the first section of the New Territories road just after the lease, the alignment passed quite close to the Cheung Sha Wan villages. The engineer reporting on the work commented:

> The inhabitants generally seem to be pretty well off and the expectation that crowds of hungry villagers would flock to the works and be glad of less wages than the Hong Kong cooly [*sic*] usually receives, was not realized. In fact higher wages are demanded and have been paid by the contractor.[29]

This implies that the standard of living there appears to have been quite high at the time. How well, and what, did the average village family eat? An informant from Sheung Li Uk has said that, when he was a boy at this time, about the turn of the century, his family of eight persons was accustomed to eating three meals a day. These were an early meal around 8 or 9 a.m., a mid-day meal at 12 noon, and an evening meal at 6 p.m. While all were of ample quantity (though the evening meal was always the largest), there was not much variety. The basic food was rice, with fresh or salt fish, and vegetables. Meat was included every two or three days, and pork, often taken in the form of a soup, was always available on the first and fifteenth days of every month. Salt fish was generally taken at breakfast and fresh fish at mid-day, and the evening meal might contain fish of both varieties. The fish and any meat consumed was bought in the nearby market centres, whilst the rice and vegetables were usually their own. He considered that though his family owned more property and were generally better-off than other village families their meals would be almost identical, and this has been confirmed by other informants whose age and memory take them this far back in time.

This relative prosperity, shared with the other Kowloon villages, was due in part to self-sufficiency and to the opportunities for marketing produce and labour in nearby Hong Kong, where a densely packed population needed to be supplied with the necessities of life. At the 1901 Census, the Chinese population of the urban districts of the Hong Kong waterfront opposite Kowloon was over 175,000 persons. As late as 1947, the *Hong Kong Annual Report* affirmed that the three basic requirements of these city dwellers were rice, firewood, and vegetables, and this must have been the case in 1901 and, indeed, ever since the establishment of the city of Victoria in 1841. Nearly all my informants, male and female, have vivid recollections of taking vegetables practically every day across to Hong Kong for sale to dealers in the Central and Western Districts. Observant foreign residents also noticed this fact of everyday life on the Hong Kong waterfront. When the former governor, Sir Henry Blake, and an eminent artist, Mortimer Menpes, collaborated to produce a book on China published in 1909, they selected for one of their illustrations the vegetable boats arriving from Kowloon.[30] As mentioned earlier, other sources of income were the sale of pigs and chickens which, like vegetables, were always in demand, whilst the sale of grass and firewood from the hillsides adjoining the villages was another way of earning cash, though more restricted after the lease.

Besides producing for income, the village families provided items for their own consumption. Some, like rice and vegetables, are still grown in New Territories villages today, though habits have changed. In 1900, if villagers could not produce sufficient rice from their own or rented fields, they had to obtain cash with which to purchase foreign rice; whereas since 1945, the practice of exchanging local rice for a larger quantity of poorer quality imported rice has become well-established. Other items grown by most village families at this time in pursuit of self-sufficiency have long since ceased to be harvested. Peanuts were grown on dry fields with good quality soil for home consumption, to vary the diet and to make special food at New Year and other festival times and not, as earlier, for oil to use in lamps or cooking. Another such plant was hemp, which seems to have been a common, and important, item of village production in the Hong Kong area for a long time. One variety, known locally as "yellow hemp" (*wong ma*), was grown to produce rope and string and was also used for darning clothes. A former Hong Kong magistrate recalls a case in which a woman recognised stolen clothes because of the hemp darns she had made on the garments.[31] Threads of another locally grown variety, "green hemp" (*ching ma*), which is not so tall a growth as the other were prepared in the form of flax (*ma sin*) and used in the earlier part of the period (of which my informants have personal knowledge) for weaving cloth which was then dyed and made into clothes. Practically every family cultivating rice fields is said to have cultivated hemp seventy years ago. However, it has gradually disappeared. One of the Cheung Sha Wan people said that his family stopped planting it when he was about twenty years old, a few years before the 1914 war, though enquiries show that the yellow variety seems to have lingered on in country districts such as Lantau until the outbreak of the Pacific War in 1941.

One of the, to me, most interesting aspects of the local scene — and now one of the most difficult to recover — is how and when the local village economy was affected by urban and commercial Hong Kong. There was, in the first place, a move away from a subsistence economy. Before the lease of 1898, though apparently not the general rule, the more enterprising inhabitants of Cheung Sha Wan would obviously grow and supply commodities which were in demand in the urban area and could not be entirely supplied from within British territory. After incorporation into the colony, the same opportunities continued to exist and expand, and gradually resulted in a general change over to vegetable marketing for profit. Second, there was an influx of manufactured goods made in, or imported into, Hong Kong which reduced the need to make certain items that would otherwise have had to be made in the villages, as in remoter country districts. The nature and extent of the export of manufactured goods from Hong Kong into the adjoining districts of Guangdong Province, and the impact this had upon local agriculture and handicrafts, need a thorough study. Regrettably, little work has been done on this subject, and the time for supplementing facts deduced from written records with oral testimony has practically expired and much invaluable information has thereby been lost.

It is interesting, in this connection, to trace the survival of old habits and ways of life at Cheung Sha Wan. Take lighting and cooking, for instance. When my informants were young, circa 1900–1910, they say that it was still common for the village houses to be lit with rush lamps fed with peanut oil; and even when kerosene lamps began to be taken into general use some time before the First World War it was still common to find both types of lamp in use in the area.[32] It was not simply convenience or expense which dictated whether households used the old or the new. One of my female informants said that some people did not like the smell of kerosene and preferred to use rush lights. The peanut oil for the old lamps was purchased in the market centres and, as stated above, was not now extracted from the peanuts still being grown by most village families for their own consumption. As for cooking, I have already mentioned that grass and firewood were used in the village kitchens. Grass was mainly for heating water for washing and for cooking pig food, whilst firewood was used in portable earthenware stoves, known as *fung lou*, for cooking the family meals and special food at festival times. Firewood is still used to this day in those few houses which survive in what is left of old So Uk Village. My friends there changed over to kerosene for cooking only three years ago and still use the firewood stove at times like Chinese New Year because, they say, it is more suited to baking cakes and other special food. A degree of selectivity was exercised even with grass. Only the coarser type was used in the kitchen; the fine sort being sold to boat people for breaming their craft.

One of the most persistent trends in the social history of these villages, from the second half of the nineteenth century onwards, has been the outside employment of the men. Even before the lease of the New Territories in 1898 which brought them under British rule, there was a definite trend for the men to seek a living away from home. Many persons from the villages of the Kowloon peninsula and what is now the adjacent part of the New Territories had gone abroad to a great variety of countries and territories where Chinese immigration was the prevailing fashion.[33] Late nineteenth-century commemorative tablets erected during major reconstructions of the local temples always list contributions from inhabitants who were abroad. In one case in the adjoining rural settlement of Tsuen Wan, a tablet of 1901 lists subscriptions from fellow countrymen in San Francisco, Jamaica, Singapore, Siam, Manila, Hawaii, and Australia, though at this time the population of the Tsuen Wan villages was probably no more than a few thousand persons.[34]

From information received, and from tablets in local temples, it is certain that the men of the Cheung Sha Wan villages shared in this exodus. In Sheung Li Uk, old Mr Li's father returned to the village in about 1870 after spending thirty years in America, during which he took part in the San Francisco gold rush and made a modest fortune by operating a general store. He was then able to build four new houses in the village and set himself up as a shopkeeper in Sham Shui Po. Mr Li's two elder brothers also went to America shortly after 1900, to San Francisco like their father, and both had died there, their deaths being reported by a fellow countryman. When he was a boy there were about ten men from his village away from home, including three or four in Singapore. This was also the case with the So families of

So Uk, some of whom are reported to have been abroad at this time, mostly in Annam.[35]

Another means of employment via Hong Kong was the sea. British and other ocean-going ships had long attracted a growing number of local Chinese who did duty on deck, in the engine room, and in the galley. In the opening years of this century, some of the men from the Cheung Sha Wan villages who were away from home were employed at sea, as some of their descendants are to this day. For reasons connected with the prevailing recruitment pattern, whereby men introduced their younger relatives and clansmen to their employers, they tended to stay with one shipping line. For instance, the men from Sheung Li Uk and Pak Shue Leung were mostly employed with the well-known "Empress" ships of the Canadian Pacific Railway.

Employment opportunities in Hong Kong also took men from their villages and, curiously enough, service with the colonial government claimed many. One of my informants from So Uk worked in the War Department's Barrack Stores for a few years before he went to sea in about 1915. Earlier, one of his uncles had been a district watchman with the Hong Kong government. The father of another informant worked as a clerk for the Kowloon-Canton Railway and the latter referred me to the widow of a fellow clansman who had entered railway service at thirty in 1914 and died shortly after going on pension in 1931 having served as a first-class locomotive driver for over ten years. Here, as in other employment, the entry and successful career of individuals would often pave the way for the introduction and employment of fellow clansmen in the accepted pattern.

The absence of many of their menfolk at sea, abroad, or in employment in Hong Kong, along with the growing economic opportunities offered by closeness to a large urban population, led to an increased freedom of movement for, in particular, married women after 1898. In addition to their work at home and in the fields and hillsides, they did the shopping in the markets of Kowloon City and Sham Shui Po and, as already described, many of them, all my female informants amongst their number, took vegetables over to Hong Kong most days, bringing back pig food on the return journey. Yet, if, through local circumstances, there was a certain measure of freedom to come and go afforded to them after marriage it seems there was sometimes severe punishment for any who used these opportunities to offend against morality. The Rev. John Hardy, a military chaplain in Hong Kong, relates that a few years before the lease of the New Territories in 1898 a friend of his happened to be in one of the villages near the British frontier, and, noticing some recently disturbed earth, asked for an explanation. He was told that two persons had recently been taken in adultery and had been punished by the elders by being buried alive.[36] This could only have been one of the North Kowloon villages, east or west. I asked my informants whether they had heard of this event. They replied that it had not happened in their villages to their knowledge but was more common in the inland districts from which their families had come. Where adultery had occurred in the Kowloon area—and they cited a case in one of the Shing Mun villages—it had been punished by expulsion from the village and from the clan.

Unmarried girls were not allowed the same freedom and were confined to tasks which could be carried out in the village and its environs away from centres of population. One of my informants told me that when she was a young girl—she was a child bride still not old enough to be married—her mother-in-law would not allow her to go with her to the nearby temple when she went to worship there or to see plays at festival times; nor was she allowed to go to markets on her own. Instead her daily tasks were to help rear the chickens and pigs, to collect seaweed on the shore for preparation as pig food, and, as she grew older, to work in the rice and vegetable fields. She was doing all this at the age of nine and had also begun to work as a grass-cutter on the hills behind the village.[37]

The enlarged cash economy of Cheung Sha Wan, and the factors that led to its emergence, is also reflected in another direction. In these villages with their small populations but comparatively large number of different clans, almost every clan, big or small, had gone to the trouble and expense, early or late in their settlement, of erecting an ancestral hall. They were not large or imposing structures and were barely distinguishable from the ordinary village houses, but their existence points to the greater cash opportunities available to local villagers and receipt of remittances from abroad, and underlines the importance attached to the ancestors. A similar degree of trouble and expense was taken over the graves of ancestors, particularly those of the first ancestors of the clan or its several branches. These were generally formal graves of brick and mortar with a slate headstone that often contained the names of the deceased's many living descendants on it. In every case a geomancer would have been called in to advise on the selection of a site, the time, and the manner of burial. His name often appears on the tablet along with the names of the family. After the welter of development and redevelopment that has swept over Western Kowloon in the last twenty years very few of these now remain.

Concern for family is evidenced, as elsewhere in the region, in the compilation of genealogical records. Amid the squatter fires and the wholesale demolition of old and new structures to make way for the redevelopment of this part of Kowloon, it is fortunate that the record of one of the clans, the So lineage of So Uk, has survived. I have already described how the first ancestor came to Kowloon in 1739 with his wife and sons after leaving his old home in another part of the Xin'an District. This record was begun by one of his grandsons, So Cho-kin, who was probably born in Kowloon shortly after their arrival in that place. In a brief introduction he states that the Kowloon branch knew very little of their family history, in particular of the names and origins of their immediate forebears, and he describes his own efforts to remedy this situation:

> The object of genealogy is to establish the beginning and end of former generations, and the purpose of a clan record is to show the origins of one's family. As an analogy, all plants grow from seeds and every running stream has its source.
>
> The original genealogical record of our So family was lost several tens of years ago [at the time of the removal to Kowloon?] after being kept for many generations by our ancestors. I have made every effort to find this record but have been unsuccessful. I have only been able to trace our descent back to the fourteenth generation to our ancestor So Nam-lok who first removed into the Xin'an district from our old home in the Dongguan district. [This happened about the end of Ming period, 1620–1644.]

Unfortunately, family history has repeated itself. As had happened with the earlier record, the main family history compiled by Cho-kin disappeared in this second major upheaval to affect the So lineage. The surviving record, now in the hands of the family, relates only to one branch (*fong*) of the five which stemmed from the ancestor who came to Kowloon in 1739. It was copied by my informant's father from the main record about forty years ago and preserves only Cho-kin's introduction and part of the descent in this branch. However, it is clear that his descendants appreciated his industry and concern for the family, for this surviving fragment states that "in view of the great efforts made by the main researcher we have named our Cho-kin Tong after him". It seems to me wholly appropriate that Cho-kin's tenacity should have been rewarded by the fact that his family's genealogical record has been the only one known to have survived the events of the last thirty years.

Since it plays a part in the Cheung Sha Wan story, the little market town of Sham Shui Po deserves a closer review. It was clearly a village when Rev. George Smith visited the area in 1844.[38] By the end of the century, it had grown by degrees, encouraged by the parallel growth of Hong Kong and, since 1860, of British Kowloon. Up to about 1900, it seems that it was not an accepted market centre for local villagers other than those living in its immediate vicinity. This position was still held by the commercial suburb of Kowloon City known as Kowloon Street which was a long-standing market centre. Local villagers were accustomed to going there for marketing and special purchases and only in the youth of my informants did a transition come about with more emphasis on Sham Shui Po—which was nearer.

In the last stages of its former existence, before redevelopment in the 1920s, Sham Shui Po consisted of narrow winding alleyways and one-storied stone hovels—hardly surprising for a village that had "grown". For purposes of comparison for present-day Hong Kong residents, an eighty-five-year-old inhabitant of Sai Kung in the eastern New Territories recalls that in his youth, Sham Shui Po much resembled the appearance of that place as it exists today. However, the advantage of this comparison appears to be with present-day Sai Kung since it is reported that some of the dwellings in Sham Shui Po sixty years ago and more had straw roofs.[39] It is also likely that the alleys of old Sham Shui Po were unpaved.

The town is said to have been Hakka in origin, but its favourable position for business apparently attracted a growing number of Cantonese shopkeepers. According to my informants, a few local people operated shops there but by 1900 their number was clearly much fewer than the number of outsiders. Some of these "local" shopkeepers must have prospered as the bell at the Mo Tai Temple at Sham Shui Po, dated 1891, is donated by a man whom my informants identified as belonging to Kowloon Tong

Village nearby. He must have done well as, judging by modern practice, only leading residents present bells to temples.

By degrees the amount of business to be done in and through Sham Shui Po became considerable. Piecing together scraps of information from official reports and from what my informants say, it appears that the civic management of the place lay with the managers of the leading temple. The growing prosperity led to disputes as to the management of temple property. According to the Registrar General's Report for 1907: "The property consists of a market and a wharf and the dispute originated in a struggle for the control of the property between the Punti and the Hakka inhabitants of the village."

What probably happened is that the Hakka element, being the original inhabitants and almost certainly the builders of the temple — and hence the persons who expected to elect its managers term after term — must have been collecting a growing revenue from the market and pier. They were incurring the jealousy and ill-will of the more recent Cantonese business element whose leaders were not being allowed to participate in the management of local affairs, a situation which clearly resulted first in frustration and then in active opposition and struggle.

Besides providing for many of their material needs, Sham Shui Po town was a centre of religious activity for nearby villages. As mentioned earlier, there were no temples in the villages but there were several popular temples in and near the little town. The villagers had not been responsible for their construction, though they were probably circularised by the organisers and were certainly requested to help when repairs were necessary, as is demonstrated on the commemorative tablets listing the names of donors to the repair of the Mo Tai Temple at Sham Shui Po in 1894, which list the names of many contributors of modest amounts from the Cheung Sha Wan villages.

The village people attended these temples for religious purposes, especially just after the New Year and the birthdays of the principal gods in whose honour they had been erected. The old people say that local villagers went especially to the Sham Tai Chi (Temple of the Third Prince) on the Cheung Sha Wan beach, probably because it was the nearest and run by their relations through marriage, the villagers of Law Uk. The temples provided the village people with a traditional and very welcome break with daily routine through the opera shows which were held there at different festival times of the year. Performances were held for the traditional four nights and five days at the time of the god's birthday in the third moon. At such times the temple surrounds and the adjoining beach were packed with people from the surrounding area, Hakka, Punti, Hoklo, and Tanka, villagers, townsfolk, and boat people alike; all intent, after performing their religious rituals, on enjoying the opera show and the other exciting features of festival time such as the gambling, fortune-telling, opium smoking, and other dubious stalls and divans which sprang up round the mat-shed stage and theatre on which the performances were given. A particular novelty was the firing of rockets which, on explosion, would scatter lucky papers. The young men would eagerly contest their possession, paying scant attention to the bystanders who would be pushed, shoved, and even struck in the excitement of trying to get hold of a lucky paper. Such times were often punctuated by disputes, either arising out of trivialities or from latent dislike between the various dialect groups which was brought to the surface through the strong drink and general excitement pertaining to these occasions. To the authorities, opera shows are suspect in Hong Kong to this day, one way or another. The local police probably breathed a sigh of relief when the development of Sham Shui Po involved the demolition of the Sham Tai Chi Temple and its removal from the former beach area, which put a stop to these proceedings.

At times of sickness recourse was also had to the gods. The images in the old temples of Sham Shui Po came in for their share of solicitations from afflicted persons and their relatives.

Application was also had to women of the class known locally as *sin po* (fairy women), of whom there were several in the market town in the early years of this century and at least one in one of the villages of the Li clan. She was an outsider and was not from one of the settled families. These women were chiefly regarded as intermediaries with the gods and were believed to be able to obtain assistance from or communicate directly with dead persons. It is related that when they prayed to gods for assistance in making a sick person well, they were generally able to quote a prescription of herbs which could be made up by the supplicants and administered to the sufferer. Whilst my informants thought that such prescriptions came to these women whilst in their trance and that they were not otherwise skilled in herbal remedies, they must have built up a basic knowledge of simples in the course of their work.[40]

Conclusion

Having traced the history and old ways of life in these villages, it seems appropriate to bring the story down to its conclusion.

I have already mentioned that old Sham Shui Po was swept out of existence and redeveloped, largely on reclamation, in the 1920s. By 1931, most of this transformation was complete and at the census of that year — the last before the 1961 Census — the population of the Sham Shui Po District (with Tai Kok Tsui) was 67,184, compared with 16,521 ten years before.

As the twentieth century wore on and the town crept nearer, village land began to attract purchasers and some fields passed out of the hands of the villagers. The landscape changed as cultivators came in greater numbers and as land was sold, either to them or to townspeople who rented it out for cultivation and pig rearing. Formerly nucleated and clearly separated by the intervening stretches of padi fields, the villages gradually became less distinguishable as cultivators built houses for themselves and their families on the agricultural land they had bought or, more usually, rented. Agricultural structures, especially pig-sties, were added. A cultivator, whose family had cultivated the So clan's ancestral land before and after it was sold to a townsman in the 1920s, stated:

> My house was a village type house, 600 feet in area, with a tile roof and a cockloft. It was there since my father's time and I was born in it [1903]. We also had six pigsties near our house, and as far as I know these were built at the same time as the house and could hold seventy head of pigs. My sister lived in a separate house of her own close by, which was built by her husband at the time of her marriage.

Another cultivator in the same area recalled that his house was built by his father and that he was born there in 1915. This stone village house, similar to the other man's, was much smaller at three hundred square feet, and they had five pig-sties covering seven hundred square feet.

As Sham Shui Po grew, the health authorities became more concerned with dangers to health from the adjoining rural area. Both pig rearing and wet cultivation came under attack. A man from one of the So Uk families states that prior to 1935 his family were rearing pigs in the old village house next door to their own. He recalls that an officer came to see them to say that they were not allowed to rear pigs nearer than twelve feet from their own dwelling and that, in addition, a permit was required for pig-sties on private land. They stopped rearing pigs, added a cockloft to the old house, and rented it out as living accommodation. It is still standing today, together with the house next door, the last two old-style village dwellings left in what little remains of old So Uk. Wet cultivation in areas adjacent to town must also have been under attack pre-war, because after the Pacific War ended in 1945 the growing of any vegetables which required wet cultivation was soon prohibited throughout Kowloon. Since many cultivators grew popular varieties for which there was a ready sale in the urban area, they opposed this measure; on the whole unsuccessfully, as they were fighting a losing battle under the conditions of the time.

But this is to anticipate. In December 1941, Japan declared war on Great Britain and shortly afterwards invaded the colony. By Christmas Day, it was all over and for the next forty-four months Hong Kong was occupied by the Japanese. It was a time of depopulation, deprivation, and death, by malnutrition and disease and occasionally by violence. The estimated population of the colony in March 1941 following an Air Raid Wardens' survey was 1,639,337. A brief notice in the Japanese-controlled *Hong Kong News* stated that in May 1945, the entire population no longer exceeded 650,000.[41]

This is not the place to discuss the events of the Occupation, save in so far as they affected the Cheung Sha Wan villages. Here, it seems, life went on much as usual, though at a tempo reduced by malnutrition. The depopulation of the colony was in accordance with Japanese policy. In order to reduce the number of mouths to feed and persons to control, they ordered recent arrivals in Hong Kong to return to whence they had come. However, as in the New Territories, many of the old-established villagers of Cheung Sha Wan, whose families had been resident for up to two centuries, were long since cut off from their ancestral villages in China and could only remove themselves with difficulty and certain hardship. They therefore stayed put. Either by luck or good judgement they were not, they say, attacked or terrorised by Japanese troops, as happened in several places in the New Territories; nor, like some other Kowloon villages, were they affected by Japanese development projects such as that to expand the Kai Tak airfield, which required the removal of several old settlements. However, pigs and chickens were occasionally taken away without payment by stray soldiers and, as one of my informants commented, the villagers thought themselves lucky to get away with that. In her village (Sheung Li Uk), many persons died of malnutrition and disease rendered more serious by an inadequate and deficient diet. She recalls that a nephew and his whole family, comprising himself, his mother, his wife, and three male children, died at different times during the Occupation, save one child sold to a person living on Tsing Yi Island. Had the liberation come a little later than it did—one month she insisted—she would have starved to death too. A man from the same village confirmed that there had been many deaths and that, whilst one branch of the lineage had died out before the war, another had become extinct during this period. Informants from other villages of the area confirm the near-starvation level of the latter part of the Occupation.[42]

In passing, it should be recorded that the Occupation had a severe effect on local village life. It was a traumatic experience which jolted the pattern of generations, if not of centuries, and its impact seems to have been felt all over the Southern District of the New Territories, which I know well. Cheung Sha Wan was no exception. From what my informants have told me at one time or another, the war resulted in a break with tradition. At So Uk, for example, there were no more of the ten yearly "pacification of spirits" ceremonies (*ta chiu*). Post-war grave worship in the So and Li clans is said to have become more of an individual concern instead of the full-scale, near total turn-outs of pre-war times. Trying to rationalise this, some So informants said that times were harder and that villagers felt, with a vague resentment, that their ancestors had not looked after them during the war. There had also been a break in worshipping in some cases, here and in other villages known to me. Some of the remoter graves were not visited during the Occupation, as the Japanese seem to have discouraged or restricted movement; and, because of guerillas, movement in hill areas was likely to be regarded with suspicion anyway. Clan records were lost or deliberately destroyed so as to deny them to the Japanese, and increasing pressures due to urbanisation and squatter influx must have also contributed to the diminished lineage solidarity.

After the war, in common with the rest of Hong Kong, the villagers had to rebuild a shattered economy, but the old times were shortly to be gone forever. Besides those persons returning after 1945, the Civil War in China, increasingly going against the Kuomintang, brought an ever growing flow of Southern Chinese and others into Hong Kong, until in 1951 the population of the colony was assessed at a record 2,250,000 persons.[43] Since these persons came mainly to the urban area, in search of work and relatives with whom to shelter, it was the twin cities of Hong Kong and Kowloon, and particularly the latter, that bore the brunt of this human onslaught. Semi-rural areas on the fringe of the city like Cheung Sha Wan soon began to be covered with temporary housing, mostly of the squatter type. Cultivators renting land soon found, as did the one quoted above, that the owners of their land wanted some of it back to build houses for their refugee relatives. Old villagers found a market for huts on such of their land as they had not already rented out, but did not always find they could collect the rent. With the influx of persons came associated problems. The village *feng shui* groves were raided by squatters in search of firewood. Trees were also destroyed by the inevitable fires that seem to occur in any area of temporary occupation. Some of the old stone houses adjacent to or surrounded by huts also suffered.

By the mid-1950s the area must have been completely unrecognisable to a returning emigrant. Here, at Cheung Sha Wan, to quote from an official report, in a one-mile strip of what was now extremely valuable building land having a depth of about a quarter of a mile, there were 65,000 squatters. They were but a part of over 300,000 squatters occupying a narrow belt of land from Lai Chi Kok in the west to Kwun Tong in the east who not only constituted a fire and health hazard but had, in addition, brought the natural expansion of Kowloon to a virtual full stop and had also denied or obstructed access to freer development areas. After a disastrous squatter fire in 1953 at Shek Kip Mei, adjacent to Cheung Sha Wan, that rendered 53,000 persons homeless within a few hours on Christmas night, the Hong Kong government decided to embark upon a multi-storey resettlement programme to rehouse squatters as land was urgently required for redevelopment. The Cheung Sha Wan District was an obvious priority for early clearance. The first big clearance came in November 1954 when 12,500 squatters were cleared for the new Li Cheng Uk Resettlement Estate. This took its name from the old village of that name. In December 1955, the clearance of a further 19,000 persons was begun: this involved the villages of Sheung Li Uk and So Uk, the former in its entirety though, as mentioned above, a small part of the latter still remained in 1969 alone of all the former villages of Cheung Sha Wan.

Before clearance, the villages were buried under what, from the surrounding hills, gave the impression of an amorphous jumble of dilapidated wooden huts. At Li Cheng Uk, staff of the Resettlement Department found that:

The squatter village had grown up around the old village of the Li Clan, and hidden among the hundreds of illegal wooden huts were old stone houses on private land, some of them dating back to the last century ... in among the buildings were about four acres given over to intensive cultivation of fifty different kinds of vegetable and fruit for the city markets.

There was more besides; for this, like most large squatter areas, was a complex and partly self-sufficient community. "Pigs were bred everywhere, and some families cultivated bean sprouts in cellars or dark rooms. Business thrived, and there were over two hundred shops and workshops in the area cleared by the department."[44]

When clearance came the change was rapid. One of my informants, a seaman, relates how he returned to find his village gone, his ancestral house demolished and his family living in the nearby resettlement estate. Old and new residents alike were offered accommodation in the newly constructed resettlement estates of the area. Private land was resumed under the provisions of the Crown Lands Resumption Ordinance, with payment of compensation according to law to owners and to tenant farmers. Squatter cultivators were given, as an ex-gratia measure, crop compensation and disturbance allowance, and many of them, like the ones mentioned above, chose to go elsewhere to take up again their interrupted calling.

This, then, is an account of the historical background and old way of life in this group of small villages on the edge of Kowloon in the early years of this century, together with a brief review of the events which led to their complete extinction under dramatic circumstances in the 1950s. Rarely can villagers have been involuntary participants in wholesale change and readjustment to the same degree as the peasant proprietors of Cheung Sha Wan in the early post-war period. Whilst it is true that the inhabitants of many other villages of New Kowloon have, since 1945, found themselves having to remove to permit redevelopment, the change was neither as dramatic nor as sudden, nor of such magnitude, as that at Cheung Sha Wan.

7

The Old Popular Culture of China and Its Contribution to Stability in Tsuen Wan

The reader of the papers in this collection is left in no doubt that they are written by a colonial government servant, but what is abundantly clear throughout, and perhaps especially so in this example, is that James saw the relationship between the administrator and the governed as a co-operative one—not of course politically democratic, but a manifestation of consensus toleration which was of benefit to both parties even where mutual understanding was imperfect. It is noticeable that he frequently uses "persons" as the plural of "person", surely a clue to his humanity—not for him the faceless mass represented by "people".

This article is aimed at investigating the very marked social stability which was so clear a feature of Tsuen Wan society in the early post-war years. What were the factors which, in the virtual absence of external controls, enabled so many people to live for so long in an orderly and peaceful manner in unhygienic and sometimes unsafe conditions in hillside

* Originally published in *JHKBRAS* 1990, Vol. 30, pp. 1–25.

squatter huts and urban hovels, or in the over-crowded conditions of the early resettlement estates? What was it that the incoming squatters shared with the indigenous villagers which allowed both groups to run their affairs so peacefully and effectively and with so little external pressure or assistance? Finally, what were the roots of the generally co-operative attitude towards removal and relocation—upheavals which were essential for development of the Tsuen Wan New Town, and a prerequisite of steady progress with construction and modernisation, but nonetheless always traumatic for those affected?

The Influence of the Past

As I see them, the answers to the questions posed above lie in the Chinese character; but more specifically in some leading features of their traditional upbringing and education.

These were deeply rooted in a reverence for the past, and for the moral standards which the heroes of the past were believed to exemplify. This reverence was invariably noted by those westerners familiar with the Chinese countryside and who had a rapport with its inhabitants, as the following statements from the 1940s show:

Every Chinese peasant is three thousand years of China in miniature. He may not peruse the books of history, but he has heard the story-teller night after night relate in detail, and with delightful embellishments, stories of the history of China from the time of the early rulers to the present day. He and his wife and children have attended the theatricals where the stories of romance, of adventure, of loyalty, and of virtue have been realistically visualised in the open-air theatre that adorns the square of every self-respecting market town. Their culture thought-patterns are not chosen from present day movie stars but from great men of old. The common people have absorbed, not read, from the master spirits of forty centuries.[1]

Most Chinese peasants are anything but stupid. Their knowledge of their own folklore and folk history is extensive, although it is far from being historically accurate. Usually the history the country person knows has been learned at the opera, and he is frequently unable to say whether a certain character is a real person who lived at a definite time, or merely the creation of a dramatist. This confusion is the more frequent because so many of the characters of Chinese drama are patterned after actual people of history.[2]

I do not wish to suggest for a moment that time has ever stood still. Rather, I am using the impressions gained by Joliffe, Winfield, and others[3] to emphasise the immense *weight* and *influence* of Chinese traditional education and upbringing upon the people until recent times. With reference to Hong Kong, I would say that their powerful, lingering vestiges here lasted until perhaps two decades ago: until the rapid modernisation and the improvements to the educational and socio-economic structure which began in the 1970s shifted the whole basis of society onto a more material level, and together with other changes greatly reduced the influence of the past upon behaviour and outlook.[4]

My own realisation of the continuing strength of traditional values and practice and their lingering influence upon the people was obtained before these changes had taken hold, and was mainly acquired at first hand in the course of observing and experiencing the responses of the early post-war generation of Tsuen Wan folk to their mostly exiguous circumstances. Among the more positive attributes seen at that time there were, firstly, their pragmatic, realistic attitudes towards their living conditions and livelihood, and the invariable availability of leaders from among their own ranks, and, secondly, their generally co-operative and accommodating response to the government's various demands upon them, especially with regard to clearances for development. At the same time, the limits of this co-operation were occasionally reached, and these cases I also had to deal with first-hand.

The Legacy of Self-management and Local Leadership

One of these legacies from the past relates to the practice and acceptance of self-management. As Lin Yutang has said, "The Chinese people can always govern themselves, have always governed themselves."[5] Local self-management characterised life in town and countryside, both under imperial rule and after. It did not amount to democracy, for much was left to a practically self-appointed group of local people, but rather they exercised their authority with the consent of the remainder.

Every town ward, every lineage, each village and sub-district had its local leaders. These men would control the people within their own circles in accordance with accepted norms, combining their wisdom whenever weightier matters demanded consultation and concerted action. In political science terms, such men constituted a genuinely local, lower-level management structure. It was a vital under-pinning of the usual and almost too well-known alliance of gentry and officials, though strange to say this fact has still not been sufficiently grasped by many of the leading historians of China.[6]

This buttressing from below, and the managerial skills that were available at the *ordinary* levels of society, were undoubtedly two of the most remarkable features of traditional Chinese society. They were found wherever Chinese were found, inside and outside China. Even though Chinese communities on foreign soil mostly comprised former coolies and erstwhile peasants, they nonetheless exhibited these features to a marked degree. It is precisely because traditional communities enjoyed them that their subsequent transition to modernity has been, on the whole, so successful.

Traditional Self-management in the New Territories

The large, indigenous, long-settled population of the New Territories possessed managerial talents in abundance, and, after 1898, the new British officials were willing to let their leaders continue to exercise them, though within a more effective framework of law and order than had been possible under Chinese rule. In the 1920s, an experienced district officer (south), Walter Schofield, saw this self-management in action among the larger communities in his district (which included Tsuen Wan) and commented: "We never went closely into details of how or why so and so acquired the status and duties of village elder; we just accepted the natural leaders we found."[7]

Decades later, in the mid-1950s, the same capabilities were still to be found among the people of Tsuen Wan. This was indeed very fortunate. Although the town's population had risen to around 80,000, it was yet without a local management office. The District Office in Tsuen Wan was not established until 1959, and, in the interim, the local people had had to cope with many problems, by themselves and largely unaided. Austin Coates, the district officer responsible for the area a few years earlier, has given a vivid account of the burden carried by the Tsuen Wan Rural Committee, the local body that filled the yawning gap between the Hong Kong government's responsibilities and its then capabilities:

As can be seen, [the Rural Committee's] duties are varied and, if done properly, heavy. In Tsuen Wan, these duties have become overwhelming, and the same may happen elsewhere. The Chairman of Tsuen Wan Rural Committee is in effect a sort of magistrate and mayor rolled into one. All day long he has a stream of problems to attend to. He is obliged to work a full day from nine to five and maintain his own clerical staff in addition to what is paid for by the Committee ... There is no time whatever for the running of his own business, so great are the demands made on his public services.[8]

There and elsewhere, the Rural Committees carried out many executive functions at that time, and in remoter places where government was less evident they continued to do so until much later.

Self-management among Tsuen Wan Squatters

Unlike the villagers, the squatter population of Tsuen Wan in the 1950s and 1960s was neither homogenous nor long-settled. It mostly comprised newcomers from parts of Guangdong and elsewhere. However, like other groups of Chinese who happened to find themselves living together in a strange place far from home, they too were imbued with the spirit and practice of these long-exercised "self-help" skills. It was, therefore, in no way surprising to find that able, willing men (and sometimes women) in the squatter areas organised themselves and their fellow residents for greater convenience, providing local services through their own efforts and giving very little trouble to the authorities.

This self-servicing was decentralised. Committees formed in each squatter area in the time-honoured way: men came forward and were accepted by the rest. There was a real need for their services. Life in such places was (and to a lesser extent still is) often fraught with dangers arising from fire, and from the floods, typhoons, landslips, and similar natural disasters to which Hong Kong is periodically subject. However, the leaders were used to taking precautionary measures and were ready to meet new crises as and when they occurred. There was an equal need for the exercise of initiative in daily life, since at that period the amenities provided by government departments or the public utilities mostly ended at the settlement fringes. The leaders had to make their own arrangements to obtain and distribute water and electricity inside the lanes of the squatter areas, and they sometimes carried out minor public works. They also formed fire-fighting teams and security patrols. Disputes between residents over a wide variety of causes had to be resolved, and sometimes triad elements had to be deterred from taking a hand in "providing" security and services for a consideration. In short, the task of the local leaders was not light, even for capable men. It needed time, effort, and the right contacts in the community and the bureaucracy, including the local police, and co-operation and support from the residents was vital.

The Legacy of Co-operation with Authority

During the seemingly never-ending process of clearances for development in Tsuen Wan and elsewhere, the demands on the family and the individual were heavy. Major personal adjustments had to be made during an initial period of strained family income at a time when expenditure on rents was higher than before and debts had to be incurred in removal costs and the expense of fitting out a new home.

The fact that, for the most part, little opposition was encountered by government staff during the process of removing persons from land needed for development, nearly always in accordance with tight schedules, could easily be, and often was, attributed to the government's efficiency. It may well be that the immediate reason for the success of the resettlement process *was* grounded in the Hong Kong government's efficient and careful approach to a potentially explosive process, and because the field staff belonging to the Clearance Division of the Resettlement Department were invariably attuned to the mood and situation of those involved. However, a moment's reflection will bring the query whether it was not just as much because of the co-operation of the people being asked to move, and to the background influences that made them generally amenable so long as the arrangements were acceptable. In this wider context, the people's behaviour has to be linked with traditional attitudes towards the government.

Officials Facing Traditional Responses

My experiences show beyond doubt that local people had a deeply engrained respect for constituted authority but this was always conditional in nature. They had high expectations of the government, but any obligations were definitely seen as being two-sided.

These twin characteristics of the Chinese people were well known outside China. An experienced British journalist visiting the country from his workplace in India had this to say following a visit to China in 1905:

> The people of China are the most law-abiding in the world; but public opinion overrides the law, being so strong that it is the ultimate court of political appeal. ... The officials maintain their position, not by force, but because of the respect which constituted authority commands. They keep up soldiers and police to enhance the dignity of their own positions, and, incidentally, to suppress rebellions and catch, castigate, torture or behead such persons as they consider to be malefactors; but all their actions are limited by what public opinion will allow.[9]

A decade earlier, the American missionary educator, Bishop Graves of Canton, long acquainted with the popular will, had explained what it was and how it had to be taken into account by the authorities at all times:

> China's government consists of two elements: the Imperial authority, as represented by Mandarins, high and low, with its underlings and police runners connected with the various official courts, and the popular will represented by the village elders, the *Kung-Kuk*, or councils of literati, and the *Kai-fong* or assemblages of householders in cities and towns. Public opinion, which is, perhaps, practically the strongest element in Chinese society, is based on local traditions, clan feeling and

provincial pride, modified by a sense of nationality founded on allegiance to the Emperor as the Son of Heaven or Divinely-sent Ruler ... No one can understand China who regards its government as a pure despotism — an Autocrat imposing his own will on subservient subjects. The popular element must also be taken into consideration in estimating the forces which bind Chinese society together.[10]

Much was expected of their rulers by the ruled. It was assumed that they would be guided in their actions in accordance with the ethical code, and rule by the moral authority and example of righteous action rather than by despotic whim or tyrannical decree. When this was not the case, it was open to the oppressed people to remove their rulers. Such conduct had been openly endorsed by the sage Mencius.[11] Apropos the overthrow of the last Xia dynasty king, he had said bluntly: "I have heard about the killing of a ruffian called Chou; I have not heard about the killing of a king". The phrase long in use for a rising against unjust rulers is *hei yi*; which means literally "to raise righteousness". The ordinary people of China justified actions against oppressive or neglectful authorities by transforming themselves from being obedient subjects into "righteous people". It was possible, as Stuart Schram has so aptly said, "to be a rebel *within* the framework of tradition".[12] It was this tradition that accounted for the people's readiness to identify unjust actions as "unrighteous" and to combine in opposition to the local authorities.

Many examples of indignant or infuriated action by the populace can be cited from the Qing period alone. It is hardly surprising that among them we should find a few local instances. A case in point from Tsuen Wan itself comes from the island of Ma Wan.

When the Chinese Imperial Maritime Customs took over the duties of the Canton Customs post on Ma Wan in 1897, there were soon serious disagreements with the local villagers. A large stone inscription in the village, bearing the enigmatic words "Seven English Feet of Leased Land to the Kowloon Customs" is a memorial of the dispute. Fortunately—because the tale that emerges has epic qualities—its enigmatic wording can be supplemented by another old text which explains what happened on that occasion:

> An access road was needed from the Kowloon Customs Station to the hills behind it and the sea beyond, and [the authorities] began excavation work without any announcement. Private land was utilised at will, and the objections of the villagers were not heeded. It was intended to build a [new] customs station also. At this time the people's tolerance had been strained to the maximum and furious anger was sparked off. Neighbouring villagers willingly joined in this righteous cause.
>
> The head Customs Office heard of this incident and feared that the incident would develop into an uncontrollable one. A special mediator was sent to the Heung [Ma Wan] to settle the dispute on the following terms:
>
> 1. Land could be leased for constructing the road, provided it was not more than seven feet wide and that its route was not circuitous.
> 2. The site of the [new] station should be kept close to the hillside and [boundary] stones should be erected to mark the four corners.
>
> Thus it was that the stones with the inscription "Kowloon Customs leased seven feet of land" and "Kowloon Customs" came into existence.[13]

This case is particularly interesting for the light it sheds on the character of the villagers; at least, as interpreted by themselves. Quick to react to injurious actions by the authorities, their concern fanned to anger by the lack of attention to their representations, they had assumed the mantle of "righteous people" and raised support from their neighbours, making the Kowloon Customs head-office realise it was best to come to an early accommodation with them. It was very typical of village behaviour in the region, and a classic case of its kind.

Thus, whilst deferential, the people were assuredly not servile. Moreover, they considered criticism of officials as part of the relationship, and one to be vigorously exercised on occasion, when it served both to remind officials of this fact and to keep their feet on the ground. In the course of my earlier official career, and in my Tsuen Wan days, I was to receive scoldings and lectures, from women as well as men, on how far short of the expected norm the government's position was thought to be in regard to particular issues. Such tirades usually included the words, "You [the] Government!" by way of introduction, and repeated several times.

However, as A.L. Lyall, an experienced Chinese Maritime Customs official and sinologue once observed, the Chinese people "are singularly amenable to moral suasion".[14] In my experience too, this was certainly the case. The villagers' basic sense of "right-mindedness" usually lead to acceptable compromises being achieved, and to a change of ground if their attitudes or behaviour turned out to be unwarranted by the facts. The Kowloon Customs did get their access, even if it was a narrow one! Moreover, the villagers were usually well aware of when their own or others' actions had transgressed the norm. Many times Tsuen Wan leaders told me that someone's behaviour was reprehensible and not supported by public opinion.

On the other hand, it was not enough for officials to proceed on the basis that Confucius and traditional values — nudged along by fair dealing, humour, and understanding — would take care of everything. The people could be stirred up by incomplete information about the government's intentions and provisions, or by their own preconceptions. When this sort of thing happened in the course of the Tsuen Wan village removals and clearances, as it inevitably did now and then, exasperation had to be eschewed and an effort made to coax the people back into a more reasonable frame of mind. The first step in the process was to check if there was anything wrong or lacking on the government's side. It was also necessary to listen carefully to what the people were saying. Besides checking for misunderstandings or misconceptions, there was what I called the "operatic" element to be considered. A talent for dramatisation and exaggeration was evident in many of the harangues one received. Also, squeezing more money out of the government was often the aim in over-reacting and making a big fuss. In short, a range of factors had to be taken into account when assessing whether a situation was serious or not. It was this intriguing combination of complex factors that made life in a District Office so interesting, even with the trials and stresses of the moment.

Villagers Even More Subject to the Legacy

The attributes and outlook described above were generally found in both villages and squatter areas, but were particularly deeply embedded in the village character. This could be attributed to their residents' long-settled and established way of life in one place and their attachment to their homes and fields. Villagers were also well aware that their cohesion and numbers made them an element to be reckoned with. Combination could be expected when there were reasons for dissatisfaction, or where there had been attempts by some parties to present a misleading or incomplete version of the government's intentions. Delays in the work could be expected in these circumstances, and immediate action was needed to clear obstacles out of the way. Where there was still no meeting of minds, some compromise and mutual accommodation was required, wherever possible, to resolve what could otherwise be an intractable situation.

Another facet of village character that is worth noting, because it was consistently encountered in my dealings with them, was that any appeal for local co-operation on account of the need of some other segment of the population, or even a general need like water for the urban masses, invariably fell on deaf ears. Once the villagers' initial anger or irritation had worn off, we were more likely to enlist their co-operation by showing that the various provisions offered for those affected by the government's decisions were reasonable and acceptable. This actually happened in Tsuen Wan in 1959, when the village population of Ho Pui, distrustful of the government and unimpressed by its need to produce more land for housing and industrial use, concluded that its own safety and legitimate interests were not being addressed. They thus opposed a particular public work, and through its power of combination withdrew its co-operation for some six months until they felt secure. Blackmail, you may ask? It might appear so, but the defence of legitimate self-interest has always been accepted in the Chinese value system and allowed for in the relationship between the government and people.

The Traditional Sources of a Positive Response to Well-conducted Government

The Confucian Ethical System

The proper relationship between ruler and people was one of the "Five Relationships" prescribed in the Confucian Classics and taught in every school room in the empire. "The underlying principle of the whole", wrote E.R. Hughes, "was the making of a man, the development of personality and the training of moral character".[15] Besides stressing the social obligations of superior and inferior towards each other, the ethical system promoted by the Classics placed a particular emphasis on "propriety". Whatever their rank or station, this was the keystone of the social system for all, since each person in Chinese society was presumed to know how to behave and what was expected. The result was, to quote Hughes again, to produce an educated man who

> took his stand before society as an expert in moral principles. In all the relationships of life, whether precedented or unprecedented, he was the man to point out the right word, the right act, the right ritual.[16]

Over millennia, this ethical system had developed immense strength and tenacity; and to such a degree, said Dr Smith, that Confucianist thinking had become an instinct that determined attitudes.[17] Nor could he over-emphasise for his readers the intensity of Chinese feeling on the subject:

> The certainty that this is the best system of human thought as regards the relations of man to man is as much a part of the thinking of every educated Chinese as his vertebrae are a part of his skeleton; *and the same may be said of the uneducated Chinese when the word feeling is substituted for thinking.*[18]

I have italicised the latter part of Dr Smith's statement, because my experience of country people from the 1950s to the 1970s has led me to the certainty that this way of thinking was still very strong among older villagers without much education. It was even more alive among their leaders, and again as much the result of *feeling* as of education and upbringing. Among the educated class, and in particular the scholar-gentry and scholar-officials, its intensity had been extreme. The scholar-official father of Yang Kang, the novelist, discussed this, and the intensity of his words can stand for the heart-felt beliefs of his whole class:

> Confucianism is in our hair, our marrow. The entire body of the Chinese people is Confucianism. What can you offer to

replace it? Without Confucianism there will be no China, no Chinese people ... Without Confucianism the country and the people will fall to pieces. Nothing worse could happen. You understand me, children? [19]

Backed by the Legal Codes

Not that the authorities had left all to the example set by Emperors Yau and Shun, or to Confucius and the Chinese Classics either. The moral code to which Dr Smith referred was, in successive dynasties, ever strongly reinforced by the legal code. The contents of Qing law, in particular, provide interesting social commentary on some of the subject matter in this chapter. There is the strong support given to family interests, with punishments prescribed for failure to observe the customary rites and social observances due to family members in the major events during life and in death. There is, too, abundant evidence for the importance of ritual in government and social life as contributing to and sustaining the desired fabric of society. This was all part of the pattern of obligations and expectations, from government to people and people to government and among themselves, that formed the basis of an ordered society and moved it forward on an even keel over the centuries.[20]

Grounded in Education by Rote

Education in these concerns began in the schoolroom and at home. This indoctrination was rendered the more effective because of the memorisation process that was such a central feature of the Chinese teaching method. Looking back on his schooldays in San Ning County, Guangdong, Dr Ng Poon-chew wrote:

In the old method when I was a boy ... we were compelled to study, but we were not required to know what we were studying about. We were simply set to memorize the Confucian classics, endeavouring hard to transform our heads into first-class phonographic records.[21]

The feats of memorisation, in a country which relied heavily on this method of teaching, often bordered on the phenomenal.[22] In 1914, after fifty years' experience with China, Archdeacon Moule not only testified to the positive qualities of memorisation but deplored its likely fate at the hands of the new Republican educators in their haste for change.[23]

Extended by Copying Teachers' Handbooks

Apart from memorisation of the classical books and the moral lessons imparted thereby, there was other work to be done in the classroom. For the smarter village boys who would go on to became the educated village elders of their generations, the process of absorption and indoctrination was intensified by their teachers' practice of making them copy their own manuscript guides to social etiquette, useful exemplars, and local traditions.[24]

Tsuen Wan fully exemplifies the old system of education (in the broad sense of ethical teaching), and its lingering force into practically our own time. Several of my friends among the indigenous population had told me about this copying before I came to realise its full importance and significance; and over a period, as the more educated elderly villagers produced their own handbooks and spoke of their education and the copying work their teachers had given them to do, the pattern became very clear to me. These men were the type of village scholar once described to me by Tsuen Wan elders as "having no degree, but scholarly (*man hok ka*), liking books and study"; persons who might themselves be schoolmasters or could otherwise maintain a reputation for being educated men. The influence of such persons in the village was correspondingly great.[25]

Augmented by Other Means of Ethical Education

Story-telling

One other means of educating children in the standard and expected norms was through story-telling and related pastimes. In response to questions put to elders in the Tsuen Wan villages about books and story-telling in their youth, various titles were mentioned, some of them surviving in hand-copied editions. It had mostly been the elderly villagers of their day who had owned such books and, in their leisure hours, had transmitted their contents to the younger members of their families. Judging from the titles listed, the moral content of many of these stories was high, emphasising such qualities as loyalty, charity and filial piety, denouncing oppression and injustice, and showing the old principle of retributive justice in operation. Though intended mainly for amusement, their contents had the effect of reinforcing the ethical indoctrination received from other sources. These customary extensions to formal education were the more influential because there had been no newspapers or periodicals on sale in the Tsuen Wan shops in their youth (i.e., in 1910–1925). Thus, the field of information had at that time been restricted to traditional reading material and its various means of transmission.

The Man and Puppet Opera Stories

We can now pass from books and stories to the opera. Even in the 1970s, it was possible to glimpse the hold which the old entertainment still exerted upon the people. In Tsuen Wan, they still flocked to see the traditional opera performances held in the temporary mat-sheds erected on waste or temporarily vacant ground at festival times, on the temple deities' birthdays, and at important events in the calendar such as the Hungry Ghosts' Festival, Mid-Autumn Festival, and the Lunar New Year.

In describing the staging of plays to celebrate the birthdays of the deities worshipped in the local temples, a Chinese author touches on one important aspect of these events:

> In raising the funds they [the organizers] talk about their god, what he did in the past and what he still means to the people. The theatricals dramatize the divine history. The idol in the temple characterizes him. The tablets and the scrolls [in the temple and the opera mat-shed] call to mind his traits and his relation to the people.[26]

It was the practice on these occasions to prepare and distribute festival brochures which contain such information. This was a tradition that was followed in some of the more popular Tsuen Wan temples.

The Surroundings

As if the process of indoctrination was not already thorough, the decoration of the temples and the better class of houses, shops, and ancestral halls provided a milieu in which cultural influences were strong and could make an impression on youthful minds. Although a small place, the Tsuen Wan District had its share of old buildings (and some not so old, dating from as late as the 1920s and 1930s) whose walls were decorated with eaves-paintings in the traditional style. Besides depicting the usual auspicious symbols for long life, good fortune, advancement, wealth, and posterity, and the flowers and animals with similar associations, they also carried paintings of well-known stories and persons known to history or from the opera. Verses from Tang dynasty poetry were also commonly included. Obviously, the better class of local buildings were not to be regarded as complete without this impressive cultural array.

The Lion and Unicorn Dance Teams

Besides what was taught in the rural schoolroom and learned outside its doors, one of the most powerful influences upon young village males was undoubtedly exercised through their training in the village lion or unicorn dance team.[27] In Tsuen Wan and other settlements in the Hong Kong region, these teams were at the heart of village ceremony. On social, political, or religious occasions, they were the personification of the village's collective respect for important visitors and the means of marking the main events in the social life of the village and its inhabitants. The dance teams would perform at the opening of ancestral halls, schools, and village offices, or when a wealthy villager built himself a new house. They were part of the ritual performances at the main festivals, at the re-installation of ancestral tablets after reconstruction of a lineage hall, or during the re-dedication of deities following a major repair to a local temple. They carried out other important functions as well. If plague menaced the village, in an old local customary practice, the lion or unicorn dancers were sent with Taoist priests in procession around the neighbourhood to dispel the threat. If the village was threatened with attack, the strong and brave lion dancers under their respected instructors formed the core of the defence. Furthermore, the dance teams were a principal means for maintaining and extending a village's status and prestige.

As part of their training, the boys would be instructed in how to carry out the dancing steps and also how to perform some basic martial arts. In discussing unicorn dancing with two village friends from Tsuen Wan, it was emphasised that the beasts (meaning in practice their human performers) had to follow *kwai kui*. For instance, there was a correct way to enter a building, a correct way to worship at a temple, and correct way to behave when meeting another unicorn. If the right decorum and etiquette was not observed when this happened, it could lead to a fight. This aspect, that of *lai* or decorum, was the most important to be taken into account in training and performance.

Boys learned the art of co-operating together, and discipline was imposed, especially self-control. This was needed during the tense excitement generated by the accompanying drumming and gonging for the dance sequences, and particularly on festival days when the element of competition was well to the fore. The dancing was exhausting for mind and body, and relays of boys took turns to dance inside the at times stifling mask and body of the "animal". Self-control was an important requirement for the participants. "We won't put up with uncontrolled temper", a kaifong friend said on one festival occasion when a dance team was performing, "If a lad can't keep it, he gets put out of the dance group". Thus, in these various ways, the village dance team constituted one of the principal means of giving practical effect to Confucian teaching.

To conclude this account of traditional instruction and entertainment with its inculcation of "right thinking", the complete process has been summed up in a few well-chosen words by Dr Monlin Chiang, one of the most prominent educationalists of the early Republican period: "These moral precepts came from the Confucian classics. Moral ideas were driven into the people by every possible means — temples, theatres, houses, toys, proverbs, schools, history and stories — until they became habits in daily life."[28]

The effect of both the legacy and the drilling was not lost on competent western observers. Writing over 150 years ago, in his standard work on China first published in the 1830s, a future governor of Hong Kong, Sir John Davis, then only lately returned to England from many years' membership of the Honourable East India Company's Select Committee at Canton, had this to say: "The Chinese lower classes are better educated or at least better trained than in most other countries."[29]

"Right Thinking" in Action in Tsuen Wan

The Tsuen Wan District (like all the rest) provides plenty of evidence for the effectiveness of indoctrination, as well as occasional examples of emulation and performance. People knew what to think and what to do, and recognised the attainment of the prescribed high standards of conduct and behaviour even if they themselves did not measure up. Men who did so were greatly respected, to the point of veneration.

It is the general opinion among Tsuen Wan natives, then and now, that one such man was the late Mr Chan Wing-on, a former Tsuen Wan Rural Committee leader and also chairman of the New Territories Heung Yee Kuk. Mr Chan, who unfortunately died comparatively young, left a fine reputation behind him. He is commemorated by a tablet in a traditional-style pavilion, named for him, which was erected the year after his death near the entrance to the Chuk Lam Sim Yuen, one of the large religious houses located above the town. The memorial tablet records his life and achievements as a teacher and as a public figure, with an emphasis on his virtuous conduct and character, and how it had influenced others for good.[30] It states:

Entering the teaching profession, he taught the village children with skill and patience. Being a teacher, he was dutiful to his parents and respectful to the elders, thereby setting a good example to his fellow villagers. Thus, being virtuous himself he caused others to establish their virtue also.

The inscription ends on this note:

> It was little expected that Mr. Chan should die from an illness last year. Upon hearing the news of his death, many persons expressed their condolences. Being sincere and virtuous, he should have enjoyed a long life. It is deeply regretted that we have lost such an honourable leader. In order to sustain the traditional morals, and to commemorate his virtuous acts, I have composed this elegy.

Notice here how the traditional morals are maintained through recording the virtuous conduct and attainments of a revered public figure. To date, the only other public memorial of such a character in Tsuen Wan is that to Yeung Kwok-shui of Yeung Uk Village (1871–1940), Qing dynasty scholar of the *sau choi* degree, graduate of the Guangdong Senior Teacher's Training College, village teacher, leading pre-war elder and a founding member of the Heung Yee Kuk. His photo-memorial, which hangs in the office of the Tsuen Wan Rural Committee, was composed and written by another surviving *sau choi* and senior rural leader of his day, the late Li Chung-chong of Kuk Po, North District. It is recorded that one of his funeral elegies contained the phrase, "He deserved to be called The Perfect Man of the New Territories".[31]

Other reminders of how deeply the Confucian virtues were esteemed and honoured, illustrating how obligations to the family and the community were keenly felt and sometimes fully honoured, can be found in a few of the inscribed tablets at the older ancestral graves of the district. One of these, located in the Shing Mun area on the slopes of Tai Mo Shan, is of special interest in the context of virtuous reputation and its ongoing influence among descendants. The person buried there had been born in about 1710 and the reburial in 1884 was carried out by all three branches of the family then living. However, retained on the new tablet were the names of the elder brothers of the deceased who had been responsible for the initial burial at this site and, it would seem, much of the wording of the original record. The inscription reads:

> The deceased was the fourth son of Ancestor Kau-yuen. He died early. Afterwards [we] his three elder brothers [only the names of two are given] took up the bones [from a coffin burial] and on an auspicious day in an autumn month in the Qianlong 4th or *ping-san* year[32] buried them above the cross road at Pak Kung Au on Tai Mo Shan [the geomantic details of the site follow]. During his life, the deceased was polite and ceremonious. He managed his family frugally and industriously, and he was straightforward and upright in his dealings with others. We his brothers and descendants flourish [*sic*: on account of his exemplary conduct and noble character]. We had hoped that he would have a long life, but his virtue is ever fragrant and he is deserving of his descendants' offerings for ever. For ten thousand years his memory will not be forgotten.

Confucian hyperbole, one might ask suspiciously? Perhaps it was, though in fact there is not much of the kind in the local grave tablets I have seen. Certainly the memory of this good man must have remained alive in the Chung family for generations after his death and formal burial in 1738; for it was nearly 150 years later that the repair to his grave took place.

Another of the basic Confucian principles was reciprocity. It had practical use amid the many uncertainties and occasional dangers of rural life: where mutual help was sometimes badly needed though not always welcomed since obligations were created and had at some time to be repaid. This awareness was well-developed. It was deemed important to know when it was appropriate to render and receive assistance, and to express or show eternal gratitude and awareness for help rendered in a time of need. These were the ideals, and it has seemed to me that many villagers did their best to put them into practice. Once assistance was given and accepted, it was both family and village custom never to forget it. Nor was gratitude to be regarded as being confined to one generation: where considered important enough, it was to be remembered and duly acknowledged long after.

The endeavours of one of my Tsuen Wan Village friends to recognise and continue to honour help given to his family in the distant past is a striking example of this. The founding ancestor of his clan had settled in a small village outside Tsuen Wan in 1724. However, as sometimes happened in the local settlements the family did not prosper, and for three or four generations just managed to produce enough adult males to survive. A crisis ensued when the only adult male in one of the later generations died when still a young man, leaving behind a pregnant wife. By great good fortune, a family from another clan living in the village took pity on her, and provided support. She gave birth to a boy who was reared to adulthood; the future of my friend's family was again secured. This happened around 150 years ago. The descendants of this other family died out or went away before the war never to return. When part of the village burial area was needed for development in the 1970s, my friend approached the District Office for a resiting of one of the old graves of the other clan. He was not applying for cash compensation as he was willing to pay all the expenses, but he *did* want another site in order to express, in tangible form, his family's continuing gratitude for the kindness done to the young widow so long ago. This was provided.

Another instance of a similar kind involved the old grave of a husband and wife, dated 1813, which had to be removed for development at Sam Pak Tsin, Texaco Road, Tsuen Wan in about 1975. Elders from another lineage belonging to Hoi Pa Village responded to our notices posted on site, stating their obligation to arrange for removal and reburial of the remains. They said that the link with the persons buried in the grave was through the female side of their family but was no longer known clearly to even its oldest living members.

In another, even older expression of gratitude for past assistance, the Ho clan of Muk Min Ha Old Village (settled in 1712) built a special hall next to their main ancestral temple to honour a man of another surname who had helped their founding ancestor. One of this man's daughters had married the newcomer, and land had been given which enabled him to make a good start in a new place. The donor's clan still lives in one of the hill villages of the district. When Muk Min Ha Old Village was removed and re-sited in the 1980s, this hall was also part of the re-provisioning. It was rebuilt on a terrace next to the Ho family's new ancestral hall, as in the old village; and honours are still paid to the benefactor's spirit tablet in the same way as to those of their own ancestors.

Conclusion: Are There Other Interpretations?

In the earlier sections of this article, I have suggested that the problems created for the Hong Kong government by continued large-scale immigration and the concurrent need to modernise were greatly mitigated by its being able to rely on a remarkably well-behaved and generally co-operative population.

I have presumed that this phenomenon was largely derived from the inherited traditions of the Chinese people of that and earlier generations. However, in making this suggestion, I have borne in mind that public and private life in China had already been subject to change in the first half of this century, and that in practice the Chinese people might at an earlier date have been more resistant to the influences described above. The degree to which peasants and other ordinary folk have shared Confucian values has always been an open question, and has drawn much attention in recent years. In his study of Cantonese ballads, of the kind to be regarded as "folklore ... written *by* simple writers, not by scholars, and *for* simple folk to be read by them or to be listened to", Professor Wolfram Eberhard has shown that "the values which the ballads represent are often not the so-called 'Confucian' values".[33] A recent survey of twentieth century Chinese peasant proverbs, which focuses on material from the north and northwest, also gives a somewhat varied impression of the extent of peasant acceptance of traditional Confucian values and shows some variation from them.[34]

However, I do not see why these should be considered to be mutually exclusive phenomena. The Chinese peasant was quite capable of absorbing and evincing *both* Confucian and non-Confucian sets of values, and this I think he did. For instance, to take a Hong Kong example, the "Extant Cantonese Children's Songs" recently studied by Helen Kwok and Mimi Chan besides revealing the "prevailing attitudes" expressed in "the speech of semi-literate peasants, direct and frank, often to the point of being coarse", did also in their opinion "help to reinforce in the young certain clearly-defined modes of behaviour and ways of looking at the world regarded as acceptable to the community".[35]

Even after making every allowance for the variable gap between Confucian indoctrination and the degree of acceptance among Chinese individuals, and for human behaviour in practice as opposed to precept, it has seemed to me that some great and tangible quality, part of the legacy of the old order of "right minded-ness" in doing and thinking, *had* manifested itself in the people of Tsuen Wan in those crucial decades. It was certainly something that made all the difference to the execution of the Hong Kong government's schemes for developments.

There is, of course, another and more pessimistic view to be taken, which would attribute the people's behaviour less to cultural characteristics and ethical indoctrination than to the fact that they were still part of the "peasant masses". In my mind at least, the "peasant masses" had still in the then fairly recent Republican period "continued to be supernumaries as they had been throughout Chinese history, the anonymous human dough that suffered and submitted, the governed" resigned to poverty and what it brought as their fate; and that moreover, in a country of whose society Dr Sun Yat-sen had once quipped that it "was composed of only two classes, the very poor and the less poor".[36] Nevertheless, whilst accepting that poverty and acceptance of fate had undoubtedly played their part in Tsuen Wan's post-war saga, I much prefer an interpretation which is more complex and accommodating; allowing more scope for the human quality that is so visible in this narrative, and for the liveliness and enterprise so abundantly observable in the people who went to live there in those spartan and difficult times.

Communities

8

Cheung Chau 1850–1898:
Information from Commemorative Tablets

This was one of James's earliest essays, marrying rescued historical inscriptions with more general background to help reconstruct the former way of life for a unique but little documented island community. It is noticeable that despite Cheung Chau being a small island dependent on the sea through fishing and maritime trade, and despite its having a greater floating population than it had people living on land for much of its known history, the boat people barely figure in this piece. It is tempting to assume that at the time this was written James was relatively inexperienced and somehow trapped into dealings principally with the land dwellers with whom he had more frequent and regular administrative contact. In the next chapter, written decades later, it is clear that he had made a determined effort to give better coverage to the Cheung Chau boat people, but "the interdependence of the land and sea populations and their daily intercourse in business matters did not lead to social fusion. The two communities kept to themselves". To some extent it seems the seafarers were

* Originally published in *JHKBRAS* 1963, Vol. 3, pp. 88–106.

discriminated against, but it was also the case that they appear not to have been eager to mix, and that must have been a disappointment to the historian.

Cheung Chau is a small island situated just over five miles west-southwest of Green Island at the western end of Hong Kong Harbour. It is adjacent to the southern side of the much larger island of Lantau from which it is separated by a strait of a little less than one mile. The island is two and a quarter miles long at its greatest extent, but takes the form of a three-ended dumb-bell, each of whose arms radiates for roughly a mile from the low beach area on which the town is built. The three arms reach a height of about three hundred feet, the northern being the highest and rockiest. The other two are flatter and more fertile, especially that to the southwest where most of the agricultural land is situated. The total area is 592 acres (0.92 of a square mile), of which 91.07 acres were registered as cultivated land at the turn of the century.

There are no large areas of cultivated fields, as most of the fertile land lies in small valleys cutting inwards from the coastal beaches or on low plateaux in the hilly areas of the island. Because of its small size and low features there is a general lack of perennial streams and this has always posed a problem for farmers and townspeople, though strangely enough it has never stopped them from staying there. The main anchorage is at Chung Wan facing due west, which together with Sai Wan to the southwest has attracted fishermen as a home port for hundreds of years. It is not an entirely safe anchorage, as recent typhoons have shown, but, again, this does not seem to have deterred fishermen from operating from the island. The 1911 Census, taken a decade after it had passed under British rule, gave a land population of 3,244, mostly Punti, and a floating population of 4,442.[1]

In the course of my tour of duty in the New Territories, I became interested in the island community and, when opportunities offered, made enquiries locally for information which would shed light on its history in the period before 1898, when it was still part of the Xin'an District. I was particularly interested in local source-material which would provide a picture of island life and society in the fifty years (1850–1898) before the lease of the New Territories to Britain. This article is based on information obtained from three commemorative tablets which date from these years, and on other information available locally relating to several district associations of long standing, besides supplementary material from a variety of different sources.

The tablets consist of slabs of slate-like stone, usually two feet by three feet in size, on which are cut characters a quarter of an inch high set out in two parts: an account of the origin and successful accomplishment of the scheme, followed by the names of all subscribers. Their object was to record the event, and to recognise the efforts of local persons, by recording the names of the donors for posterity. Tablets in this old form were quite common — they are found all over the New Territories — and could record any undertaking, such as the construction of a road or bridge, the repair of a temple, and so on. They were set up, no doubt, with the appropriate commemorative ceremony which is still current practice for such occasions. We have the well-developed Chinese sense of the historical element in everyday life to thank for the existence of such interesting records, which, by their nature, are immune from the ravages of white ants and the damp summer weather. They are not, however, free from the attentions of the man in the street as the present state of these three tablets show: in that the first was hidden by a double bunk, the second is exposed to the elements at a street corner and is often hidden by wood from an adjacent timber yard, and the third was serving as the back of a stove, part of which had to be demolished and the tablet cleared of a heavy deposit of soot.

The first of the Cheung Chau tablets is in the office building of the Dongguan Association and records the repair of the Po On

Study or School in the fifth year of Tongzhi (1866); the second, dated the fourth and thirty-second years of Guangxu (1878 and 1906) stands in the street outside the Fong Pin Hospital telling how it came to be established; and the third, in an old house in Tai Shan Street, commemorates the establishment and repair of a Defence Office in the second and tenth years of Tongzhi (1863 and 1871).

The three tablets give information about the island population towards the end of the Qing dynasty and, for instance, tell something of the various sections of the community, especially those where local leadership and authority rested; their links with other parts of the Xin'an District and Guangdong Province; their relations with the district government and other officials, civil and military; and the way in which such local communal needs as a hospital, schools, and a defence corps or local militia were met.

The nucleus of Cheung Chau society seems always to have been the community of fishermen and shopkeepers, the two being interdependent to a great extent though separated by many basic differences. There has, in addition, always been a farming community, but it has ever taken a third place. A hundred years ago it is likely that the majority of the land dwellers were connected with the island's shops, as proprietors or *fokis* (employees), and in subsidiary trades and occupations (such as ship-building) associated with the three main sections of the community. Cheung Chau also served as the market town for over a dozen villages on the central and southwest coast of Lantau, the largest of which was Shek Pik with a population of 363 in 1911, and for the inhabitants of the outer islands. The Fong Pin tablet states that there were two hundred shops in the 1870s, from which it can be deduced that Cheung Chau was a flourishing commercial centre at that time.[2] This is borne out by the house in which the Defence Office tablet was found, which is long, narrow, and surprisingly large, with a small open courtyard in the middle.

It has changed very little in the last hundred years like many other houses in the town which date from this period and before.

In this urbanised community local power lay with two groups: the members of the Wong Wai Chak Tong of Nantou and Cheung Chau, and the larger traders and shopkeepers. The two were probably intermingled to some extent, in that some *tong* members would be businessmen, but more investigation is needed on this point. The *tong*'s position commands a special mention. It is the family organisation of the Wong clan who are now in the twenty-seventh adult generation at Nantou, their principal seat. By allowing a twenty-five-year generation period, this will place their origin in Guangdong in the early Yuan dynasty (1280–1368). However, the introduction to their genealogical record was written by a descendant of the tenth generation in the eighth year of the Hongzhi reign (1492–1493), so that it seems likely that the generation periods are slightly longer and that the family dates from late Song times. The *tong* itself stems from an eighth-generation ancestor, Wong Hing-cheung, a scholar of the *cheun si* degree who had six sons, giving the *tong* six branches, of which only the first and third are now represented on Cheung Chau.

When the *tong* acquired the Cheung Chau property is not stated, but since it was the sole ground landlord on the island in 1898 and all the other inhabitants held their leases from it and not direct from the Crown,[3] it must have been at an early date, and very likely before the formation of the *tong* in the mid-fifteenth century. Whether the whole island was given to the *tong* by one grant, or whether, having first acquired a substantial grant of land, it pursued an assiduous policy of aggrandisement which eventually resulted in total ownership, is not certain; but, if a grant, it seems to have been a not uncommon thing in the Xin'an District.[4]

The island community was not as isolated as its geographical position on the fringe of an outlying district might suggest. It was on the main route between Macau, the West River, and Hong Kong which, as the century drew on, was a factor of increasing importance. Cheung Chau began to share in the prosperity of Hong Kong though it would probably be going too far to say that it owed its rise to the increasing fortunes of its neighbor.[5] Besides its original families, it began to attract settlers in larger numbers, among whom were many persons from adjacent parts of the province, such as Choi Leung, "the kind-hearted man of Dongguan", who originated the Fong Pin scheme in 1872. According to the tablet, he had already been trading on the island for several decades before he began his philanthropic work, probably one of many such, since the Po On tablet (1866) also mentions that "our Dongguan natives are flowing in for business". The lists of donors on the various tablets in temples and old buildings underline Cheung Chau's business and kinship links with the outside world.[6] The local members of the Wong Wai Chak Tong seem to have maintained close contact with their parent body in Nantou; and, in much the same way, persons who had come to Cheung Chau to farm or do business, and had prospered during their stay, kept in touch with their families and friends in Xin'an, Dongguan, Huizhou, or from whichever district of the province they happened to come.

Relations with the minor officials in the immediate area also seem to have been close, as one might expect. The officers of the Dapeng (Mirs Bay) battalion of the regular land forces, which was scattered in forts and guard posts throughout the eastern half of Xin'an, seem to have contributed quite often to various repair schemes, whilst the salt, stamp, and Customs posts on the island automatically became victims for the collection of funds.[7]

Some of these contacts were useful when it came to collecting subscriptions and also when it was necessary to contact or bring pressure upon the district government—in this case the district magistrate of Xin'an whose *yamen* was at Nantou, the seat of their own Wong Wai Chak Tong. Fortuitously, the tablet in the

Defence Office provides an instance of an approach to the district government. Four graduates, three of them almost certainly members of the *tong*, and the managers of four large shops besides other persons, petitioned District Magistrate Wu when piracy and lawlessness threatened the lives and property of island people in the Xianfeng reign (1851–1861). It is interesting to note that they did not request direct assistance from the magistrate, but asked only that he issue a public notice urging the people of Cheung Chau to unite and provide "brave and strong village guards" for the defence of their island. One of the reasons why the magistrate was approached when this security organisation was being debated was likely because his permission was required to raise and arm any body of men for defence purposes.[8]

Otherwise, the local leaders do not seem to have requested the magistrate's permission to carry out their various projects or even to have invoked his assistance. In the case of the repair of the Po On Study in 1866, they seem to have acted without consulting the *yamen*. Again, there is no mention of the district magistrate on the tablet commemorating the establishment of the Fong Pin Hospital in 1872–1878, though this act seems to have owed much to an enlightened and energetic military official, Lai Chun-pin, who was commander of the Kowloon garrison at the time. According to the tablet, Lai stated:

> I happened to be stationed in Kowloon in 1877 and was so pleased to hear about this man (Choi Leung) that I paid a visit to him. I found him to be a merchant with an untiring devotion to philanthropic works, so I compiled a subscription book urging contributions by officials, gentry, scholars and merchants to help make this scheme a success.

The names of the donors on the commemorative tablet show that Lai had cast his net wide but he did not secure the district magistrate, even as a subscriber.

Whether the magistrate knew officially of these proceedings is not known, but perhaps the sponsors did not inform him. Had they done so, particularly in respect of schemes for a poorhouse-cum-hospital and a school, both public amenities for which he had a measure of personal responsibility by virtue of being district magistrate, he would probably have been obliged to show his interest in one form or another. Perhaps he chose to ignore them as it was likely that he had lost face by Lai's actions; or he may well not have known what was going on.

A considerable degree of self-help seems therefore to have been both necessary and unavoidable in isolated communities like Cheung Chau. Whilst the district government might take an interest in local schemes, it could not be expected to do much more, partly because of poor or inconvenient communications, but principally because there was very little money available to assist deserving projects. Local communities were expected to help themselves and to set aside the means whereby an institution could be perpetuated and the structure kept in good repair. Cheung Chau was no exception to this general requirement and the tablets state that upon its establishment, the Po On Study was endowed with a shop and a house, both with their title deeds, while the Fong Pin Hospital was endowed with two shops.

This abstention from many of the basic duties of local government on the part of the district authorities could lead to abuses when a powerful group of local leaders became unscrupulous through continued exercise of power, and lack of control and supervision from above. On Cheung Chau, as I have said, this group was represented by the Wong Wai Chak Tong, with whom the larger shopkeepers and important individuals were probably prepared to make common cause. The *tong* owned all the land; its parent branch at Nantou must undoubtedly have included senior graduates and possibly retired officials; and the tablets show that some members of the Cheung Chau branch were junior graduates by examination or purchase. This group must have been able to exert considerable pressure on the district magistrate and his secretaries regarding Cheung Chau affairs, and during their short three-year tour most magistrates must have felt that the *tong* and the Cheung Chau people were capable of looking after themselves on what was, after all, a small and remote island, with a population less than that of many of the larger villages in the district. In short, Cheung Chau interests were well represented if the *tong* was honest and well-meaning, but not if its members were corrupt and ill-intentioned.

Turning again to the tablets, that relating to the Po On Study is of great interest because of its connection with a prominent feature of Cheung Chau society which has so far only been mentioned in passing: the district association.[9] The district association is a social and charitable organisation organised on the basis of mutual assistance for natives of the same district when living in another place. In a mixed settlement like Cheung Chau, where Hoklo and Tanka rubbed shoulders with Hakka, Chaozhou, and Punti from various districts of Guangdong Province, with consequent language difficulties, it was a distinct advantage to be part of a community which had troubled to organise itself for welfare purposes, as had several district groups on this small island a hundred years ago. These traditional media of mutual assistance warrant a closer look, especially as their existence is proof of the diversity of persons settling on Cheung Chau, its popularity with businessmen and others, and of the degree of wealth and general prosperity there in the middle of the last century. District associations, like present day kaifong in the urban area, can only operate effectively (and, indeed, come into existence) inside a community which possesses these prosperous elements. The district associations must also have been a useful counterpoise to the political dominance of the Wong Wai Chak Tong.

The association for natives of Dongguan is the largest, richest, and probably the oldest of the Cheung Chau societies. It seems to have been established in 1800, and in 1898 owned five shops, office premises, and an ancestral hall which had been in existence for at least forty years, judging by an incense holder dated 1859. Members and destitute persons of Dongguan origin could receive relief assistance from its funds and contributions, with which the Po On Study, the ancestral temple, and later three large communal urn graves were also managed. Practically all the way from the cradle to the grave the member and his children could benefit from the operation of his association. He was born into membership and participated in activities by subscription, as required.

Because of their loose organisation and lack of proper safeguards, the associations often ran into trouble over money. To quote an elder's reminiscences from the manuscript notebook of the Dongguan Association (which the present chairman has kindly allowed me to see and use), compiled in about 1928 but referring to the previous sixty years:

> In the past there were upright managers, but there were also embezzlers, who appropriated public funds without authority. When X was in charge of our association's funds he reported that he had lost the account books, so nothing could be audited. It was through my persuasion he produced fifty dollars to end the matter.

Similarly, he records how, on the death of a leading member who had been instrumental in purchasing new property for expanding the association, the members asked his family for the accounts and title deeds. The relatives refused to part with them unless a payment was made first. Members naturally refused "which is why no title deeds or accounts are available from the early period".[10]

The association laid emphasis on social cohesion and the observance by its members of the customary proprieties. There was the traditional feast for all members every year at the lantern festival on the fifteenth day of the first moon, on which day the managers for the new year were elected, and the yearly worship of Kwan Tai, the God of War and patron god of the association, on his birthday on the thirteenth day of the fifth moon, when each subscribing member received a share of roast pork. Confucius's birthday and the two grave sweeping festivals were also celebrated by members gathering together.

Commemorative tablets existed until only a few years ago which would have provided useful information about two other similar associations of long standing; those of people from Huizhou and Chaozhou (combined) and from Siyi. One in the Huizhou clansmen's office was turned out during repairs after Typhoon Mary in 1960 and not replaced; and what was probably the foundation stone of the Yik Sin Tong, an association for Siyi natives, was taken down and not put back when the house next door, which shared a party wall, was renovated about ten years ago. There is now no trace of these tablets.

However, two inscriptions still remain from these institutions. One, removed to the Huizhou section of the Kwok Man School in 1952, is dated 1908 and is an ornamental granite head-slab with two side pieces, all with carved and painted characters upon them, the gift of wealthy members or else a sign of general prosperity in the Huizhou community. The present leaders of the association say that the date refers only to the handsome inscriptions and not to the establishment of their school, which is believed to have been in operation for many years before. This is likely as the office building is an old one and was already registered at the time of the lease of the New Territories as the Huizhou and Chaozhou Club, and the association has a reputed existence of over two hundred years.[11]

Similarly, a headstone is still in position inside an old building on the Praya belonging to the Siyi Yik Sin Tong, which records its repair in the twenty-third year of Guangxu (1897), the inscription being the work of Wong Wai Sam, said to be a teacher in the *tong*'s school. This *tong* has an interesting origin, if the tale told by its present managers is reliable, in that it arose from a shipwreck which washed up a body carrying money on one of the Cheung Chau beaches. The ship was supposed to have been carrying emigrants back to China from San Francisco. The body was given a decent burial by some Siyi persons who hit upon the idea of forming a *tong* for the unity and betterment of their fellow countrymen on the island, and with additional subscriptions the initial windfall was used to build or purchase the present building, which was the only property owned by the *tong* in 1898. A feature of the building was the establishment of an altar on the ground floor on which were placed the tablets of the original organisers and principal subscribers, but these have now all gone, though a shrine remains.[12]

The fourth of these district associations of long-standing is the Po On which has no connection with the old Po On Study run by the Dongguan Association. Its leadership in 1898 rested with the senior members of the Wong Wai Chak Tong, as it does today. It controls the old Defence Office which is rented out and the proceeds added to the association's funds. Very little information is at present available concerning its history beyond the fact that it existed in the Qing period[13] and that it had a close connection with the members of the *tong*, who were its principal patrons and sponsors.

Two other instances of communal enterprise remain to be mentioned. There was, before the outbreak of the Pacific War in 1941, an organisation of local leaders known as the kaifong, which is now represented in most things by the Cheung Chau Rural Committee. The kaifong had an informal constitution and its leaders were generally those persons who were already playing a leading part in the affairs of the four old district associations. The kaifong had a general concern in Cheung Chau affairs whereas the district associations may be said, in the best sense, to have had a sectional interest.

The history of the kaifong is less easy to trace than that of the associations, likely because it was a less tangible body. However, it seems to have existed before 1898 because the land registers list a clubhouse or *kung sor*, which was described as public property. This must have been built and administered by somebody and the kaifong is the most likely candidate. In the early part of this century, the building probably housed a school and is known to have served as a headquarters for the town's watchmen.[14] These were both likely activities for a kaifong, and it is probable that it ran these and other central services before the British lease. Presumably, too, it administered Choi Leung's Fong Pin Hospital, which the registers describe as an asylum (*chai lau sor*) and as public property.

Whilst I am satisfied that there was a kaifong on the island before 1898 which organised various functions on behalf of the whole community, there is, as yet, no information as to the date of its origin, though there is one clue which takes its history back at least another twenty years. This was the provision of what are still known today as "kaifong junks" or "*kai tou*" which are managed by prominent persons for a group of financially interested local parties who support the venture which is designed to assist the public by providing a safe, regular, and reliable means of conveying cargo and passengers between the island and, in this case, Hong Kong. An agreed percentage of the profits is supposed to be contributed towards charitable and welfare purposes. Four junks appear on the list of donors to the Fong Pin Hospital, and one of these, together with a fifth, appears on the list for the repair of the Tin Hau Temple a year later, in 1879. They have business names such as *Tung On* (Universal Peace), *Kung Cheung* (Public Prosperity), *Yi Tai On* (Righteous Peace), *Kung Yik* (Public Welfare), and *On Shun* (Peaceful Tranquility), all propitious names for sea and river travel. It is likely that the two which made donations to the repair of the temple were kaifong junks since their generous contributions placed their names almost at the head of the list.[15]

Scrutiny of the tablets and other sources of information mentioned in this brief account of Cheung Chau just before the British lease leaves a vivid impression of a lively, bustling community, largely dependent upon its own leaders and local resources for initiating works of communal benefit, but making use of its links with the outside world, both by business and kinship, to help achieve its ends. So far as I know, there are no studies of the internal structure of a community of similar size and location in the same period available in any western language and it is therefore difficult for me to say whether Cheung Chau is similar or dissimilar to the general pattern of small coastal towns in South China. It does, however, present a basic pattern of association and an enforced reliance on self-help which is typically Chinese. In this respect, the community has altered little to this day.[16]

9

Notes and Impressions
of the Cheung Chau Community

A total of thirty-two years separate this paper from the previous one, and the time difference is clearly shown in the increased sophistication and depth of treatment of the subject.

When serving as district officer (south/islands) between 1957 and 1962,[1] I usually spent the Lunar New Year period at the District Office bungalow on the island with my family. During the festival, all members of the Cheung Chau Rural Committee used to come in a body to the house to pay a courtesy call and to express their best wishes for the coming year. It was a large committee, on which the leaders of the various resident landsmen's groups were well represented, and practically anyone who was anybody on the island was a member or had been co-opted as an adviser. That is, save for the boat people in the anchorage. In management matters, they did not count, as I shall explain.

* Originally published in David Faure and Helen F. Siu (eds.), *Down to Earth: The Territorial Bond in South China* (Stanford 1995) pp. 89–103 and 243–247.

Through contacts made at that time, I was able to learn about Cheung Chau's diversified community and its organisations, along with their origins and history. The Rural Committee itself, although a newly established organisation, had venerable antecedents. It was the direct lineal successor to the former Cheung Chau Kaifong, a managerial body for the community at large whose continuous history can be traced back at least to the middle of the nineteenth century. During the three-and-a-half-year wartime occupation by the Japanese (1941–1945), under changes made by the military government in the captured territory, the kaifong had seemingly been displaced by another body, styled the Cheung Chau Residents Association. However, this was merely the old kaifong under a new name; it appears to have operated under the same leadership and to have remained the owner and manager of all the property accumulated by the kaifong in the past to defray the various expenses incurred in carrying out its duties in the public interest.

The Rural Committee had been established in 1960. Indeed, as district officer of the day I had had a lot to do with its formation, through canvassing and negotiating support for the establishment of the new body. Only after considerable effort, and with some compromise over the committee's composition, had it been possible to hold elections in accordance with an officially imposed but locally accepted constitution. These elections had ended the five-year hiatus due to the withdrawal of official recognition from the Cheung Chau Residents Association in 1954. Recognition had been withdrawn in response to unauthorised pre-election changes to the constitution by the association's officeholders in a bid for electoral advantage at a time of continuing rivalry within the leadership. In the interim, the Cheung Chau Chamber of Commerce had carried out the managerial duties of the Residents Association with the recognition and support of the New Territories District Administration.

Despite the general support for our efforts to replace the Residents Association with the Rural Committee, I was unable to arrange for the transfer of funds and property from the older management body to the new, owing to the unwillingness of the association's leaders to allow the transfer and the lack of legal powers to require it. Recognised or not, the Residents Association had clung to life, able to perform some of its former functions—such as management of the Fong Pin Hospital and dying house—by refusing to turn over the public property to the Rural Committee.[2] On the other hand, management of the boat shed used to store the three dragon boats raced by the local boat population each year, hitherto in the hands of the Residents Association, had been transferred to the fishermen's representative on the new committee.

The partisan behaviour inside the Residents Association that had led to the withdrawal of official recognition highlights the factional and personal feuding to which the island community was subject at all times. Besides the animosities and rivalries between individual leaders that affected their public and working relationships,[3] the mixed composition of the land population and the continuance of old antipathies between its groups complicated the work and functioning of the kaifong and its managers. Even so, the very difficulties of the situation seem to have been a challenge and an inspiration for some of them over the years.

A Diverse Population on Land and Sea

On land, nineteenth- and early twentieth-century Cheung Chau was noteworthy for the variety of settlement among a population that by 1911 numbered no more than a few thousand. The most numerous as well as probably the earliest among its settlers over the previous few centuries were Hoklos from Northeast

Guangdong. First arriving in local waters as seasonal fishermen, they came by degrees to settle on the island. Although living on land, they maintained their connection with the sea, which, after generations of settlement there, still provided their principal livelihood even into the 1950s. Some among them also worked as marine hawkers in the anchorage, selling vegetables and other commodities to the Tanka families living on their fishing boats. Others became shopkeepers and businessmen on the island, catering to their own people, to the local boat population, and to visiting craft from the wider area, and setting up businesses as varied as shrimp paste manufacturing and ropewalks. Their leaders established the Pak Tai Temple (1783) and built a clubhouse that also served as a school.

However, sustained population growth continuing throughout the nineteenth century brought linguistic diversity and some cultural differences to the island community. The 1911 Census shows that Punti speakers outnumbered the Hoklo residents by more than two to one.[4] By then, the land population included many people from other parts of Guangdong Province, from equally long-settled groups that were different in language and customs from the Hoklo residents. These were especially to be found among the local shopkeepers and businesspeople who, unlike the Hoklos, had mostly been attracted to Cheung Chau by its favourable location on the trade routes and the many opportunities available in all lines of retail and wholesale business connected with the boat people and the fishing industry.

Inquiries among old persons indicate that in a place like Cheung Chau, with a lot of coming and going in the region, there was a degree of assimilation in individual cases. One of the Hoklo elders (born in 1885) was by descent a Punti from Dapeng City in eastern Xin'an; but, living among Hoklos and sharing the same occupation (a sea fisherman), and with a Hoklo mother and wife, he, the first settler's grandson, had become one with them, regarding the Hoklo dialect as his natural speech.

By the early twentieth century, the Tanka boat population outnumbered the land residents. People in this major group lived their lives entirely on the water; only in death did they move ashore. Whole families lived on board their craft, which varied from the largest seagoing trawlers to the sampans which fished only in local waters.[5] A leading shopkeeper and old kaifong told me that the fishing craft using the Cheung Chau anchorage before the Pacific War had between twenty to fifty persons of all ages on board, the number depending on size and including old people, children (since very few went to school), and a few hired hands.

At the 1911 Census, the floating population of the Cheung Chau District was stated to be 4,442, and at the next decennial count it was 3,550. The census officer for the latter said that the count in the New Territories was not as satisfactory as that for the urban boat population, "as it must be remembered that at Tai O and Cheung Chau a large proportion of the fishing fleet is at sea at any given time". At other times, the number would have been swelled by boats from other districts, come to off-load fish and take on supplies, and in 1931 the count was much higher, at 7,045 (4,041 males and 3,004 females). There was much coming and going among the fishing craft, and indeed generally. After the British takeover, the Hong Kong harbor master's new out-station on the island recorded the number of arrivals and clearances in the anchorage as well as the number of licenses and permits issued, and some figures are provided in the *Annual Reports* and *Sessional Papers*.

A good description of the Tanka boat people is given in the *Hong Kong Annual Report for 1938*, at which time little had changed:

To these [junks] they have confined their entire lives for generations, regarding them not only as their sole means of support but also as their only home. The fact that there are some 100,000 persons living in 5,500 boats, the largest of which does not exceed 85 feet in length, and the majority of which are less than 60 feet long shows the extent of the overcrowding to which their traditional occupation subjects them. A boat of 70 feet in length provides space for the accommodation of 40 to 45 persons of all ages, besides space for fish, salt, gear, food and miscellaneous cargo. The average earning capacity of a single able-bodied fisherman is $70 per annum. This general low standard of living combined with the hidebound allegiance to a centuries-old tradition has prevented the infiltration of modern methods and the adoption of modern appliances.

However, as in other places, the interdependence of the land and sea populations and their daily intercourse in business matters did not lead to social fusion. The two communities kept to themselves. This even applied to the long-established land-based Hoklo fishermen's families and marine hawkers. From my interviews with their old people, it was obvious that Hoklo of this group regarded themselves as totally distinct from the Tanka fishermen. The difference lay in the fact that, though the sea provided a lifelong occupation, the Hoklos were essentially landsmen, mostly congregated at Pak She near their own Pak Tai Temple. The style of fishing was also different. The Hoklo boats ("over a hundred when I was young", said a man born in 1894) went out for only a few hours at a time, and, significantly, "no rice was [cooked or] eaten on board" (according to a man born in 1885).

In the Hong Kong region, the existence of groups of sea fishermen other than Tanka was quite common. I encountered a degree of occupational blurring in my widespread inquiries. On nearby Peng Chau, both Cantonese and Hakka villagers undertook sea fishing from boats, as did many of the families in some of the Hakka coastal villages of Tsuen Wan. However, in all such cases, it is important to note that occupational blurring did not mean social intercourse or intermarriage between the Tanka and these land-based fishermen, who clung to their own kind.

With the rest of the land population, the land-sea dichotomy must have been even more marked. The only means open to Tanka to rise to social and political influence on land was by engaging in business and becoming wealthy, as some among them were reported to have done in the lifetime of my elderly informants.[6] Then, and only then, could they attain membership on the kaifong committee, which in local landsmen's eyes was surely the supreme manifestation of success.

Perhaps as a result of this long-established social divide, the Tanka boat people of Cheung Chau were excluded from participation in the organisation and ritualistic elements of the *ta chiu* festival. They were also excluded from any say in the political arena, that is, in the management of the island's affairs. In keeping with what was clearly old practice, this exclusion of the Tanka came to the fore during the discussions with local leaders leading up to the formation of the new Rural Committee in 1960. The floating population, indigenous or not, was not included in the island-wide electoral roll. While the constitution approved by the New Territories District Administration provided for two representatives from among the boat people to be appointed by the district officer to the General Assembly of thirty-nine members and one to the seventeen-man Executive Committee, these men could not vote on matters not pertaining to the boat people that might come up for discussion in either body. They were basically observers.

At the same time, we must take into account several factors that made such practices rather different from mere discrimination. The boat people lived in a completely different environment, as reflected in their occupations, customs, and lifestyle. Moreover, their numbers were at all times subject to fluctuation, according to the seasons and the fortunes of the catch. Even as late as 1960, it would not have been realistic to include them in an organisation that was mainly concerned with the management of a land-based community. At the same time, it is wrong to think of them as universally poor and downtrodden. Some Tanka trawler owners were comparatively rich, and a run of good catches could put a good deal of money in their crew's hands.[7]

Separate Loyalties, Intergroup Rivalries, and Ill Feelings

The resident land population of nineteenth-century Cheung Chau was particularly noteworthy for its highly segmented organisational development. By 1898, there were established communities of Cantonese speakers from the nearby counties of Xin'an and Dongguan and others from the more distant Siyi complex in the southwest part of the province. Each of these groups provided its own mutual help association and clubhouse; and, as in the case of the older Hoklo population, their separate identities had been preserved and perpetuated by their having named each of the district societies for its own area.[8]

The premises of the district associations were located in the streets from which they drew their membership. This was no coincidence, since the different sections of the population had tended to settle in separate parts of the residential and business areas of the growing township. In time, as the numbers in each locality increased, this would lead to the establishment of street offices and associations.[9]

Offsetting the undoubted assistance and mutual support that the district associations provided to fellow countrymen, their existence as important elements in the organisational structure of the community must also have served to accentuate and solidify linguistic and cultural differences among the mixed population. They did nothing to discourage divisive and separate loyalties, since each of the groups remained distinct and self-directing. Socially and politically speaking, their members had little in common. Other than a self-interested need for co-operation in the maintenance of law and order to sustain stability and prosperity, the only shared concern among shopkeepers of different origin was the pursuit of gain. However, that was, presumably, for the most part an individual matter.

Separate identities had much to do with the underlying general antagonisms and suspicions between members of the Cantonese and Hoklo groups. Documented in the records of Christian missionary work on the island, these antipathies had not originated with the two groups' shared residence there, but had been nurtured by centuries of mutual antagonism in and away from their home areas. However, the excitements and rivalries connected with the events of local temples were undoubtedly an aggravating factor in their perpetuation. During the processions and congregations that characterised the *ta chiu* festival and other celebrations, there were often minor scuffles and larger-scale fights between the different groups, especially when they competed for prized or lucky objects. Besides the deeper causes of strife, the heat of the moment so readily generated on these occasions also heightened old antipathies and helped perpetuate ill feelings.

The general roughness of the population owed something to the turbulence and uncertainties of the times. As a flourishing coastal market centre, known to people all over the outer parts of the Pearl River delta, Cheung Chau attracted the attention of robbers and pirates even into the period of British rule.[10] In earlier days, with or without the consent of the local people, it had itself been a base for pirate bands.[11] It is also quite likely that some of the island's shopkeepers had dealt regularly in stolen cargoes and had assisted in the provisioning and fitting out of fishermen-turned-pirates.[12] Whenever the opportunity presented itself, any kind of smuggling was also a welcome source of gain and excitement.[13]

Temples and Shrines

Any curious visitor to the island in the late nineteenth century would have noticed its many temples. Dedicated to a variety of Taoist deities, they were prominent features in their localities. By 1898, there were seven of them. In step with population growth, this was more than at the beginning of the century. In the interim, the three oldest had been rebuilt or extended. Besides the Pak Tai Temple already mentioned, there were two other eighteenth-century temples, both of them dedicated to Tin Hau, the Empress of Heaven. However, only the Pak Tai Temple had island-wide importance, serving as the principal venue for the important yearly *ta chiu* rituals performed to protect the land population from epidemics and supernatural harm, and for the associated and other opera performances. Although both land and boat people patronised all the temples, there was one that was particularly linked with the floating population. This was the Tin Hau Temple at Sai Wan, which, from the perspective of one walking from the town (but not of one approaching from the sea), was located in an outlying part of the island. Here, the firing of lucky rockets (*cheung pau*) was still taking place annually in the second lunar month when I was district officer, as I knew from invitations to attend the event and set off the principal rocket.

In the course of my inquiries, it became apparent that each of these temples had its own geographical boundaries. The people living within them were aware of the limits and would normally seek advice and protection from their local temple's deities. At the same time, the temples' clientele was probably varied. In addition to people from the locality seeking help from the temple gods, other worshipers might come from any of the resident ethnic landsmen's groups or from the fishing fleets. In keeping with the "shop around" attitudes common to this type of worship, the efficacy of the god in meeting requirements and performing miracles were the primary considerations in the supplicants' minds. Only in the case of the island's earth-god shrines did a more specific territorial jurisdiction apply: because each shrine was associated with a particular street or locality, the devotees were usually confined to the families in residence there.

The Kaifong and Local Self-management

Despite their importance as places of religious resort by the people, and notwithstanding the considerable sums of money raised to build, extend, and restore them periodically, neither the temples nor their managers were part of the infrastructure for managing the island community's affairs. This important role was played by the district associations and the Cheung Chau Kaifong.

It has already been noted that, in imperial times, local communities were expected to make their own arrangements for management. In neither town nor countryside were government officers charged with such duties, or even with coordinating management among villages or groups of townsmen. Although there had been a Customs post on Cheung Chau from 1868, and for much longer a small body of island-based soldiery whose surveillance was supplemented by occasional visits by patrolling naval vessels, none of their personnel participated in local management. Yet in places like Cheung Chau, where, in addition to the mixed population, there were many visiting outsiders to give rise to or complicate problems, some kind of commonly accepted authority was clearly needed across the board to help keep order and sustain progress. There, as in other towns and cities large and small, the responsibilities of local management were shouldered by a kaifong committee.

In accordance with the usual practice, the local kaifong committee was drawn from the ranks of the shopkeepers and businessmen in the various speech groups. Each leader commanded the respect and obedience of his own people and worked with others of his kind to provide local management. The kaifong committee's duties ranged over a wide field. They comprised the provision of watch and ward in the business streets (which, as was customary in the region, were barred off and patrolled at night), the operation of a hospital-cum-dying-house, the supply of free medicines and coffins, and the maintenance of a communal grave for the indigent dead without relatives.

The kaifong also made some provision for education, though this responsibility was undertaken mainly by the district associations. The water supply and local public works were among its other concerns, according to need. The head of the kaifong also represented the community to the outside world, especially to the imperial officials. Less enviably, its leading members bore the brunt of any unpleasantness to be encountered in emergencies, ranging from attacks by pirates to the onslaught of contagious disease. The performance of these miscellaneous but important duties can be detected from various sources, and especially from the information provided by old or retired kaifong members and other elderly residents. However, although the kaifong's position and contribution to good government were crucial, it did not possess authority, only influence. It relied upon the district associations, lineage elders, and family heads for co-operation and support in all its actions, and could not act responsibly nor guarantee the continuation of local order without this sustained backing. In such a structured and generally ordered community, the presence of the government was in normal times practically superfluous. The district magistrate's principal responsibility, the maintenance of law and order and the avoidance of major popular unrest and disturbance, was carried out in practice by other hands through the good work being done day in day out by the kaifong leadership. His other main duty, the collection of the land tax, was also made lighter by the fact that the Wong Wai Tsak Tong of Nantou (Xin'an, the district city) was the sub-soil owner of much of Cheung Chau, including its principal sand beaches. As such, the *tong* was responsible for making the regular land tax payments for its holdings, and thus relieved the magistrate from the necessity of chasing after a mass of individual owners.

Though largely left to their own devices, the merchant kaifongs of Cheung Chau could not avoid dealing with the local authorities from time to time. Besides the officers of the military and Customs posts located on the island, occasional visits could be expected from other officials in the course of their duties. From time to time, as the need arose, representations would have to be made to them on behalf of the local people. By the later nineteenth century, such liaisons were facilitated by the ease with which ranks and degrees could be purchased from the government. The information provided on the still surviving commemorative tablet for the establishment of a Defense Office in 1870 shows that, in line with the general practice of the time, some of the Cheung Chau leaders had taken this step, improving their social status and gaining better access to officials.

The largely obligatory liaison with officials continued into British times. A former district officer, Austin Coates, states it well, though in exaggerated form to make a point:

> For example, it may happen that the District Officer visits Cheung Chau on Monday, the Divisional Superintendent, Marine Police on Tuesday, the Assistant Director of Education on Wednesday, the Chief Engineer, Port Works, on Thursday and the Medical Officer of Health on Friday. If prior notification is given, as it sometimes has to be, to enable local discussions to be held, this means, by local etiquette, a substantial restaurant lunch every day of the week, which for the Chairman is a very considerable outlay.[14]

The frequent repair or extension of the island's temples, and of public buildings such as the Fong Pin Hospital (1877 and 1908), provided a convenient means for local leaders to forge and maintain those informal connections with officialdom which, in a traditional Chinese social and cultural milieu, were so important to individuals and communities alike. Either upon request or on their own initiative, some officials were donors to these projects, and their titles or appointments appear on the commemorative tablets set up to mark such events. Others presented honorific boards or couplets for the buildings, or themselves wrote the characters for them. These valued indications of interest and respect would be pointed out to their successors in office, and no doubt would help to smooth relationships with minor officials and thus promote the public business of the place.

Though widely operative, the kaifong *per se* had no part to play in the organisation of the opera performances and the performance of the protective rituals in the *ta chiu* festival or other such occasions. Such duties were left to individual leaders in the ethnic and street groupings, although these men were more than likely also to be leading members of the kaifong. Herein lay both the strengths and the weaknesses of the traditional kaifong organisations of the day.

Men Rather Than Institutions

In any discourse upon the nature of local authority on the island as it was in the nineteenth century, or indeed as I found it in the late 1950s, it would be misleading to give any account of the kaifong and other principal institutions that purported to show a ranking between and among them. As already mentioned, it was individual men who mattered, and they often carried more weight than the institutions to which they belonged and which they led. Their influence and activities were widely distributed. It was quite usual for the top kaifongs to hold posts in the district associations, street bodies, annual temple committees, and any *ad hoc* working groups that might be formed to meet the needs of a particular occasion or purpose. Since it was also the leaders who made the financial contributions required to keep the kaifong committee and the district associations in existence and able to carry out their various projects and responsibilities, the financing of many activities assumed a semi-private nature. This gave rise to a good many problems, especially upon the death of a leader. The resulting melding of public and private affairs could also lead to misappropriation and malversation.

This confused dichotomy in financial matters is significant because it emphasises the importance of the merchants and men of business in local management. Their financial contributions and personal effort were crucial to its operation and continuance, as carried out through the kaifong and the four district bodies. Each and every local association had to rely on donations from the wealthier merchants and businessmen for their very existence. Often this took the form of purchase and presentation of property that provided a regular basic revenue. At other times donations would be made towards running expenses or special projects. As a rule, public subscription was required only for major repairs to buildings and reconstructions. Even then, any shortfall had to be made up by the leadership.

The Sinews Provided by Business

It follows that the leaders' continued success in business underpinned the whole system of local management on Cheung Chau. It is therefore worthwhile to indicate the ultimate sources of the island's prosperity, which provided the funding for public and community purposes.

First and foremost must come Cheung Chau's popularity with the boat population and the fishing fleets of the region. This stemmed from its favourable location for business. By the mid-nineteenth century, the island was well-positioned in the trading triangle formed by the ports of the Pearl River delta — Guangzhou, Macau, and the flourishing new entrepôt of British Hong Kong. Merchants were quick to seize on its potential for trading in fish and other marine products with these places, as well as for catering to the various needs of the fishing fleets themselves. Among their number were representatives of the big Hong Kong firms dealing wholesale in marine products. The junk masters, too, must have recognised the advantages of a place that so conveniently met all their requirements, for the fleets that used the island anchorage to sell their catches also needed to reprovision their stores of salt and victuals as well as to repair and refit their craft. Thus, in business matters, the relationship between the land and sea communities was (and had to be) strikingly close and symbiotic.

The Cheung Chau boatyards flourished accordingly, as did those shop-keepers who supplied ship chandlery services and salt to the boatmen and their families and who dealt in the basic staples of daily life (rice, salt, soy, firewood, and oil, which were needed by all, whether afloat or ashore). They also dealt in the large volume of fish landed by the fishing fleets, sending it fresh or mostly salted to markets in Hong Kong and the large towns of the Pearl River delta. These prospering concerns were carried out in roomy premises, often with internal courtyards.

I was fortunate to be able to see some of these old shop premises during my visits to the island in the 1950s and 1960s. Constructed with imported blue-grey bricks, they were functional rather than elegant. Typically narrow-fronted, they were long in depth with one or two internal yards. By the time I saw them for the first time, most had been partitioned into front and rear parts and were being used for other purposes. Long dilapidated or in ruins, some had been partly rebuilt as temporary structures.

Cheung Chau's business net was cast wide. The principal shopkeepers were not content to sit in their shops waiting to deal with the catches that the fishing fleets brought to their doorsteps. Widespread inquiries reveal that the ties of business stretched all around, from the village settlements on nearby Lantau and adjacent islands to the much wider area to the south and west among the outer island port villages of the Ladrones. Besides dealing in the catches landed on Cheung Chau itself, shopkeepers also collected fish from the many village fishermen operating stakenets throughout the whole area. The larger retailers also supplied goods to the smaller shops in the islands. However, because of the mark-ups there and the greater variety of items on sale in the Cheung Chau shops, the boat and land people preferred to shop in Cheung Chau whenever they had the opportunity. The island's principal shopkeepers also made loans to villagers and boat people, with land or catches pledged against failure to repay.

It was these various lines of business that enabled the leading men of the place to participate effectively in local affairs, to pay a considerable part of the routine public expenses, and to make major donations to worthy causes; but ultimately, of course, it was the presence of the boat people, local and visiting alike, that was the basis for good business prospects on the island. Thus, any increased prosperity ashore must ordinarily have been a reflection of greater prosperity afloat, given the constant and close connection between these two main sectors of the local economy.

Another aspect of their contribution to the local scene was that during their periodic stays in port the visiting fishing fleets added to the community's already diverse social mix. Swelling the considerable number of locally based boat people, their crews and family members came ashore at the main festivals. At such times, they must have landed by the thousands to enjoy the colour and excitement of opera performances and take in the competing attractions of eating, gambling, and opium smoking, together with the other diversions provided by the land population and other persons drawn in season by the rich pickings to be found there.

Dynamics in the Leadership Group

Given the growth in the island's population and the steady increase in its business over the years, it is hardly surprising to find that these changes were eventually reflected in the power structure at the centre, that is, among the kaifong leadership that performed managerial duties on behalf of the community as a whole.

A significant change took place in the early twentieth century, when the leadership of the kaifong shifted away from the Hoklo, who had predominated up to that time. This change was ascribable to the growing number of prosperous merchants in the Cantonese-speaking groups, to their undoubted financial clout, and probably to a less than altruistic desire to take their fair share of local management in order to further their own interests. Curiously enough — and perhaps more significantly — the leadership struggle took place outside the kaifong, though the results were soon reflected in its composition. It came about in connection with the Pak Tai Temple.

Despite competition from other old temples, the Hoklo community's Pak Tai Temple had always been regarded as the main one on the island. Established by them in 1783, it had remained largely if not solely under their management for the whole of the next century. The nineteenth-century kaifong is reported to have held its meetings on the premises. This circumstance would be a sure sign of the Hoklo inhabitants' political predominance in that period, and it is corroborated by the fact that for long Hoklos had formed the majority of the kaifong committee. However, upon the occasion of the temple's repair and enlargement in 1908, the commemorative tablet erected to mark the event shows that, for the first time, the list of organisers included people from Guangzhou Prefecture.

Whether the Cantonese element had insisted on having a say and paid their dues, or whether their financial assistance had been requested, is not now known. Another record that relates to the time states that the Hoklo managers approached the Guangzhou leaders in order to raise sufficient funds, together, to maintain the temple fabric. Either way, help with the cost of enlargement and maintenance of this important building was likely given in exchange for certain agreed-upon changes in the kaifong's management. Thereafter, the leadership is reported to have been broadened by the inclusion of non-Hoklo persons, and the head post to have become subject to rotation among the principal men of the main speech groups. These managerial adjustments reflected the new balance of power within the business community, thereby achieving a more realistic sharing among the various speech groups in regard to the management of communal affairs.

The dramatic change at the top probably made little difference to the "rank-and-file" leadership in the other managerial bodies within the community. The leadership group as a whole had ever been subject to slow but constant change. Any vacancies of a routine kind in any of the managerial bodies were filled by co-opting deserving assistants, of whom there were always a number learning the ropes by carrying out routine work for their bosses. This applied to the kaifong as well as to the committees of the various speech group associations. The *ad hoc* committees that managed the temple festivals and activities connected with the street shrines were also manned and renewed in this way.

Conclusion

The longtime vitality of the island community, intensified as it was by the continuous presence of the boat people, offshore and occasionally on land, is evident both from historical sources and from the reminiscences and information provided by local residents. Yet there was always a sharp division between its principal components on land and sea, and a partisan approach to affairs among its residents owing to their diverse origins and divided, self-contained loyalties.

In recent decades, the land community has greatly increased in number and diversity, while the number of casual visitors to the island seeking good food and recreation has also risen significantly. In sharp contrast, the fishing fleet has greatly diminished, and many boat people have come to live ashore. Within today's much wider community, the lines of ethnic division have become blurred. However, as Choi Chi-cheung has shown,[15] the *ta chiu* festival, still so popular with old and new residents alike, retains its traditional organisation, reflecting the divisions and prejudices of an earlier age.

10

A Mixed Community of Cantonese and Hakka on Lantau Island

This was the text of a Symposium address to the Royal Asiatic Society, Hong Kong Branch delivered in May 1964. The theme crops up several times in these essays and may not seem to warrant so much attention. However, the Hakka are interesting. They speak a different Chinese language from the Cantonese, their dress is slightly different, they have some different customs in observing ancestor worship, their women never bound their feet, and those men who were not farmers seem to have favoured semi-skilled labour-intensive trades. For the most part, they moved into the Hong Kong area from the north later than the Cantonese, found the best land already taken, tended therefore to settle on higher or marginal land, and were consequently poorer. In the middle to late nineteenth century, there was widespread and very bloody feuding between the two groups, particularly in Guangdong Province, but it seems that the New Territories were almost free of such trouble, and James's research confirms a much more peaceful situation here.

* Originally published in *Aspects of Social Organization in the New Territories* (RASHKB 1965) pp. 21–26.

Over the whole period of the settlement of the New Territories since 1100 AD, Hakka arrivals have formed a considerable proportion of the new population. When the area was leased from China in 1898 the first report on the "New Territory", by J.H. Stewart Lockhart (1858–1937) the colonial secretary of the time, estimated that there were 64,140 Cantonese (Punti) living in 161 villages and 36,070 Hakka living in 255 villages. The painstaking Hong Kong Colony Census of 1911, which was the first accurate count of the population of the New Territories, produced figures of 47,990 Punti and 44,375 Hakka, and is more likely to be correct. My point is that the number of Hakka settlers was a considerable part of the whole and represented successive migrations into the district over many centuries.

Who are the Hakkas? A good description comes from a member of the Hong Kong Cadet Service, J. Dyer Ball (1847–1919), who wrote at the turn of the century:

The author remembers, when a boy, travelling in the interior, and coming across a village where the people spoke quite a different speech from that of the other inhabitants round them; it is like this that the Hakkas are often situated in the midst of a population, quite distinct from them in language, differing in customs, to a slight extent in dress, and even in some of the idols worshipped. Those found in the South of China were not originally of that region, but their family genealogies show that they have come from the North ... settling in some cases in different places till they have finally established themselves in their present surroundings. In certain districts they have monopolized the whole country-side ... while in other places they form a half, a third, or more of the population, being interspersed among the Pun-tei [Punti], as the older Chinese inhabitants are termed. In some places partly peopled by them they have settled on the higher land, leaving the Pun-tei to the low-lying lands, and from this circumstance they have been called Chinese Highlanders by some, but the name is a misnomer, as it is only capable of local application, for in other places they are spread over the plains as well as the hilly ground. They are not confined to the Canton [Guangdong] Province, where they are considered to form a third of the inhabitants, but are found in different parts of China — in Kwang-si [Guangxi], in Fuh-kien [Fujian], and in Che-kiang [Zhejiang].[1]

In his report Lockhart wrote: "The Hakkas are a hardy and frugal race and are generally found in the hill districts, their chief pursuits being agriculture and quarrying." He goes on to say: "As a rule, their villages are inhabited solely by members of their own race, just as the Pun-tei villages are inhabited only by Cantonese, though there are a few villages in which both races are represented." I shall return to this point in a moment, as it is a material one for this short paper.

It would not be surprising if these dissimilar groups were sometimes animated by mutual suspicion and dislike; or that, when fanned by economic and other grievances, this antipathy sometimes erupted into violence, started now by the one then by the other. In fact, there are many records of fighting between the two races in Guangdong Province, especially in 1840–1870, when trouble began in varying circumstances for a variety of different reasons.[2] The New Territories, then part of the Xin'an District, may have witnessed these troubles, but they are not well documented, and I have not started delving into newspaper and other records to see what can be found.[3]

The area I wish to examine is the district of Pui O on Lantau Island. Within an area of some ten square miles, there is a Cantonese-Hakka complex of settled villages whose origins go back to the seventeenth century. There are nine separate villages or hamlets which, under the Qing dynasty, were linked to form a sub-district or *yeuk*.[4] Here Hakka and Cantonese have lived side by side for three hundred years. In two or three of the villages they actually live together as neighbours in the same village. This was the phenomenon noted by Lockhart in 1898, though it is unlikely that he was referring to the same area. It is an important one, however, because the accepted view of relations between Hakka and Cantonese in traditional rural life is that they were somewhat different, kept to themselves, did not intermarry, and, indeed, did not particularly like each other. Besides giving a general account of the settlement, it is these particular features I wish to discuss.

The villages in question are all small and have populations of about a hundred persons each. The present population of the sub-district is around one thousand persons, which is probably much the same as it was in 1898, though with the difference that the older villages used to be larger than they are today, with bigger populations. I ought to mention that two of the four at Pui O itself were formerly located on the hillside and have moved down in the last fifty years to more modest buildings on the padi fields below. Another of the villages of the group moved as recently as 1931 to a position nearer the sea. In each case the removal was for *feng shui* reasons, which seem to carry equal weight with Hakka and Punti alike.

The Hakka clans predominate among the ten clans, large and small, which live in these villages. One of them has branches in five of the nine villages, and is easily the most important.[5] The four main Hakka clans settled in the seventeenth and early eighteenth centuries, whilst the Cantonese clans appear to have come into the district in two waves. The earlier Cantonese probably came about the same time as the first Hakkas in the late seventeenth century, or may even have been living in the area before they arrived; it is difficult to say. The second and less important wave of Cantonese settlers arrived in the mid-nineteenth century and represents late-comers who picked up the remoter or poorer parcels of land left to them by the earlier settlers. One of the smaller and poorer villages was founded by such persons, whose ancestor seems to have come first to the area as a shopkeeper.[6]

Whether the principal Hakka clan arrived before or at the same time as the early Cantonese clans, it soon grew to a position of importance. Whilst Hakkas are traditionally famous for their energy and thrift, this clan's lead seems also to have been favoured by numbers. Their genealogies list a surprisingly large number of male descendants since the time the founding ancestor arrived in the seventeenth century, and today one can find their horse-shoe graves scattered throughout the Pui O area, and even outside. Their rise was also due to the availability of land at the time their numbers increased so much, either empty land suitable for farming but not yet developed, or cultivated land belonging to other persons who wished to sell. As early as 1774 a member of this clan bought twelve acres of padi fields from members of a Punti clan which is still living in the district today.[7]

In the period just before 1898, about which it is still possible to gain some information from elders who were boys or young men at the time,[8] the principal person in the Pui O area was a Hakka from the main clan. He was a prosperous shopkeeper, trader, and money lender.[9] Through giving mortgages to farmers who needed money, he became the owner of many fields and was generally looked upon by everyone in the neighbourhood as *san si* or village gentry. He played a prominent part in village affairs and settled disputes within the Pui O *yeuk*, and beyond its boundaries too. He and another member of the same clan kept the only shops in the neighbourhood. A direct indication of their clan's prosperity and local superiority in the nineteenth century was the possession of minor titles of rank by at least two of its members.[10] Though they probably bought them from the Chinese government — a fairly common device which brought money to the treasury as well as "face" to the purchasers — it added considerably to the family's local status.

Earlier I mentioned intermarriage between Cantonese and Hakka, and the general feeling that it seldom happens. This was not the case at Pui O. By questioning men about their parents and grandparents it became evident that there were many cases in this locality of Punti men taking Hakka wives, as well as the other way around, which is held to be even more uncommon. Numerous examples from the last sixty years can be cited and the various genealogical records of the district, listing marriages from the seventeenth century onwards, seem to show that the same thing has happened since the early days of the settlement. When I put to the elders for confirmation what was, for me, this somewhat novel proposition, the response was immediate: they almost nodded their heads off in agreement. In short, the ancestry of the present villagers, whether they claim to be exclusively Hakka or exclusively Punti, appears to be rather mixed.

The reason for this mixture of the races at Pui O and elsewhere is probably simple enough. In the early days of these settlements in remote coastal regions, villagers were always liable to attacks by robbers and pirates. Two brothers founded one of the local Hakka clans, and family tradition has it that one of them was killed in a pirate raid in about 1710. The necessity to combine against danger, likely reinforced by the need to take wives from the few settlers who must then have been in the area, seems to have started something which has continued to this day. I do not know if this state of affairs is repeated widely in the New Territories, but I do know of other instances, for example on the Kowloon peninsula where a study of six small villages, both Hakka and Punti, shows the same phenomenon in the past hundred years.

J. Dyer Ball, whom I have already quoted, lists some differences between Hakka and Punti. He writes:

In dress the women differ somewhat from the Cantonese, their jackets being longer and reaching down nearly to their knees; their shoes have squarer toes; they wear a peculiar hat consisting of a broad brim with a valance of cloth round it; the bunch of hair, done up on the top of the head, goes through the open crown. The women's ornaments are somewhat dissimilar, such as their bangles, which are made of thick silver, and of different patterns from those in use among the Pun-tei population. The earrings are also of curious construction; one kind, of silver, hooking through the ear and thickening up to the other end, while every short distance they are embossed with rings of silver; another kind of earring is formed of tassels of silk. The Hakka children often have a ring of silver round their neck; Cantonese children do not wear the same, but one or two of the attendants of the Chinese idols have such a ring.

These words were heard in silence when I read them to the elders recently, and I was told that at Pui O, at any rate, differences were slight. The elders say that before the Pacific War differences in dress between the Hakka and Punti women were negligible, and in fact the well-known Hakka hats with their hollow crown and cloth fringe were not worn. Instead an expensive Punti hat, made locally by one or two Lantau villagers, was kept for weddings and high holiday use. For ordinary wear, the local Hakka and Punti both wore flat bamboo hats. On the other hand, there are said to be slight differences locally in making the ancestral sacrifices at the two grave festivals. The Cantonese villagers offer cooked rice, whereas the Hakkas do not offer rice at all. The former slice any meat offered to the ancestors, whilst the Hakkas offer a whole chicken or whatever is being offered. I was also told that the Hakkas do not carry out *ta chiu* festivals to placate unrestful spirits as the Punti villagers did at regular intervals until the Pacific War. However, these things are a little beyond my ken, and I offer them with some reservations.

In most respects there has obviously been co-operation for a long time. For example, repair tablets and other dated material, mainly from the nineteenth century, from the two temples of the Pui O area show that, together with the local fishermen and any outsiders whom they could persuade to contribute, the Hakka and Cantonese clans have participated jointly in the various repair projects. Again, before and after 1898, children from the different villages seem to have been allowed to attend schools held in the ancestral halls of clans other than their own; usually because there was no school in their village or because the teacher hired by the elders had moved elsewhere. I know of cases where Cantonese children sometimes went to a Hakka teacher in a Hakka clan's hall. This sort of thing, and a general "togetherness", accounts for many of the local Punti people speaking Hakka quite naturally — or so I was told. A few miles away, however, the people of the adjoining Cantonese villages cannot speak Hakka, though, as I have said earlier, they may have the occasional Hakka among their female ancestors.

In conclusion, I ought to say that Pui O is not necessarily typical of mixed areas. Along the Sai Kung Road, the large Cantonese villages stand in the plains with Hakka hamlets on the higher and less fertile land in the foothills, and, as far as I am aware, there is no mixed settlement of long standing inside the individual villages as at Pui O. Again, though the whole area centred on Sai Kung Market is a mixed area of settlement, the wide, hilly, eastern part of it is almost entirely inhabited by Hakkas. Thus, as Dyer Ball says, there is considerable variation in the pattern of settlement, and this appears to be equally the case with a small area like the New Territories; so that one must, I think, beware of generalisation.

To recapitulate, for the Pui O area it appears that, in the traditional period, there were few differences between Hakka and Punti; in some cases they lived in the same villages, they did not keep to themselves, they frequently intermarried and seem to have got on together over a long period without too much trouble.

11

The Settlement and Development
of a Multi-Clan Village

This chapter includes the text of a second talk James gave at the weekend symposium of the Royal Asiatic Society, Hong Kong Branch in May 1964. Family, locality, and ethnicity were major elements defining identity in Chinese society. In the more fertile and prosperous areas of the New Territories, the greatest cohesion and success was, and to some extent still is, found where members of one clan, all speaking the same language, lived together in one village. Potentially, where there was not such shared identity or community, the likelihood of disharmony, and even feuds and fighting, was stronger. James finds persuasive evidence that this correlation is too facile, and that co-operation and harmony can also be found in mixed family settlements, just as in the previous chapter he has shown that mixed ethnicity in a small community does not necessarily equate with harmful competition and confrontation.

* Originally published in *Aspects of Social Organization in the New Territories* (RASHKB 1965) pp. 10–15.

A previous speaker has mentioned the "typical pattern" of a multi-clan village. I wish to go a step further now and discuss an actual example of such a village, following, as far as is possible, the available data, the process of its settlement and development. The village in question is inhabited entirely by Cantonese people; or rather it *was*, since Shek Pik no longer exists. Together with a small single-clan village[1] in the same valley on Lantau Island, it was removed four years ago to make way for the Shek Pik reservoir. It was a village of some two hundred persons in 1960, but its population had previously been much higher. At the carefully conducted Hong Kong Colony Census of 1911, its inhabitants numbered 363 and it seems that there were even more than this number fifty years before when, for various reasons,[2] it began its long decline.

When did the first settler arrive at Shek Pik? In multi-clan villages, families have (for the historian) the disconcerting habit of dying out.[3] It is therefore difficult to state with any certainty when the first settlement was made. However, the first ancestor of the oldest of the present clans arrived in the later years of the Ming dynasty (1368–1644), and his descendants were reinforced by successive additions from other clans in the seventeenth and eighteenth centuries. At the time of the villagers' removal from the valley there were six clans, all Cantonese of Xin'an or Dongguan origin. The founding ancestors had all come from other places in the province, to which, in turn, they had come from somewhere else. For each of these clans it was the last of a series of moves which their earlier members had made over a long period extending from at least the Song dynasty (960–1278). Family history in China, then, usually involves a series of removals, ever southwards.[4]

Why did people come to Shek Pik, a remote valley on an off-shore island? Persons in dispute or out of favour with their family, or those who for one reason or another had fallen foul of the government of their native place, would naturally seek refuge in such a remote area if they had decided to leave their homes for good.[5] There was vacant land there too, which would encourage people to come from more densely settled areas in which there was too little land per family to provide an adequate livelihood. Most of the Shek Pik elders do not remember the reasons which led their ancestors to remove to Lantau, but the first member of one of the clans is said to have come there as a pottery hawker. Others who arrived in the mid-seventeenth century may have come because of the disturbances which accompanied the fall of the Ming dynasty. In a neighbouring village, for example, the first ancestor of one of the clans, so it is said, came at this time to avoid conscription in his native place and brought his widowed mother with him. In short, the Shek Pik settlers were probably either political refugees, fugitives from justice, or persons who were dissatisfied with life and prospects at home.

Where would the first settlers make their homes? Since, in the main, they were dependent upon their own efforts to secure their safety, newcomers to coastal areas usually placed their first simple dwellings at the heads of valleys, or on high ground. Certainly they would keep away from the coast, from which quarter danger was most likely to come, since pirates have always been an intermittent scourge of the coastal dwellers of South China. At Shek Pik, the first settlement was nearly two miles from the sea probably right at the top of the valley, from which their descendants later removed a little lower down to the more permanent settlement of Shek Pik Wai, which means the "walled village of Shek Pik".

With the removal to lower ground the real development of Shek Pik as a rural settlement could begin. It must have been prompted by the confidence which came with the growing number of villagers caused by births and by new arrivals from other clans. Though judging from recent cases, newcomers may not have been entirely welcome and may have had to spend some time outside the settlement before they were grudgingly admitted.

A period of peace would also have assisted the expansion of the village, and this, in fact, was provided from the early years of the Kangxi until late in the Qianlong reign, roughly from 1670 until 1790, after which, times again became more unsettled. A clan record from a nearby village[6] emphasises this long period of quiet which stands in sharp contrast to the twenty years of unrest and uncertainty which followed, when prolonged cruises by pirate fleets off the coast of Guangdong became a regular feature of life.

Turning to the village in its permanent location, archaeological evidence suggests that the first houses were built at the end of the seventeenth century. Thereafter the village expanded rapidly and probably reached its greatest size by the mid-nineteenth century. The land survey undertaken shortly after 1899 shows that there were then about four hundred houses in the village, though some of them were already in ruins, and, as is usual in the country, many were used as cow-sheds and pig-sties. An interesting feature of the village layout is that the clans do not appear to have occupied separate sections of the village, as is considered usual, but were mixed together. A nineteenth-century deed of sale for a village house shows this quite clearly. It reads: "The house in question is situated in Shek Pik village, facing south, with Cheung Yung-tai's house on the left, Kung Kwai-fat's house on the right, Chan Wang-ho's house in front and Tsui Lung-choi's house at the back".[7]

We cannot assume that the early Cantonese settlers were the first on the Shek Pik scene. Besides dealing with each other, they probably had to establish a working relationship with other earlier inhabitants. It is possible that there was some assimilation of local non-Chinese tribes, whilst some understanding would also have to be established with the boat people who used the anchorage and may have been there long before the village was established.[8] There is also no doubt that the settlers were approached by the important Li family from the neighbourhood of Guangzhou, who showed them an imperial deed dating from the Song dynasty granting them land on Lantau and then asked them to pay rent on that account. Land deeds surviving from the nineteenth century indicate that the villagers accepted the situation and that, probably for centuries, the Li family sent their representatives every year to Lantau to collect.[9] Two eighteenth-century leases issued by the Li's show that the villagers were expected to pay their rent without fail in two equal amounts in the early and late seasons of the year. The tenants had additional duties to perform, for the leases state that "the lessee shall not evade his responsibility to receive, to see off, to provide meals, and to carry personal effects for the lessor when he comes to the farm to collect rent".[10] It was probably cheaper to pay them promptly. Otherwise the collectors stayed longer, and it cost more in the long run.

During the long period of peace in the eighteenth century and through the bad times thereafter, more and more land was opened as the number of villagers grew. Over time the steady rhythm of agricultural life became well established with two crops of padi harvested in July and November and some vegetables grown on land near the village in the winter months. The numerous terraces cut high into the hillsides of the main valley and the exploitation of areas in adjoining bays testify to the large amount of land, about 180 acres in all, which was under cultivation by the Shek Pik people by the middle of the nineteenth century. As a village, Shek Pik was known locally for its wide acres and plentiful water; so much so that an old Lantau maxim advised men from other villages to marry their daughters into a Shek Pik family in preference to elsewhere.

What of land tenure at Shek Pik? The land settlement after 1899 shows that possession of land was almost universal, though few people were rich. The village was composed of peasant proprietors, who sometimes held land sufficient for their family needs and sometimes had to rent from other villagers to meet their wants. Their plots were often scattered wide, which led them to rent land from other villagers which lay nearer to their main holdings, and rent out their more distant ones. Each clan had an ancestral trust or *tso*,[11] which held land, and this was usually rotated annually between families or rented to its poorer members, though land was mainly in individual hands. In the nineteenth century, farm land seems to have changed hands frequently by sale or mortgage.[12] Surviving deeds show that the government was not always informed, but the need for the purchaser to pay the Li family's tax was always specified, where applicable. The village pattern is not complete without some mention of outside proprietors. Shek Pik was a big valley, and in 1898 a Buddhist nunnery, a *tong* of merchants from Tai O Market, and several villagers from adjoining places all held land there, which they rented to the Shek Pik people.

Village life was closely interknit. As well as taking wives from other villages, the Shek Pik clans intermarried and child brides were sometimes taken into each other's households, even until as recently as the village's removal from Lantau.[13] This must have increased the solidarity of the village unit, despite the inevitable squabbles of a small community. Though several clans had their own ancestral temples the focal point of village organisation was the Hau Wong Temple to one side of the houses.[14] Meetings were held there and notices posted, including accounts of income and expenditure at festival times which (by tradition) were put there for public scrutiny. The elders were also responsible for building a substantial two-room village school which flourished in the nineteenth century but was destroyed by a typhoon in the 1920s and not rebuilt.

This activity on the part of the elders provides the key to rural life under the Qing dynasty. The district government at Nantou[15] appears to have been mainly interested in collecting its taxes and otherwise had little to do with the internal affairs of the villages. Provided people paid the land tax and there was no serious crime or disturbance, the government left the people to their own devices. In a multi-clan village like Shek Pik this meant government by a consortium of elders. All the various clans were usually represented. Villages had their own rules and ways of dealing with offenders from their own or other villages. A board dated 1893 which still hangs in a temple at Tung Chung on North Lantau is visible proof of this,[16] and the Shek Pik elders recall their own village rules, with an appropriate scale of fines for stealing crops, grazing animals on other people's fields, felling private trees, disturbing graves, etc. The elders also dealt with disputes, both public and private. An eighteenth-century deed and a subsequent petition to the elders show that they even dealt with disputes over clan fields which were, strictly speaking, the business of the clan concerned and no one else. Presumably the view was taken that disinterestedness was some guarantee of impartiality. The clans seem generally to have been on good terms with each other and if the present elders' memories are to be trusted, there appear to have been no real internal trouble or serious difficulties with other villages, of which there were a dozen, Hakka or Cantonese, within a few hours' walk, for a long time past.

With the village well established and life set in an orderly mould, it is time to close this brief account. However, the story would not be complete without a reference to the removals which took place from time to time. It usually happens, in the history of any long-established settlement, that in time some families will move to adjoining areas and either set up subsidiary hamlets or join existing villages. This also happened at Shek Pik. There are today communities at Silver Mine Bay and on South Lamma Island, whose ancestors left Shek Pik many generations ago,[17] and there must be others who have left no trace behind them. Now, as if to complete the process, the whole community has left the old village, and at their own request its members are living in modern flats in the large township of Tsuen Wan, where under the name of Shek Pik New Village they are beginning a new and different chapter in their long history.

12

Village Credit at Shek Pik 1879–1895

This is an appetizer which gives interesting detail without blunting hunger. Many of the general treatments of traditional Chinese society devote space to this topic, not always achieving accuracy or elucidation, but James refers to just two sources, and offers here only what he has sound evidence for. Of course, this fragment does not measure up to some of the weightier pieces presented in this volume, but it is fitting that attention should be drawn to the number and value of his Notes and Queries *contributions which quietly preserve little known details that others can refer to and gain insights from.*

Shek Pik appears to have been established in the Ming dynasty (1368–1644), and in the late nineteenth century was inhabited by about a dozen different clans. At the 1911 Hong Kong Census its recorded population was 363, although for various reasons, it seems likely that numbers had been decreasing for several decades.

* Originally published in *JHKBRAS* 1965, Vol. 5, pp. 119–122.

One of the villagers has kindly allowed me to see a few papers which survived the removal of the inhabitants in 1960 to make way for the Shek Pik Reservoir. Some of these relate to credit arrangements made by local people more than six decades ago. Although their context and meaning is not always clear — some documents appear to have been only *aides memoire* for the writers — they provide useful information on this interesting subject. They concern the activities of several money loan associations (*ngan wui*) and loans made by an organisation belonging to one of the clans, the Chi Wing Shing Tong.

Money Loan Associations

These are described by J. Dyer Ball in the various editions of his *Things Chinese*[1] and, with more local application, by G.N. Orme in Appendix E to his *Report on the New Territories, 1899–1912*.[2] A few of the Shek Pik papers directly concern these associations and in others they figure indirectly. For the three money associations for which some details are available, the following facts may be noted:

1. The number of participants was small (sixteen, thirteen, and nineteen), although the village was comparatively large.

2. Membership was not restricted to one clan or even to the members of the village. In the thirteen-member association, eleven villagers came from five different clans, and the remaining two members were outsiders. This suggests that the groups were formed on the basis of a mutual and contemporaneous need for funds — which would explain why they were not composed of members of the same clan.

3. Participation was sustained. The two men whose names figure most often in the papers were engaged in various money-raising activities through most of 1879–1895.

4. Land and house deeds were sometimes used to guarantee security (i.e., the payment of the periodic instalments which all participants in the association agreed to make upon entering it).

5. Three media were used in drawing up the accounts: silver dollars, silver by weight, and cash, but the reckonings were always made in terms of weight calculated in taels (*leung*: Chinese ounces).[3]

6. The rate of exchange was constant during the period and was 1 dollar = 0.72 taels = 1,000 cash.

Loans Made by the Tong

This organisation belonged to the Chi clan which had been settled at Shek Pik since the middle of the seventeenth century. A *tong* is a Chinese customary association usually set up for business purposes to acquire and administer funds and property for private or family gain.

The various papers show that:

1. money loans were made *on payment of interest*;

2. the loans on interest terms were made both to clan members and to other villagers of Shek Pik;

3. interest rates were high, usually amounting to fifty percent principal per annum in simple interest, although the rate was mostly listed at a monthly figure;

4. members of the Chi clan could borrow on more favourable terms, at twenty-four percent interest per annum;

5. loans were often outstanding for a long time (e.g., two separate cases appear in the papers where loans were not concluded until thirty-eight months had passed), and where

such delays occurred fields were taken during the course of the loan as additional security for it, or on settlement in lieu of repayment in cash;

6. money loans were also made *under different initial arrangements* (i.e., on the security of a deed of mortgage of land to the *tong*, a procedure which was presumably adopted in cases where repayment in cash was doubtful), and where it occurred a debtor paid no interest for the loan but lost the use of his fields which were placed at the complete disposal of his creditor; and

7. sometimes a time limit was placed on repayment of the loan (e.g., this was done in one case relating to a man from an adjoining village, whereby his fields were to become the property of the *tong* if repayment was not made within a two year period).

A *tong* such as this would only come into being and flourish where a member of the clan was literate (i.e., could keep written accounts) and possessed business acumen. This particular *tong* appears not to have survived the death of its architect. It was not known of by the present Chi elder (born in 1900), nor did it appear in the schedules of ownership completed by the Hong Kong government after the land settlement which followed the lease of the New Territories to Great Britain in 1898.

Other Points

1. The papers give no indication of the objects for which villagers sought to raise money by joining a money association or getting a loan on repayment of interest. However, where land was given as security by way of

mortgage, or where land was sold, reasons were usually given in the deed of transfer and some of these were specific (e.g., debts incurred by a younger brother, the need to pay government taxes, money to pay for a father's funeral; capital for business, etc.).

2. With the high rates of interest on loans and the continuing need over several years to have money ready to pay the instalments in a money loan association, it is not surprising that people got into difficulties and there are illuminating instances of this in the papers. One man borrowed thirty-four silver dollars from the *tong* at the end of 1886, and three years and two months later owed eighty-eight dollars, representing principal plus interest. Of this sum ten dollars had already been paid off by selling land to offset the debt. The remainder was extinguished by the debtor waiving his turn for payment in a money loan association in favour of his creditor. Yet this experience was not a case of "once bitten, twice shy" for either side, for in the month following the settlement of his affairs with the *tong* he asked it for, and secured, another loan of sixteen dollars "due to dire need of money". This loan was made on the mortgage of more of his inherited farmland. We do not know the sequel. Another villager who had failed to pay his share or instalment in a money loan association mortgaged a house in pledge and was to lose it if he had not paid the money by the end of that lunar year.

3. The *tong* was not the only source of money loans available to the Shek Pik villagers. Shops in the neighbouring market centres of Tai O and Cheung Chau would advance credit, or give loans as would two other local *tongs*. They were not organisations belonging to Shek Pik, one being composed of merchants from Tai O and the other a family organisation belonging to a clan in another village.

4. These papers came from only one of the clans living at Shek Pik and there is reason to think that similar activities were taking place in other clans and amongst other groups of persons in the village.

13

San Po Tsai (Little Daughters-in-Law) and Child Betrothals in the New Territories of Hong Kong from the 1890s to the 1960s

James prefaces this article with four quotations from the writings of previous scholars. He was perhaps steeling his readers against the shock of discovering that a custom seldom documented in contemporary writings was still being observed in the last decades of the 20th century. They make for disquieting reading:

[E]arly betrothals and early marriages are common ... especially among the Hakkas, who have, moreover, the custom of sending the betrothed, as soon as she is able to walk, say when three or four years old, to the family of her future husband, where she remains until her marriage.[1]

It is perhaps superfluous to state that ... a girl is really, even at a very early age, a marketable commodity.[2]

This is the most economical, most looked down upon type of marriage arrangement.[3]

* Originally published in Maria Jaschok and Suzanne Miers (eds.), *Women and Chinese Patriarchy: Submission, Servitude and Escape* (Hong Kong 1994) pp. 45–76.

> *Why don't they wait another two or three years and carry you through their gate formally, in the red embroidered sedan chair and with the horns blowing and the gongs beating? Then our family also could add something at least to your trousseau. It'd be better for our reputation. Zhongyao [her betrothed] has many younger brothers, and a formal wedding would give you more standing among your sisters-in-law.*[4]

The practice has received little attention in Hong Kong, very likely for the reason that it was not ever particularly common. Since 7 October 1971, the only form of marriage that can legally be contracted there has been that in accordance with the provisions of the Marriage Ordinance, and there can now be comparatively few potential informants alive to recount their first-hand experience of being a san po tsai. *Understandably neither James nor the people of Hong Kong have shown regret at the loss of this custom, but the article is a very worthwhile contribution to our understanding of the workings of traditional Chinese society.*

In the 1950s, when I first served in the New Territories District Administration, the villagers of the Hong Kong region were still leading a traditional rural existence based on agriculture. The two rice crops a year were still of major importance to most settlements, and the market towns catered largely to the village populations and their agricultural pursuits. Indeed, in most places the position had scarcely changed since pre-war times. In this very conservative and old-fashioned society, it was still usual to find various traditional kinds of betrothal and transfers of children. There were *san po tsai* staying with their future husbands' families. There were little girls already betrothed but still living with their own parents. There were young, recently betrothed female adults, and there were newly married women who had come into the village from nearby settlements. In practically all cases, the traditional patterns of bride-finding, betrothal, and marriage had been observed.

In the practice of what has been styled "major marriage", the employment of "go-betweens", specialists in fate and letter writers versed in the various forms of documentation needed on such occasions was still *de rigeur*. Bride price, dowry, and presents were obligatory. Use of the bridal red sedan chair to take the weeping bride to her new home was still quite common in the 1950s, and in outlying places it persisted into the 1960s. The traditional bridal laments could also be heard on these occasions.

While information is available concerning major marriage, it has not been easy to collect first-hand information on "minor marriage", the conditions of life, and the rituals associated with *san po tsai* in the Hong Kong region. There are only a small number of persons alive today who were either former *san po tsai* or knew much about them. Also, when compared with betrothal and major marriage, there was much less ceremony attached to the *san po tsai* transfer and the later marriage. Outside the basic ritual essentials, what *was* done to celebrate these occasions seems to have varied from family to family. Even in cases of adult marriage, according to some informants, brides knew little of the details since the arrangements were made by their parents, so former *san po tsai*, transferred as small children, were even less likely to know about them.

The basic information and the personal histories in this chapter come from three areas of Hong Kong: the Cantonese-speaking farming and fishing village of Shek Pik on Lantau Island, the former Hakka stonecutters' settlement of Ngau Tau Kok in East Kowloon, where I collected them in the late 1950s and mid-1960s, and, more recently, the Hakka settlements of the Shing Mun and Tsuen Wan areas of the mainland New Territories.[5]

Infant and Child Betrothal in Chinese Marriage

On the subject of marriage and betrothal, Archdeacon Gray noted in 1878 that around Guangzhou the age of betrothal was between seven and fourteen, except among the Hakka, whose children were "affianced in infancy".[6] One of the early district officers in the New Territories reported in 1912 that the average age of marriage was about nineteen for husbands and seventeen for wives, but infant betrothal was common among the poorer Hakka population. He added:

> The girl in such case [*sic*] is regarded as belonging to her destined husband's family, but continues to reside with her parents, until she is of an age to cohabit with her husband: unless her parents die first, when she enters the house of her future husband as an "expectant" wife.[7]

It will be noted how in this and other accounts it is always the Hakka who are singled out for notice, yet early betrothal seems to have been a universal practice in nineteenth- and early twentieth-century China. R.F. Johnston, an authority with a keen interest and much first-hand experience, writing at the close of the Qing (1910) about Shandong Province but with general reference, goes so far as to state that "the majority of marriages are the outcome of longstanding betrothals".[8] This is affirmed by another impeccable source, the translator of and commentator on the Qing Code, Father Guy Boulais, who writes: "*Les pères de famille ont l'habitude de fiancer de très bonne heure leurs enfants; ils n'attendant même pas toujours qu'ils aient atteint l'age de raison*" (Fathers of families are in the habit of betrothing their children very early, not even waiting until they reach the age of reason).[9]

Father Boulais adds that betrothals *before* birth were also made: "*quelque-fois même ils les unissent hypothètiquement avant leurs naissance, pendant qu'ils sont encore dans le sein de leur mère*" (sometimes they even hypothetically unite them before their birth, while they are still in their mother's womb). In this connection, it would appear that these were to be found in Guangdong too. My wife's mother, born in Foshan near Guangzhou in 1907, has told me that such betrothals in the womb were a feature of family life in some well-to-do households there in her youth. There was yet another form of betrothal found in Southeast China:

> There are also some superstitious women, who, being afraid that they may not be able to conceive, take in a young girl child to rear and then wait for a son to be born. When this happens, there will already be a wife ready for the son when he comes of age. They think that once this kind of girl is in the household—known as "a girl who waits for a son" or the "girl waiting to be the brother's wife"—there will be more chance of having sons. In this kind of marriage the female is always older than the male.[10]

In the New Territories, Rubie Watson mentions children "matched" when they were eight or nine years old in the 1940s.[11] By the late 1950s, early betrothals were almost certainly less usual than in the recent past, but I came across a few cases in Shek Pik of couples who had been betrothed in childhood but were only married as adults. I never heard of any betrothals in the womb or "of girls who wait for a son", although these practices may have existed.

San Po Tsai in Chinese Marriage

A *san po tsai* is a child transferred from her natal family in a particular form of early betrothal. The term is Cantonese for a "little daughter-in-law". In Hakka, the other long-standing local language of the Hong Kong region, she is known as a *sim pu tsai* (same characters). In the written language, she was more often referred to as a *tung yeung sik* (daughter-in-law raised from infancy).

The *san po tsai* held a special and intermediate position in the household, of lesser status than a bride or a regularly betrothed girl, but not to be confused with the *mui tsai*—a female sold, pledged, or leased into domestic service or worse, who was a servant by status and was married outside the household—she was part of the taking-in family, brought in with the specific intention that she should marry one of its sons when she was old enough.

This traditional institution—for such it may be called—was not merely a phenomenon of the New Territories of Hong Kong, but was known in many other parts of China. Olga Lang states that it was well known in old China, and was even mentioned in the legal code of the Yuan dynasty. It is clear that it was common in nineteenth- and twentieth-century Fujian, as reported by Christian missionaries, and Van Der Valk's researches have identified cases from a number of different provinces.[12] Such marriage transfers seem also to have been plentiful in Hunan and in central China where the girls were called *xiao xi* (little daughters-in-law), and doubtless they were known elsewhere by other names. In Guangdong itself, the transfer of young children was common[13] and was apparently not a custom of recent origin.

The *San Po Tsai* Condition and its Associated Rituals

The essentials of the *san po tsai* condition in Guangdong and Guangxi are brought out very clearly by the following extract from the collected papers of Hsieh K'ang, born in central Guangxi in one of the poorer areas of South China in 1901:

The Little Daughter-in-Law is the most economical and least respected form of marriage, and only to be found among poor people. The girl can be a few years old up to the age of ten when she enters her future husband's family as a "not yet married wife". Upon entry, she and her husband-to-be will be about the same age. She will help with the household duties, and the two will be wed when they are old enough. The boy's father will then ask for the consent of the girl's father, and a celebratory feast will be held, after which they will be considered man and wife.[14]

Lou Tzu-k'uang, writing in 1968 about Hakka marriage customs on Taiwan, says:

When a boy is young, his parents purchase a little girl to be a Little Daughter in Law. When the two are of age, they will be given new clothes and ornaments, and the marriage will take place on the eve of the new year. But before the marriage, the families on each side must secure the other's consent, and the girl must be willing. This type of marriage, though still to be found, is seldom encountered nowadays. The reason is that girls are unwilling to marry in this way.

A similar statement also comes from Taiwan, couched in much the same vein, but emphasising the difference between major and minor marriage:

Tong-yang-xi: A proper marriage involves betrothal money, and much expenditure on guests, feasts, wine, and the like, to a not small amount. Therefore in a number of poorer families, in order that out of poverty their sons do not lose the chance to be married, the parents assist them by taking other people's young daughters into the family as *tong-yang-xi* (a child reared as the son's future wife), so that in due course they may be married to their own sons.[15]

As practised in the Hakka villages of the New Territories, the *san po tsai* institution appears to have been characterised by the following features and "conditions". There had to be a middleman or "go-between", as for a major wedding. There was also a transfer paper which was given to the taking-in family. My informants said that it was most usual to send away a girl-child "one hundred days" after birth. I suspect this is a way of saying "early in life" rather than an exact length of time. Whilst transfer in infancy was stated to be common in the early part of this century, it will be seen from the cases cited here that it was just as common for the transfer to be made later, especially if it was dictated by the death of a parent. The transfer was to be accompanied by a suit of clothing, as a token of the girl's or infant's "not needing her own mother's milk". In some cases, a small sum of money and other auspicious small gifts were sent with her, to get her off to a good start. The two families would henceforth regard themselves as relatives.

When the transition from *san po tsai* to the married state was decided, the girl would receive a hat decorated with flowers, as implied by the description used to indicate the marriage of a *san po tsai*. This was styled *sheung tau* or "Placing [the decorated hat] on the Head". The hat in question had "flowers" stuck in it, but it seems from descriptions given that these were made of gold or silver wire rather than being real flowers. In preparation for the *sheung tau* ceremony, the girl, who had hitherto worn her hair in a pigtail, would put up her hair in the *kam kai* style with the flowered headdress. The hairstyle was called *tau shik*.

The marriage would be signified by the couple going to worship before the husband's family's ancestral tablets. In the case of *san po tsai* marriages, this would usually be done on the last day of the old year or at the Winter Solstice. Other than this and performing the *sheung tau* ritual, no other celebration was required; though if money was available and if the family felt so inclined and well-disposed, some little show might be attempted and there might be a dinner for family on the male side.

The Mother-in-Law

Towering over the *san po tsai* even more than in the case of an adult bride was the awesome figure of the mother-in-law. Discussion of the status and condition of the child "bride-to-be" would not be complete without taking into consideration the practically unfettered authority of the mother-in-law. Her power over the *san po tsai* was that much greater than over older female members of the household, though some women were able to exert their personalities and vent their temper on all regardless of whether they were adults or children. Her authority aside, the nature of the mother-in-law, whether she was kindly or cruel and vicious, was everything to the incoming girl and was not tempered by the blood tie as with a natural daughter.

The prevailing attitude and expectation of older women in traditional rural life was that the advent of a younger woman in the household would free her from menial duties in and around the home and improve her life in other ways. I recall asking one old village woman when she had stopped cutting grass and firewood on the hills and received the prompt answer: "When I got a daughter-in-law." It was also traditional for a mother-in-law (and sometimes a father-in-law) to bully a son's wife.[16]

The petty tyranny of a mother-in-law (*ka po* in Cantonese) was of course well known and probably expected. In Hong Kong, and no doubt elsewhere, it was embodied in local folklore. Thus, the irritating cries of a bird on Lantau Island are likened to the words "*Ka-kung Ka-po, tak-tsui-Lou-po*" ("Father-in-law, Mother-in-law, always finding fault with their Son's Wife") and linked to a story about a young wife whose husband went abroad and whose mother-in-law mistreated her so badly that she died or committed suicide.[17]

It seems plain that the harshness often exhibited towards daughters-in-law was extended to "little daughters-in-law". Ill-treatment and tears are encountered in a wide variety of literature. Hsieh Ping-yang, for instance, mentions a "tea garden", seemingly more of a plantation, where she was sent to pick tea leaves along with other girls, most of whom were "child daughters-in-law". Their lives at the hands of the mothers-in-law who had sent them out to work to bring money into the family were hard. "Rarely did they have a good meal ... they were as thin as skeletons ... and they cried a great deal about their sad lot". Lena Johnston's little daughter-in-law was only three at the time of her transfer, yet her mother-in-law "kept telling her she must be of use", and she received slaps and beatings if she was clumsy or slow, even though her father sometimes came to see that she was not ill and to say that she must "not be beaten too heavily".[18]

Some accounts in Christian missionary works also make sad reading. The Catholic Vicar Apostolic of Zhejiang noted that one little baptised daughter-in-law was "afraid of going to heaven, for fear she should find her mother-in-law there ... but we succeeded in convincing her that in heaven her mother-in-law could never ill-treat her again".[19] The woes of the little daughter-in-law were also celebrated in folklore. The break for older children who had to leave their homes must have been traumatic for some girls, and for their mothers. Adele Fielde's "Aunt Luck" from Swatow was sent from her mother at seven years old.[20] Though not harshly treated, she had to work very hard at spinning from daylight to dark and so missed her own family that she "kept crying more or less for years" and "never really stopped crying" until she had her own children.[21]

Interestingly, however, I have not had a strong impression of the unkindness of mothers-in-law from my many female informants over the years, though they often mention the hardness of their early lives. They were probably among the luckier children, or perhaps their memories of "hardness" encapsulated any severities experienced at the mother-in-law's hands, for in those days it was the general practice to be authoritarian in the home and to beat children for real or imagined transgressions.

Cases of *San Po Tsai* and Other Betrothals in Childhood from the Rural Areas of the New Territories

The Shek Pik Villages on Lantau Island

In the 1950s, the Shek Pik Valley contained several villages and hamlets. The main village, Shek Pik Wai, had shrunk from 363 inhabitants in 1911 to just over two hundred by 1957. The smaller settlement of Fan Pui had exactly fifty-nine residents at each count. Elders said that the population had been much larger in their grandfathers' time, but had been greatly reduced by disease. The larger settlement was multi-lineage, whereas Fan Pui was a single-lineage village.

The villagers were Cantonese-speaking, in the particular patois that K.M.A. Barnett called "Nantou Punti". However, the marriages listed in genealogical records or ascertained by enquiry show Hakka- as well as Punti-speaking brides and a complex speech situation.

These settlements were remote. Lantau Island, though much larger than Hong Kong and located closer to Guangzhou and Macau, had not been developed by the 1950s. Save at Silver Mine Bay with its regular ferries from and to Hong Kong, which had attracted immigrant vegetable cultivators, its villages had remained intact and undiluted by outsiders. Life followed pretty much the same patterns as it had done for centuries. This particularly applied to the women, some of whom, up to the time of their resettlement in Tsuen Wan had never left the island. Perhaps it should be recorded that the women did most of the farm work as well as the domestic work. This was not uncommon in the region, especially among the Hakka communities whose menfolk had gone abroad in search of less unpredictable means of livelihood than farming.

In my enquiries, I found three *san po tsai* living with their future husbands' families. One was six, the second was ten, and the third, taken in during the removal negotiations, was also six.

Their prospective husbands were twelve, nine, and eleven *sui*, respectively. The first two girls came from clans in the village. In the third case, surely the last of its kind in the long history of this old village, the girl of six was the daughter of an immigrant farmer in nearby Upper Keung Shan, whose father had come there to settle in 1934. There were three other daughters in the family. The girl's father was paid $600, there were "all the usual papers", and the boy's family gave a celebration dinner in the big village [Shek Pik], attended by "all the relatives, clan elders, and the village head". These relatives came only from the boy's side.

Looking for pre-war cases, I found another family in which the wife, now thirty-three years old, had come into her husband's family in 1934 when she was five. Conceivably, there may have been a few more of these former *san po tsai* among the village wives, especially among the older women.

Ngau Tau Kok Village and Neighbourhood, East Kowloon

Ngau Tau Kok Village and its residents, together with the neighbourhood to which they belonged, differed greatly from the long-settled, chiefly agricultural settlements at Shek Pik. The East Kowloon Sub-district included rice and vegetable farmers, duck breeders, fishermen, and the like, often from areas in eastern Guangdong, but the Ngau Tau Kok stone quarries are of particular interest. These were part of a larger group of quarries in East Kowloon known as the "Four Stone Hills".[22] In the early years of this century there were said to be more than ten quarries in the Ngau Tau Kok section of the "Four Hills" alone, each employing twenty to thirty persons, all Hakkas from the Tung Kong (East River) area of northeastern Guangdong. The quarries engaged stone cutters and polishers, together with the blacksmiths who supplied and repaired the tools of the trade. Ancillary workers, comprising locally recruited casual labour, women, and girls from the quarrymen's families, broke the cut stone into aggregate and carried it to junks at the shore. The more prosperous quarry masters also owned junks which took the cut blocks and broken stone to their clients.

Both male and female recruitment was very selective. The quarry workmen were mainly recruited from the home area in China. They served as apprentices at Ngau Tau Kok, and once trained went back to their home villages to marry, after which they returned to work in East Kowloon. In the case of quarry workers whose families were already settled in the village, their wives might have been living with their parents from the time they were small, having been brought into the household as *san po tsai* from the home area, or in some cases locally. It was this clear preference for women and girls from the home areas instead of from the local Hakka villages which differentiated the stonecutters' settlements from the farming villages around them.

The greater emphasis laid on bringing in *san po tsai* seems to have been connected with the fact that most of the Ngau Tau Kok quarries of the time were small family concerns. There was a continual need for labour in and around the home and quarry.

My best female informant had a clear memory of her childhood, perhaps because it had been so dramatic. She was born in a hamlet at Hang Mei, To Kwa Wan, Kowloon, about 1888. Her father died when she was very small. Her mother, a Poon from the village of Ha Kwai Chung, Tsuen Wan, died when the daughter was in her twenties. However, the girl had been sent to Ngau Tau Kok as a *san po tsai* when she was seven years old, and thereafter lived with her husband-to-be's family there. The boy was two years her senior.

As she grew in size and strength her duties in her new family were to feed pigs and cut grass and firewood for the family stoves. She also helped to grow vegetables and had to struggle with the essential regular watering of the plots using two buckets on a carrying pole. For the first few years, being little, she did not go out of the house, which was located beside the family quarry, but later went with a sister-in-law to the village shop. In her twenties she carried cut firewood to the market at Kowloon City, a two-hour walk along the shore or over the hill.

Her father-in-law died only two years after her arrival, but her mother-in-law, who, she said, "had been brought up at the quarries and knew all about the work", ran the business in her husband's place. Soon after the mother-in-law began cutting stone at a well-known *feng shui* spot, in the face of warnings that it would bring misfortune, four of her husband's seven brothers died, after being ill for only a few days. This momentous event, occurring when my informant was still young, left a number of widowed sisters-in-law at home, who kept a close watch on her and told her mother-in-law of her doings, real or imagined. She was not well treated by her mother-in-law and included the presence of the sisters-in-law among her catalogue of the "disasters" suffered by the family.

Another female informant, also a *san po tsai*, was born in 1892 at Ngau Tau Kok, the daughter of a duck farmer. Her father died when she was small, and so did her only brother. She was then transferred as a *san po tsai* to a Lau family in Hang Hau town, Junk Bay, when she was eight years old. However, her first husband died, and at the age of twenty-four she remarried, to a man living at Sai Wan Ho, Shaukeiwan, on Hong Kong Island. Her tale is of interest because she often visited her own mother, both from her new family at Hang Hau, and later from Shaukeiwan. The visits were mainly at festival times.

Another elderly woman, again a *san po tsai*, was born at Hui Yang in about 1894. She had been orphaned when very small and was brought up by a relative, and then sent with an uncle to Ngau Tau Kok at the age of seven. The uncle had come to join kinsmen in the quarries, but later returned to the country.

She was sent to a Lin family as a *san po tsai* soon after her arrival at Ngau Tau Kok.

Yet another elderly lady, born in 1903, had come to Ngau Tau Kok in her early teens to be a *san po tsai* in the Ko family. She was from Tong Mei Village near Tam Shui, and an uncle had brought her from there, and then returned. The Ko family came from a village near to her native place, and were known to her own people there. Her husband-to-be was ten years her senior.

The Purchase of Children for Adoption

The stonecutters' community also bought in children, girls as well as boys, who were neither *mui tsai* nor *san po tsai*. One old lady had bought a granddaughter, the child of a stranger, one of the quarrymen employed at Hung Hom. She had bought the girl as a baby in the 1930s. She had met them one day when buying rice at Hung Hom, and upon becoming better acquainted had learned that they wished to dispose of the girl.

Another of the Ngau Tau Kok families had bought a girl and three small boys in the few years prior to the Japanese attack on Hong Kong in December 1941. They were intended as grandchildren after the only son of the family had died without issue. They were bought from "human traffickers" in Hong Kong.

Shing Mun and Other Villages of Tsuen Wan

The Shing Mun Valley, above the former market town of Tsuen Wan in the western New Territories, was home to eight villages and hamlets. These had been built in scattered locations in and above the main valley. The great majority of the villagers belonged to one lineage which was represented in most of the settlements, including the largest, Tai Wai. There were several other, smaller lineages. All the villagers were Hakkas, and the main lineage, the Chengs, had been settled there since the mid-seventeenth century. At the repossession of the land by the Hong Kong government for a reservoir project in 1928, the population was recorded as 855 persons.

The Shing Mun families were all farmers, growing rice and pineapples. Pineapple growing provided many households with an extra cash crop to supplement the produce of their fields and the sale of grass and firewood in the local market towns, and later in urban Kowloon. This was necessary since many of their fields were on small upland terraces and yields were poor.

By the late nineteenth century, despite a bitter three-year "war" with their fellow Hakkas in the Tsuen Wan villages in the 1860s, the families at Shing Mun were again finding wives and little daughters-in-law from Tsuen Wan. At the same time, their women and female children were being married-out to the villages of the sub-district. Their numbers "in" and "out" represented a considerable percentage of all such marriages. This was probably due to proximity, and also to the fact that much of their marketing, especially of a heavy export crop like pineapples, had to be done in or through Tsuen Wan with its cargo junks, which encouraged social intercourse and facilitated marriage transfers.

Here I found one woman who had been a *san po tsai*. She was born a Chan of Kwan Mun Hau Village, Tsuen Wan, in 1920, the youngest of four sisters, and had two younger brothers. Her mother, who died in 1983, was also a Tsuen Wan native, a Lau of Yi Pei Chun Village. Her father died at about the time she was sent at the age of five to a family of Chengs at Fu Yung Shan, Shing Mun, and this could well have been the reason for the transfer. There was a *san ka*, or "body money" as she described it, of ninety-nine silver dollars; this number whose sound is homonymous with the Cantonese for "long, long" [*sic*, life] being, as she said, very auspicious. Her husband, who was the eldest son of the family and about five or six years older than herself, had two younger brothers and three sisters. The mother-in-law was another Tsuen Wan person, a Tsang from Hoi Pa, as was her husband's grandmother, a Lau from Wo Yi Hap Village just below Shing Mun. Both had been adult brides, not *san po tsai*.

She began to work from the start, looking after the family's cows and calves, cutting grass and firewood, helping with the pigs and with housework. She was kept very busy. Every day was the same, and life was hard for all. Being fed and kept fully occupied, she did not have the time or any reason to think much about her own home, she said. Her parents-in-law seem to have been generally kind, calling her "Chan Tsai" or "Little Chan", and she addressed them as a daughter would her own parents. Her husband's next younger brother, who was still alive and in fact sitting in on my interview with her and joining interestedly in the conversation, said he had addressed her as "Ah So", the term for elder brother's wife, right from the start, showing that the married state of both parties was recognised in the family from the time of her entry.

The *sheung tau* ritual was carried out on the thirteenth day of the tenth lunar month in her case. Her husband wore the clothing that would be worn at a major marriage ceremony: a long gown with black riding jacket and a sash, and an old-style "gold" hat. The couple bowed to the ancestors in the ancestral hall. There was a feast the night before the ceremony, and the husband's relatives (not hers) were invited.[23] Music was played and her husband's family slaughtered their own pigs and chickens.

Whilst a *san po tsai* she was taken to visit her own family in Kwan Mun Hau for several nights over the Lunar New Year period both when she was in Shing Mun, and after the move to the new village in 1928. Visits at other times were fewer, she said.

This was the only former *san po tsai* I found in these villages, although the mothers of some of my informants had been *san po tsai*. It would seem, therefore, that there were very few of them.

However, there were cases of childhood betrothals. One was a Tang of Lo Wai, born in 1909. Her mother was a Cheng, the main lineage at Shing Mun, from Pei Tau To in that area. She had been betrothed soon after birth through a female go-between named Tang from her own clan in Lo Wai to a Yeung of Yeung Uk, Tsuen Wan. The betrothal money was $2. She was married at thirteen, and went in a bridal chair to her husband's village. He was two years older than she was. Her elder sister, also betrothed in infancy, had been married to a Lau of Yee Pei Chun below Lo Wai when she was seventeen or eighteen.

Another old lady was a Yau of Kwan Mun Hau, Tsuen Wan, born about 1902, who had been betrothed when she was about four to a Cheung of Ho Lek Pui, who was a year younger. The usual two dollars was paid — she called it *lai see* (lucky money) — and her bride price on marriage was $160. The horoscope papers had been exchanged and compared before the betrothal, she thought. It had come about because one of the Cheung wives at Ho LekPui was a Yau and knew of her. This "go-between" had arranged everything. The marriage had been "blind", and she had not seen her husband until the bridal chair arrived in Shing Mun.

San Po Tsai from Other Parts of the New Territories.

I came across a few other *san po tsai* cases among elderly residents of the former villages of Northwest Kowloon when making enquiries there in the early 1960s. An old lady who entered her future husband's family in 1898 at the age of six — he was then eleven — recalled that her (in effect) bride price had consisted of one hundred pieces of silver, two chickens, two slices of pork, nine eggs, nine salted fish, and two bottles of a fine medicinal wine called *ng ka pei*, sent over to her parents by her new family. Her future mother-in-law had treated her harshly, and she was kept very busy helping with pig rearing and cooking the pig food, cutting grass and firewood, carrying vegetables and the like. It seems that all the women in this small Hakka village of Cheng Uk worked in the fields, growing vegetables for the urban market.

Another lady, born in 1892, had lived with her parents in an old house in Law Uk Village, Sham Shui Po. They were casual workers on building sites in the area and had come from the country before she was born to find work in Hong Kong because her father, a compulsive gambler, had lost all his property at home. At the age of three, she was sent to a farming family in the nearby village of Sheung Li Uk. She led the usual life of a young village girl, helping to rear the pigs and chickens, cutting grass and firewood, and assisting in the rice and vegetable fields. Because her village was close to the sea, she also collected seaweed from the shore in the winter months and prepared and cooked it for the pigs, to eke out the swill obtained from food shops and stalls near the market to which the villagers took vegetables and livestock to sell.

One of the most curious cases that has come to my attention concerned a *san po tsai* in one of the Tuen Mun villages. She had been taken into another family when small, but in 1940 when the time came for her to marry, the husband-to-be wished to marry another girl. The *san po tsai* must have been strong-willed, or else the husband and his parents were unusual. Perhaps both — but the outcome was that he married both of them. Both ceremonies took place on the same day and at the same time, and the two wives were accorded equal status thereafter as *ping chai*.[24]

It is also of some interest that Mr To Tim-fuk of the large and long-established To lineage of Tuen Mun recounted that his teacher, a Pat Heung man from an area of long-settled mixed Hakka-Punti settlement, had told him that Hakka girls made the best *san po tsai* as they were more likely to settle down sensibly and happily, as well as to flourish and have children.

San Po Tsai in **Shenzhen**

Finally, to complement the information given by former *san po tsai* from Shing Mun Village, there was the story told to me on 1 July 1990 by a splendidly cheerful and robust elderly village woman at Kwor Yuen Sai Kui, near Shenzhen. She was seventy-six, born a Lok in the village of Mong Ngau Kong in about 1913–1914, and sent as a *san po tsai* at the age of four. She had been carried on the back of one of the women from her own village who, from her description, appeared to be the equivalent of a *tai kam* or mistress of ceremonies, a person well-versed in marriage rituals and customs. The journey to her new family's village had taken half an hour, and she had been accompanied on the way by her own close relatives. The husband-to-be was the second of three brothers. He was two years her senior. All three brothers had *san po tsai* brought into the family for them and there were more than ten persons in the household. Her husband's family had sent over the following gifts to mark the taking-in: ten catties of pork, 110 catties of bean curd, two catties of bean vermicelli, two chickens, two fish, four catties of rice, and two jars of rice wine, but small ones and more like bottles.

When I mentioned the *sheung tau* or putting on the floral headdress to mark the transition to married woman, her face lit up. She motioned to her head and indicated having worn a flowered or decorated hat. She said there had been bowing to the ancestors and to earth and heaven, in the prescribed way, but the ceremony had taken place at the beginning of the year, not at year-end as mentioned in other accounts.

When asked about her childhood, she mentioned being scolded by her father- and mother-in-law to be, and being beaten and denied food on occasion; but it was impossible to tell from her cheerful manner whether this had been the normal childhood experience or an individual bias. With two other *san po tsai* in the family, it may have been the former.

San Po Tsai in Cities

I have little or no information about *san po tsai* in cities. Given that the basic reasons for taking them into households must have been much the same in town or country, there is no reason why they should not appear in accounts of urban as well as rural life. Indeed, Olga Lang cites the case of a Shanghai worker who told her co-researchers: "We had no daughter so we decided to buy a little girl in order to marry her later to our son. A little girl is cheaper than the grown-up one and we sent her to work in the factory meantime."[25] However, in an early post-war survey of 516 households in an urban location on Hong Kong Island, whose results are now being examined by Maria Jaschok, not one *san po tsai* came to light, though the survey questionnaire specifically included a question on this topic. The question remains unanswered. Clearly, we need more information on the subject.

The Social Aspects of *San Po Tsai*

It is clear that *san po tsai* was a minor, muted form of marriage, with the glory and colour removed along with the expense.

A *san po tsai* lived alongside the brothers and sisters of her intended husband. Her position was worsened if her mother-in-law favoured her own children and treated her with open discrimination or even with harshness, or if older members of her own generation took a dislike to her. The position would obviously have varied from person to person, and family to family.

In regard to status, it is of particular interest that there seems to have been no discrimination against the *san po tsai* in the mode of address used within the family. In the local Hakka families, the *san po tsai* was treated and addressed as a daughter, no different from those of her future in-laws. As one old lady described it to me: "before marriage, she was addressed [by the parents] as a daughter: and after marriage, as a bride." We have also noted how a prospective brother-in-law used the married form of address for his child sister-in-law to be. Though this evidence is slight, it is likely to be accurate. It is also significant that none of my informants over many years, whether speaking of themselves, their mothers, or other relatives who had been *san po tsai*, showed any reluctance to state this fact. One may deduce from this that the *san po tsai* status was for them just one of the traditional forms of local marriage—minor maybe, but to be accepted by all concerned as a feature of family life.

However, there was a great difference in how minor and major marriage was celebrated. In major marriage, the betrothal could take place in infancy or childhood, as well as in the months or years prior to the wedding, and it appears that the age of betrothal made no difference to the customary ceremonies. For the *san po tsai* there was seemingly no exchange of horoscopes or even choosing of a lucky day for the little daughter-in-law to enter her future husband's home, nor was there a dowry or present-giving.[26] The "lucky money" or token gifts given on the occasion of the *san po tsai*'s transfer as an auspicious gesture normally sufficed for both her transfer and later marriage. Whereas an adult marriage could take place on any auspicious day throughout the year, the *san po tsai* marriage was said usually to have taken place at a fixed time. This was at year-end, on either the evening of the winter solstice or the last day of the Old Year.

In Chinese traditional society, these differences in the ceremonies of betrothal and marriage were truly significant, and directly reflected the low-income and financial stringency always associated with the practice of giving and taking in *san po tsai*. This difference was also underlined by the fact that in an age when infant and child betrothals were common in the local villages and poverty was general, many girls were not sent as *san po tsai*, despite the fact that it would save the cost of the girl's upbringing. The implication is that the sending-away family had to be poorer than most, tying in the *san po tsai* status to inferior financial and, therefore, low social status in her native village. Yet the *san po tsai* did not suffer the stigma that was generally attached to *mui tsai*.

Whether or not the *san po tsai*'s position was intrinsically inferior because of these differences, and whether or not she held an inferior position in certain households, I was assured by some informants that her situation and status improved on marriage.[27] After the *sheung tau* ceremony, she was an acknowledged wife, with the same status as other daughters-in-law, in the same way as her husband was his brothers' equal.

My enquiries into situations in which either the *san po tsai* or her husband-to-be died before the marriage ceremony reveal some important facts about *san po tsai* status. First, in the context of death, both parties were regarded as having been married. Second, where the prospective husband died before the *sheung tau* ceremony had taken place and another marriage was arranged for the girl, she was still not entitled to any of the formalities of major marriage on her entry to her new home upon what was considered her remarriage. In such cases it was usual for the girl to return to her natal family on the death of her prospective husband, but if this was not possible or desired, then the taking-in family would find her another husband. However, there was no obligation on either side and the outcome would depend on circumstances. Third, if the *san po tsai* herself died during childhood or girlhood, her funeral arrangements were the responsibility of the boy's family, and burial would take place in his village area. The *san po tsai*'s family would be informed and invited to the funeral.

It is of parallel interest that a betrothed girl, however young when death occurred, would for ritual purposes also be regarded as married. A girl who lived in a village on Tsing Yi Island had been betrothed to an informant's father (born in about 1890) when a babe in arms. Sadly, she had died when still young, and another young girl was found in her place. However, in circumstances of this kind, it was the local practice that before a new betrothal could take place, a *san chue pai* or ancestral (spirit) tablet had to be prepared for the deceased girl and brought into the boy's home to be placed on the family altar. The children of the replacement partner in the marriage would be brought up to reverence her along with the other ancestors of the clan, in accordance with the general custom.[28]

Logically, the same formalities should have been followed for a deceased *san po tsai* when her husband-to-be married someone else, but I have no information on this point.

The Financial Aspects of *San Po Tsai*

The difficulties of obtaining reliable information about the financial aspects of *san po tsai* transfer are obvious, especially in my near total lack so far of supporting documentary evidence. However, my informants recalled or received statements about payments made to the taking-in family or sent with the girl are probably sufficient to show that the amounts were usually token in nature. They comprised a small sum of money and sundry items which were regarded as contributing to the *san po tsai*'s future good fortune.

They appear to have been similar in kind and amount to the payments and the accompanying gifts made in village circles to the girl's family when betrothal took place in infancy or early childhood and there was a long wait before the marriage transfer took place. However, as already stated, in cases of major marriage, the celebrations at the time of the marriage ceremony were very different from the simple, unobtrusive *sheung tau* ritual.

The difference in the financial approach is made clear in another way. In the ordinary betrothals for major marriage, whether made in infancy or childhood, payments were made (and expected) at the two ends of the long progression from child betrothal to actual marriage. This contrasted with the absence of a bride price when the *san po tsai* was married. A few examples will indicate the position.

One of my oldest female informants, born in 1880 and interviewed in 1969, had been betrothed when not more than a babe in arms. She came from the Punti-speaking village of Ho Chung in the Sai Kung Sub-district, and was married into another Cantonese family living in Chuk Yuen, one of the old villages of Kowloon. She was carried there in the traditional bridal chair when sixteen years of age. The dowry (*ka chong*) upon marriage was $70, but she had been told that $2 and some *cha kwo* cakes had been given to her own family at the time of the betrothal. In my more recent enquiries, I have found other, later, instances of the same kind in the Tsuen Wan Sub-district. The survivor of two sisters born at Lo Wai (circa 1905–1909) told me they had been betrothed in infancy to boys a few years older than themselves, and were married into their local villages when they were thirteen years old in the one case and probably a little older in the other. The betrothal money had also been about $2, but the *lai kam* or bride price paid upon marriage had been over $100. Another informant, born in Kwan Mun Hau Village in about 1902, had been betrothed when small to the younger son of a family in Ho Lek Pui Village, and reported the betrothal money as the same $2. However, she described it as *lai see* or "lucky money" which it probably was. In her case, the bride price upon marriage at sixteen had been $160.

It thus seems likely that these token levels of payment to the girls' families upon early betrothal, followed by a larger bride price upon marriage, were the norm among peasant families in the region, and grounded in the realities of life. The emphasis placed on the financial aspects of traditional Chinese marriages, together with the severely practical view of these transactions taken by the families concerned, indicate that the customary payments at the different stages of the progression would be fixed at sums considered to be appropriate to the ages of the children. In the case of infant betrothal, the time that must elapse before the betrothal could be replaced by marriage, and the possibility that death might intervene, would be taken into account. This would explain the token nature of the financial exchange, and its characterisation as "lucky money", marking a happy event and hoping for the best.

Logically enough, the existence of the *san po tsai* type of marriage arrangement had the effect of keeping the bride price in major marriages at a high level. In this regard, though without reference to the *san po tsai* institution, the experienced and knowledgeable American missionary John L. Nevius wrote at an earlier time:

> Parents of the lower and middle classes, whose daughters live with them till they are married, feel that they are entitled to some remuneration from the parents of the husband for all their expense and trouble in bringing her up. For this reason, when a girl is betrothed with the expectation of her remaining in her own family, her parents expect a considerable amount of money; so that the transaction has very much the appearance of a matter of buying and selling.

This, in turn, had a dampening effect on the marriage prospects of some men, Nevius continued: "Many men are doomed to a life of celibacy because they are too poor to buy and support a wife."[29]

Gender Inequality

Attitudes to Traditional Marriage Arrangements and Female Subordination

No discussion of the various aspects of Chinese marriage in traditional society can avoid touching on the subject of gender inequality. The more reading and interviewing one does on the subject of marriage arrangements among a conservative-minded rural population, the more one comes across immensely deep-rooted attitudes which conditioned the individual according to his or her gender. These attitudes were not rooted only in community values and tradition, but were equally grounded in the prevailing economic system and the uncertain life expectancy. Together, these dictated the continuance of social institutions like infant and child betrothals for both sexes, as well as the "little daughter-in-law" practice, the buying and selling of women and girls, and much else that affected the female sex adversely. Just as importantly, they ensured the women's continued acceptance of these subordinating and demeaning traditions.

Dr Hu King Eng, graduate of the Woman's Medical College in Philadelphia and a regular medical missionary of the Woman's Foreign Missionary Society from 1895, wrote of the first female student graduation from Woolston Memorial Hospital, Foochow, in 1902: "Seeing a Chinese young woman receiving her diploma made many Chinese parents regret that their daughters were engaged, or married, or drowned."[30] Her words indicate the extent of early betrothals and the enormous burden placed by traditional social practices upon the wives and daughters of her day, at all levels of society. In some ways these were worst for the better-off women who mostly stayed at home, inhibited by custom and by their bound feet from venturing abroad or receiving other than women guests in their houses.

During one of my discussions with an old lady of eighty-seven from Yau Kam Tau, conducted with the help of three men in their sixties from her late husband's lineage, we discussed *ping kam* and *lai kam*, the sums paid to the girl's family at betrothal and marriage. Running through the conversation like a brightly coloured thread on a plain ground was the clear indication that, for the menfolk of the villages, these transactions amounted to sales. As one of them explained to me: "A man takes a wife but a girl is sold out." Indeed, they said, the common term in ordinary use in the villages of the Tsuen Wan Sub-district to describe a girl leaving the family on becoming a bride, *was* that she was being sold out. Groping for comparisons, in a flash of inspiration, one of the men said that betrothal money was like putting down a deposit on a new house!

My notes of conversations with village elders at Shek Pik nearly thirty years ago show equally illuminating glimpses of how men there regarded the marriage market. Searching for a meaningful comparison for bride prices recalled for his father's generation, the village head (born in 1899) noted that they were "about three or four times the selling price of pigs at that time". Talking about the purchase of village land during the late Qing, he mentioned that the prevailing price of farmland had then been "several tens of dollars", adding gratuitously that "a wife could be had for the same sum at the time".

Thus, from these and similar discussions I was obliged, like Johnston in Wei Hai Wei eighty years ago and Kulp in the Swatow region of Guangdong in the 1920s, to conclude that these were *clearly* money matters. In recording hagglings over the financial aspects of betrothal and marriage, Kulp commented: "Such tactics sometimes cause the monetary aspects to become pure purchase of a bride. Cases have been known where purchase was effected as coldly as that of any chattel in the market place."[31] George Jamieson, British Consul-General at Shanghai in 1897–1899, also emphasised the monetary side of the "marriage presents":

This is an essential part of every engagement, and the amount is not left to the goodwill of the parties as the term "present" would suggest but is exactly stipulated by the negotiators of the marriage. Though the Chinese will not hear of its being called "price", it is exactly tantamount to the purchase money in a contract of sale, and is no doubt a survival of the time when the transaction was one of ordinary bargain. Actual money always constitutes a substantial part of the "presents" and of course is paid by the bridegroom's family to the bride's.[32]

In places, it appears that these practices could be taken to extremes. For example, custom in Fujian even allowed for the outright "buying" of wives, and for a wife to be sold to another person by her husband.[33] There is an echo of this in a case from Tsuen Wan, recalled by one of my elderly female informants from one of the local villages. In the 1930s, a man from the mainland, who was an opium addict, had sold his wife to another man, whereupon his daughter commented that her mother "had disappeared into the mouth of the opium pipe".

As far as my female informants were concerned, they all seemed to have accepted the monetary aspects of their betrothal and marriage as part of their lot in life, along with other aspects of the traditional forms of marriage and betrothal. Male attitudes towards women and girls thirty years ago in Shek Pik were clearly stated by the elders, who said that a man renting part of his fields to others "might find himself with a new daughter-in-law and have to take back the land for her to work". The relative status of men and women was also revealed when the village head recalled that when he was a boy, his family had a new daughter-in-law and had to give a large dinner. "But", he added, "women were excluded on that occasion because of the expense." At the same discussion, the elders had laughed when, rather naively, I had enquired about bound feet among the women of their fathers' and grandfathers' generations. They said that sixty years before, not one woman in the village had bound feet "because they had to cut grass and firewood, carry them to market along with other things to sell, and cultivate the fields". They also emphasised that women took no part in the management of village affairs "as they did not know how to write or keep accounts" since none went to school.

The Lack of Education for Females

The traditional Chinese discrimination against women in regard to the provision of educational opportunities is well known. It was still very much in evidence in post-war rural communities in Hong Kong. A number of reasons prevented children from attending school, including lack of schools, the difficulty for small children of walking over rough terrain to get to school, and most important, the poverty of the parents at a time when schools were not free. After becoming district officer in 1957, my visits to villages showed that although a good many boys were not going to school, many more girls were not attending. In one of the Tung Chung villages on Lantau, I recorded that only four children of school age were studying—three boys and one girl. In 1961, at Yuen Tun, one of the outlying hill villages of the district with a hundred inhabitants of all ages, the census commissioner reported that thirteen children (two boys and eleven girls) were not attending school, compared with six boys and four girls who were. Of the fifty-six who had passed school age (here defined as over fourteen), only eighteen had at some time been to school (seventeen males and one female).

This difference of treatment had a long history. The 1911 Census of Hong Kong showed that in the Southern District of the New Territories, 231 females were "able to read and write" compared with 7,760 who were illiterate. In the Northern District, only 235 out of 25,664 were literate. I doubt whether these figures are comprehensive. The greater discrimination in the northern New Territories where the big lineages were is corroborated in Hugh Baker's study of the large Cantonese-speaking lineage village of Sheung Shui, where he says:

> [I]t may be said with certainty that very few [daughters] received any education prior to 1932 [when a new-style school was opened in an ancestral hall] while no daughter of school age born after 1945 has gone without education.[34]

The Relationship of *San Po Tsai* and Married Women with Their Natal Families

In older accounts of Chinese society, it was usual to paint a uniformly dark picture of women's lives after marriage and the fact that they were cut off from their own families was reported as a particular hardship. However, my local enquiries indicate that it was, in fact, quite usual for village women to make regular visits to their home villages and to maintain ties with their natal families.

In one case that seems to illustrate the situation nicely, I learned that three girls from a village in the Lam Tsuen Valley married into the Shing Mun villages had all returned to their own families several times a year, taking their children with them. These occasions had included the major festivals, such as the Lunar New Year (the fourth day was the customary date) and also the marriages of their own relatives on their mothers' side. In this instance and many others of the kind, the villages in question were quite distant. Elderly men from Shing Mun had also all been with their mothers when small to visit the mothers' natal families. It was usual to visit at the main family festivals (New Year, the fifth and eighth moon festivals, and the Winter Solstice) and to go whenever their mothers were invited to wedding celebrations among their own kinsfolk. Such visits were called *fan ngoi ka*. Both men and women said this phrase meant "visiting one's own people, something we treasure in Chinese village life".

Furthermore, Frances Lee's account of the lives of the women of her family over the past three generations shows that contrary to anthropological literature, which treats married women as members of their husbands' and not their own natal families, the women members of her family included daughters as well as daughters-in-law. She states that:

Firstly, a difference must be drawn between the women's feelings and commitments to the family of their birth and their customary obligations to the family of their marriage. Moreover, many regular activities were maintained with the village of their origin, such as visiting the parents' family at New Year, and social visits paid to one another. One result of the social network that grew out of these activities was that some women could act as marriage go-betweens.[35]

These links, and the good feeling that clearly existed in different areas between village families related on the female side, are worth remembering, for they have a bearing on the condition of the *san po tsai*. They were not all cut off from their parents by the transfer at a tender age, partly because of the social network of ties and visits. Some even made extended visits to their own families. Thus, Adele Fielde notes that an informant in Swatow, having been transferred as a *san po tsai* at the age of seven, returned to her father's house for four months of every year between the ages of eleven and fourteen—when she was married. Moreover, the absence from many Hong Kong villages of men abroad or working on ships further strengthened ties in such communities between women, children, and old people.

Avenues of Escape

Even if they were often not completely cut off from their natal families, it can be seen how the transfer of *san po tsai*, early betrothal and marriage, and female disposability without consultation or consent, meshed with hard work, the lack of an education, narrow confines, and an inferior status. All had to be accepted as the long-established way of life for women in rural communities. As my mother-in-law has observed on a number of occasions: "Patience was an essential part of being a woman in the old society."

Patience was the more necessary as there were few avenues of escape from unhappiness at home for married women and girls. In extreme cases some were driven to suicide.[36] Another alternative was to run away. However, this was a last resort since the likely result was that the girl would be shunned by society and all right-thinking people, possibly including her natal family, and then how was she to maintain a livelihood? Even if her own family supported her, the two families would become involved in wrangles and recriminations that could lead to worse troubles. Only the very strong-minded might rise above their situation and effect a measure of change by staying and resisting. A notable case was reported by G.L. Bendelack, who was principal of the Church Missionary Society's St Hilda's Girls Middle School in Guangzhou in the 1910s. Among her pupils was a Christian girl who declined to marry the "wealthy heathen" chosen for her by her grandmother (her father being dead and her only brother at school in England). Her only escape was to "put up her hair as a married woman does, have a great feast in her home similar to a wedding one, and announce her decision to all the family and friends assembled there". This she did, and the author was invited to attend, at the mother's invitation, "the decided unmarriage of her daughter Wing Yi at 6 p.m. on May 25, at the home of the bride", and did so.[37]

Such cases, of course, were rare; but although Chinese women usually accepted their inferior lot in life, they were well aware of it. Thus, William Martin, an American missionary in Ningpo, reported finding two or three thousand women all reciting prayers to Buddha, praying that they might be born into the world as men "so unhappy, as well as inferior, are they taught to consider their present condition". The funeral laments of women in one of the Tsuen Wan villages are equally revealing.[38]

Reasons for the Persistence of *San Po Tsai* in the Hong Kong Region

Why were *san po tsai* marriages so prevalent in the Hong Kong region until several decades ago? The direct, and obviously over-simplistic, answer must be that this was a traditional form of marriage and that the area was itself cast in a traditional mould for longer than might otherwise have been the case owing to its having passed under colonial rule. However, this is only part of the story.

Poverty

With regard to the institution itself, most writers on the subject indicate that it was only to be found in poor families. This is also the view expressed to me by village representatives and other local leaders. There were, in truth, many poor families in the villages of the Hong Kong region. Whether in a farming village or one with specialised employment, life was hard for most people. For persons dependent on the farm, the weather was uncertain, crops were subject to disease, natural disasters were not uncommon, and sickness and early death were among the normal expectations of people living in country places. In many village households, cash was usually in short supply, and economy had to be practised most of the time. In particular, all means to reduce the obligatory and normally heavy expenses of marriage had to be considered, out of common prudence.[39]

However, poverty had been accentuated and prolonged by local conditions. From a number of sources, it would appear that from around the 1850s, many villages in the Hong Kong region were afflicted with stagnation and decay. Owing most probably, in the final analysis, to overpopulation—the result of two centuries of peace—the production of staple foods became inadequate in many places.

Malnutrition may have set in, creating a greater susceptibility to disease, which was often followed by death. Individual and collective vitality and enterprise dipped, and material prosperity was reduced in proportion.[40] Many signs point to a continuation of this downturn into the early decades of the twentieth century.

The connection between this and *san po tsai* is made clear by Michael Palmer who states that elderly men of the Liu lineage of Sheung Shui in the northern New Territories, one of the former "Five Great Clans", told him that

> the 1930s were times when the local standard of living was so depressed that many villagers had to eat sweet potatoes instead of the orthodox staple food of rice *and were driven to marry their children by means of the low-status mechanism of a minor marriage.*[41] [emphasis added]

Thus, continuing poverty as well as custom explain the continuation of the institution of *san po tsai*, adoptions, infant and child betrothals, and the purchases, sales, and presentations of children, especially of girls, that were evident to me in the villages of the region in the 1950s.

The Exodus of Males

Another factor that encouraged the continuation of traditional transfer and marriage practices was the absence of many men from the villages, before and after the British takeover of the New Territories in 1898–1899. Some worked as cooks and waiters, and others as stokers and seamen, on ocean-going ships of many nationalities from the 1840s onward. Others left to seek work, and it was hoped riches, in many countries of the world. Whilst their absence was often balanced by the receipt of remittances by their families, it also resulted in the whole burden of maintaining a livelihood at home falling mainly on the womenfolk. The 1917 Report of the London Missionary Society's "Hong Kong and New Territories Evangelisation Society" contains a striking testimony to the resulting situation in one such area, the Lam Tsuen Valley in the present Tai Po District: "Over considerable areas the women and girls do, practically, all the field work, heavy and light, including the plowing [*sic*] of the soil." Such telling phrases as "the struggle for existence is keen", "poverty-stricken folk", and "the great majority of persons at [church] services are women and girls" appear in this section of the report.

Clearly, the hard-pressed women, and the men who remained because they preferred their fields to going overseas, could use additional help; and since the *san po tsai* institution brought an extra pair of hands into the depleted family, it surely had its practical side.

Female Isolation and Ignorance

Yet another reason why *san po tsai* transfers, child betrothals, and even the sale of children were still encountered in the post-war New Territories was the restricted horizon of the women, especially in the remoter districts like Shek Pik, where some of the older females, born and married on Lantau, had never left the island. Until the reservoir construction work brought a road and vehicles to its rural solitudes, they had never actually seen a motor car. Limitations on female movement were apparently the norm in the China of their day. When telling me in 1963 about women's work at home, a male informant born in 1877 in a large single-lineage village in the Kaiping District of Guangdong, said with great finality that "women were too busy to go outside the village". In his home area, it was usual for women to have bound feet. Though his own father was only a poor tenant farmer of the lineage, the boy was married at eighteen to a girl from an adjoining village complex, whose feet were bound.

Even though bound feet were not common in the Hong Kong region, women were constrained by the narrow village concepts of what was proper for females, especially unmarried ones. I have been told by many persons, male and female alike, that in the earlier part of this century more distant marketing was usually done by men. Thus, women were confined to the village and its environs, only marketing locally produce from farm and hillside and returning as soon as all was sold.

Added to this was the innate conservatism of country people. Women were often consulted about important family decisions, such as land transactions, but they seem to have accepted traditional institutions uncritically.[42] Commenting on infant betrothals, the *san po tsai* institution, and other features of Chinese traditional marriage and family that now seem so far removed from present-day life, my mother-in-law has reminded me that there was no effort of will, no conscious decision, to be made in settling these matters. They were the norm because they had formed the pattern of behaviour for so long. Thus, none of the Shing Mun or Tsuen Wan informants in the last few years ever lamented their "blind marriages", and indeed, in some cases they chuckled over them. Clearly, they were still inclined to regard the whole thing as perfectly normal, as indeed it was at the time. An old lady from Yau Karn Tau explained that she had not seen her husband before her wedding day but as was usual she knew something about his family from the go-between (*kai siu yan*) who was her neighbour and came from her prospective husband's village and whom she trusted. The *tai kam tse* or knowledgeable woman who guided her through the ceremonies was also from her husband's village. She had felt comfortable about the event, therefore, and it had never crossed her mind to be frightened, although she had to go in a closed bridal chair to a place and family completely unknown to her. It was an old custom and that was that.

So long as economic conditions in the villages remained unchanged, custom and tradition would persist.

Changes in Recent Decades

Whilst the overall economic position of the New Territories may, through increased commercial activity in those areas around the market towns, have gradually improved to some extent in the two decades before the outbreak of the Pacific War, it was not uniform, since the remoter parts experienced little amelioration in their condition from pre-war days. The privations and shortages of the Japanese Occupation were keenly felt in most places and starvation was widespread in the final year. In some places both the people and the economy took a long time to recover from the war years. In short, poverty was still widespread, and helped to perpetuate traditional practices that had for centuries been grounded in the old harsh realities of life.

Though the subject of women's life in urban Hong Kong has not been treated here, in fact the countryside was far behind the city by the 1950s. In many country places there was no significant degree of modernisation or development until recent decades, and women and girls in the villages led very different lives from those in the city until well after the Second World War. These differences in status and opportunity remained until the end of traditional farming in the early 1970s, its demise hastened by the spread of education among females and the new opportunities for women and girls to gain a living outside the home without any stigma, or interference from the men of their families. Followed by the widespread urbanisation and modernisation of the whole territory of Hong Kong in the later post-war period, such changes in the economic and social life of the community intensified, leading to the disappearance of the old customary marriage arrangements and practices from the villages.

The Frequency of *San Po Tsai* Transfer in the Hong Kong Region

In the Hong Kong region, the *san po tsai* practice has been specially linked to the Hakka population, and was reported to be "prevalent" in 1921.[43] However, neither fact is entirely borne out by my enquiries, which covered the several decades before and after 1921. The number of cases I have encountered directly or by report has not been large. As we have seen, the elderly ladies with whom I have spoken on the subject did not think there were many *san po tsai* in their home or married-in villages. It is significant that all the older headmen and elders consulted about it have given similar replies. Also, the majority of marriages mentioned by my many other female informants, in their own and reported cases, suggest that, though still fairly common, *san po tsai* were certainly the exception rather than the rule during the long period under review. Moreover, they were to be found in Punti-speaking as well as Hakka-speaking villages.

The Validity of the Evidence

In determining the incidence of *san po tsai*, one has to decide whether all the facts have been disclosed. The scarcity of documents on minor marriage led me to consider whether concealment was likely. Was there any reluctance to reveal minor marriage among my female informants, either for themselves or for their mothers and aunts, grandmothers and great-aunts on both sides of their families, because it might carry a social stigma?

Generally speaking, I think not. From long experience of interviewing, I believe that women who came into a household as *san po tsai* would always mention it when asked about the age of marriage. Conversely, it may be assumed with confidence that women who reported an adult marriage had not been *san po tsai*. Moreover, the elderly men who answered my questions on this topic would have had less reason to "fudge", and in any case, over the years, I have formed a particularly favourable impression of the reliability of information given by most village representatives in view of their extensive knowledge of village affairs acquired over long periods in the post. It also seems that *san po tsai* status was accepted as a fact of life, an established part of old village customs.

The most likely explanation for the received notion that *san po tsai* transfers were common is that they had been more numerous in the nineteenth century, and declined as the twentieth century drew on. It does seem that just before the Second World War there were not a great many of them, and that by the early post-war years there were fewer still. There is clear support for this in the figures recorded at the Hong Kong Censuses of 1931 and 1961. In the 1931 Census no fewer than 1,365 persons under fifteen were reported as married or widowed, including 284 under the age of ten. The 1961 Census shows only fourteen persons under fifteen (three boys and eleven girls) as having reported themselves as married.[44] Of these, five were Hakka from farming families, five were Tanka boat dwellers, one was a Cantonese village girl from the Sheung Shui District, and three were from the fringes of New Kowloon. All but one were born in Hong Kong. There were also a few married women who, though over fifteen at the time of the census, had clearly been married before that age. These were all Hakka farming women or Tanka boat women. The census commissioner noted: "It would appear that though the practice of child marriage, once so prevalent in these two communities, has not entirely disappeared, it is almost a thing of the past."[45] However, he was probably over-sanguine as it seems unlikely that there were *quite* so few *san po tsai* left in 1961, given that I had found three in one village only a few years before.

Conclusion

Whilst the general pattern of *san po tsai* transfer, infant and child betrothal, and the sale of children, especially girls, is generally well known, little has been written on the subject for this part of Guangdong, especially in the former rural area of Hong Kong that lay undeveloped on the city's doorstep for so long. Therein lies the main justification for this chapter. The firsthand information it provides can also be set alongside other recently published accounts of life in urban Hong Kong for those girls who came there for domestic service, or worse, at the dictates of others.[46]

However, this chapter is merely a first look into a subject that deserves a deeper and wider treatment. Apart from conducting other interviews with elderly informants like those appearing in these pages, it would be possible to gain more information from the hundreds of handwritten genealogical records from the New Territories which are now available through the efforts of David Faure and the Hong Kong History Project. Displaying considerable variety in format and content, these provide an opportunity to glean useful information on *san po tsai* transfer, infant and child betrothals, and the other family-related practices of the region.

There is also the matter of documentation, discussed further in the annex following this chapter. It will be clear from its contents that there is scope for a lot more work on the documentary side of minor marriage, as well as on the rituals and formalities of infant and child betrothals, bride price, and the like, whereby our understanding of the parameters of life for women and girls in the rural parts of the Hong Kong region up to the recent past may be enhanced.

Finally, this chapter sets out to be more descriptive than analytical, in the belief that there is a pressing need for more information on the customary family practices and domestic strategies of the region. When this is available, it will be possible to consider them with more confidence within the wider geographical and theoretical contexts provided by other scholars.

Chapter 13 Annex
Documentation for Child Betrothals, *San Po Tsai*, and the Sale, Pledge, "Presentation", and Adoption of Children

The Hong Kong History Project and Documentary Evidence

Documentation was a striking feature of Chinese social life and was practised at all levels, down to the ordinary strata of Chinese society, however poor. I have found printed guides and handbooks on domestic rituals, letter writing, forms, and documents and the like in bookshops and second-hand stalls in the central districts of Hong Kong Island. These all came from Guangdong, although some had been published in Shanghai. A few handwritten guides of a similar kind are also available. At my suggestion, scholars at the Chinese University of Hong Kong searched the mainland New Territories for such printed and handwritten documentation, utilising the then-ongoing Hong Kong Oral History and Historical Inscriptions Project, conducted in the early 1980s with student help, to widen the search.[47] An impressive amount of documentation was recovered from the villages, copied and bound into 130 volumes (at the last count) and placed in various libraries in Hong Kong and overseas. The Project proved that the handwritten books giving detailed guidance on the forms to be used in correspondence and the documentation connected with the family and its various concerns, as well as some of the printed ones, were indeed commonplace in the New Territories villages.

Documentation for *San Po Tsai* Transfer

Despite the wealth of documentation available in the many guides I have seen, dating from the eighteenth century to the early Chinese Republic, the only document encountered which deals with *san po tsai* transfer, actual or in specimen format, came from Shek Pik. My notes indicate that some "taking-in" papers were reported for the three Shek Pik cases. However, I was only able to obtain the one for the 1959 transfer, and then only the text rather than a copy of the actual paper. A translation is provided below. It covers the main aspects of the transfer, which is specifically stated to be the transfer of a "little daughter-in-law" (here called a *sik fu*).

Although a recent search for documents in the Tsuen Wan District was unsuccessful, my informants stated that, as for betrothal and marriage, documentation was the rule for *san po tsai* transfers. They said that the transfer document [usually known by the term *sung tip*] would record *inter alia* the parents' names, the name and birth details of the girl (year, month, day, hour), the go-between's name, the taking-in household head's name, and the price paid upon transfer. The paper would be drawn up for the boy's family and was handed to the girl's grandfather, father, or paternal uncle, whichever of them was the surviving senior member of the household This tallies with the contents of the paper from Shek Pik which, given the time and place it was written, is more than likely to be in the traditional format.

Documentation of Infant and Child Betrothals

The absence of *san po tsai* formats from the printed and manuscript handbooks seems to have a parallel in the lack of specimen documentation for betrothals effected in childhood. After enquiry among some of my elderly informants, my tentative conclusion is that there was no special form of documentation for them. The customary set of procedures governing betrothal and marriage known as the "Three Documents and Six Ceremonies" were followed whether the future bride was one year old or 20 years of age. However, we may be reasonably sure that, as in the cases listed above, the financial arrangements of the betrothal, especially the *ping kam*, were adjusted to match the age of the children concerned, and also reflected the economic standing of the families involved in the arrangements.

Opportunities for Further Documentary Research

Finally, it must be made clear that I have confined my search for written formats and documents on *san po tsai* and infant and child betrothals to those areas in which I have conducted research and have detailed knowledge. I have not yet examined the 130 volumes of the Hong Kong History Project's documentation nor have I been able to extend my research to other areas of China or to Taiwan, where there are extensive collections of documents. These would be rewarding fields for research, as would a survey of novels on the family.[48]

Translation of a Transfer Document for a *San Po Tsai*, Shek Pik, Lantau

Everlasting Good Fortune Presentation Card

> The person drawing up this deed of presentation of a girl [name], with his wife, agrees to send her to [name] of Shek Pik Village,

who is willing to accept her, and to rear and bring her up as the future wife of his son [*sik fu* or daughter-in-law].

Both sides have discussed and are clear on the giving of a decorated cloth and a *lai kam* [bride price] of 600 Hong Kong dollars. [Name] received it in person and returned home with it. The girl was sent forthwith to [name] to be reared as a [Little] "Daughter-in-Law".

Henceforth there can be no regrets. This [transaction] has been agreed by both families, and was not done in connection with debts or any other similar situation. May Heaven bless [it].

Lest verbal agreement be insufficient, this document is provided as evidence of the transaction.

Dated the 30 March 1959; that is the twenty-second day of the second month of the *chi hai* year of the Chinese Republic.

The true signature of the person presenting the girl [name].

14

Geomancy and the Village

This and the following chapter illustrate the ambivalence with which James viewed feng shui. *There is no indication that he himself believes in it, but there is also no doubt that he accepts that the people of the New Territories do. Fascination and frustration are both evident from these accounts, but his pragmatic approach ensures that we learn more about the* effects *of the belief than we do about its inner workings, though he does not entirely neglect the latter.*

Much of what I have to say in this short paper is within my own experience. The immediate occasion was the interference by outsiders — in this case building contractors — with the local landscape in the course of carrying out major public works required by the Hong Kong government. I recount these events as an observer looking more at people's reactions than at the theories which produced them.

* Originally published in *Some Traditional Chinese Ideas and Conceptions in Hong Kong Social Life Today* (RASHKB 1967) pp. 22–30

My experiences convinced me that the local response to what was taking place was based on genuine feeling, whatever subsidiary motives there may have been in addition.[1] Moreover, as I shall try to show, it had its roots, reasons, and precedents in the past.

The principal events noted in this paper took place on Lantau Island mostly in connection with the Shek Pik Water Scheme between 1957 and 1960. In the course of the work, two villages were moved in their entirety from the valley in which the dam was constructed. Nine other villages surrendered some of their private agricultural land for the construction of the extensive catchwaters and other works necessary for the scheme. Before the engineering works began, the area was almost entirely rural and undeveloped and, judging by the several examples that have come to my notice, it is likely that some of the inhabitants, particularly among the women, had never left the island.[2]

Feng shui—the meaning of these two words is literally "wind and water"—may be described briefly as the combined effect of "natural" influences upon a landscape and the people who dwell in it.[3] A site possesses good or ill fortune insofar as its geomantic properties allow.[4] An ideal site is situated on the higher ground, facing water, and protected by encircling hills. If any of these natural features, particularly those in direct view from the village, are disturbed, it is held to be, potentially at least, a serious matter for those who live there. If anyone or anything should fall sick, be it man, beast, or fowl, it is considered that a baleful influence is at work and that worse will follow unless it is turned away by the performance of appropriate rituals. This is why, when ground is turned in order to construct a new house or outbuilding, it is practically obligatory to employ a Taoist priest or *nam mo lou* to conduct a propitiatory ceremony on the site, just to be on the safe side. In 1885, a Christian convert stated the position thus:

When any villager builds a house, he must select a lucky day, and employ the priests to drive away the evil spirits. If we, who believe in Jesus, refuse to do this, and then any of the villagers are taken sick and die, the responsibility of the death is laid at our doors, and we are required to make a recompense for the man's life.[5]

That failure to take steps could cause trouble is demonstrated for our area by events in two Lantau villages some twenty and thirty years ago, when ceremonies were held following deaths in the villages that were attributed to cutting stone and building a cow-shed on ground with *feng shui* properties.[6]

Disturbance of the local *feng shui* was not only something that followed from unwise human action. Where there was no ostensible reason for protracted bad luck, the deduction was drawn that the *feng shui* had changed, and was no longer favourable. Under such circumstances action was sometimes taken to move an ancestor's bones, whether in a formal grave or in an urn, to another location. This even extended to dismantling houses, taking the tiles and wooden fittings to a new site, and removing thereto. The inconvenience and expense of so doing can well be imagined, and yet this is precisely what at least four Lantau villages have done in the past fifty years on the grounds that the *feng shui* had become harmful.[7]

Let me turn now to Shek Pik. From the *feng shui* angle, Shek Pik was probably the worst place to construct a reservoir and so interfere with the local landscape on a really drastic and irrevocable scale. I say this with the advantage of hindsight because it was only by degrees that I accumulated the historical material which shows this to be the case.

There is good evidence to show that the village had been in decline for a long time, probably for as much as a hundred years. Two kinds of proof bear out the otherwise unsubstantiated statements of the older village men. In the first place, the land survey and registration of titles that followed immediately upon the lease of the New Territories to Britain in 1898 show that there were many unclaimed and ruined houses among the four hundred listed at that time, whilst no less than fifty acres of abandoned agricultural land behind the village went unclaimed. At a time when village people depended almost entirely on the land for a livelihood it is curious that so many fields were abandoned and I can only think that depopulation was the prime cause. There is some evidence for this too. There were 373 people in the village at the 1911 Census and local tradition credits it with a larger population in the nineteenth century; yet in 1960 only 202 persons removed from the village to new homes in Tsuen Wan, the place of their choice and a fast developing New Town.

Depopulation seems to have brought demoralisation and there are signs of this from the 1920s onward. The two-roomed village school was demolished by a typhoon in about 1920 and was not rebuilt. The villagers gave up the regular rites to placate wandering spirits about this time. Some of them became Christian converts, and a chapel was opened in a village house. It is recorded that the first step was not the fruit of determined preaching but the result of their own approach to a mission in Tai O, perhaps through disillusionment with their own gods and in the hope of better fortune.[8] In 1936, a severe epidemic occurred which is said to have killed many people.[9] This finally goaded the villagers to take drastic action against what they considered to be the cause of their misfortunes; namely the bad *feng shui*. They removed themselves from the site where, in all probability, their ancestors had lived since the seventeenth century or even before and built for themselves new but poorer quality houses on the edge of the padi fields, some few hundred yards below the old village. We may therefore agree with Samuel Wells Williams when he stated in 1883 that *feng shui* was "a source of terror".

It may be argued that this dramatic act did not change their fortunes. The Japanese Occupation of South China followed on the heels of the epidemic. It made the seaways dangerous and restricted the visits of Hoklo fishermen who, before 1937, seem to have come yearly to Lantau in the winter months to catch shrimp. This affected the local economy since the villagers had derived seasonal employment and a little business from the manufacture of shrimp paste on the beaches. The war also led to an incursion of refugees from Japanese-occupied territory who were a plague to the villagers. Finally, the Occupation of Hong Kong led to great hardship and even to killing. Life for the Japanese and villagers alike was complicated by the presence of guerilla forces. Crops were taken equally by the Japanese troops and the guerillas, the village headman was shot by the guerillas for helping the Japanese and they, in turn, arrested three villagers who died in prison in Tai O. During this time village people lived on sweet potatoes and roots; some died of malnutrition and children were sold. Many fields were sold to obtain money, most of them to a profiteer in Tai O Market.[10]

Therefore, in the mid-1950s, when the Hong Kong government announced that it wished to investigate the possibilities of building a reservoir at Shek Pik, the news must have been viewed locally as the culmination of a long period of decline and misfortune that was the direct result of bad *feng shui*. The news, and certainly its confirmation in 1958 at the close of the tests, was received passively. It was, all along, specific violation of *feng shui* which led to difficulties rather than determined opposition to the scheme in general.

As luck would have it, practically the first thing the engineers wished to do resulted in a confrontation with the village people. It was necessary to build a pier and an access road from it to their wooden huts at the testing site in the middle of the valley. This involved blasting a rock beside a temple. Unhappily this was the very spot which, by village tradition, was regarded as the source of the ill-fortune that had dogged the village since their fathers' and grandfathers' time. Under the circumstances it is hardly surprising that the road had to "edge" past this place and that it remained "sensitive" throughout the period of the work until the villagers had been removed from the valley. In consequence, no blasting ever took place there.

The same difficulty was experienced with other places specifically related to the *feng shui* of the valley. For instance, it was necessary to leave a small hill in the floor of the valley inviolate until the villagers left. This was because of the *feng shui* properties attributed to it by the local people and the respect they gave to the place. No villagers were permitted to bury their dead there or to cut trees or grass on pain of being taken before the elders and fined. It is highly unlikely, of course, that anyone would have dared to do so.

The same problem arose with the thickly wooded hill immediately behind Fan Pui, the smaller of the two villages. This village stood directly along the axis of the dam and had to be removed earlier than the big village which was not so much in the way of the engineering works. It was imperative to conduct early drilling investigations into the hill behind Fan Pui because the right wing of the dam would rest upon the original earth at this point, and before building the dam it was necessary to "grout" here, as everywhere along its entire length, to prevent underground seepage. Attempts to begin this work met with opposition from the villagers. It was clear that to ignore their feelings was to invite real trouble. Accordingly, work on the hill was delayed until the last possible moment in the hope that they would come to see its inevitability. Despite much persuasion, this day never dawned. Eventually it became necessary to expedite construction of their new houses and fields in an adjoining bay, and convince the villagers to remove themselves there, before any work could begin. These difficulties were undoubtedly intensified by the hill in question being the *feng shui* grove which is nearly always found behind a village, and as such, to use military parlance, is "a protected place".

I would like, now, to stress the connection drawn by villagers between disturbing ground and the occurrence of illness. When it is borne in mind that the valley was malarial; that housing conditions were poor with damp walls and earth floors, leaky roofs, and insufficient light and air; that men and animals drank stream water; and that local cattle were not fed adequately but were turned out on the hills to fend for themselves — suffering thereby from the weather, malnutrition, and, inevitably, disease.[11] It is clear that the occasions when villagers might be alarmed by the engineering works would not be few: quite apart from any grievances they might have about more tangible things.

Against this background it will not surprise you that there was intermittent trouble with the village people when the engineers began to dig numerous trial pits at various places in the upper and lower valley. It so happened that some cows fell sick and died. The villagers held up the work and informed the District Office; so did the engineers. When work was hindered in this way, it was usually a toss-up who got a word in first. For the engineers time was money. Their main concern was not to hold up the progress of the investigations and not to have expensive labour and equipment lying idle. For the villagers these considerations meant nothing. Their main concern was to avert the train of harm that appeared to have been set in motion by the drilling. On this occasion the trouble dragged on for a week or ten days with intermittent starts and stops to the engineering works as more animals fell sick and died. A veterinary team sent out to ascertain what was wrong with the village cattle met with little co-operation in tracing sick or dead animals. Eventually I went out again and prodded the villagers into indicating where the dead cattle were buried. With their help we located and disinterred the bodies of one large cow and one calf and carried them down to the shore where they were put onto a police launch to be taken back to Kowloon for a post-mortem. The remains did not permit diagnosis but as it happened no more animals died and the drilling was able to proceed. Similar but less protracted difficulties were experienced from time to time.

Feng shui considerations also affected the construction of the new houses for the smaller village. I have mentioned the evidence of a Christian convert as showing the importance attached to ceremonies to avert evil influences when building a house. It was equally important to see that a new building was adjusted in accordance with the best geomantic qualities of its surroundings.[12] At their own expense the villagers consulted an expert in *feng shui* to vet the site chosen for their new houses. Whilst he did give general clearance to the site, I recall that just before the contractor began work, a request was made, on the geomancer's further advice, for the layout to be re-orientated by no more than a few feet here and as much there so as to alter the direction in which the houses faced. This request was complied with—though it meant re-pegging and some delay—because it was important not to give cause for trouble when it came to removal time that might further affect the engineering schedule. In any case it was clear that it was a matter of importance to the villagers.[13]

I encountered other examples of opposition allegedly based on *feng shui* during my five years as district officer (south) in connection with the opening of jeep tracks over hilly ground near villages, various road works, and the construction of catchwaters for the Shek Pik water scheme on Lantau Island. I also recall a number of objections to the grant of prospecting and mining licences at various places in the district. With regard to mining in China proper, William F. Collins states in his *Mineral Enterprise in China*: "In view of the obstructionism wielded by geomancers, it is not surprising that the work of mining on a large scale has, from the earliest time, been impossible for individuals and only practicable by the state".[14] He speaks of "unending obstruction to railway and mining development under the Manchu regime" and opines that *feng shui* had until 1912 as legal a status as "ancient lights" in British law.

Some difficulties with *feng shui* I cannot now recall in detail. There was, I am sure, frequent preoccupation with these matters locally in the early days. I saw nothing of this, being an occasional visitor to the valley from my office in Kowloon, whereas the District Office field staff must have encountered it often, usually in the form of grumbling from the villagers. By degrees, however, their will to object was weakened by the sheer inevitability of it all.

Lest you might think that Shek Pik was an extraordinarily sensitive place let me quote from my notes the case of another village on South Lantau where depopulation and voluntary removal from a long settled site took place by degrees early in this century.

The decline of the village is attributed to a temple to the God of War which appears to have been built at the beginning of the 19th century, when it was erected on the advice of a geomancer to give protection against pirates who were the scourge of the area at the time. The story goes that this particular geomancer (an outsider) had no love for the people of Lo Wai and sited the temple in such a way as to cause harm rather than do good. At any rate, the temple was regarded by many villagers as a source of harm, and it was not rebuilt when it became dilapidated in the years before the move.

Late in the century, another geomancer picked on a large boulder outside the walls of Lo Wai as the cause of ill fortune and, on his advice, each family in the village brought a pile of firewood and placed it around the stone. At a given signal this was ignited and the stone was sufficiently heated to explode, as was the intention. However, the ill fortune of the village did not abate and another geomancer was consulted by the elders. This man gave his opinion that the first geomancer had been mistaken but added, with a deprecatory air, that it was too late to do anything about it now. When pressed to give an opinion, he said he thought that a sixty-year cycle of bad luck would give way to a period of new prosperity.

I hope I have said enough to indicate the degree of belief in *feng shui* among village communities on Lantau in recent years and the extent to which they were prepared to act upon it themselves and to expect others to respect their beliefs.

15

Feng Shui and Road Works at Tong Fuk Village, South Lantau, in 1958

That feng shui *was and is the cause of much difficulty and misunderstanding is a fact of life all too familiar to administrators in the New Territories and urban Hong Kong. Here James focuses on one small settlement and a series of events which led to or arose from* feng shui *disputes. He reports his own irritation when trying to deal with such problems, but there is a sub-text which reveals that he does not subscribe to the cynical view that dismisses the subject as merely a ploy to extract money from the authorities. His views are further highlighted in the annex to this chapter, which provides additional details concerning one of his experiences.*

In my memoir of government service, *Friends and Teachers, Hong Kong and its People 1953–1987*, I recounted the periodic confrontations with the villagers of Shek Pik over the drillings and soil excavations needed to establish the viability of the proposed design for the dam, along with the similar difficulties experienced later on, during construction

* Originally published in *JHKBRAS* 1999–2000, Vol. 39, pp. 225–259.

work on the reservoir, its access roads, and catchwaters. Bringing obstruction and delays, the local people's opposition stemmed from their strongly rooted belief in geomancy, or *feng shui*, and in the adverse effects for man and beast certain in their minds following any tampering with the landscape.

Similar problems were also encountered in adjoining old villages during the extension of the South Lantau Road to the reservoir site. Five miles of new motor road were required, and the line passed through several settlements. There were difficulties with the villagers at each of these places, particularly at Tong Fuk Village, to which at one point I and my land staff had to make frequent visits because of the villagers' continual interference with the contractor's workmen on site, regardless of promises made and assurances given.

Needless to say, the appearance of Tong Fuk Village today, with its array of smart "Spanish Villa" type houses, restaurants, and shops bears no resemblance to its former self. In 1958, every house was old and built in the traditional architectural style, occupied by humans or livestock, or used for storage, and all its inhabitants were engaged in agricultural work, mainly in raising the two annual rice crops on which they depended for subsistence.

Getting to Tong Fuk at that time was a slow business. After taking a scheduled ferry from Hong Kong and travelling along the new South Lantau Road to the road-end at Cheung Sha, half the distance to Shek Pik, we had to walk along old country paths and ford large and small streams. One of the stream courses was wide and boulder-strewn, and crossing it in full flood after heavy rain, as well as several smaller ones, was guaranteed to give one a thorough soaking. However, being young and active, and in high spirits, we thought nothing of it. In fact, I enjoyed it! Nonetheless, when visits were so time-consuming and there was plenty of work to do in the office and elsewhere in the district, the need to go out so frequently in that short time was not appreciated.

On this occasion, local opposition was centred on one especially sensitive spot, where the villagers insisted that rock and boulders be broken up by hand instead of being removed by blasting with explosives. My reluctant acquiescence made the District Office unpopular with the government engineers from the Roads Office, who thought we were pandering to the villagers. So it might have seemed, but there was otherwise certain to be a conflict with people who were quite numerous, united in their opposition, and capable of taking the law into their own hands, not omitting sabotage of contractors' equipment and installations. In this respect, they were no different from the majority of New Territories villagers of the day.

To run such a risk was not advisable in circumstances where both the senior police and civil authorities were based in Kowloon, several hours' journey from the site. Violent confrontations would not have been acceptable to my seniors; and in any case, it was part of my personal responsibility as district officer to avoid that kind of thing. Moreover, further and more prolonged delays would be certain to ensue. This was unthinkable.

Our experiences on this particular occasion were certainly rather trying. The full story, on two and a half closely typed pages, was contained in a minute to the district commissioner dated 27 May 1958. I do not know whether it has survived in the Public Records Office of Hong Kong, but fortunately I kept the copy on which this account is based.

As I reported to Mr (later Sir Ronald) Holmes, the villagers had changed their mind about letting the work proceed "a further three times" in the four days that had elapsed since my first visit to the village to deal with the difficulty. Enquiring into the reason for the renewed stoppage of work, I was told by the village representative and elders that the deities in the two local temples had been consulted, and that the propitious day for resuming work would be a day or two later.

Frustration and annoyance are writ large in my report:

> I replied that I certainly hoped this would be the case since I was not possessed of second sight sufficient to enable me to know what they had *not* said to me on my first visit [about the need to consult the deities].
>
> Nor could I be expected to understand their frequent changes of mind during the past two weeks when they would say one thing to Mr Abbas [the land bailiff], quite another thing to the contractor and the Roads Engineers when they wished to resume work, and yet another to myself; not once but several times all round.
>
> Masters indeed in the art of creating confusion and uncertainty!

On this visit, it had soon appeared that the villagers had thought up extra reasons for causing us delays. On our way to Tong Fuk, passing by the South Lantau Rural Committee's office at Pui O, we had been given letters from the village representatives of Tong Fuk and the adjoining village of Shui Hau, making some additional points in the ongoing dialogue with the District Office. These concerned what I described as "an entirely new series of complaints" about the crop compensation to be paid in connection with the engineering works, the villagers professing themselves worried about the compensation schedules and about rates of compensation:

> All this, mark you [as I told the commissioner], though in their large-scale airing of perplexities on the Monday not one word of these matters had been breathed, saving only their concern about [the date of] payment.

Viewed in retrospect, my report is rather ponderously expressed. My prose tended to be "turgid", the boss once told me, and I resolved to do better. However, turgidity could not disguise my exasperation, which still shines through the contents of the report, loud and clear, thirty-nine years on.

Looking back on that period, my exasperation was increased by the fact that I had to put up with (and more to the point, get over) similar difficulties with village communities in other parts of a far-flung district, from Sai Kung in the east to Lantau in the west. With road works going on at each extremity, I was sometimes rushing here and there, backwards and forwards, dealing with problems of this kind.

There were special difficulties in getting the new extension to the Sai Kung road past Tso Wo Hang Village in regard to the road line, and also with cutting stone at a certain spot where, my notebook says, "the Village Representative was to say when work could start". It sticks in my memory that none of the other villages affected by construction work for the new road were as temperamental or difficult as this one, and this seems to be borne out by my notes.[1]

As I have written elsewhere, patience and resolution, leavened with an essential saving dash of humour, were qualities in demand on these occasions. The Tong Fuk episode was certainly one of those in which all of these had to be deployed by my land staff and myself. Mercifully, an antidote was sometimes supplied by the villagers themselves, since their ill humour could be turned to laughter by themselves or even by one of us, and lead to an amicable compromise. When all is said and done, it was fun! What was equally important for me as a young district officer was that in Ronnie Holmes I had an ideal boss, someone who was immensely able, perceptive, and compassionate, and a good Chinese linguist, a man who could see both sides of any situation. Also, he would welcome me home for a drink, listen and laugh at my predicaments, and (usually) endorse my solutions to them.

By way of a postscript to the above, we were by no means finished with Tong Fuk. Later, there were similar difficulties over blasting during construction of the access road to the new catchwaters above the village. This time, perhaps owing to location, the position must have been deemed more serious for the villagers, and at their request expenditure for a protective ritual was approved to take care of village concerns.

A year or two after these events, the catchwaters for the new reservoir were under construction behind Tong Fuk Village. Mindful of the need to provide water for irrigation, pipes and taps were installed to ensure this supply before any flow from the stream courses was taken for the reservoir. However, displeased with the whole business, some villagers sawed off the heads of the water taps, so as to maintain a continuous flow of water to their fields, as hitherto, freeing themselves from irksome constraints and engineers' decisions as to what constituted "enough".

Chapter 15 Annex
A Ceremony to Propitiate the Gods at Tong Fuk, Lantau, 1958

This account by James appeared in the "Notes and Queries" section of JHKBRAS Vol. 5, 1965, pp. 122–124, and provides some of the descriptive detail for the occasion mentioned above.

In the course of opening new roads and other works developers usually run up against *feng shui*. This happened recently at Tong Fuk, a multi-clan Cantonese village with a population of 198 at the 1911 Census. Its present population is about the same number.

In 1958, the scheme to build a new reservoir at Shek Pik was confirmed and work went ahead on the dam and associated works. Behind Tong Fuk there were catch-waters for which an access road had to be constructed to the west of the village. This led to difficulties with the villagers, because in *feng shui* ideology the place was held to be the seat of the White Tiger. They therefore requested a ceremony—known locally as a *tun fu*—to propitiate the gods and spirits who would, as they thought, be aroused by digging earth and blasting stones in this particular spot.

Precedents were cited by the village elders. They said they had carried out such a ceremony thirty-five years before, following several unexpected deaths in the village. The inhabitants had worshipped at the Hung Shing Temple on the beach nearby, praying for the removal of the malignant influence. It transpired that a villager had cut stone from the same spot to build a house. The elders then invited a Taoist priest—a Hakka—to come from one of the neighbouring villages to carry out the propitiatory observances usually made under such circumstances. They said that a similar ceremony had also been conducted twenty years before in the adjoining Cantonese village of Shui Hau, this time by a priest engaged from the urban area. Deaths had also occurred there and had been traced to one of the villagers having constructed a cow-shed in front of his house on ground with *feng shui* properties.

Returning to the 1958 case, the elders proposed to call in the services of the nephew of the priest who had supervised the ceremony thirty-five years before. He was a man of forty years of age who had followed in his uncle's footsteps. Such persons are known locally as *feng shui sin sang*.

This ceremony was supposed to cause considerable inconvenience for the villagers, in theory if not in practice. One week of vegetable diet was obligatory for all and there was also a three-day prohibition on entering and leaving the village—that is, if the ceremony was to realise its full value. This meant that no cows could be grazed or grass or firewood cut on the hills, nor, presumably, could men go out to work in the fields.

For the priest the ceremony was to involve two days' work: on the first day of the ceremony and on the last. On the opening day, I was told, he comes to the village and prepares various pots. Into each pot he puts five bamboo sticks. Each of these sticks carries an inscription which he writes especially for the occasion and is then covered with lucky red joss paper. Before being placed in the pot the sticks are dipped in the blood of a live chicken. The priest decides how many pots are required. The pots then have to be placed at various spots in the works area and must stay there until the operations have been completed. A procession of village people follows the priest to the places he has chosen to put the pots. With them they bring various articles for worshipping, such as candles, incense sticks, joss paper, and offerings of drinks and food, including chicken and roast pork as well as fresh and preserved fruits.

Since the object of the ceremony is to appease all the gods who may conceivably be offended by the proposed works, especially the local earth-gods, the priest issues a general invitation to them to partake of the offerings. In so doing, it is hoped to dispose them favourably towards the village despite the offence given by the works. It is interesting that the ceremony is not connected with either of the two village temples, one of them dedicated to Hung Shing and the other inside the village wall dedicated to Kwan Tai, the god of war and agriculture. It only takes place on the hills and not inside these temples, although the effigies of the gods are taken around with the procession which deposits each of the pots.

On the conclusion of the engineering works, the priest returns to the village. On this day, each family prepares a plate of roast pork and chicken to thank the gods for turning evil away from them during the period of the work. The priest visits all the pots in turn, dismisses the gods, and burns the pots.

This account is taken from my notes of what was supposed to happen during the ceremony. Pressure of other duties prevented me from seeing the ceremonies on either day—but I did see some of the pots in their appointed stations!

A similar ceremony took place at Keung Shan near Tai O in 1960 during the construction of another road, and I know of two such cases from the Sai Kung District in 1960–1961.

16

The New Territories Twenty Years Ago:
From the Notebooks of a District Officer

*It is more than a full traditional sixty-year cycle since the time
that James is remembering here. In those days there was still
quite a lot of rice being grown in the New Territories, village
houses were almost universally one storey high, with a cockloft
reached by a wooden ladder, dark with no windows, without
running water, without electric power to run refrigerators or
air-conditioners (though a few homes had electric light). The
Kowloon-Canton Railway was single-tracked—one train each
way each hour drawn by diesel locomotives—and it terminated at
the Star Ferry pier, where the harbour was dominated by the Peak
and not yet by high-rise buildings. It was the start of "interesting
times" for the leased territory, and it is fortunate that a few
historians like James have recorded and striven to understand
details of a way of life that now often seems quaint, but which
was real and serious for those living it.*

* Originally published in *The Hong Kong Journal of Public Administration* 1980,
Vol. 2, No. 1, pp. 60–70.

Twenty years ago, I was district officer looking after the islands and the Sai Kung and Clear Water Bay parts of the mainland New Territories. Twenty years is not a very long time but, in Hong Kong where, over that period, the population has doubled and the economy and the physical environment have dramatically changed, these years marked the end of an era. What, in many places, was still the traditional style of rural life—described by the Hong Kong agronomist C.T. Wong as "the quasi-subsistence pattern of padi cultivation"[1]—was to be exchanged for another. This article describes the work of one part of the administration at a time and place when change was scarcely visible and improvements to rural life and livelihood were its main concern, at any rate in the Southern District. Thus, this article is primarily concerned with my first year in office rather than with the changes which were effected later in my term.

The responsibilities and duties of the New Territories Administration in the 1950s are well described in the *Annual Departmental Report for 1957–1958*:

> The District Administration stands in particularly close relationship to the people of the New Territories, and thus finds itself concerned intimately in the activities of other departments even though these departments are not directly responsible to the District Administration. Close co-ordination is therefore maintained with the Police Force, and the Agricultural, Co-operative and Marketing, Education, Medical, Public Works, Social Welfare, Labour and Mines Departments.

District officers were empowered to hold Small Debts Courts and Land Courts under the New Territories Ordinance and were available for emergency duty as magistrates. They also performed "the customary duties of the office in settling family disputes and personal troubles". They had wide responsibilities for the occupation of Crown land under lease or permit whether for agricultural, building, or other purposes and collected revenue on numerous permits and licences as well as Crown Rent on all private land.

The District Office (South) was located in a large temporary building in the grounds of the South Kowloon Court on Gascoigne Road, Kowloon. The area it administered was sizeable, containing over one hundred and fifty villages and hamlets and several market towns and boat people's anchorages, but its staff was small. Like the other district officers of the time, during my first year of office I was "assisted by two or more Land Bailiffs, and a small clerical and outdoor staff numbering less than thirty in all". The district was still mostly rural, and the post-war influx of population from China not much in evidence, save in the main centres like Cheung Chau, Peng Chau, and Sai Kung where many semi-urban squatters in wooden huts were to be found and in a few villages near to main roads or, in the somewhat unusual case of Mui Wo on Lantau, near a ferry service to Hong Kong, where immigrant vegetable growers were cultivating some of the land. Otherwise the villages were still compact social entities, long settled and closely knit, relying heavily on twice yearly rice cultivation and other traditional rural occupations, and on remittances[2] from menfolk absent abroad or serving at sea.

The district officer's post was my first appointment in the Hong Kong civil service after a year's language study at the University of Hong Kong.[3] I knew nothing of the background beyond what I had read in the *Hong Kong Annual Reports* and seen on occasional trips to the New Territories. During my first official visits to the small towns and villages of the district in late 1957 and early 1958, I kept a notebook in which, seeking to gain a basic knowledge quickly, I recorded the answers to my various questions and the points which village leaders and the kaifong committees of the market towns brought to my notice. It was necessary to do this: there was no handbook on the district to consult. True, there were the office files[4] and my predecessor's handover notes, but the first did not tell me what I wanted to know and the other, as was usual, covered current assignments and their associated problems and did not provide the detailed record of the district and its people that I needed.

My notebooks helped to fill out the picture. Reading them today, and recalling that I was new to the New Territories and Chinese rural life, it is hardly surprising to find that they are strong on some aspects of village society, and aggravatingly scanty or lacking on others. I seem to have been interested, from the start, in the basic details of each settlement. Population figures, family history, farming livelihood, and education fill the pages. It is interesting that the village representatives and elders were able to respond in detail to my questions, so that records were seemingly being kept, if only to satisfy a succession of curious incumbents of my post. Some useful facts are, however, available, especially those relating to schooling or the lack of it, the numbers of cattle and pigs, information on rice and vegetable land under cultivation by villagers, and facts on rice exchange[5] and general livelihood.

Other items of interest that appear in the notebooks are requests made on behalf of individual villagers. The District Office was conceived (and saw itself) as benevolent and paternalistic. In 1961–1962, the district commissioner of the New Territories, for example, could still write: "It is still the custom that a villager wishing to approach the Government on almost any matter should normally do so through the District Office." The New Territories Administration was encouraged in this attitude by the common people who from time immemorial have addressed the local officials as *fu mou kwun* ("father and mother officials"). Indeed, when invoked, the phrase is often to be construed as a form of reproach. It was a tacit reminder that such officers were expected always to look after ordinary folk, and had a duty to do so. Thus, villagers were not slow to put forward applications for employment or introductions to employment, for post-registrations of birth to facilitate application for travel documents to go abroad,[6] for medical treatment, and also for financial assistance in maintaining daily livelihood, such as that provided through the generosity of the Kadoorie Agricultural Aid Association.[7]

There are occasional glimpses of the pre-war work and travel of New Territories inhabitants, people who had worked overseas, and ex-sailors, old men who brought out their service papers, and, in one case, I recall, a membership card for the Liverpool branch of the Hakka General Association. A plausible piece of evidence for wide travel by local men was the broken early Victorian railway mug, from its design no later than the 1840s, which I picked up one day beside a well in Tai Long in East Sai Kung. There were many elderly seamen to be found in the villages of Tung Chung, Lamma, and Sai Kung and one old man even had general service medals from the First World War. Their sons and nephews were sometimes still at sea as stokers and seamen, but the demand for their services had declined.

Another link with the pre-war period was the recruitment of villagers for overseas contracts by large concerns. Many men continued to go to the British Phosphate Commission on Nauru and Ocean Islands in the Western Pacific in the early post-war years, and there was, during my own term, a recruitment drive by an agent of the Royal Borneo Company. Whilst the conditions of this type of employment were probably better than they were pre-war[8] it still conjured up bitterness for older men: "selling little pigs" (*mai chue tsai*) was the common term used, and a venerable one as it was common Cantonese parlance by at least the 1860s.

Again in retrospect, it was of interest that, on my brief attachment to the District Office (South) when I first arrived in Hong Kong in 1956, I went with the district officer to Tung Chung and Sha Lo Wan, on North Lantau, in connection with sand-taking by government contractors from the Sand Monopoly. This undertaking, regulated by permit, was usually cleared in advance with the district officer and the elders, to try to save trouble later, but it often gave rise to a crop of difficulties. Villagers feared that the cultivated land behind the beaches would be damaged by the sea if protective sand bars were removed. This was a long-standing problem. One of my predecessors as district officer (south), Mr Walter Schofield, mentions it in his reminiscences of the 1920s, and things had changed very little in this respect in my time. Sand-taking from remote beaches continued throughout my service as district officer, and when the time came to get sand from local beaches for construction work on the Shek Pik reservoir in 1960, I recall difficulties with villagers on South Lantau for the same reasons.

The time needed for travel was a prominent feature of District Office life in those days, as it always had been for the villagers. There was still a lack of roads in the late 1950s and it was necessary to use footpaths along the shore and over the hills to get to and from the remoter settlements of the mainland districts and the larger islands. The greater part of the extensive eastern section of the district was entirely without roads. For military reasons, the Clearwater Bay Road was still closed to the public from its junction with Hiram's Highway, and the latter, an improved version of a military road constructed by the wartime Japanese authorities to link Kowloon with Sai Kung, was only open to one-way traffic with a twenty to thirty minute wait if one missed the "in" times. This had the effect of making Sai Kung Market seem remote from Kowloon. Beyond the market, one relied on village tracks and coastal junk service to travel. On Lantau, the short stretch of road from Mui Wo to Cheung Sha had just been built, but most of the island was still inaccessible save by boat or on foot. Thus, the existence of local ferries or *kai tou* as they are still called, was vital to those many areas not served by the ferry company. Concern for their safety and the prevention of overloading were the constant preoccupation of the Marine Police, Marine Department, and the District Office and my notebooks contain information and proposals for more piers and improvements to existing ones.

The Second World War and Japanese Occupation had not been long over, and the effects of impoverishment and disease during the Occupation continued in some places. There were villages that had been burnt, and others were still in a depressed and poor state. The peace had not brought law and order immediately. There had been some post-war insecurity, leading to authorised possession of rifles in places far from police stations, and the issue of alarm rockets to summon help when needed. The former had been withdrawn by police before the time of my visits, but villagers were still anxious to have them restored. There were also reminders of courage and disaster during the Occupation years. A few elders produced certificates of merit for services rendered to Allied military personnel, and in some villages, widows and orphans whose husbands and fathers had been killed or had died in prison during the Occupation were receiving monthly payments from the Hong Kong War Memorial Trust, paid by my staff on their field visits to the district.

The health of the villagers was not very good. Many children had boils and sores, and requests for referrals for medical treatment were regularly encountered on visits to villages at that time, especially in the outlying areas. This situation can, in large measure, be attributed to work in the padi-fields, the habit of going barefoot in the warmer months, and to the water supply. Villagers then relied heavily on streams and wells. It was not until I got to know Tsuen Wan in these past few years that I was informed how dangerous reliance on stream water could be, since in passing under shrubs of the *strychnos* family it could take in their poisonous seeds; and stagnant parts of streams helped to breed malarial mosquitoes. Thus, until the days of a piped water supply, the provision of well-constructed, covered wells was a major prerequisite of health.

The government's Local Public Works Scheme, for which funds were greatly increased in the late 1950s, therefore, concentrated on the improvement of village water supplies and on bettering communications.[9] In villages with alert leaders, much of the Local Public Works effort was devoted to the provision of a piped supply taken from the upper reaches of the nearest stream. This was the best that could be done at the time, since the circumstances of most villages in the Southern District, isolated and often remote, made the provision of a piped supply difficult enough, and a mains supply mostly impossible.

The situation was yet more critical in the towns of the area, especially those where both a permanent and visiting boat population competed for the available supply. Islands like Peng Chau and Cheung Chau were still reliant on water boats in most winter seasons in the early 1950s. I recall that the latter got its first cross-sea supply from a small reservoir on Lantau in 1955, and that the Tai O community also got its first reservoir supply in 1958, having previously relied on piped stream water.

Community organisation was well established in the villages and leadership was effective. Wherever I went there were village representatives, and in the smaller towns a committee of shopkeepers and businessmen managed the community, acted as its intermediaries with government officials, and often organised basic services not otherwise provided. Many of these men were clearly knowledgeable, experienced, and able, especially the men at the top of the kaifong committees in the market towns. In the villages they usually emerged without election, and where elections were held, mainly in the market towns, the same men often held office for years on end. Such had been the case since the earliest years of British management in the New Territories, and long before.

It was these men who took offers of cement, sand, aggregate, piping, old railway tracks, and steel bars from the District Office and the Kadoorie Agricultural Aid Association. With the help of village labour, they converted them into a steadily growing list of all-weather paths and tracks, small bridges, irrigation bunds, water intakes, and the like. Some places, notably Cheung Chau, took more than others since we gave where there was a will and capacity to act.

Education was another field for joint efforts. By 1957, when I joined the District Office, most villages of any size had primary schools built under a vigorous programme that in ten years had taken education from being, in most places, a burden on the village elders and the richer families and placed it on a subsidised basis in simple but suitably designed and constructed buildings built to a standard plan. The new schools were financed largely by the government which paid half the capital (or more) and much of the recurrent cost. When a village wished to obtain a subsidy to build a school the application had to be considered in the first instance by the district officer and the Education Department. If the subsidy was approved, the district officer supervised the calling for tenders, the signing of the contract, and the payment of the government subsidy. By the late 1950s, my task was mainly to fill in the gaps. We had then to persuade the smaller villages to share schools, and the bigger ones to seek replacements for older buildings of their own financing that were now too small to meet the growing pressure for universal primary education. In either case, finding a suitable site was a major requirement, and where two or more villages were involved, it was sometimes difficult to secure agreement.[10]

The village programme was matched by a similar one for boat people's children, through the Fish Marketing Organization which financed and ran these schools.[11] Unlike those in the villages, it could not be said that they brought a primary education to most children of school age. In those days many families still lived and worked at sea in their boats, and were often based on small anchorages where there were not enough children to justify the expense of constructing a school. Where the landsmen had a school of their own, it was seldom that a boat family could get a boy into school, even if they were willing to pay and spare a needed pair of extra hands. At Shek Pik, for instance, where a small number of boats had been locally based for generations, the elders said that no Tanka children were admitted to school right up to 1959. Only in major local anchorages like Tai O and Cheung Chau, where the Fish Marketing Organisation's own or assisted schools were located, was this then possible.

Another concern for improvement in rural conditions took the form of requests for electricity. The remoter parts of Sai Kung and most of Lantau and the other islands were still reliant on kerosene for lighting. I recall writing to the electricity company about the villages close to Sai Kung and going to see the general manager on the subject, to be met on one occasion with reports of theft of expensive copper cable (by persons unknown) that temporarily put paid to progress. It was not until the early 1960s that significant steps were taken to improve the situation with the introduction of a rural electrification scheme by the China Light and Power Company. I have no figures for the Southern District, but the Annual Departmental Reports show that one hundred villages were included in the first stage in 1961–1962, 140 in the second stage in 1962–1963, and 131 in the third stage.[12]

The marine police were, as they had been earlier in the District Administration's history, an indispensable adjunct to the District Office and the people it looked after. The police launches and the men of the land stations under the charge of the Marine Division, were the friends and helpers of both. They were always invited to rural functions and it paid a new district officer to be friends with them because of their contacts and influence with the rural people and their leaders, and sometimes it secured a timely lift to or from a remote spot. The villagers and fishermen could be sure of their help in time of personal need or natural disaster, and in the days before local hospitals and helicopters, accident cases and complicated deliveries were often rushed to urban hospitals by police launch. This history of co-operation was a valuable asset to the government, and I was very conscious of its importance.

This review of the work of the District Office in the 1950s, the communities it served, and the joint endeavours with other departments has much in common with the pre-war reports of the district officers (north and south). For myself, however, it is the human element, the recollected words, the remembered faces, which give life to the printed record. I have many memories of my time as district officer (south) of the beauty and peace of the countryside, the bustle of busy anchorages, the gaiety of the regular festival times, the friendliness of many people in remote places and what I came to recognise as, for all its occasional difficulties, the privilege of working with and for the Chinese rural population.

Notes

Introduction

1. See Bibliography, pp. 383–396.

2. The name was changed to *Journal of the Royal Asiatic Society Hong Kong Branch* in 2003, and to *Journal of the Royal Asiatic Society Hong Kong* in 2016.

3. Royal Asiatic Society Hong Kong, G.P.O. Box 3864, Hong Kong.

4. See Chapter 2, paragraphs 1 and 3.

5. See Chapter 11, note 13.

Biography

1. Data taken from *Hong Kong Annual Report for 1956* (Hong Kong, The Government Press, 1957).

2. Stephen Selby, "Everything you wanted to know about Chinese customary law (but were afraid to ask)", *Hong Kong Law Journal* 1991, Vol. 21, pp. 45–77.

3. James Hayes, *Friends & Teachers: Hong Kong and its People, 1953–87* (Hong Kong, Hong Kong University Press, 1996), p. 270.

4. May Holdsworth, quoting James, *Foreign Devils: Expatriates in Hong Kong* (Hong Kong, Oxford University Press, 2002), p. 274.

5. Elizabeth Sinn, "The Study of Local History in Hong Kong: A Review", *JHKBRAS* 1994, Vol. 34, p. 152.

6. James Hayes, "Profile", *The Asian Arts Society of Australia Review* 1993, Vol. 2, No. 2, p. 7.

7. James Hayes, "The Royal Asiatic Society Hong Kong Branch", *JHKBRAS* 1994, Vol. 34, p. 130.

8. Hayes, "Profile", *op. cit.*, p. 7.

9. Citation (for James's honorary doctorate), awarded October 1992 by the University of Hong Kong.

10. Holdsworth, quoting James, *Foreign Devils, op. cit.,* p. 196.

11. Hayes, "Profile", *op. cit.,* p. 7.

12. *South China Morning Post,* "Planners aim for tech hubs amid the farms", 22 June 2018, A4.

13. Citation, *op. cit.,* p. 7.

14. Robert Nield lived in Hong Kong for almost 40 years before moving to Canada in 2019. He joined the Royal Asiatic Society in 1988, serving as its President from 2005 to 2011. Retiring as a partner in a major accounting practice in 2002, he pursued an interest in the history of China's former treaty ports. He has published two books on the subject—*The China Coast* (2010) and *China's Foreign Places* (2015)—and has contributed to a number of other publications. In 2019, he gained an MPhil degree from the University of Bristol.

Chapter 1

1. James Haldane Stewart Lockhart (1858–1937) became a Hong Kong Cadet in 1878. He was appointed colonial secretary in 1895, the post he held at the time of his Report (8 October 1898).

2. Extracts from the Report are given between pages 181–209 of Papers laid before the Legislative Council of Hong Kong 1899 (Hong Kong, Government Printer, 1900).

3. See *Eastern No. 88 Correspondence relating to the Kowloon-Canton Railway* (London, Colonial Office), 1907.

4. See the tablet at the Chow-Wong School in Kam Tin.

5. I have compared customary deeds of sale and mortgage from the New Territories between the years 1898 and 1958 with those cited by R.F. Johnston for Wei Hai Wei in Shandong and find that they invariably follow the same form (see his *Lion and Dragon in Northern China,* London 1910, pp. 144–145).

These deeds are known as "white deeds" as in Qing times and had not been put through the formal process of registration in the District Office which would turn them into legal documents; or, as formerly in Qing days, in the magistrate's *yamen* when they became "red deeds".

6. This is recognised in the provisions of the New Territories Ordinance where the registration of a *tso* manager in the Land Office is obligatory. A change of manager can only be secured after the vacancy has been filled at a properly advertised clan meeting and notices of selection, posted by the District Office, have expired without objection. Prospective sales of *tso* land have to be reported to the District Office and advertised, again without objection, before a sale is allowed. This authority, with powers of discretion, was given to the district officer to help preserve the traditional way of managing land within the clan, and to provide a cheap and impartial arbiter in case of dispute.

7. The text of a stone tablet outside the Tin Hau Temple at Kat O uses similar picturesque phraseology. Contrasting their sorry lot with the power of the *yamen* officials the villagers had written in a petition to the viceroy: "We, civilians, whose lives are cheap as ants … who are we to start a lawsuit against the district *yamen*'s worms?"

8. Lockhart does not mention officers other than those at the two Lantau forts, but there was another fort on Lantau at Fan Lau, still standing, which may or may not have been occupied at this time. There were also posts on Lamma and Cheung Chau officered by *sun tei kwun* ("guardpost officers"). There must also have been *sun tei kwun* in the mainland part of the district. As far as I know they were military officers of low rank who controlled ten or twenty men in an out-station.

9. The councils of the *tung* may not have existed in the remoter and more sparsely populated areas. On Lamma, for instance, the village elders appear to have administered summary justice individually and not in unison. There were four *tung* in any district: north, south, east, and west.

10. J. Dyer Ball, *The Chinese at Home* (London, Religious Tract Society 1912) p. 189.

11. Sir Robert Douglas, *Society in China* (London, Ward, Lock & Co. 1901) pp. 120–121.

12. These affected the coastal and riverine regions of Guangdong. The pirates spent a considerable time on and near Lantau, which must have suffered from their depredations. The clan record of the Ho family of San Tsuen, Pui O, on the south side of the island mentions pirate raids and a decision to fortify the village with walls which can still be seen, with several embrasures for canon. Piracy continued until a much later date. The Cheung Chau police station was attacked and burnt in 1912, necessitating its removal and enlargement, one of the Cheung Chau ferries was pirated in 1923, and in 1925 a band of sixty robbers from the Delta entered Tai O by way of Po Chue Tam creek, killed a

woman, and made off with young men and a fair amount of booty without any difficulty. The Police Station is situated at the other end of the town and knew nothing of the attack until it was over. See *Administrative Reports, District Officer, New Territories* 1912, 1923, and 1925.

13. Salt was smuggled into China from Tai O as the government monopoly and price ring made it profitable to do so. In 1905, Governor Sir Mathew Nathan reported rice smuggling from Shum Chun and Deep Bay into Hong Kong. The export of rice from China was forbidden, and checked by the Imperial Maritime Customs.

14. *Foreign Office Trade Report No. 1778* for 1895.

15. *Foreign Office Trade Report No. 1983* for 1896.

16. *Foreign Office Trade Report for Canton No. 1606* for 1894.

17. These feuds, often of long standing, persist today. See paragraphs 77–79 of Mr K.M.A. Barnett's annual administrative report for 1955–1956 as district commissioner of the New Territories for a good instance of traditional hostility. See also the reports for 1957–1958 and 1958–1959.

18. According to J. Dyer Ball's *Things Chinese*, published in 1903, "a dreadful internecine strife, in which 150,000, at least, perished, took place between the Hakkas and the Punteis in the southwestern districts of the Canton province, from 1864 to 1866 AD, and arms and even armed steamers, were procured from Hong Kong by both parties".

19. The semi-official District History is also known as the *Xin'an (San On) Gazetteer*. Two editions, dated 1688 and 1819, are extant, containing rich detail on the history, geography, economy, and government of the district, with sections on natural and man-made disasters (*choi*), lists of examination passers, local products, customs, biographies of officials, village names, military strength, landscape features, distinguished natives, and so on. For details, see Peter Y.L. Ng, *New Peace County: a Chinese Gazetteer of the Hong Kong Region* (Hong Kong 1983).

20. These extracts are from stones located in places as far apart in the New Territories as Kat O, Yuen Long, Peng Chau, and Tung Chung.

21. An ancestral temple is not open to the public, it is for the private use of the clan, for whom alone it has any meaning. Most villages of any age and consequence have ancestral temples, and in multi-clan villages there are sometimes several. As a general rule they are small buildings, but the major clans have constructed large high spacious buildings with several courtyards and side rooms. Among the largest in the New Territories are the ancestral temples of branches of the Tang clan at Ping Shan and Ha Tsuen near Yuen Long. These are fine and impressive buildings but are not, unfortunately, kept in good repair. Much of the

opposition to the British troops in 1898 was planned in the ancestral hall at Ha Tsuen. Beside the Ping Shan hall there is a school/library building, now used as a private residence.

22. The reason is always said to be lack of funds, though I suspect a lack of leadership is also a prime factor. The clan usually waits until something is seriously wrong, by which time it is often too late: a storm completes the ruination. There seems to be some truth in this as I have found newly built ancestral halls in several villages (e.g., the Cheung clan ancestral hall at Pui O which was rebuilt in 1960 on a new site, the old one having been in ruins for twenty years).

23. Clan worship at the graves still goes on, but is much more informal than in 1898. A retired schoolmaster from Fui Sha Wai, who was born in 1894, tells me that when he was a boy the ceremony was taken very seriously. Everyone wore the long robe, elders were carried to the grave in sedan chairs, and male members of the clan were drawn up in ranks by generations and worshipped in strict seniority, under the direction of a master of ceremonies.

24. For some, these obligations could mean up to several days' travel for the whole family. I am told by a man born on Lamma in 1883 that his grandfather settled on the island from his native village in the Lam Tsuen Valley in the present Tai Po District. Ever since he can remember, and until old age interfered with visits a few years ago, he has gone back to his ancestral village at least three times a year, as dictated by custom. For the first twenty-five years there was no railway and his family used to go by junk to Kowloon and walk the rest of the way, children included. Others went further afield. The chairman of the Peng Chau Rural Committee told me that his family went regularly to their ancestral village in Po On, north of the border, and were interrupted in their journeys first by the Japanese and later by the Communists. He has been twice since 1942, and an uncle has been visiting fairly regularly up to last year. His family travelled to Kowloon by junk, then used the railway and had a long walk from Shenzhen Market to their native village.

25. They were full at any time. In *Correspondence relating to Kowloon-Canton Railway*, there is an interesting count of travel on the Shenzhen ferries and the colony's border roads taken on 11 and 12 December 1905. The first was a market day, when the count of persons, with and without goods, roughly doubled the figures for the second, or ordinary day. On the two main ferries, for instance, the count on 11 December was "with goods 1,126, without goods 1,379" and on the Shum Chun-Sha Tau Kok road "521 and 1,302". On the day following, the figures were "468 and 1,124" and "158 and 550", respectively. At New Year and the two grave festivals the number must have been very much increased.

Chapter 2

1. The New Territories were ceded by the Convention of Peking signed on 9 June 1898, but were discussed until March 1899, and some hostilities took place in March and April of that year when the Hong Kong government took possession.

2. This figure is given on p. 145 in *Sessional Papers for 1906* included in "New Territories: Land Court, Report on Work from 1900 to 1905". The figure is for all private plots demarcated, and includes house lots as well as agricultural land. The land-mass measures 56.62 square miles.

3. See "Extracts from a Report by Mr Stewart Lockhart on the Extension of the Colony of Hong Kong" in *The Hong Kong Government Gazette*, 8 April 1899, p. 541.

4. It is indeed a worthy subject for future research, and one which is becoming more attainable through the growing body of local genealogies being established in the Chinese Library of the University of Hong Kong and in the Library of the Genealogical Society of Utah. It is unfortunate that in an otherwise comprehensive coverage, the Lantau villages to which the leaders who will be discussed in the coming pages belonged, together with many others on the island, were not included in the listings of committee members.

5. See Chapter 12 of this collection for interest rates of fifty percent of principal per annum, simple interest, from a money-lending *tong* in the same area.

6. Ho Ping-ti, "The Examination System and Social Mobility in China, 1368–1911" in *Proceedings of the Annual Spring Meeting of the American Ethnological Society*, 1959, pp. 60–65.

7. I have written more about him in *The Hong Kong Region*, 1977, pp. 134–137 and 230.

8. The Kungs were in their sixth generation at Yi O in Kung Fong Chai's time, according to his spirit tablet, which gives a likely arrival date of about 1725, and certainly in the first half of the eighteenth century.

9. One *tso* of the Kung lineage held 1.84 acres of fields at Shek Pik, and two Kung *tongs* held 3.41 acres at Yi O. Kung Fong Chai himself was the registered owner of another 3.41 acres there. All these Kung estates had been built up by purchase or through giving mortgages.

10. The Census of 1911 lists 5,694 Cantonese and only 944 Hakka out of an estimated land population of 6,710. I have my suspicions about the Hakka figure but have not yet counter-checked by other means. For alleged Cantonese domination, see *inter alia* G.N. Orme, "Report on the New Territories 1899–1912" in *Sessional Papers for 1912*, where he says that the imposition of British rule led to the freeing of the neighbours ("especially the Hakkas") of many Punti villages from "squeezes" formerly levied on them.

11. In 1911, the market town of Tai O had a land population of 2,248 and a boat population of at least several thousands, many of whom lived in mat-huts over the water and were therefore part of the settled population; *Sessional Papers for 1911: 103*. There were said to be eight schools in the Tai O District at a New Territories School Census in April 1912, with an average attendance of 21. See Appendix G to Orme's Report in *Sessional Papers for 1912: 63*.

12. The schedule of ownership attached to the Block Crown Leases for 1898 New Territories villages shows this general pattern of peasant ownership very clearly. They are kept in the District Offices of the New Territories Administration.

13. Stewart Lockhart, "Report on the New Territory for the Year 1901", *Sessional Papers for 1902*, p. 4.

14. *Hong Kong Government Gazette*, 8 April 1899, p. 546, under the heading "Local Government in the Villages". The information about the number of *tung* per administrative district comes from a former magistrate mentioned in the same text. He was in charge of Junzhou and Anlufu in Hubei for part of the first decade of the twentieth century.

15. In 1962, there were six lineages in Sha Lo Wan, and at least one of the earliest to settle had died out. At Yi O, there were four lineages: beside the Kungs, there were the Chengs (the first to arrive), the Tans, and the Lams, and two other lineages registered there in the Block Crown Lease had died out or gone away by 1962. In the Pui O group, there were as many as eleven lineages. For details see my *The Hong Kong Region*, p. 131.

16. In Sha Lo Wan, the Chans had an ancestral hall, and so did the Lis and the Mans, but I was told in 1962 that the last belonged only to the branch descended from one of the brothers who founded their family. It was built, or repaired, at the beginning of the 1850s. The Chan hall must have been built not long after, judging by its fittings and appearance. All four lineages at Yi O had ancestral halls. At Pui O, the Cheungs had four halls and the other large lineages one each.

17. Some of these lineages must have had great wealth, or at least been prepared to spend a great deal on the outward manifestations of the ancestral and lineage cult. A Lo lineage of Xinhui lists sixty-seven ancestral halls (*chi tong*) and two *ka miu* (family temples) in its 1947 revision of the lineage genealogy. The Chiu lineage of Taishan lists fifty *chi tong* in the 1902 revision of its family record, and another large lineage from the same district, the Kwan, includes no fewer than 105 *chi tong* in its eighteen-volume genealogy published in 1894. These are merely examples from printed Guangdong works collected in Hong Kong in the past few years, and now located in the libraries of the Genealogical Society of Utah and the University of Hong Kong.

18. See Maurice Freedman, *Lineage Organization in Southeastern China* (London 1958) pp. 131–133.

19. My small lineages are, in size alone, at one end of Freedman's model, and show something of the "rudimentary genealogical segmentation, low level of corporate property and a lack of social differentiation" that he postulates for model "A". However, they also show a far greater degree of organisation and integration than is allowed for, bearing out his observation that "these polar models may never have had their analogies in reality". Freedman himself, of course, was aware of this possibility showing itself when a body of good historical and field material on southeast China had been built up, and was typically provocative in suggesting such a model in the presence of slender material on the basis that "it may explain much because it knows so little" (Freedman 1958, p. 133).

20. Paradoxically, it also caused disputes within lineages where conduct was thought to be unethical or to harm others, by intent or accident. Such cases are plentiful in local families of long settlement.

21. When the new Civil and Criminal Codes were being elaborated by the Kuomintang government, the place of local custom in the matter of irrigation and other rights was much in its mind. The Introduction to the Civil Code states (p. xvi): "It was the wish of the Commission that many traditional agricultural customs, which had grown out of the geographical or economic conditions of particular districts, should be preserved so long as they were not contrary to public or good morals." It is noteworthy that the articles of the Civil Code in this and related matters allow for local custom to have precedence over the Code if there be a difference in provision.

Chapter 3

1. See Peter Wesley-Smith, *Unequal Treaty 1898–1997, China, Great Britain and Hong Kong's New Territories* (Hong Kong 1980).

2. For a convenient account of the place of customary law in late imperial China, see Sybille van der Sprenkel, *Legal Institutions in Manchu China* (London 1962) Chapter 8.

3. For what was available for guidance and local use, see my "Specialists and Written Materials in the Village World" in David Johnson, Andrew J. Nathan, and Evelyn S. Rawski (eds.), *Popular Culture in Late Imperial China* (Berkeley 1985) pp. 75–111.

4. The periodic rituals that have for so long played an important part in New Territories village life are described in Chapter 12 of my *The Rural Communities of Hong Kong* (Hong Kong 1983) pp. 156–164.

5. This promised, and still does, "once in a lifetime" grants on concessionary terms to male villagers over eighteen to permit village extension within agreed

boundaries. The grants can be by conversion of an applicant's agricultural land, or by sale of Crown land, both to be located in the village environs.

6. The "Letter of Exchange" was an alternative to cash compensation introduced by the Hong Kong government in about 1960 to facilitate development works. Cash compensation for agricultural land did not take into account any potential development value, and this led to strong objections and representations from the Rural Consultative Council (the Heung Yee Kuk). By introducing the Letter of Exchange, which could be sold to developers for a higher sum than the cash compensation, the authorities secured the cooperation of the reluctant village landowners. The purchasers could assemble portfolios of Letters that could be used to obtain sites for commercial, industrial, or residential development. Later, when the number of Letters on the market was high, values were ascribed to Letters of different age and they could be used in Crown land auctions. No more Letters were issued after 1983, by which time compensation rates for agricultural land had been revised upwards under a zoning scheme, revised at regular intervals.

7. I have written more on this subject in "Government and Village: Reactions to Modern Development by Long-settled Communities in the New Territories of Hong Kong", in Hugh Baker and Stephan Feuchtwang (eds.), *An Old State in New Settings: Studies in the Social Anthropology of China in Memory of Maurice Freedman* (Oxford 1991) pp. 107–136.

8. Shek Pik is, or rather was before a large reservoir was constructed there between 1958 and 1963 by the Hong Kong government of the day, a widely cultivated, long-settled valley situated on Southwest Lantau Island. It rose gently back from sea level, and nestled under the 933 metre high Lantau Peak. Two old farming villages and one hamlet had occupied the site for centuries. Early in the construction work on the reservoir, their 260 residents were moved to new homes built for them elsewhere from public funds. According to local elders, the population of the valley had been much larger in the nineteenth century and had been reducing in number for many decades due to endemic disease, to such an extent that the inhabitants of the larger village had abandoned it in the 1930s, in favour of a site deemed more favourable for human habitation lower down the valley.

When I first met the people of the valley in 1957, they were without benefit of piped water, electric light, or any other modern amenities, as was still the case in much of the then-rural New Territories. In keeping with their unchanged surroundings and traditional life style, their villagers and leaders were still adhering to an accumulation of norms that catered for the entire range of daily life and activities in the two villages from cradle to grave and beyond. Among them were the family matters that are the subject of the case studies in this annex. Administered in the villages by family/lineage elders and village headmen under what must surely, in that time and place, have been viewed by all those involved as long-standing local customary laws, usages, and practices, their subject matter was also to be found in the Qing Code, and when still under Chinese imperial rule up to 1898 had been liable to adjudication by the district magistrate.

Under British rule, district officers, as magistrates, would also have handled civil cases if taken to them. However, we have no means of knowing if any were, because all pre-December 1941 New Territories office files were lost or destroyed during the Japanese Occupation, whilst very few cases went on appeal from the district officers, either pre- or post-war up to 1961, when their legal function was transferred to the professional judiciary.

9. This all took place *after* the mass updating and re-registration of titles to property had been carried out by the government. Irrespective of the terms of the agreement, the government was obliged to re-house all registered inhabitants of the valley displaced by the reservoir. Being now *persona non grata*, the couple could not be re-housed in the Shek Pik New Village in Tsuen Wan and had to be accommodated elsewhere. The daughter married a fellow villager in the normal way and received the cash compensation as her dowry, but the estate (the housing entitlement) could not revert to the lineage. The unique circumstances of the time had dictated part of the outcome.

10. Whereas, pre-war, the village schoolmaster had mostly been a native from Shek Pik or from a local village, as engaged by the village elders, in the post-war years when the Education Department of the Hong Kong Government supplied the teacher, he was more likely, as here, to be an outsider.

11. This term, translated here as "will", does not have the legal force implicit in English common law.

12. To *kowtow* is to kneel and touch the ground with the forehead in worship or submission as part of Chinese custom.

13. In actual fact, marrying into the wife's family (uxorilocal marriage) was found in many parts of China; see, for example, Arthur P. Wolf and Chieh-shan Huang, *Marriage and Adoption in China, 1845–1945* (Stanford 1980), especially Chapter 7 which is devoted to uxorilocal marriage, Chapter 9 which discusses the incidence of marriage types, and the detailed index at p. 425. In regard to Hong Kong, it is of interest that James and Rubie Watson found that the two major lineages of their New Territories studies seriously discouraged or banned outright deviations from what they took to be the "proper" mode of life, prohibiting customs such as uxorilocal marriage, widow remarriage, minor ("little daughter-in-law") marriage, and non-agnatic adoption, in contrast to the position in these lineages' dependent or "satellite" villages where they found high rates of such practices; see James L. Watson and Rubie S. Watson, *Village Life in Hong Kong: Politics, Gender, and Ritual in the New Territories* (Hong Kong 2004) p. 445.

14. Their text is reproduced and translated in Patrick H. Hase, *Custom, Land, and Livelihood in Rural South China* (Hong Kong 2013) pp. 367–374, with related remarks at pp. 125–126. The explanations and conclusions reflect our joint consultations on the subject with the help of such genealogical aids as were available.

15. Explaining why the two copies were made in the same hand and on similar paper as the appeal, as ascertained at our request by Professor Peter Lam, former director of the Art Museum, The Chinese University of Hong Kong.

16. See Kathryn Bernhardt and Philip C.C. Huang (eds.), *Civil Law in Qing and Republican China* (Stanford 1994) pp. 4–6.

17. Chan Yam-chun was the eldest son of the founder of the clan in the village. The two brothers were descended from the third son of Yam-chun.

18. See, for example, Ann Waltner's study of adoption in the late Ming and early Qing, *Getting an Heir: Adoption and the Construction of Kinship in Late Imperial China* (Honolulu 1990). For adoption in a New Territories lineage, see James L. Watson, "Agnates and Outsiders in a Chinese Lineage", in Watson and Watson (eds.), *Village Life in Hong Kong*, pp. 53–71.

19. The spoken term *chiu long yap she* used by the headmen and lineage elders for the first of these arrangements is rendered *chiu sai yap mun* in the written document, and is more precise.

20. They were among a group of papers given to me unexpectedly by an elder of the Chi lineage just before the villagers of Shek Pik removed to their new homes in 1960. The group included some forty-five original land deeds from the nineteenth century together with other miscellaneous documents relating to land, and the papers of a late nineteenth century money loan association. All are now held by the Art Museum of The Chinese University of Hong Kong. The texts of many of the land deeds were reproduced and translated by Dr Patrick H. Hase in his book, *Custom, Land, and Livelihood in Rural South China*.

21. Using case studies from Qing Taiwan and Republican North China, this subject is dealt with exhaustively in David Wakefield's *Fenjia: Household Division and Inheritance in Qing and Republican China* (Honolulu 1998).

22. This feature, and the capabilities that made it possible, was the theme of my doctoral thesis of 1975, later published under the title *The Hong Kong Region 1850–1911* (Connecticut 1977).

23. See, for example, Philip C.C. Huang, *Civil Justice in China: Representation and Practice in the Qing* (Stanford 1996).

24. I seem to recall a similar position within the main *tso* of So Uk Village, Cheung Sha Wan, New Kowloon, as stated to me in interviews from the early 1960s.

Chapter 4

1. Ann Arbor, University of Michigan Press, 1979.

2. See my *The Hong Kong Region 1850–1911* (Connecticut 1977) pp. 9–16, 181–193, and *The Rural Communities of Hong Kong* (Hong Kong 1983) pp. 3–15.

3. Ramon Myers, "Taiwan under Ch'ing Imperial Rule 1684–1895: the Traditional Society" in *Journal of the Institute of Chinese Studies of the Chinese University of Hong Kong* 5, No. 2, p. 422.

4. G. William Skinner (ed.), *The City in Late Imperial China* (Stanford 1977) pp. 264–265. He writes of "the wide range of occupational specialists (traders, artisans, religious specialists, scribes, pettifoggers, geomancers and so forth) many of them literate, who were neither of the peasantry nor yet of the elite, who existed in the villages and the standard marketing communities". The point is, he concludes, "that the little local tradition of the standard marketing community was essentially the only culture of the peasant".

5. An overall statement on literacy in the New Territories is given in the *1911 Hong Kong Census Report* at p. 103. It lists 7,006 males "able to read and write" and 4,646 unable to do so in the Southern District and 14,162 and 11,517, respectively, in the Northern District.

6. It is unlikely to have changed much from the traditional form of education reported in the village schools of Hong Kong in the early 1860s by the colonial educational authorities of the day, and distinctly undervalued by them. "To the majority the language is an end, not a means. It is an accomplishment which may be very showy in the eyes of the Chinese themselves, but which contains within it none of the elements of the useful or of the improving." The masters, too, came in for comment. "A Chinese Schoolmaster is truly an object of pity. He is simply a drudge. He is expected to be in his desk by six o'clock in the morning and to continue there till nearly the same hour in the evening—always ready to teach his scholars when it suits their parents' convenience to send them to him." *Hong Kong Government Gazette* Vol. XII, 24 March 1866 (GN 43). For evidence of little change after fifty years, see the report on rural schools in the New Territories in *Hong Kong Administrative Reports 1913*, pp. N 13–17. Both the earlier and later reports show bias against the traditional education system.

7. *Elementary Studies*, a popular anthology of easy pieces for the classroom.

8. See Hayes 1977, *op. cit.*, p. 47. Several elders have been most emphatic on this point, including the man from Sha Kok Mei mentioned in the text who said that the Sai Kung people had to take their land deeds to the Lung Chun School in Kowloon City where the British assistant land officer had set up an office and that they were not returned.

9. They relate to ownership of the surface, whereas registrations in government offices related only to the sub-soil which at Shek Pik was owned by a family from Guangzhou. The division was recognised in Qing law. See pp. 46–47 "Fond et Surface" of Guy Boulais, *Manuel du Code Chinois* (Shanghai 1924). Penalties for non-registration of sale attached only to the sub-soil.

10. From Shek Sun (Fan Lau) to the west, Shui Hau and Tong Fuk to the east, Tung Chung to the north, and Yee O to the northwest. For these places, see *A Gazetteer of Place Names in Hong Kong, Kowloon and the New Territories* (Hong Kong 1960).

11. Copies of manuscript genealogies of the Chan lineages of Chung Mei, San Uk Tsuen, and Yim Tin Kok, and of the Tang lineage of Tai Wong Ha, Lam Tin, and Lo Uk are kept in the Chinese Library at The University of Hong Kong.

12. These forms for conveyances on sale, mortgage, Chinese mortgage, assignment, etc. can be found with the consolidated New Territories Land Ordinance, No. 34 of 1910 in Chaloner Grenville Alabaster's edition of the *Laws of Hong Kong*, 3 Vols. (Hong Kong, Government Printers, 1913).

13. The Japanese drew up printed forms for entering and registering transactions on land. Specimens can be found in Series No. 1, HKRS 116 in the Public Records Office of Hong Kong, serials 4, pp. 65–66.

14. The Annual Reports of the District Commissioner, New Territories for 1948–1949, 1949–1950, and 1950–1951 mention the disputes over transactions entered into during the Japanese Occupation. There was a large number of such cases to be settled, both by conciliation and by the district officer sitting as assistant land officer, and I recall some even from my time as district officer (south/islands) in 1957–1962. There are eighty-nine case files from the Southern District dealing with these transactions, mostly in respect of land in New Kowloon, Tsuen Wan, Sai Kung, and Hang Hau in the Public Records Office of Hong Kong, Series No. 1, HKRS 116.

15. Delays in registering succession, or change of ownership, were common in country districts pre-war; see *Hong Kong Administrative Reports 1912*, District Officer, New Territories, p. 11. I well remember the red-faced indignation of one villager when presented with a bill for charges on this account when bringing land titles up to date prior to effecting compensation for land required for the Shek Pik reservoir scheme in 1958. In one celebrated case where a valley on Hong Kong Island was needed for redevelopment, the titles to property had become so muddled by neglect, some "innocent forgery" by persons with customary but unregistered title, and some fraudulence, that a special ordinance was required. The Crown Lands Resumption (Chai Wan) Ordinance, 1959 provided for a Land Tribunal to settle ownership. Out of 739 village lots, police enquiries found 272 (thirty-seven percent) with good title

and 467 (sixty-three percent) with defective title (enclosures 104 with 105 in Lands and Surveys Office file 6/HCA/63, Part II).

16. See my "Popular Culture in late Ch'ing China; Printed Books and Manuscripts from the Hong Kong Region", in *Journal of the Hong Kong Library Association* 1983, No. 7, pp. 57–72, especially pp. 59–63.

17. This is my experience from research and collecting in the New Territories, and it is certainly borne out by the results recorded by the Oral History Project at the Chinese University of Hong Kong. Many bound volumes of photo-copied material of all kinds from the Project are held in the City Hall Library, Hong Kong.

18. See my *The Rural Communities of Hong Kong, op. cit.*, pp. 275–276, quoting from the *South China Morning Post* for 2 June 1982.

19. See Hayes 1977, pp. 121–122; and David Faure, "Saikung, the Making of the District and its Expansion during World War II", *JHKBRAS* 1982, Vol. 22, pp. 161–216.

Chapter 5

1. I saw her traditional square of red cloth on which, as usual, was written the date and hour-cycle of birth of herself, her husband, and all her children.

2. G.B. Endacott, *A History of Hong Kong* (London 1958) and his more recent *Government and People in Hong Kong* (Hong Kong 1964) have gone into the official side of managing the local Chinese population, but so far as I know no detailed work on the individual villages of Hong Kong Island has been attempted, at any rate in a western language.

3. See the brief mention in the useful "Note on the Island of Hong Kong" by A.R. Johnston, HM Deputy Superintendent of Trade, first published in the *London Geographical Journal*, Vol. XIV and reprinted in the *Hong Kong Almanack and Directory* for 1846.

4. The family graves indicate their long settlement at Tai Tam Tuk. It may also be deduced from the land records, which give no names, that the Chans and Yaus may have been there too in 1841.

5. Genealogical records are still kept by clans in old villages in Hong Kong and the New Territories, though in many cases they are bare recitals of family descent and dates of births and deaths.

6. See Mr Chadwick, *Reports on the Sanitary Conditions of Hong Kong*, Eastern No. 38, printed for the use of the Colonial Office in November 1882, p. 43.

7. From various pieces of information, it may be deduced that the village was probably either Pokfulam or Tai Tam Tuk.

8. The original (about 1841) registered holdings of the village, *in toto*, are listed at pp. 40–41 in the appendix to the *Report from the Hong Kong Land Commission of 1886–87*. There are also Village Rent Rolls from 1856 onwards whose value is limited by the fact that they give numbers and rents for houses and the corresponding agricultural holdings but provide no names or areas — though they do show that most villagers must have been peasant proprietors living in their own houses and cultivating their own land. The first registered holdings show that a population known to be around fifty persons relied upon 115,500 square feet of agricultural land (approximately 2.65 acres). By the time of the Land Report in 1887, a greatly increased amount of land is said to have been cultivated (equivalent to sixteen acres) and it is specifically stated that none of this land was in the occupation of licensed or unlicensed squatters. Yet the agricultural yields for padi and vegetables are very low by comparison with the returns of adjacent areas. The figures given in the *Hong Kong Hansard: Session 1914*, p. 51 show that in 1914 the villagers were compensated for approximately 6.6 acres.

9. The villagers also kept bees. The house in which Mrs Chung lived had three of the usual cylindrical rattan basket hives hanging under its eaves. G.N. Orme, "Report on the New Territories 1899–1912", in *Sessional Papers for 1912* says that "the honey is sold almost entirely to the local chemists, by whom it is utilized as medicine".

10. See *Hong Kong Annual Report for 1938* (London 1939) p. 59. [Editor's note: cwt. = hundredweight = 112 lbs.]

11. The land population of Shau Kei Wan was 1,355 and the boat population 2,102 in December 1858 (see the Census Returns in the *Hong Kong Government Gazette* for 5 March 1859). Numbers rose steadily. In 1911, the land population was 11,727 and the boat population was 6,440. See *Sessional Papers for 1911*.

12. There were no periodic market days in Shau Kei Wan from 1900–1914, nor apparently previously either. Every day was a business day, probably because of the presence of a large fishing population.

13. For this god, see V.R. Burkhardt, *Chinese Creeds and Customs* (Hong Kong 1958) Vol. III, pp. 105–107.

14. See E.T.C. Werner, *A Dictionary of Chinese Mythology* (Shanghai 1932) pp. 412–415 under *She Chi*.

15. It would be more correct to say that they were always at Tai Tam Tuk during the main typhoon season from the fifth to the eighth lunar month of every year, fishing the surrounding waters for the rest of the year.

16. The boat people only fished in the surrounding area and generally did not go any distance from their base. Fishing at night with bright lights was common in Hong Kong and Kowloon at this period and before. See J.H. Gray, *China* (London 1878) Vol. 2, p. 295. The Hung Shing god is described in Burkhardt,

op. cit., Vol. III, pp. 106–107. By 1914, fishermen were apparently using dynamite in local waters.

17. Even allowing for the advanced age of my informants it is necessary to emphasise this fact. I have come across the same thing in the New Territories where similar communities of farmers and fishermen have lived side by side for several generations.

18. See my article on Peng Chau Island in the New Territories in *JHKBRAS* 1964, Vol. 4.

19. Miss C.F. Gordon-Cumming, *Wanderings in China* (London 1886) Vol. 1, p. 24.

20. See A.R. Johnston, *op. cit.*, for salting fish at Stanley in 1841–1842.

21. Orme, *op. cit.*, Appendix F, p. 63.

22. Rev. W. Lobscheid, *A Few Notices on the Extent of Chinese Education and the Government Schools of Hong Kong* (Hong Kong 1859) p. 45. I am grateful to Mr J.M. Braga who made this rare book available to me. Rev. Ph. Winnes, writing in the *Report of the Morrison Education Society for 1863–64*, says: "Popular education in this (Xin'an) District ... is, generally speaking, in a deplorable state as regards the Hakkas. We may find small villages in which scarcely *one* person is to be found who can read and write." He attributed this state of affairs to poverty.

23. See Dalrymple, *Observations on the Southern Coasts of China and the Island of Hainan* (London 1806) p. 20.

24. Robert Fortune, *Three Years Wanderings in the Northern Provinces of China* (London 1847) p. 17. He qualifies his remarks slightly, but the substance is as stated.

25. K.S. Mckenzie, *Narrative of the Second Campaign in China* (London 1842) p. 160.

26. For the Chinese and English versions of the proclamation, see Government Notification 41 of 1860 dated 24 March 1860 in the *Hong Kong Government Gazette.*

27. Captain G.G. Loch, *Closing Events of the Campaign in China* (London 1843) p. 21.

28. E.J. Eitel, *Europe in China* (Hong Kong 1895) p. 166, writes: "Yet although this (the *tepo*) system is now officially not recognized and has been replaced by the Registrar General's Office the Chinese secretly adhere to their own system faithfully. The Chinese people in town are at the present day under the sway of their own headmen (the Tungwa Hospital Committee) and the people in the villages are ruled by their elders, as much as ever."

29. The section of the *Blue Books* dealing with the agriculture of the New Territories gives useful figures for produce in respect of areas between 1905–1908, but

thereafter only gives total figures. Moreover, the files of the New Territories District Administration for the period up to 1941 were destroyed during the Japanese Occupation.

30. See, for instance, p. 5 of a *Report on the Sanitary Condition of Hong Kong and Kowloon for 1864* prescribed to both Houses of Parliament by Command of His Majesty in 1865 (Military).

31. See the Harbour Master's Report for 1887 in *Sessional Papers for September 1887–December 1888*, p. 258.

32. This subject is not well-documented nor is very much known of it at the present time. The Tang family, a rich and powerful Cantonese clan whose main estate lay in the present New Territories, were apparently the registered owners of most of the cultivated areas of Hong Kong Island before 1841 (see Sung Hok-pang, "Legends and Stories of the New Territories", Part III, Kam Tin, in *The Hong Kong Naturalist* 1935, Vol. VI, pp. 212–218, and 1937–1938, Vol. VIII, pp. 201–207). Lobscheid, *op. cit.*, p. 36, was told by the headman of a Hong Kong village near Aberdeen in the 1850s that his first ancestor to arrive there (circa 1668) took a lease from a Tang, "the acknowledged owner of the soil". To what extent the Tangs levied legitimate rent charges, or exacted rent for greater areas than they were in fact the proper owners of, is not known but they were seemingly guilty of the latter elsewhere, albeit these charges were inconsiderable.

The Tangs' ownership of land on Hong Kong Island seems to have gone back before the establishment of the Xin'an District in 1573 as in his article quoted above Sung Hok-pang states that the entries were in the land registers of the Dongguan District, which before that date embraced the whole of the later Xin'an District.

Chapter 6

1. Lieutenant Christopher Cradock, R.N. (later Rear-Admiral Sir Christopher Cradock) (1862–1914), *Sporting Notes in the Far East* (London 1889) p. 180.

2. See *Sessional Papers for 1912*, G.N. Orme, "Report on the New Territories, 1899–1912", para. 61 for instances of the havoc these beasts could cause.

3. The survey sheets and schedules for any area, together with the conditions of the grant, are bound together to form what is known as the Block Crown Lease. These are kept in the District Offices of the New Territories Administration.

4. I am sometimes asked to assess the reliability of my informants, bearing in mind their age, village background, and, in particular, the almost total lack of education of the women among them. Whilst these are handicaps, I should

explain that my questions are directed at their personal experience and family knowledge; and whilst it is only right to query the value of oral sources, I must record that I am left with a keen sense of their honesty and their ability to answer accurately if a question is correctly aimed and is within their experience. I am well aware of the potential hazards of the oral approach but have always sought to minimise them by careful questions based on acquired knowledge, checked against the testimony of others, retested at intervals on crucial points, and set against such printed materials as are available. The resulting synthesis, whilst not proof against error, is at least as accurate as I can humanly endeavour.

5. For a description of these groups and their background, see S.F. Balfour, "Hong Kong before the British", *T'ien Hsia* 1941, Vol. 9, pp. 330–352, 440–464. See also my article on Peng Chau, an island on the west side of the New Territories, in *JHKBRAS* 1964, Vol. 4, pp. 71–96.

6. At the 1891 Census, the number of boat people in adjacent British Kowloon was given as 6,447. See *Sessional Papers for 1891*, p. 374.

7. In 1911, the population of the villages with which this article is mainly concerned were: So Uk 157, Pak Shue Leung 151, Sheung Li Uk 68, Cheng Uk 55, and Un Ling Tsai (also known as Tse Uk) 61.

8. A tomb dated to the Later Han dynasty (25–220 AD) was discovered at Li Cheng Uk in 1955 while site formation for a resettlement estate was in progress, and is now preserved as a museum. See *Hong Kong Annual Report for 1955*, pp. 183–189.

9. E.J. Eitel, *Europe in China: the History of Hongkong* (London and Hong Kong 1895) p. 132.

10. Translation of a petition from villagers of Tsuen Wan, New Territories, 1936.

11. Charles Gutzlaff, *Journal of Three Voyages along the Coast of China in 1831, 1832 and 1833* (Second Edition, London n.d.) p. 141.

12. See *China, Imperial Maritime Customs, Decennial Report 1892–1901* (Shanghai 1906) Vol. 2, pp. 202–231.

13. The main trade in these products was done by the Shatin villagers from north of the Kowloon hills who used the track which crossed the So Uk area and in one year (1902) brought over the hills as many as 66,521 loads of firewood, each load being estimated at seventy piculs in weight. See *Sessional Papers for 1903*, p. 209.

14. See W.F. Mayers, N.B. Dennys, and C. King, *The Treaty Ports of China and Japan* (London 1867) pp. 19–23.

15. Eitel, *op. cit.*, p. 380.

16. James Johnston, *China and Formosa, The Story of the Mission of the Presbyterian Church of England* (London 1897) p. 266.

17. See L.C. Arlington, *Through the Dragon's Eyes* (London 1931) pp. 151 ff and W.F. Tyler, *Pulling Strings in China* (London 1929) pp. 31–32.

18. *Sessional Papers for 1900*, p. 278.

19. See T'ung-tsu Ch'u, *Local Government in China under the Ch'ing* (Harvard 1962) pp. 8–13.

20. A good description is given in *Hong Kong Annual Departmental Report by the Social Welfare Officer for the Period 1948–54*, para. 72, which states: "'Kaifong' is a Cantonese expression meaning the residents of a particular street or locality. Under one name or another Kaifong have been known in South China for a very long time, and have existed in parts of Hong Kong throughout the colony's history. At its best, a Kaifong was always something more than a chance collection of neighbours. It had its own spontaneous leaders who for all practical purposes were the Kaifong. Those unofficial Kaifong of old had very practical social responsibilities, which included repairing bridges, mending roads, promoting educational facilities, providing free medical aid for the poor, and providing free coffins for the indigent dead. Another undertaking which fell to the Kaifong was the organisation of holiday festivals on the birthday of a popular local god, and of processions to avert or diminish the effects of a disaster attributable to a god's negligence or anger."

21. Information from elders (born in 1884 and 1885) of Nga Tsin Wai and Sha Po, Kowloon.

22. See note 19 to my "Chinese Temples in the Local Setting" in M. Topley (ed.) *Some Traditional Chinese Ideas and Conceptions in Hong Kong Social Life Today* (Hong Kong 1967).

23. Rev. George Smith, *A Narrative of an Exploratory Visit to each of the Consular Cities of China and to the Islands of Hong Kong and Chusan* (London 1847) p.79.

24. J.L. Buck, *Land Utilization in China* (Shanghai 1937) p. 362, gives 5.9 as the average number of persons per household in the double cropping rice area to which Hong Kong belongs. Buck defines "household" on p. 475 as "all persons living and eating together, including non-relatives, such as hired laborers".

25. See "Report of the Anglo-Chinese Land Commission" attached to a despatch from Robinson to Newcastle, No. 82 dated 30 April 1862 in CO 129/85, Public Record Office, London.

26. *Hongkong Government Gazette*, 1901, pp. 1403–1404.

27. Rents were rendered in kind, in respect of the local measure of land, the *tau chung*. According to information received from old Lantau people the yield of *kuk* ("unhusked rice") about this time was 1–2.5 piculs per crop per *tau chung* depending on the class of land. Allow 2 piculs per crop, 2 crops a year for reasonable land, giving a yield of 4 piculs per *tau chung* per year.

Now, 36.2 mau = 7.5 acres = 45 *tau chung*. For 45 *tau chung*, then, the yield might be 180 piculs, against a stated Tang rent of 40 piculs (i.e., less than 25% of the crop). By comparison, the Lantau figures show an annual rental of 33.3%–50% of the estimated yield. For more information about local measures of land, see W.A. Taylor, "A Note on Land Measurement and Tenant Rentals in Hong Kong", *JHKBRAS* 1966, Vol. 6, pp. 165–171.

28. This subject, which the New Territories Land Court styled "the outstanding feature of the [land] settlement problem" is explained in para. 82 of the paper "New Territories; Land Court, Report on Work from 1900 to 1905" in *Sessional Papers for 1906*, pp. 143–152, which talks of "Tax-collecting families or Tax lords". See also Gompertz, "Report on the work of the Land Court up to the 31 December 1901", in *Sessional Papers for 1902*, pp. 557–564, para. 14, where these persons are referred to as "tax lord" or "rent charge owner" and the Chinese term *leung yuen yan* is used in the Claim Form attached as Appendix B to the Report, p. 564. "Tax lord compensation" is described in para. 21(1) of G.N. Orme's report in *Sessional Papers for 1912*, pp. 43–63.

29. *Sessional Papers for 1900*, p. 241.

30. Sir Henry Blake and Mortimer Menpes, *China* (London 1909) pp. 119–120.

31. Private communication from Mr Walter Schofield, Cadet Officer, Hong Kong, 1911–1938.

32. Writing in 1840, J.F. Davis (Sir John Davis, Bt., Governor of Hong Kong 1844–1848) on p. 332 in his *The Chinese: a General Description of China and its Inhabitants*, (Revised edition, London 1840) refers to the groundnut as being "extensively cultivated for the sake of its oil, the common food of their lamps". By 1900, things had greatly changed. J. Dyer Ball, *Things Chinese* (London 1903) p. 732, writes: "Kerosene is such a bright light compared with pea-nut oil and the tiny wick formerly used so largely."

33. See S. Wells Williams, *Chinese Commercial Guide* (Fifth Edition, Hong Kong 1863) pp. 220–227 and 234–236 for an account of the Chinese passenger trade and the coolie trade principally from Macao and Hong Kong. With regard to the latter, he estimates that "the total number taken from all parts of China, since 1847, can hardly be less than one hundred and fifty thousand persons, of whom not more than a thousand were women and children". He adds: "The free emigration during the same period was more than twice this number."

34. The commemorative tablet in the Tin Hau Temple at Miu Kong, Tsuen Wan is dated the equivalent of 20 January–18 February 1901. The population of Tsuen Wan is given as 3,270 some years later.

35. For a good description of returning emigrants on board a steamer between Penang-Singapore-Hong Kong in 1886, see Rev. J.A. Turner, *Kwang Tung or Five Years in South China* (London 1894), where 281 of them "were perched on the cargo in the holds fore and aft, in the galleyways, and on deck all over the

ship, thick as bees ... their whole luggage consisting of a red blanket, grass or cane mat, fan, umbrella, and a narrow box about eighteen inches long with a curved lid to serve as pillow and money-box".

36. E.J. Hardy, *John Chinaman at Home* (London 1905) pp. 80–81.

37. All my female informants recall the many days they spent gathering fuel on the local hills, doing so "until", as one woman said, "my daughter-in-law took over the job". Villagers continued with this practice after 1898, although the colonial administration planted out the Kowloon Hills and appointed forest guards to curb damage of the plantations by grass and fuel gatherers. The district officer (south) commented: "The conservation of the Government forestry area on the Southern slopes of the Kowloon range causes trouble owing to trespass by grass cutters and cattle from the villages. Some hardship is inevitable since the practice of grass cutting has gone on for centuries and is a chief source of support to many of the villagers who must now give it up or go much further afield for grass." *Hong Kong Administrative Reports*, 1913, Vol. I, 12.

38. Rev. George Smith, p. 78.

39. See article by Sir Robert Ho Tung, at pp. 72–74 of *Hong Kong Centenary Commemorative Talks 1841–1941* (apparently Hong Kong, 1941, being broadcast talks on Hong Kong Studios of ZBW).

40. For a short list of local herbs in use in the New Territories villages at this time see Appendix F of Orme's Report in *Sessional Papers for 1912*.

41. Taken from S.G. Davis, *Hong Kong in its Geographical Setting* (London 1949) p. 14; Kathlean J. Heasman, "Japanese Financial and Economic Measures in Hongkong", *Journal of the Economics Society, The University of Hong Kong* 1957, pp. 65–92, p. 71 considers the population as only 500,000 in March 1945.

42. For a brief account of aspects of the Japanese Occupation in the Southern District of the New Territories, see my article in the *South China Morning Post* for 15 December 1967. See also Heasman, especially pp. 72–76.

43. *Hong Kong Annual Report for 1952* (Hong Kong 1953) p. 27.

44. For the above, see paras. 66–67 of the Commissioner for Resettlement's *Annual Departmental Report, 1954–55*.

Chapter 7

1. R.O. Joliffe in Yi-fang Wu and Frank W. Price (eds.), *China Rediscovers Her West, A Symposium* (London 1942) pp. 20–21. An almost identical view was given nearly forty years before by Arthur H. Smith in *The Uplift of China* (London 1908) pp. 49–50.

2. Gerald F. Winfield, *China: The Land and the People* (New York 1948).

3. See R.O. Joliffe, *op. cit.* See also Gerald F. Winfield, *op. cit.*

4. A useful survey is given in Chapter 4 of Ian Scott's *Political Change and the Crisis of Legitimacy in Hong Kong* (London 1989).

5. Lin Yutang, *My Country and My People* (New York 1938) pp. 203–206.

6. James Hayes, *The Hong Kong Region 1850–1911* and *The Rural Communities of Hong Kong* are directed at this theme. See especially the former at pp. 11–13, and also David Faure, "The Hong Kong History Project", *JHKBRAS* 1987, Vol. 27, p. 261.

7. Personal letter from Walter Schofield (1888–1968) dated 27 July 1962.

8. Coates was district officer between May 1953 and July 1955. [Editor's note: His final report, *Summary Memorandum of the Southern District of the New Territories, 1955*, was not published at the time, but was lodged with the Hong Kong Public Records Office. Much of its content has subsequently appeared in John Strickland (ed.), *Southern District Office Reports* (Hong Kong 2010), *passim.*]

9. Everard Cotes, *Signs and Portents in the Far East* (London 1907) pp. 110–111.

10. Rev. R.H. Graves, *Forty Years in China, or China in Transition* (Baltimore 1895) pp. 1819.

11. Mencius was a Confucian philosopher who lived 372–289 BCE. His principal writings are known simply by the title *Mengzi* (The Master Meng)

12. Stuart Schram, *Mao Tse-tung* (Harmondsworth 1967) p. 21.

13. I am uncertain whether this record was engraved on a stone which has since been lost, or whether it only ever existed on paper. The original is now lost, and I cannot recall who was kind enough to give me a copy.

14. Leonard A. Lyall, *China* (London 1944) p. 99.

15. E.R. Hughes, *The Invasion of China by the Western World* (London 1937) p. 157.

16. *Ibid.*

17. Arthur H. Smith, *China in Convulsion* (Edinburgh 1901) Vol. I, p. 6.

18. *Ibid.* Striving to convey to his readers the power of these teachings, he explained that "the tenets of Confucianism, as a whole and in detail [are] intellectually and psychologically appropriated by the Chinese as on a par with a law of nature".

19. Yang Kang, *Daughter: An Autobiographical Novel* (Beijing 1988) pp. 225–226, and see also pp. 67–74 and 80–83 of this fascinating book.

20. Sir George Thomas Staunton, a member of the 1793–1794 Macartney Embassy, had been at pains to emphasise this in *Ta Tsing Leu Lee: Being the*

Fundamental Laws ... of the Penal Code of China (London 1801) p. 185. For cases translated with commentary, see Derk Bodde and Clarence Morris, *Law in Imperial China, Exemplified by 190 Ch'ing Dynasty Cases* (Philadelphia 1967).

21. Cited in Corinne K. Hoexter, *From Canton to California. The Epic of Chinese Immigration* (New York 1976) p. 136.

22. Dr William Lockhart of the London Missionary Society cites the case of the old scholar who so greatly assisted Dr W.H. Medhurst with his translations and research. See his *The Medical Missionary in China* (London 1861) pp. 21–22, where he states: "He was a living concordance of the entire range of Chinese literature. He could find any passage without hesitation, repeat page after page of most of the works, and could easily take up any citation which had been begun in his hearing, and finish it without hesitation. This is not an uncommon thing amongst the educated Chinese, but this man possessed the faculty in a remarkable degree."

23. Arthur Evans Moule, *The Chinese People, A Handbook on China* (London 1941) p. 262.

24. Some types of literary material found in villages of the Hong Kong region are described in Patrick Hase, "Research Materials for Village Studies", in Alan Birch, Y.C. Jao, and Elizabeth Sinn (eds.), *Research Materials for Hong Kong Studies* (Hong Kong 1984) pp. 31–46, especially pp. 32–37.

25. By great good fortune, some of their libraries have survived and are in safe keeping. One of them came from Hoi Pa Village, Tsuen Wan, and had belonged to the builder of the traditional village house there which is now a listed monument. He lived between 1865 and 1937, and after his return from Jamaica engaged in educational pursuits in a literary club and at the Luen Fong School in Hoi Pa-Kwan Mun Hau. When what had survived of his library was presented to the Urban Services Department in 1982, it consisted of some two hundred books of various kinds, as well as manuscript essays and poems, including some of the famed "eight-legged essays" written in preparation for the imperial examination: all providing valuable documentation for the educational, social and intellectual activities of their period. *South China Morning Post*, 26 May 1982. See also the Chinese press of that date.

26. Francis C.M. Wei, *The Spirit of Chinese Culture* (New York 1947) p. 149.

27. In the Hakka villages of Tsuen Wan, this "animal" was always a unicorn. In Cantonese villages, the lion was usual. However, their purpose and motivation was clearly the same. Informants said there were differences in the dance performances of lions and unicorns: unicorns "crept, bobbed and weaved", whereas lions would "stand up and prance". The musical accompaniment, drums and gongs, was the same, and in the past firecrackers had been an indispensable part of any performance by lions or unicorns.

28. Monlin Chiang, *Tides from the West* (New Haven 1947) p. 9.

29. John Francis Davis, *The Chinese: A General Description of the Empire of China and its Inhabitants* (London 1836) Vol. 2, pp. 29–30.

30. From the memorial tablet to Mr Chan Wing-on, chairman of the Tsuen Wan Rural Committee and chairman of the Eighteenth Term, New Territories Heung Yee Kuk 1950–1952, at the Wing On Pavilion, Fu Yung Shan, Tsuen Wan. See *Annual Department Reports, District Commissioner, New Territories*, 1953–1954, para. 56, and l956–1957, para. 119.

31. From a "Short History of Yeung Uk Village" (in Chinese), published at the time of the village re-siting in 1965 and written by Yeung's eldest grandson, Mr Yeung Cho-ling.

32. 1736: in fact, *ping san* was the first year of Qianlong.

33. Wolfram Eberhard, *Cantonese Ballads (Munich State Library Collection)* (Taipei 1972) p. 2.

34. R. David Arkush, "Orthodoxy and Heterodoxy in Twentieth-Century Chinese Peasant Proverbs", in Kwang-Ching Liu (ed.), *Orthodoxy in Late Imperial China* (Berkeley 1991) pp. 310–335.

35. Helen Kwok and Mimi Chan, *Fossils from a Rural Past: A Study of Extant Cantonese Children's Songs* (Hong Kong 1990) pp. 17, 29.

36. Lucien Bianco, *Origins of the Chinese Revolution 1915–1949* (Stanford 1971) pp. 94–95, 126.

Chapter 8

1. This article is mainly concerned with the land population, but for a good short description of the life, work, and general background of the boat people, see G.N. Orme "Report on the New Territories 1899–1912", in *Sessional Papers for 1912*, pp. 53–55.

2. The number of Cheung Chau shops subscribing to the various schemes recorded on the tablets is as follows: Po On Study (1866) 38; Defence Office (1863–1870) 66; Fong Pin Hospital (1878) 98, and Tin Hau Temple (1879) 125, from the 200 odd mentioned in the Fong Pin preamble.

3. The whole of the island "was adjudged to belong to the Wong family and it is let out to various tenants on lases renewable every five years. All these leases were registered in 1906". *Hong Kong Administrative Report for 1909*, District Office, New Territories. See also G.N. Orme's unfavourable opinion of the initial survey and Crown rent roll; *op. cit.*, p. 46.

4. For example, before its tax-lord rights were extinguished (along with others') by the Hong Kong government after 1898 as "not compatible with the principles

of British administration" (Orme, *op. cit.*, p. 6), the Li kung Yuen Tong of Sha Wan appears to have owned a considerable proportion of all the cultivated land on Lantau Island under an imperial grant made in the Song dynasty (see Lo Hsiang-lin, "The Sung Wang T'ai and the location of the Travelling Courts by the sea-shore in the Last Days of the Sung", *Journal of Oriental Studies III* 1956, No. 2, p. 217). Nineteenth-century land deeds from the village of Shek Pik show that much of the village land paid tax to the Li family, a burden which was passed on to the purchaser when a "sale" took place. It is not known whether this *tong* owned land elsewhere in the present New Territories, but its main estates lay elsewhere. It is curious how the Wong Wai Chak Tong maintained its tax-lord position whilst the Li family's was extinguished.

5. It is a pointer to the island's increasing prosperity, as well as to its favoured geographical situation, that when the Chinese Maritime Customs first began to operate in the Hong Kong region in 1887, they set up a post on Cheung Chau. Old villagers on the Lantau coast opposite Cheung Chau can remember having to pass through the Customs every time they came to the island to buy daily necessities and sell their produce in the market. Available information points to a community which was already well established and prosperous by the Xianfeng reign (1851–1861), which would be rather early for Cheung Chau to owe its rise mainly to Hong Kong. The tablet in the Defence Office mentions that "our forefathers came and lived m Cheung Chau several hundred years ago"; whilst the attention of pirates in the early years of Xianfeng, also mentioned in the tablet, seems more conclusive proof of the island's established prosperity than any other. A spate of repairs and expansion seems to have been going on apace in the Tongzhi period (1862–1875) when most of the island's temples were repaired, the Chu family ancestral hall was enlarged, many old houses were built or reconstructed, and the public buildings erected which these tablets commemorate.

6. Of the shops which contributed to the Po On Study, thirty-six were from Hong Kong, twenty-eight from Peng Chau, and fifteen from Tai O (presumably all or mainly of Dongguan origin); a few outside shops contributed to the Defence Office; but the subscriptions for the Fong Pin Hospital came from a wide area and the list included over twenty shops and forty individual persons and *tongs* from Dongguan, Heshan, Guangzhou, Panyu, Nanhai, Shunde, Macau, and other areas of the province.

7. For mention of these Cheung Chau posts, see the following tablets: salt (Tin Hau and Fong Pin), stamp (Tin Hau and Fong Pin), and Customs (e.g., tax on kerosene) (Fong Pin). There was also a Customs post on Lamma (Fong Pin), and there were various patrol boats (both tablets). The officer in charge of the military post on Cheung Chau is mentioned on the Tin Hau tablet, whilst the Fong Pin tablet lists eight officers of the Dapeng battalion.

8. See Kung-Chuan Hsiao, *Rural China; Imperial Control in the Nineteenth Century* (Seattle 1960) pp. 294–306 for defence organisations in this period.

9. District associations are of considerable antiquity in China and were known in Song times. See J. Gernet, *Daily Life in China on the Eve of the Mongol Invasion 1250–76* (London 1962) p. 222, as well as Y.K. Leong and L.K. Tao, *Village and Town Life in China* (London 1915) pp. 78–79 for "the guild of co-provincials"; and H.B. Morse, *The Gilds of China* (London 1909) pp. 35–48 for the provincial club with a mercantile bias.

10. The manuscript also contains interesting material which illustrates difficulties faced by conscientious managers. For example: "This house was originally the property of X. Unfortunately he was murdered and the body could not be found. His relative Y donated the house to the association. At first no tenant would take it and the fabric deteriorated. In the second year of the Xuantong reign (1911) repairs were suggested, but there were no funds. Loans of five and ten dollars were raised from district members at 1.5 percent interest. I loaned over a hundred dollars interest free, but it was still insufficient, so the association joined a ten dollar (share) money association and drew the necessary balance. The repair then started and the front is now let for $5.50 per month and the rear for $4 per month."

11. In the Crown Rent Rolls, the association is termed *kung sor* in Chinese and "club" in English. An inscription on one of the stone lions outside the Pak Tai Temple, the largest on the island, states that it was donated by the Huizhou and Chaozhou community in 1861. Mr Leung Yau, born on Cheung Chau in 1875, attended the Hui-Chao School in the association's premises for two years (1885–1886).

12. There was also a shrine in the Po On Study. The tablet states that "a small fixture, known as the Tun Sin Temple ('promote charity') has also been placed at one side of the hall, where wooden tablets bearing the names of the organisers are placed in commemoration of their devotion to the cause, irrespective of their parentage and place of origin".

13. The Dongguan Association notebook says that there was a Po On Wui Sor in the Qing dynasty, but since this had always led to confusion their association (the Po On Shue Sat) was renamed the Dongguan Wui Sor in the twelfth year of the Chinese Republic (1923).

14. A tablet (1953) in the Free School says that this institution dates back to 1921 and local leaders say that the *kung sor* was rebuilt then. The old *kung sor* was also known as the *hon kang lau* (watchmen's building).

15. Mr Leung Yau recalls that there were two kaifong junks operating a daily service between Cheung Chau and Hong Kong before the lease (1898). One left Hong Kong (Sai Ying Pun) at 11 a.m. whilst the other left Cheung Chau at the same

time. Both were sailing junks and took three hours to make the journey under good conditions and the whole day if otherwise. They were subscribed and run by a number of local gentlemen for public use. A steam kaifong vessel was bought with public subscriptions in 1910. *Hong Kong Administrative Reports, District Officer, New Territories*, 1910.

16. There are now eight district associations on the island for natives: Po On; Dongguan; Hui-Chao (combined); Siyi ("The Four Towns"); Wuyi ("The Five Towns", i.e., Heshan plus Siyi); Shunde; Zhongshan; and Chaozhou (separate). The last four were formed since 1945. All of these offerred a variety of social, educational, and charitable services to members.

Chapter 9

1. The author remembers with gratitude and affection the many local leaders of the Cheung Chau Kaifong of the 1950s and 1960s, knowledgeable men who gave him their assistance and friendship, especially the late Messrs Chau Li-peng, MBE, JP; Fung Pak-choi, BH; and Kwong Ping-yau, JP.

2. For the Fong Pin Hospital, see Hayes, *The Hong Kong Region 1850–1911* (Hamden 1977) pp. 67–68, 69, and 219 n. 42.

3. Austin Coates recalls the chronic disagreements of the Residents Association in his day: "As one of its older members (in the days when it was a committee of seven) said to me: 'We're not a committee. We're seven warring states.'" *Summary Memorandum of the Southern District of the New Territories, 1955*, p. 42.

4. The census breakdown in 1911 according to "dialect spoken in the home" was Punti, 2,443; Hakka, 564; and Hoklo, 957. See *Sessional Papers for 1911*, p. 103.

5. The major work on Hong Kong's Tanka boat people has been done by Barbara E. Ward. See the collected papers in *Through Other Eyes: Essays in Understanding "Conscious Models" Mostly in Hong Kong* (Hong Kong 1985) and her "Kau Sai, An Unfinished Manuscript", published posthumously in *JHKBRAS* 1985, Vol. 15, pp. 27–118. See also V.R. Burkhardt, "The Water People", in J.M. Braga (comp.), *The Hong Kong Businesses Symposium* (Hong Kong 1957) pp. 271–275.

6. See Hayes, *The Hong Kong Region, op. cit.*, p. 79.

7. This is borne out by the lists of contributions made to the repair of temples in the area; see Hayes, *ibid.*, pp. 97–102 for examples where the boat people's donations were larger than the landsmen's in joint funding exercises. Another

commentary on the situation is that one of my Cheung Chau friends collected Tanka fishermen's money belts, which were waterproof and apparently of a special kind. In 1976, he told me that there were no more to be found in Cheung Chau and that he had to look for them in Macau.

8. The Hoklos had named their association the Wai-Chiu Club, indicating that their fellow countrymen had come from the two prefectures of Chaozhou and Huizhou to the east of Hong Kong. The rest were named either for single counties (Dongguan and Bao'an) or for recognised groups (Si yi, or the Four Counties of Kaiping, Enping, Xinning, and Heshan).

9. Hayes, *The Hong Kong Region, op. cit.*, pp. 69–70 and note 43.

10. In the 1860s–1870s, the local people found it necessary to maintain a "Security Bureau"; see Hayes, *ibid.,* pp. 63 and 68. The full text of the commemorative tablet can be found in *Historical Inscriptions* (Hong Kong 1986) Vol. 1, No. 55. As late as 1912, the police station was attacked by a band of robbers; see G.R. Sayer, *Hong Kong 1862–1919: Years of Discretion* (Hong Kong 1975) p. 113. A fuller account is given in the Captain-General of Police's annual report for 1912 in *Hong Kong Administrative Reports*, 1912.

11. In 1844, in British Hong Kong, it was reported that "a notorious nest of pirates was known to lurk" on the nearby island of Cheung Chau. The pirates had attacked passing British small craft three times in less than three months, and the governor had requested that the British naval commander send a force there to deal with them. By then, these pirates were reported to have 150 fighting boats and to be "in open defiance of the [Chinese] authorities and exacting blackmail from all passing native craft". They had "captured the official in charge of the Bogue, cut off his ears and carried away his seals". From Captain A. Cunynghame's *The Opium War* (Philadelphia 1845) p. 208.

12. Hayes, *The Rural Communities of Hong Kong* (Hong Kong 1983) pp. 26–31, and especially pp. 29–30 for the high rate of piratical activity in local waters reported by the officer in charge of the Chinese Imperial Maritime Customs post on Cheung Chau in 1893–1899.

13. In the nineteenth century, salt and opium were government monopolies, farmed out on tender, which attracted smuggling. The smuggling of banned commodities into China was rife in the early 1950s. Coates, *Summary Memorandum, op. cit.*, p. 119, states: "As occasion offers, Cheung Chau makes large profits out of smuggling ... Cheung Chau smugglers made a great deal of money out of fuel oil smuggling in 1950 and 1951, and many of the large European [style] houses on the [Cheung Chau] Peak rest on kerosene foundations." Some of the gains were also ploughed back into community projects (*Ibid.*, pp. 119–120).

14. Coates, *ibid.*, p. 115.

15. Choi Chi-cheung, "Reinforcing Ethnicity: the Jiao Festival in Cheung Chau", in David Faure and Helen F. Siu (eds.), *Down to Earth: the Territorial Bond in South China*, Stanford 1995, pp. 104–122.

Chapter 10

1. J. Dyer Ball, *Things Chinese* (Fourth Edition, Hong Kong 1903) p. 323.

2. See Kung-Chuan Hsiao, *Rural China: Imperial Control in the Nineteenth Century* (Seattle 1960) p. 421 *seq.*

3. Fighting between Hakka and Punti villagers at Tsim Sha Tsui in the Kowloon peninsula in 1862 is recorded in E.J. Eitel, *Europe in China: The History of Hong Kong from the beginning to the year 1882* (London 1895) p. 380.

4. The meaning of this term is not clear in its Pui O context. In Kowloon and the surrounding district, there were *yeuk* which appear to have been set up by the government at some time previous to the nineteenth century, but in the Taipo District there are also *yeuk* which seem to have been alliances formed between villages for mutual assistance and defence, that is, they have a non-government origin.

5. Confusingly, the main clan is actually two, having been founded by two persons of the same clan name—but allegedly not with a common ancestor—from the same village in Fujian Province. The descendants of these two persons set up their separate ancestral halls which are spoken of locally as "the upper and lower halls" (*sheung ha tong*). One of them has branches in four villages whilst the other has branches in three. They are jointly represented in five of the nine villages of the group. I have, nonetheless, felt justified in describing them as one in view of their same origin, their close links during their long settlement at Pui O, and their united weight of numbers.

6. Apart from the main clan, the other nine removed to Pui O from places within Guangdong Province, the majority coming from the western part of the Xin'an District beyond Nantou, the district city, twenty to thirty miles from Pui O.

7. From a "white deed" dating from that year. This purchase was afterwards registered with the district magistrate, who issued a "red deed" dated fourteen months later.

8. This information was obtained principally from interviews with elders of the area who were born in 1884, 1886, 1888, and 1889.

9. [Editor's note: This is Cheung Kwong-chuen, who figures more largely in Chapter 2 of this collection.]

10. According to the genealogical record they held the titles of *kwun hok shang* (Pupil of the Banner School) and *kwan kung* (Military Merit).

Chapter 11

1. The village of Fan Pui. At the 1911 Census, the population was fifty-nine, and sixty-two at the time of its removal in 1959. All these persons were of the Fung clan.

2. For example, it is interesting to note that the survey and land settlement conducted shortly after the lease of the New Territories in 1898 showed that a large area of former padi fields behind the village had already been abandoned and were not claimed by any of the villagers living at that time.

3. Members of two clans now extinct lived and owned land in the village in 1898. The elders credited them with being earlier settlers than the Tsui family who are the oldest of the present clans.

4. The Tsui clan claim twenty-seven generations in Guangdong and fifteen in Lantau. The first ancestor to live in the province came from a village in the Nanchang District of Jiangxi Province and settled in the Dongguan District. A Tsui of the thirteenth generation removed to Shek Pik and was buried there. The Fung clan of Fan Pui, now in their twenty-second adult generation, arrived there from Ma Tau Wai, Kowloon, in the eleventh generation after their first ancestor had entered Guangdong Province.

5. A map of Lantau and the adjoining area included in Ruan Yuan's *Guangdong Tongzzhi* (*Guangdong Gazetteer*, 1822) describes one of the places on the island as a good hiding place for bad characters, but equally this could apply to the whole island.

6. The old man (apparently born in 1721) who wrote the early record of the Cheung family of Lo Wai, Pui O, emphasises the peace and prosperity of the greater part of his long life until continuous trouble with pirates began in the fifty-third or fifty-fourth year of Qianlong (1789–1790).

7. From a "white deed" dated (the Chinese equivalent of) 17 December 1887.

8. Shek Pik had its own anchorage and its own long-established fishermen. In 1957, there were six families of Tanka fishermen, all from the same clan, whose fathers and grandfathers (at least) had been born in the anchorage.

9. The deeds usually mention the necessity to pay tax to the Li family. The earliest deed with this requirement included is dated 1832 and the latest 1894, which covers the whole period of the deeds I have seen.

10. These leases do not come from Shek Pik but from the adjoining area of Pui O about six miles to the east. They are dated 1728 and 1807.

11. In Shek Pik Village, the Tsui, Cheung, and Chi family *tsos* held 1.1, 0.39, and 0.04 acres of agricultural land in 1898. These holdings were still intact in 1959. The Tsui *tso* probably dates from the fifteenth generation, and is therefore three hundred years old. The Fung *tso* in Fan Pui held 0.92 acres in 1898 but this was sold in 1953.

12. The entries in the Block Crown Leases show that 144 individual fields were mortgaged about the time of the lease out of a total of around 4,000 lots.

13. In 1957–1960, there were three *san po tsai* in the village. Two of them had been taken from other clans in the valley and the third came from an immigrant family living in the hills above Tai O. See also Chapter 13 of this collection.

14. In a multi-clan village, the Taoist village temple sometimes assumes a primacy over the ancestral halls in the direction of public affairs. The Hau Wong Temple at Shek Pik was in this position and was endowed with several houses and 1.67 acres of agricultural land in 1898.

15. It was the seat of government in the Xin'an District. As usual, it was a walled city with civil and military officers within its walls and the civilian suburb outside.

16. See "The Pattern of Life in the New Territories in 1898" (reprinted as Chapter 1 of this collection).

17. There are today families of the Tsui clan living in Tai Tei Tong Village, Silver Mine Bay, whilst several families named Chan live in Tung O on South Lamma. Both settlements are multi-clan villages.

Chapter 12

1. [Editor's note: J. Dyer Ball insists that they "seem complicated, but when once understood are simple enough". He then embarks on eight pages of explanation, which some might consider not to be "simple".]

2. See the Hong Kong Government's *Sessional Papers for 1912*.

3. This profusion of media seems to have been general at the time; see Rev. J. MacGowan, *Lights and Shadows of Chinese Life* (Shanghai 1909) pp. 179–180.

Chapter 13

1. E.J. Eitel, *Report 1879*, p. 54.

2. H.A. Giles, *The Civilization of China* (London 1911) p. 98.

3. Hsieh K., *K'ang Lu San Wen Chi* (Taiwan 1962) p. 255.

4. Wang Ying, *The Child Bride* (Beijing 1989) p. 148.

5. I interviewed the elderly former inhabitants of the Shing Mun Valley, who had been resettled elsewhere in 1928 to make room for a reservoir, and their relatives from the Tsuen Wan villages in the last four years. I am greatly

indebted to my friend Yeung Pak-shing, village representative of Yau Kam Tau Village, Tsuen Wan, for his help with these interviews.

6. J.H. Gray, *China* (London 1878) Vol. I, p. 189.

7. G.N. Orme, *Hong Kong Sessional Papers for 1912*, p. 15.

8. R.F. Johnston, *Lion and Dragon in Northern China* (London 1910) p. 203.

9. Guy Boulais, *Manuel du Code Chinois* (Shanghai 1924) p. 258.

10. Chang Chi-Ch'ien, *Enquiry into Hakka Creeds and Customs* (Taipei 1960) pp. 26–27 [in Chinese].

11. Rubie Watson, *Inequality Among Brothers* (Cambridge 1985) p. 120.

12. Marc Van Der Valk, *An Outline of Modern Chinese Family Law* (Beijing 1939) pp. 76–78; also his *Interpretations of the Supreme Court at Peking, Years 1915 and 1916* (Batavia 1949) pp. 101, 167, and 204.

13. One must always be prepared to find the exception from time to time, such is the diversity of the Chinese countryside. In Guangdong, while the transfer of young children was widespread, it was strikingly absent in a few places, as reported by anthropologists. Villagers in the Chashan District of Dongguan belonging to a cluster of three natural villages and two hamlets, with a population of about five thousand, have stated that marriages based on the adoption of a child daughter-in-law never occur, and have never been known to occur in the past. They could not believe that such a practice could be Chinese; see S.H. Potter and J.M. Potter, *China's Peasants: the Anthropology of a Revolution* (Cambridge 1990) p. 207. Janice E. Stockard notes with reservations that the Customs sections of local gazetteers provided little information on minor marriage, but adds that it was not reported from the home areas of her informants; see her *Daughters of the Canton Delta* (Stanford 1989).

14. Hsieh K., *op. cit.*, p. 254.

15. Lou Tzu-k'uang, *Chieh-hun Chih* (Taiwan 1968) p. 17; Chang Chi-Ch'ien, *op. cit.*, p. 17.

16. Little daughters-in-law very definitely thought along the same lines! See Elizabeth L. Johnson, "Song about a small daughter-in-law", in Mary Sheridan and Janet Salaff (eds.), *Lives: Chinese Working Women* (Indiana 1984) p. 91.

17. From Mr Ma On of Pui O, Lantau.

18. Lena Johnston, *China* (London 1922) pp. 24–26.

19. C.M. Reynaud, *Another China* (Dublin 1897) p. 95.

20. A.M. Fielde, *Pagoda Shadows* (Boston 1884) pp. 157–161.

21. *Ibid.*

22. For an account of the village of Ngau Tau Kok, together with the "Four Stone Hills" and their organisation, see my *The Hong Kong Region 1850–1911* (Hamden 1977) pp. 151–162. Some of the men were also itinerant masons.

23. In the case reported by Lena Johnston, *op. cit.*, some little show was also attempted, as explained on p. 26: "When she was 16 she was married. The mother-in-law did not want much expense, but, still, there was a feast, and some new clothes, and for three days she did not need to work."

24. Elizabeth Johnson (*op. cit.*, p. 253) reports a similar case from Kwan Mun Hau Village, Tsuen Wan, also apparently pre-war.

25. Olga Lang, *Chinese Family and Society* (New Haven 1946) p. 127.

26. It is still unclear whether or not horoscopes were exchanged for *san po tsai*, though they probably always were for child betrothal with a view to major marriage.

27. Such a transformation was noted in Zhejiang in the case of girls "purchased for a dollar out of a heathen orphanage as future daughters-in-law. But if the girl grows up well in spite of the inhuman usage, she is married to the son for whom she has been purchased and instantly is treated with consideration in the household, and in due time her own turn arrives to have a daughter-in-law to maltreat in precisely the same manner" (Reynaud, *op. cit.*, p. 95).

28. Confirmed by my wife's mother, for the Guangzhou-Foshan area. Documentary evidence of such recognition is provided by an entry in the genealogy of the Fung clan of Fan Pui. A betrothed girl who died at the age of six in 1903 is entered together with the intended husband and his replacement wife. The girl is categorised as a *sin pui* and the wife, as usual in these records, as a *yuen pui*. This custom is mentioned in an early Protestant missionary work on China; see S. Kidd, *China: or Illustrations of the Symbols, Philosophy, Antiquities etc.* (London 1841) pp. 179–180.

29. J.L. Nevius, *China and the Chinese* (Philadelphia 1882) p. 253.

30. I.T. Headland, *China's New Day* (West Medford 1912) pp. 198–199.

31. R.F. Johnston, *Lion and Dragon in Northern China* (London 1910) p. 208; D.H. Kulp, *Country Life in South China* (New York 1925), pp. 166–186.

32. G. Jamieson, *Chinese Family and Commercial Law* (Shanghai 1921) p. 33.

33. Maurice Freedman cites Van Der Valk on the 1930 compilation of customs published by the Chinese government in connection with legal reform (unfortunately Guangdong is not covered in the survey) in regard to the "outright buying" of wives in some districts, especially in Fujian. He reports of Nan-an in Fujian that the husband, having "paid" for his wife, was entitled by custom to "sell" her to another person, her own family having no right to interfere (*op. cit.*, p. 32).

34. H.D.R. Baker, *Sheung Shui* (London 1968) p. 77.

35. Frances Lee, "The Careers of Village Women", in *Eighth International Symposium on Asian Studies*, Hong Kong 1986, Vol. I.

36. See for instance M. Wolf, "Women and Suicide in China", in M. Wolf and R. Witke (eds.), *Women in Chinese Society* (Stanford 1975) pp. 11–41.

37. G.L. Bendelack, *The City of Rams* (London 1921) pp. 60–61.

38. W.A.P. Martin, *A Cycle of Cathay* (New York 1896) p. 82; E.L. Johnson, "Grieving for the Dead", in J.L. Watson and E.S. Rawski (eds.), *Death Ritual in Late Imperial and Modern China* (Chicago 1988) pp. 35–66.

39. For an account of marriage expenses in Guangdong and Hong Kong, see my *The Rural Communities of Hong Kong* (Hong Kong 1983) pp. 227–230.

40. This is part surmise and part based on the received history of many old settlements like Shek Pik and other places on Lantau where the elders have described the resulting depopulation in graphic terms. I have gone into some of the physical evidence for depopulation in the second half of the nineteenth century in a long note in *Hong Kong Region, op. cit.*, pp. 213–214.

41. Michael Palmer, "Lineage and Urban Development", in Hugh Baker and Stephan Feuchtwang (eds.), *An Old State in New Settings* (Oxford 1991) p. 82.

42. Wives, mothers, and grandmothers were consulted over the sale and mortgage of land, and in some cases their names and fingerprints appear among the persons witnessing nineteenth-century deeds that have survived from Shek Pik. Mothers were often actual parties to the transactions, along with their sons.

43. *Hong Kong Sessional Papers for 1921*, pp. 60–61.

44. The entries for married or widowed persons under fifteen years of age by western reckoning, which produced these figures on "child marriage" for census purposes, by then included married *and* unmarried *san po tsai* living with the boy's parents; Conversation with Mr Benjamin N.H. Mok, ISO, JP, Commissioner for Census and Statistics, 27 June 1990.

45. *Report on the 1961 Census*, Vol. II, pp. LXIV–XLV.

46. See, *inter alia*, Maria Jaschok, *Concubines and Bondservants* (London 1988); Janice Stockard, *op. cit.*; and my "Women and Female Children in Hong Kong and South China to 1949: Documents of Sale and Transfer", in Joseph S.P. Ting and Susanna L.K. Siu (eds), *Collected Essays on Various Historical Materials for Hong Kong Studies* (Hong Kong 1990) pp. 33–47.

47. See Peter Yeungs, "Bibliography of New Territories Historical Literature", *JHKBRAS* 1985, Vol. 25, pp. 192–206. This is described as "a partial bibliography of historical documents collected by the Oral History Project at the Centre for East Asian Studies, Chinese University of Hong Kong, between 1980 and 1982".

48. Some have been translated into English. See, for instance, Wang Ying, *op. cit.*, Beijing 1989; Xiang Hong, *Tales of Hulan River* (translated by H. Goldblatt, Hong Kong 1988); Wu Zuxiang, *Green Bamboo Hermitage* (Beijing 1989).

Chapter 14

1. It is always easy to assert that *feng shui* is merely an excuse for squeezing money out of the government or its contractors and, indeed, anyone with cash to spend on building, but though this is true to the extent that money is paid openly (or privately by a contractor, for whom time is money) it is rarely the case that there is no underlying fear of disturbing the local *feng shui.*

2. Until the first road was built on the island in 1955–1956, some of them had never seen a motor car.

3. For a discussion of *feng shui*, particularly in relation to ancestor worship, see Maurice Freedman, *Chinese Lineage and Society: Fukien and Kwangtung* (London 1966) pp. 118–154.

4. J.L. Nevius in *China and the Chinese* (New York 1872) comments at p. 169: "The advantages expected from the vitalizing influences of such places [i.e., *feng shui* sites] are vigor of body, family prosperity, and success in business, to be enjoyed by those living in close proximity to them; but the blessings which are most prized and sought for are those which result to children in consequence of the bodies of parents being buried in these auspicious spots."

5. Arnold Foster, *Christian Progress in China* (London 1889) p. 87.

6. See the annex to Chapter 15 in this volume.

7. See my "Movement of Villages on Lantau Island for Fung Shui Reasons", *JHKBRAS* 1963, Vol. 3, pp. 143–144.

8. Thomas F. Ryan, *The Story of a Hundred Years, the Pontifical Institute of Foreign Missions (P.I.M.E.) in Hong Kong 1858–1958* (Hong Kong 1959) p. 201.

9. [Editor's note: Elsewhere in his writings James has stressed the role of endemic disease in the long process of depopulation. Most graphic is the comment in his *South China Village Culture* (Hong Kong 2001) pp. 42–43, where he says of Shek Pik: "The population of the villages began to fall from the mid nineteenth century onward. From a claimed peak population of nearly 1,000 ... falling to around 260 (by the mid-twentieth century). There had been no significant removals to other places, and few men had gone to work overseas. The dramatic reduction had been due to repeated epidemics of a disease, unidentified but recorded from elsewhere in the New Territories, in which pig-like bristles and fish-like scales pushed out from the skin and death could follow within several days ... Lacking effective medical remedies and at the mercy of circumstances beyond their control, the villagers concluded that the local *feng shui* had changed for the worse and that the ancestors in their tombs had become malevolent towards the living ... Several lineages consulted geomancers and moved their founding ancestors' graves to other locations, to calm them and restore good fortune to their descendants. Another dug up its first ancestor's grave and placed the burial urn separately in another spot. In yet another, a geomancer had recommended retention of the old location, with adjustments to the orientation of the grave tablet." He adds in a note: "This

disease appears to be within the trichothiodystrophic spectrum of diseases in which scaling of the skin, brittle hair and nails, and sudden hair loss when the temperature exceeds 41°C, all occur during high fever."]

10. This paragraph is based mainly on the oral statements of local people and private land papers of sale and mortgage.

11. There was a severe outbreak of disease (*Haemorrhagic Septicaemia*) among cattle at Shek Pik and the adjoining villages soon after the New Territories were transferred to British rule in 1898; see *Sessional Papers for 1905*, p. 61.

12. *Feng shui* did not relate only to the selection of an auspicious site. Nevius, *op. cit.*, pp. 173–175, describes the *feng shui* of Chinese buildings in respect of the siting of their several parts and the internal disposition of doors and amenities.

13. When the eight Shing Mun villages were removed pre-war for the construction of the Jubilee Reservoir, the Hong Kong government expended $700 to cover "extra travelling expenses in connection with the move and payments to *feng shui* doctors for their services in siting wells and houses". See "Move of the Shing Mun Villages" in *Hong Kong Sessional Papers for 1928*, pp. 21–23.

14. William F. Collins, *Mineral Enterprise in China* (London 1919) pp. 38–44.

Chapter 15

1. See my chapter "The Traditional Background: Hong Kong Villages in the 1950s", in Elizabeth Sinn and Patrick Hase (eds.), *Beyond the Metropolis: Villages in Hong Kong* (Hong Kong 1995).

Chapter 16

1. C.T. Wong, "Uses of Agricultural Land:Some Changes in New Territories Farming Patterns", in D.J. Dwyer (ed.), *The Changing Face of Hong Kong*, HKBRAS 1971, p. 25.

2. New Territories men have long been included among the number of emigrant workers, traditionally remitting money through shops and agencies in Hong Kong and the market towns. After a temporary post-war decline in overseas migration, a very marked increase began in the late 1950s. The *Annual Departmental Report, District Commissioner, New Territories 1961–62* states that an estimated 1,300 Chinese restaurants in Britain were employing more than twenty thousand Hong Kong Chinese, the majority of them from the New Territories. The total remitted income was not known, but the eight New Territories post offices opened by then cashed 109 million dollars in postal and money orders in that year.

3. It was the practice, as far as possible, to provide new Cadet Officers (as Hong Kong Administrative Officers were called between 1862 and 1958) with Chinese language training. During the pre-war period, a two-year stay in Guangzhou was the prevailing arrangement, but unsettled conditions post-war, the change of government in mainland China in 1949, and the heavy demands on the service in the difficult years of large population influx thereafter reduced this to one year at the Chinese language school of the University of Hong Kong.

4. These only covered the period from the post-war military administration on. The pre-war files had, with trifling exceptions, been lost or destroyed during the Japanese Occupation.

5. This was the then common practice whereby families owning or cultivating insufficient land to provide a supply of rice all year round exchanged unhusked rice grains (*kuk*) with a rice shop in their market town for the same weight of imported lower grade husked rice to stretch the amount available for home consumption.

6. New Territories natives born after the Lease of 1898 were British subjects by birth and entitled to Hong Kong passports. The reporting of births (and deaths) was required under the Births and Deaths Registration Ordinance and included a provision for summary conviction and fine in case of failure to do so. This particular ordinance was more honoured in the breach than in observance, and of course lapsed during the Japanese Occupation. Even as late as 1958, I recall that the then district commissioner of the New Territories, Mr K.M.A. Barnett, minuted to me asking why there were so many children in the Clear Water Bay villages none of whom, officially speaking, had even been born! Hence the need for post-registrations.

7. For a full, illustrated record of the first twenty years of its work, see W.J. Blackie, *Kadoorie Agricultural Aid Association 1951–71* (Hong Kong 1972).

8. See Arthur Grimble, *Return to the Islands* (London 1965) pp. 159–198, for an account of the life and troubles of Chinese labourers on Ocean Island in the 1920s.

9. For a good account of this work see, the *Annual Departmental Report District Commissioner, New Territories 1959–60*, paras. 163 and 170. The vote was raised from $60,000 for the whole New Territories in 1956–1957 to $420,000 in 1958–1959, to $1,000,000 each in 1959–1960 and 1960–1961, to $1,500,000 in 1961–1962, and to $2,000,000 in 1962–1963.

10. By 1961–1962, it was possible for the district commissioner to write in his report "Government's policy of subsidizing schools in rural areas has brought primary education to practically every corner of the New Territories, even to remote hill villages"; see *Annual Departmental Report District Commissioner, New Territories 1961–62*, para. 184.

11. By 1962–1963, "2,233 children were attending the eleven FMO [Fish Marketing Organization] Fishermen's Children's primary schools, a further 905 were attending other primary schools on FMO scholarship, and thirty-six were at secondary schools on FMO grants" (para. 50 of the *Annual Departmental Report District Commissioner, New Territories* for that financial year).

12. *Annual Departmental Report District Commissioner, New Territories 1961–62*, para. 222, and *Annual Departmental Report District Commissioner, New Territories 1962–63*, para. 158. However, places like Cheung Chau, Tai O, and Peng Chau had their own electricity generating plant under kaifong or private management.

Bibliography of Works by Dr James Hayes

** indicates items included in this book

Books

The Hong Kong Region 1850–1911: Institutions and Leadership in Town and Countryside (Hamden, Archon Books, 1977). Reprinted with new introduction (Hong Kong, Hong Kong University Press, 2012) in the series *Echoes: Classics of Hong Kong Culture and History.*

The Rural Communities of Hong Kong, Studies and Themes (Hong Kong, Oxford University Press, 1983).

Tsuen Wan: Growth of a New Town and its People (Hong Kong, Oxford University Press, 1993). A Chinese version《蒼海桑田話荃灣》was published in 1999 by the three rural committees of Tsuen Wan, Tsing Ye and Ma Wan, together with the Yuen Yuen Institute, Lo Wai, Tsuen Wan.

Friends and Teachers: Hong Kong and its People 1953–87 (Hong Kong, Hong Kong University Press, 1996).

South China Village Culture (Hong Kong, Oxford University Press, 2001), in the series *Images of Asia.*

The Great Difference: Hong Kong's New Territories and its People 1898–2004 (Hong Kong, Hong Kong University Press, 2006). Paperback edition published 2012 with new preface (ix–xiii) and a new review of material culture in Hong Kong from the 1950s to 2004 (pp. 179–181).

新界百年史 (Hong Kong, Chung Hwa Book Company, 2016). This is the Chinese edition of *The Great Difference: Hong Kong's New Territories and its People 1898–2004*. It contains 45 more plates, 16 of them of agricultural tools collected from the Tsuen Wan District, mainly connected with rice farming and kept at the Civil Aid Services Camp Site at Yuen Tun Old Village since 1977, together with information on Yuen Tun and its inhabitants.

National Service Revisited, 1952–1954: UK, Hong Kong, Korea, Gibraltar (unpublished). Copies in Regimental Museum, The Duke of Wellington's Regiment (West Riding), Banksfield House Museum, Huddersfield, Yorks., UK; and in The National Library of Australia, Canberra, ACT.

Papers in Books

In Marjorie Topley (ed.), *Aspects of Social Organization in the New Territories* (Hong Kong, Royal Asiatic Society Hong Kong Branch, 1965):

> "The Settlement and Development of a Multiple-clan Village", pp. 10–15.**

> "A Mixed Community of Cantonese and Hakka on Lantau Island", pp. 21–26.**

> "Report on Visit to Villages in the Sai Kung Area", pp. 41–42.

In Marjorie Topley (ed.), *Some Traditional Chinese Ideas and Conceptions in Hong Kong Social Life Today* (Hong Kong, Royal Asiatic Society Hong Kong Branch, 1967):

> "Geomancy and the Village", pp. 22–30.**

> "Chinese Temples in the Local Setting", pp. 86–95.

> "A List of Temples in the Southern District of the New Territories and New Kowloon, 1899–1967", pp. 96–98.

> "Notes on Temples and Shrines of Tai Ping Shan Street Area" with Marjorie Topley, pp. 123–141.

"Chinese Village on Hong Kong Island Fifty Years Ago: Tai Tam Tuk, Village under the Water" in I.C. Jarvie (ed.) in consultation with Joseph Agassi, *Hong Kong: A Society in Transition: Contribution to the Study of Hong Kong Society* (London, Routledge and Kegan Paul, 1969) pp. 29–51.**

"Hong Kong, A Tale of Two Cities" in Marjorie Topley (ed.), *Hong Kong: The Interaction of Traditions and Life in the Towns* (Hong Kong, Royal Asiatic Society Hong Kong Branch, 1975). Brochure for Symposium 25–26 November 1972, pp. 1–10.

"Building a Community in a New Town: A Management Relationship with the New Population" in Leung Chi-keung, J.W. Cushman, and Wang Gungwu (eds.),

Hong Kong, Dilemmas of Growth (Hong Kong, Centre of Asian Studies, University of Hong Kong, 1980) pp. 309–340.

"Chinese Clan Genealogies and Family Histories: Chinese Genealogies as Local and Family History" in Series 824, Panel on Chinese Clan Genealogies and Family Histories in *Proceedings of the World Conference on Records*, Salt Lake City, 12–15 August 1980, Vol. 11, Proceedings, Asian and African Family and Local History.

"The Nature of Village Life" in David Faure, James Hayes, and Alan Birch (eds.), *From Village to City: Studies in the Traditional Roots of Hong Kong Society* (Hong Kong, Centre of Asian Studies, University of Hong Kong, 1984) pp. 55–72.

"Collecting Business Papers of Chinese Enterprises in Hong Kong" in Alan Birch, Y.C. Jao, and Elizabeth Sinn (eds.), *Research Materials for Hong Kong Studies* (Hong Kong, Centre of Asian Studies, University of Hong Kong, 1984) pp. 47–55.

"Rural leadership in the Hong Kong Region: Village Autonomy in a Traditional Setting" in Göran Aijmer (ed.), *Leadership on the China Coast* (London, Curzon Press, 1984) pp. 32–52.**

In *Proceedings of the Sixth International Symposium on Asian Studies, 1984* Vol. 1, China (Hong Kong, Asian Research Service, 1986):

    "Chairman's Introduction, Panel on Rural Management in the Hong Kong Region in Late Ch'ing and Early Republican China", pp. 539–541.

    "Education and Management in Rural South China in the late Ch'ing", pp. 575–592.**

"Specialists and Written Materials in the Village World" in David Johnson and Judith A. Sperling (eds.), *Popular Culture in Late Imperial China* (Berkeley, University of California Press, 1985) pp. 75–111.

In *Proceedings of the Eighth International Symposium on Asian Studies, 1986*, Vol. 1, China (Hong Kong, Asian Research Service, 1986):

    "Chairman's Introduction, Some Aspects of Traditional Village Life in Hong Kong", pp. 549–550.

    "Stakenet and Fishing Canoe: Hong Kong and Adjacent Islands in the 19th and Early 20th century. The Sea and the Shore in Social, Economic and Political Organization", pp. 573–598.

"Some Aspects of Traditional Life in Hong Kong: The Village Fisheries" with Jack Tin, in *Proceedings of the Ninth International Symposium on Asian Studies, 1987*, Vol. 1, China (Hong Kong, Asian Research Service, 1988) pp. 53–63.

"Rededication of the Ho family's ancestral hall at Muk Min Ha Old Village, Tsuen Wan, March 3, 1987" (Hong Kong, publisher unknown, 1987).

In *Proceedings of the Tenth International Symposium on Asian Studies, 1988*, Vol. 1, China (Hong Kong, Asian Research Service, Hong Kong, 1989):

"Chairman's Introduction, Panel on Customary Law in South China", pp. 453–454.

"Chinese Customary Law in the New Territories of Hong Kong", pp. 455–476.**

"East and West in Hong Kong: Vignettes from History and Personal Experience" in Elizabeth Sinn (ed.), *Between East and West: Aspects of Social and Political Development in Hong Kong* (Hong Kong, Centre of Asian Studies, University of Hong Kong, 1990) pp. 7–24.

"Chinese Customary Law in the New Territories of Hong Kong, Part II: The Background to the Operation of the New Territories Ordinance 1899–1987" in *Proceedings of the Twelfth International Symposium on Asian Studies, 1990*, Vol. 1, China (Hong Kong, Asian Research Service, Hong Kong, 1991) pp. 97–136.

"Women and Female Children in Hong Kong and South China to 1949: Documents of Sale and Transfer" in Joseph S.P. Ting and Susanna L.K. Siu (eds.), *Collected Essays on Various Historical Materials for Hong Kong Studies* (Hong Kong, Urban Council, 1990) pp. 33–47.

"Government and Village: Reactions to Modern Development in Long-Settled Communities in the New Territories of Hong Kong" in Hugh D.R. Baker and Stephan Feuchtwang (eds.), *An Old State in New Settings: Studies in the Social Anthropology of China in Memory of Maurice Freedman* (Oxford, JASO, 1991) pp. 107–136.

"San Po Tsai (Little Daughters-in-Law) and Child Betrothals in the New Territories of Hong Kong from the 1890s to the 1960s" in Maria Jaschok and Suzanne Miers (eds.), *Women and Chinese Patriarchy: Submission, Servitude and Escape* (Hong Kong, Hong Kong University Press, and London and New Jersey, Zed Books Ltd., 1994) pp. 45–76.**

"Notes and Impressions of the Cheung Chau Community" in David Faure and Helen F. Siu (eds.), *Down to Earth: The Territorial Bond in South China* (Stanford, California, Stanford University Press, 1995) pp. 89–103.**

"The Traditional Background: Hong Kong Villages in the 1950s" in Patrick H. Hase and Elizabeth Sinn (eds.), *Beyond the Metropolis: Villages in Hong Kong* (Hong Kong, Joint Publishing (HK) Company Limited, 1995) pp. 19–25.

In Patrick H. Hase (ed.), *In the Heart of the Metropolis: Yaumatei and its People* (Hong Kong, Joint Publishing (HK) Company Limited, with Royal Asiatic Society, Hong Kong Branch, 1999).

"Working in Yaumatei in the 1950s", pp. 44–49. This is part of "Outsiders in Old Yaumatei: Reminiscences of Europeans Living and Working in Old Yaumatei" with Graham Cochrane, pp. 40–49.

"Nineteenth Century Yaumatei" with Carl T. Smith, pp. 101–109.

"Colonial Administration in British Hong Kong and Chinese Customary Law" in Elizabeth Sinn (ed.), *Hong Kong British Crown Colony, Revisited* (Hong Kong, Centre of Asian Studies, University of Hong Kong, 2001) pp. 63–101.

"A Short History of Military Volunteers in Hong Kong" in *Serving Hong Kong: The Hong Kong Volunteers* (Hong Kong, Hong Kong Museum of Coastal Defence, 2004) pp. 10–37. [A revised and updated version of the article originally published in the *Journal of the Hong Kong Branch of the Royal Asiatic Society* 12 (1972).]

"Collecting Chinese Calligraphy: A Personal Journey" in Liu Yang, with Edmund Capon and James Hayes, *The Poetic Mandarin: Chinese Calligraphy from the James Hayes Collection* (Sydney, Art Gallery of Sydney, 2005) pp. 36–42.

"Author Introduction" to my Village Notes, both published in John Strickland (comp.), *Southern District Officer Reports: Islands and Villages in Rural Hong Kong 1910–1960* (Hong Kong, Hong Kong University Press, 2010) pp. 24–32, with the Familiarization Notes from my visits to the approximately 180 Villages in the district in autumn-winter 1957–1958, interspersed with village names throughout.

Papers Published in the *Journal of the Hong Kong Branch of the Royal Asiatic Society*

Note that from Volume 1 to 43, the journal was titled *Journal of the Hong Kong Branch of the Royal Asiatic Society*; then until Volume 57 the title was *Journal of the Royal Asiatic Society Hong Kong Branch*. From Volume 58, the title was and still is *Journal of the Royal Asiatic Society Hong Kong*.

(Arranged in chronological order of publication)

"The Pattern of Life in the New Territories in 1898", 2 (1962) pp. 75–102.**

"Preliminary Report on the Findings at Shek Pik", 2 (1962) pp. 122–124

"Cheung Chau, 1850–1898: Information from Commemorative Tablets", 3 (1963) pp. 88–106.**

"Movement of Villages on Lantau Island for Fung Shui 風水 Reasons", 3 (1964) pp. 43–144.

"Peng Chau between 1798–1899", 4 (1964) pp. 71–96.

"The Tung Chung Fort", 4 (1964) pp. 146–150.

"Village Credit at Shek Pik 1879–1895", 5 (1965) pp. 119–122.**

"A Ceremony to Propitiate the Gods at Tong Fuk, Lantau, 1958", 5 (1965) pp. 122–124.**

"Old British Kowloon", 6 (1966) pp. 120–137, with sketch of Hong Kong viewed from Kowloon by Lt Collinson, 1846.

"Land and Leadership in the Hong Kong Region of Kwangtung in the Nineteenth Century", 7 (1967) pp. 91–103.

"Visit to Places of Historic Interest in the Aberdeen Area", 7 (1967) pp. 161–170.

"Notes on Some Vegetarian Halls in Hong Kong belonging to the Sect of Hsien-T'ien Tao: (The Way of Former Heaven)" with Marjorie Topley, 8 (1968) pp. 135–148.

"A Reaping Knife from Lantau Island, Hong Kong", 8 (1968) p. 161.

"Itinerant Hakka Weavers", 8 (1968) pp. 162–165.

"The Tung Chung Fort (Lantau Island, Hong Kong)", 8 (1968) pp. 165–167.

"Removal of Villages for Fung Shui Reasons: Another Example from Lantau Island, Hong Kong", 9 (1969) pp. 156–158.

"The Occupancy Level of Village Houses in the Hong Kong Region", 9 (1969) pp. 158–160.

"Visit to Old Shau Kei Wan—24th May, 1969", 10 (1970) pp. 183–188.

"Hemp", 10 (1970) pp. 188–190.

"Coach Tour of Eastern Hong Kong Island 18th October, 1969", 10 (1970) pp. 190–193.

"The San On Map of Mgr. Volontieri" with Rev. S. Volontieri, 10 (1970) pp. 193–196.

"A Casualty of the Cultural Revolution", 10 (1970) pp. 196–197.

"A Short History of Military Volunteers in Hong Kong", 11 (1971) pp. 151–171, with ten black and white pictures.

"Visit to the Tung Lin Kok Yuen, Tam Kung Temple, Happy Valley and Tin Hau Temple, Causeway Bay, 7th November 1970", 11 (1971) pp. 194–197.

"Rope-making and Dyeing/Calendering on Ap Lei Chau, Hong Kong", 11 (1971) pp. 198–199.

"Charcoal Burning in Hong Kong", 11 (1971) pp. 199–203.

"'Letting Go the Wooden Goose'", 12 (1972) p. 207.

"Programme Notes for the Visit to Pokfulam, Hong Kong Island, 29th July, 1972", 12 (1972) pp. 207–212.

"The Hong Kong Region: Its Place in Traditional Chinese Historiography and Principal Events since the Establishment of Hsin-an County in 1573", 14 (1974) pp. 108–135.

"Programme Notes for Visits to Places of Interest in Hong Kong Island (Urban Areas) and to Kowloon, 1974" with Carl Smith and Helga Werle, 14 (1974) pp. 196–234.

"The Pottery Kilns at Wun Yiu, Tai Po", 15 (1975) pp. 291–292.

"Chang Yu-tang and an old Hanging Scroll from Cheung Chau" with Francis S.Y. Sham, 15 (1975) pp. 311–318.

"Hung Hom (紅磡): an Early Industrial Village in Old British Kowloon" with Carl T. Smith, 15 (1975) pp. 318–324.

"Visit to Tung Wah Group of Hospitals' Museum, 2 October 1976" with Carl T. Smith 16 (1976) pp. 262–263.

"Sandal Wood Mills at Tsuen Wan", 16 (1976) pp. 282–283.

"Chinese in the Volunteer Forces of Hong Kong", 16 (1976) pp. 283–284.

"A Missing Chinese Library?", 16 (1976) p. 284.

"Royal Asiatic Society—Visit to Tai Mo Shan 3rd April 1976 Scientific Notes" with L.B. Thrower and Stella L. Thrower, 17 (1977) pp. 157–179.

"Royal Asiatic Society—Visit to Tang Family Graves, Saturday, 11th December 1976" with David Liu, 17 (1977) pp. 179–185.

"Royal Asiatic Society—Visit to Tsuen Wan, 10th December 1977 'A Village War'" with J.A. Fraser, 17 (1977) pp. 185–198.

"Two Bibliographical Notices", 18 (1978) p. 213.

"More Notes on Tsuen Wan", 19 (1979) pp. 204–213.

"Local Reactions to the Disturbance of 'Fung Shui' on Tsing Yi Island, Hong Kong, September 1977–March 78", 19 (1979) pp. 213–216.

"The Nam Pak Hong (南北行) Commercial Association of Hong Kong", 19 (1979) pp. 216–226.

"Editorial", 20 (1980) pp. viii–ix.

"Lychees of Tsang Shing County, Kwangtung", 20 (1980) pp. 153–154.

"Local Reactions to the Disturbance of 'Fung Shui' on Tsing Yi Island, Hong Kong, March 1978–December 1980", 20 (1980) pp. 155–156.

"Another (Missing?) Library", 20 (1980) p. 157.

"Yet Another Library", 20 (1980) pp. 158–159.

"A Missing Chinese Library" with H.A. Rydings, 20 (1980) pp. 159–162.

"Maryknoll in China", 20 (1980) p. 162–164.

"The Popular Culture of Late Ch'ing and Early Twentieth Century China: Book Lists Prepared from Collecting in Hong Kong", 20 (1980) pp. 168–183, with help from Peter Yeung.

"Address by Dr James Hayes, at the Annual General Meeting, 17th February" (as incoming president), 22 (1982) pp. xiv–xvi.

"The Village Watch in the Hong Kong Region", 22 (1982) pp. 294–297.

"Village Rules: Firecrackers in the Settlement of Disputes and in Token of Fines", 22 (1982) pp. 297–302.

"President's Report 1983–84", 23 (1983) pp. viii–xiv.

"So Kon Po (棉桿埔): Notes for the Visit Made by Member of the Society, 26th November 1983", 23 (1983) pp. 7–11.

"Secular Non-Gentry Leadership of Temple and Shrine Organisations in Urban British Hong Kong", 23 (1983) pp. 113–136.

"A Ch'ing Cannon from Wyndham Street, Hong Kong", 23 (1983) p. 208.

"Chue Mo Peng (猪乜病), A Fever Reported from Villages in the Hong Kong Region, and Its Cure, Together with Other Village Remedies for Excess Heat", 23 (1983) pp. 209–211.

"The Kwun Yam—Tung Shan Temple of East Kowloon, 1840–1940", 23 (1983) pp. 212–218.

"A Community Shooting Bungalow near Chinkiang, Kiangsu, and Its Library about 1905", 23 (1983) pp. 218–221.

"President's Report: 1984–85", 24 (1984) pp. viii–xv.

"Hong Kong Island Before 1841", 24 (1984) pp. 105–142.

"Traditional Tea Growing in the New Territories" with P.H. Hase and K.C. Lu, 24 (1984) pp. 264–281.

"The Soldiers at the Tung Chung Fort on Lantau Island in Late Ch'ing Times", 24 (1984) pp. 305–306.

"Wai Cheung (圍長), a Kind of Rural Leader in the 19th Century Hong Kong Region", 24 (1984) pp. 307–309.

"Village Shops in the Hong Kong Region", 24 (1984) pp. 310–311.

"President's Report: 1985–86", 25 (1985) pp. vii–xv.

"The Nixon Scroll", 25 (1985) pp. 217–222.

"President's Report 1986–87", 26 (1986) pp. vii–xiii.

"Lantern Festival, Cheung Chau, 10th February 1971", 26 (1986) pp. 267–270.

"Visit to the Mitsukoshi Department Store, Muromachi, Tokyo, Japan, June 1986", 26 (1986) pp. 270–271.

"President's Report 1987–88", 27 (1987) pp. vii–xii.

"Obituary of K.M.A. Barnett", 27 (1987) pp. 1–4.

"Hong Kong History Project" with David Faure and Patrick H. Hase, 27 (1987) pp. 254–277.

"Hong Kong's Own Boat People", 27 (1987) pp. 280–282.

"Visit to the Iwataya Department Store, Fukuoka, Japan", 27 (1987) pp. 283–285.

"Notes on Temples and Shrines, Hong Kong Island", 27 (1987) pp. 285–291.

"President's Report 17 March 1989", 28 (1988) pp. vii–xvii.

"The Tai Sheung Lo Kwan Temple, Chai Wan", 28 (1988) pp. 217–218.

"A Note on Rice Hullers (穀磨)", 28 (1988) pp. 226–228.

"A Glimpse of the Land Settlement at Shek Pik Village, Lantau Island, Hong Kong", 28 (1988) pp. 228–233.

"Royal Asiatic Society, Hong Kong Branch President's Report for 1989–90", 29 (1989) pp. vii–xx including Letter to the Chairman, Consultative Committee for the Basic Law, pp. xvi–xvii, and Address to Annual Dinner, pp. xviii–xix.

"The Old Popular Culture of China and Its Contribution to Stability in Tsuen Wan", 30 (1990) pp. 1–25.**

"Old Chinese Graves from the Tsuen Wan District of Hong Kong's New Territories", 32 (1992) pp. 164–179.

"The Royal Asiatic Society, Hong Kong Branch", 34 (1994) pp. 129–145.

"The Characteristics of Chinese Religion Mainly Taken from 19th Century Writings, but yet Relevant for Contemporary Hong Kong", 39 (1999) pp. 195–209.

"'That Singular and Hitherto Almost Unknown Country' Opinions on China, the Chinese and the 'Opium War' among British Naval and Military Officers who Served During Hostilities There", 39 (1999) pp. 211–233.

"Feng Shui and Road Works at Tong Fuk Village, South Lantau, in 1958", 39 (1999–2000) pp. 255–259.**

"A Torn Scrap of Paper: Relating to a Money Loan Association, Small Loans, or What?" 39 (1999) pp. 261–267.

"Model Village, Kowloon Tsai, Hong Kong", 40 (2000) pp. 269–283.

"Hong Kong's Chinese Associations: their Ceremonial Occasions and their Helpers", 42 (2002) pp. 67–80, 81–99 (photos).

"Afterthoughts on 'South China Village Culture' (Hong Kong: Oxford University Press (China), 2001)", 42 (2002) pp. 393–398.

"Canton Symposium: The World of the Old China Trade: the Locales and the People", 43 (2003) pp. 29–62.

"Obituary for Ian Diamond", 43 (2003) pp. 225–227.

"Introduction to 'Reminiscences of a Hong Kong Herbal Doctor: Life at Seventy' by Tim Ko", 44 (2004) p. 129.

"A Further Note on Hong Kong's Chinese Associations: their Ceremonial Occasions and their Helpers", 44 (2004) p. 144.

"Tony Rydings—an appreciation", 44 (2004) p. 155.

"Fertile and Fortunate: Shanghai before the Treaty Port Era", 48 (2008) pp. 175–203.

"Yip Hing Fai and the Training of an Optometrist in Postwar Hong Kong" with Ko Tim-Keung, 49 (2009) pp. 93–103.

"Manuscript Documents in the Life and Culture of Hong Kong Villages in Late Imperial China", 50 (2010) pp. 165–244.

"'Small Papers': More on the New Territories Cadastral Survey and Settlement of Titles to Land 1900–1905", 52 (2012) pp. 297–300.

"The Education of Boys in Hong Kong Villages", 52 (2012) pp. 300–309.

"Paul Tsui's Note on Ham Tin Village, Pui O, South Lantau 1950", 52 (2012) pp. 310–314.

"Purchase of Degrees, Rank, and Appointment in Late Qing China: Some Impressions from Contemporary Sources", 53 (2013) pp. 31–88.

"Memories (a contribution to obituary for Solomon Matthew Bard)", 55 (2015) pp. 230–232.

"Chinese Customary Law Revisited /重探中國習慣法", 56 (2016) pp. 111–132.

"An Appreciation (contribution to obituary to Deric Daniel (Dan) Waters)", 56 (2016) pp. 253–254.

"Chinese Customary Law: Family Cases from Shek Pik, Lantau, New Territories of Hong Kong", 57 (2017) pp. 206–225.**

"Chinese Customary Law: Family and Customary Trust Cases from Tsuen Wan District and New Kowloon 1961–1982", 59 (2019) pp. 190–199.

Book Reviews in the *Journal of the Royal Asiatic Society Hong Kong Branch*

Review of *The Awakening of China 1793–1949* by Roger Pelissier and Martin Kieffer, 8 (1968) pp. 174–175.

Review of *Strangers at the Gate, Social Disorder in South China, 1839–1891* by Frederic Wakeman Jr, 9 (1969) pp. 170–174.

Review of *Hong Kong Studies: a Bibliography* by M.I. Berkowitz and Eddie K.K. Poon, 10 (1970) pp. 203–204.

Review of *Golden Guide to Hong Kong and Macao* by P.H.M. Jones, 10 (1970) pp. 213–214.

Review of *Premodern China, A Bibliographical Introduction. Michigan Studies in Chinese Studies No. 11* by Chu-shu Chang, 12 (1972) pp. 235–236.

Review of *Tai Yu Shan: Traditional Ecological Adaptation in a South China Island* by Armando da Silva, 13 (1973) pp. 182–184.

Review of *Village and Bureaucracy in Southern Sung* China by Brian E. McKnight, 13 (1973) pp. 184–185.

Review of *The Taiping Revolutionary Movement* by Jen Yu-wen, 15 (1975) pp. 344–345.

Review of *The Impact of Chinese Secret Societies in Malaysia—A Historical Study* by Wilfred Blythe, 19 (1979) pp. 232–234.

Review of *Ancestral Images, More Ancestral Images and Ancestral Images Again* by Hugh Baker, 20 (1980) pp. 166–167.

Review of *New Peace Country: A Chinese Gazetteer of The Hong Kong Region* by Peter Y.L. Ng and Hugh D.R. Baker, 22 (1982) pp. 346–350.

Review of *Histoire de l'Asie de Sud-Est, Révoltes, Reformes, Révolutions* by Pierre Brocheux, 22 (1982) pp. 350–351

Review of *Transferring Technology to China, Prosper Giquel and the Self-strengthening Movement* by Steven A. Leibo, and of *Prosper Giquel, A Journal of the Chinese Civil War 1864* edited by Steven A. Leibo, 27 (1987) pp. 296–299 repeated in 29 (1989) pp. 417–420.

Review of *Pirates of the South China Coast 1790–1810* by Dian H. Murray, 28 (1988) pp. 234–236.

Review of *Ancestors, 900 Years in the Life of a Chinese Family* by Frank Ching, 27 (1987) pp. 299–301, repeated in 29 (1989) pp. 420–421.

Review of *Report from Xunwu, by Mao Zedong* by Roger R. Thompson, 29 (1989) pp. 422–423.

Reviews of *China 1890–1938, From the Warlords to World War, A History in Documentary Photographs* by Eric Baschef and *China, A Photohistory 1937–1987*, edited with commentaries by W.J.F. Jenner, 31 (1991) pp. 206–209.

Review of *Heaven is High, the Emperor Far Away: Merchants and Mandarins in Old Canton* by Valerie M. Garrett, 41 (2001) pp. 423–426.

Review of *From Rice to Riches: A Personal Journey through a Changing China* by Jane Hutcheon, 42 (2002) pp. 472–474.

Articles in Other Journals and Periodicals

"The Japanese Occupation and the New Territories", *South China Morning Post*, 15 December 1967.

"Finds of Sung Coins and Porcelain at Shek Pik, Lantau Island, 1962" with J.C.Y. Watt, *Journal of the Hong Kong Archaeological Society*, (1968) pp. 19–23.

"Old Ways of Life in Kowloon: the Cheung Sha Wan Villages", *Journal of Oriental Studies*, 8:1 (January 1970) pp. 154–188.**

"Rural Society and Economy in Late Ch'ing: a Case Study of the New Territories of Hong Kong (Kwangtung)", *Ch'ing-shih wen-ti*, 3:5 (November 1976) pp. 33–71.

"The New Territories Twenty Years ago: From the Notebooks of a District Officer", *Hong Kong Journal of Public Administration*, 2:1 (June 1980) pp. 60–70.**

"Popular Culture in Late Ch'ing China: Printed Books and Manuscripts from the Hong Kong Region", *Hong Kong Library Association Journal*, 7 (1983) pp. 57–72.

Review of Michael Moser's "Law and Social Change in a Chinese Community", in *Hong Kong Law Journal*, 14:1 (1984) pp. 131–135.

"The Yu-hsueh Ku-shin Ch'iung-lin (幼學故事瓊林) A Long-lived Popular Educational Text", *Hong Kong Library Association Journal*, 8 (1984) pp. 39–43.

"Popular Culture in Late Ch'ing China: Printed Books and Manuscripts from the Hong Kong Region. Part II", *Hong Kong Library Association Journal*, 9 (1985) pp. 59–74.

"Book Publishing and the Popular Culture: Kwangtung and Shanghai", *Hong Kong Library Association Journal*, 13 (1989) pp. 65–72.

"Customary Law in the New Territories of Hong Kong: The Background to the Operation of the New Territories Ordinance, 1899–1987", *Asian Profile*, 19:2 (April 1991) pp. 97–136.**

"Ancestral Graves and the Popular Culture of China, Some Examples from Hong Kong's New Territories", *International Association of Orientalist Librarians*, Bulletin 39 (1992) pp. 10–21.

"Social History and Ethnography in Hong Kong", *The Hong Kong Anthropologist*, 9 (1996) pp. 32–36.

"Hong Kong's Own Boat People, Vignettes from Life and History", *The Hong Kong Anthropologist*, 11 (1998) pp. 2–12.

"Calligraphy—a very fine art", *Look* magazine (Sydney, Art Gallery of New South Wales, September 2005) pp. 28–31.

"The Great Difference, The Great Rift, and The Great Need: The New Territories of Hong Kong and its People, Past and Present", *The Asia Pacific Journal of Public Administration*, 30:2 (December 2008) pp. 139–164.

Short articles in *TAASA Review*, the Journal of The Asian Art Society of Australia:

"For Better or for Worse: Chinese Ancestral Graves in a Landscape", 2:3 (1993) two pages with one image.

Review of *China 1890–1938, From the Warlords to World War: A History in Documentary Photographs* by Eric Baschet and of *China: A Photo-history 1937–1987*, edited with commentaries by W.F.C. Jenner, 2:4 (1994) two pages.

"Western Photography in China: The Historical Background", 3:3 (1994) four pages with three images.

"The Lion and Uniform Dance Teams of Hong Kong", 5:1 (1996) two pages with one image. Reproduced with small additions, and with permission, in the *Hong Kong Museum of History's Newsletter* (January–March 1997) pp. 16–20.

Contributions to the *South China Research Resource Centre Newsletter*, Humanities Division, Hong Kong University of Science and Technology:

"The Ng [Wu] Lineage of Man Lau Heung, Sun Wui County [Wenlou Xiang, Xinhui County] and its Regulations of 1921", 34 (15 January 2004) pp. 20–22. With the Chinese text of the Regulations in a Supplement, pp. 23–36.

"Notes on 'The Heung Regulations of the Ng Tsung Yeung Tong of Man Lau'", 35 (15 April 2004) pp. 15–16.

"Some Suggestions for Research Studies in the Present Day New Territories of Hong Kong", 52 (15 July 2008) pp. 1–7.

"The Chung Yee Tong and Tuen Mun District [of the New Territories of Hong Kong]" with Poon Suk-wah, 64 (15 July 2011) pp. 40–49.

Short Introductions in English to four book-length publications in Chinese of collections of land deeds and family papers. These were published in the series 許舒博士所藏土及商業文, South China Research Press 華南研究出版社. The booklets contain information on how the documents were collected, etc. They were assembled by James Hayes and edited by scholars working in association with, and under arrangements made by, the South China Research Centre at the Hong Kong University of Science and Technology. Plus an Introduction to an earlier two-volume collection published by the University of Tokyo in 1988–1989.

Puzzles

"'Good Morning Mrs Thompson': A Chinese-English Word-book from 19th Century Sydney" in Paul Macgregor (ed.), *History of the Chinese in Australasia and the South Pacific*, 8–10 October 1993 (Melbourne, Chinese History Museum, 1995) pp. 113–128.

Unpublished Materials

Talks given to The Asian Arts Society of Australia:

"On the Exhibition 'Chinese Country Craft: Domestic Utensils, Furniture, Textiles and Folk Paintings from the Late Nineteenth and Twentieth Century'", Fire Station Art Gallery, 24 November 1993. Text pp. 1–21 plus reminders of useful materials, with pp. 22–25 of Notes.

"The Material Culture of Southern Chinese, at Home—and Overseas", July 1995. Full text with finished Notes: text pp. 1–20, notes from pp. 20–27.

"An Introduction to Valery Garrett's Talk on Collecting Traditional Dress in Hong Kong's New Territories: some Historical, Social and Ethnographic Background", TAASA Textile Seminar, 18 March 1995. Text, plus "Things to Remember" and notes, 10 pages.

"Multiculturalism and the Asian Arts Society of Australia", unpublished talk to the Royal Asiatic Society, Hong Kong Branch, 30 October 1993. Transcript includes 20 pages of text and 3 of notes.

"Notes for the TAASA Visit 'ASIA IN SYDNEY'", Saturday, 13 April 1996. The theme of this visit was the attraction for and influence of Asia upon some notable Australians of their day, as seen through their personalities and interests, and the properties associated with them. Includes 6 pages of text plus 10 notes.

Other unpublished items:

"Books on Asia bought in Sydney", unpublished text, February 1996. Includes 4 pages of text and 1 of notes.

Compiled by Colin Day
Associate Editor of the *Journal of the Royal Asiatic Society Hong Kong*, editor of John Pownall Reeves *The Lone Flag: Memoir of the British Consul in Macao during World War Two*. He joined Cambridge University Press in the United Kingdom and then became Editorial Director of the Press's American Branch. He later became Director of the University of Michigan Press and President of the American Association of University Presses. He retired as Publisher of Hong Kong University Press.
October 2020

Index

R

Rawski, Evelyn 98, 113

S